THE ENCYCLOPEDIA OF
BRITISH BIRDS

This is a Parragon Book
This edition published in 2000

Parragon
Queen Street House,
4 Queen Street,
Bath BA1 1HE, UK

ISBN 0-75254-159-5

Produced for Parragon Books by
Foundry Design & Production, part of
The Foundry Creative Media Company Ltd,
Crabtree Hall, Crabtree Lane,
Fulham, London SW6 6TY

Special thanks to Polly Willis.

A copy of the CIP data for this book is available in the British Library.

Printed and bound in Indonesia

THE ENCYCLOPEDIA OF
BRITISH BIRDS

DONALD CAMPBELL

CONTRIBUTING EDITOR
MARTIN WALTERS

Contents

How to use this book

This book contains a number of important features:

- **An introductory section** 'The World of Birds' containing detailed information on all aspects of birds and ornithology. Photographs, illustrations, informative captions and 'bird fact' boxes provide extra detail on every page.
- **Descriptions of over 300 bird species** organised by habitat within one of seven groups, such as Town and Garden or Mountain and Moorland.
- **'Species Information' boxes** cover scientific names for species, details of related species, behaviour, bird calls and habitats.
- **Icons provide additional information** about size, identification marks and population.
- **The reference section** comprises a reading list, useful contacts, a glossary of vital terms and an extensive index.

KEY TO SYMBOLS

SIZE

SMALL

MEDIUM

MEDIUM-LARGE

LARGE

VERY LARGE

IDENTIFICATION
Arrows point to distinctive features of the outlined bird

HABITAT
Six main headings of habitat have been identified that relate to the sections within the book. Within these there are, therefore, further categories:

BUILDINGS	CLIFFS	CONIFEROUS	DECIDUOUS	ESTUARY	FIELDS	GARDENS

GRASSLAND	HEDGES	ISLANDS	LAKES	MARSHES	MOORLAND WTH MOUNTAINS	MOUNTAINS

OPEN WATER	REEDS AND EMERGENT VEGETATION	RIVERS	SAND	SCRUB	SHINGLE	HEATH

POPULATION

ABUNDANT 50,000 PAIRS OR A MILLION IN WINTER

LARGE 50,000 OR 100,000 IN WINTER

MEDIUM 5,000 OR 1,000 IN WINTER

SMALL 500 OR 1,000 IN WINTER

PRESENT BUT A SMALL POPULATION

DISTRIBUTION
A green outline map of Britain and Ireland using the following colours:
> **red** to show the species is present in summer – breeding
> **blue** to show the species is present in winter
> **pink** to show the species visits during spring or autumn migration but will not spring or overwinter in Britain and Ireland
> **orange** to show the species will visit but only in very small numbers

Introduction

THIS ENCYCLOPEDIA PRESENTS a concise introduction to British birds, and is aimed primarily at the amateur or general reader with an interest in birds and natural history. In part it is intended to help with the identification of birds in the field, and therefore to act as a companion to the many excellent detailed field guides which are now available. It also explains something of the biology of birds, with accounts of their anatomy, ecology and behaviour, and thus presents birds as active, living animals, rather than simply as species to be ticked off a list and named.

At the heart of the encyclopedia is a conservation thread, reflecting our awareness of the vulnerability of so many of our bird species to changes in the landscape, be these agricultural, industrial, or perhaps climatic. The work of various organisations – notably the British Trust for Ornithology (BTO) and the Royal Society for the Protection of Birds (RSPB) – constantly helps to support birds and their habitats and monitor the changes (often quite subtle) in their populations, some of these findings are reflected in the book.

One of the unusual features of the book is that the identification section is divided up by habitat. Thus, those species most likely to be seen in woodland are grouped together, whilst those more typical of the coast will be found in a different section. This gives the reader a valuable insight into which species to expect to see in a given habitat. Of course, birds are mobile (often highly so) and will cross over between these somewhat artificial compartments, but this habitat approach helps to accentuate an ecological view of wild birds, so vital for successful conservation.

Naturally, many species would qualify, perhaps equally, for inclusion in more than one habitat – thus great spotted woodpecker is increasingly a bird of gardens as well as woodland, and other birds, such as wren and chaffinch, are at home in a wide range of habitats. However, the choice in the main is of those species most typical of each habitat.

The first part of the book covers the biology of birds – topics such as how birds evolved, their anatomy, reproduction, flight, migration, and songs. It then goes on to look at their ecology, with information about changes in bird populations, before discussing techniques of birdwatching and identification, and ending with a short section about the main groups (orders) of birds and their classification.

The main part of the encyclopedia contains the bird descriptions and illustrations, grouped by main habitat. Each section opens with an introduction to that habitat and its associated birdlife. Then, within each habitat, the species are presented roughly in conventional 'systematic' sequence, with, as far as possible, related species put close together, for ease of comparison.

Each species is described concisely, with information about size, related species, calls, main habitat, and status. Occasionally, a literary reference relating to the species in question is also included here. The species descriptions are enhanced by colour photographs, clear diagrams indicating size and habitat, and by distribution maps showing the main geographical range of each bird within the British Isles.

The final two sections in the main part cover rare or local birds, those which are only likely to be seen under exceptional circumstances, or where one knows exactly where or when to search for them. The first of these looks at those species which breed in Britain or Ireland, but only in small numbers. Some of these are at the edge of their range, and in many cases the numbers breeding here fluctuate from year to year. The other main category of rare species are those birds seen mainly as occasional migrants or as vagrants blown off course by adverse weather.

Evolutionary Background

THE EARTH IS about 4.5 billion years old. The oldest sedimentary rocks, originally laid down in layers, as sediments accumulated on the bottom of the seas, are 3.75 billion years old and contain some of the first signs of life. Fossils of bacteria and blue-green algae appeared in these rocks 3.5 billion years ago. Then, for over 2 billion years, little appears to have happened in terms of evolving life, but in rocks 1.4 billion years old the first true cells appear.

APPEARANCE OF ANIMALS

MOST OF THE cells found in rocks of this age, and for the next 0.8 billion or 800 million years, are fossils found in the last 40 years. Until then it was thought that the life of the Cambrian period, which included most of the present day animal phyla, or major groups of related animals, appeared as if from nowhere. The Cambrian, began some 570 million years ago.

The animals did appear suddenly in geological terms, and so did a whole host of soft-bodied groups that didn't survive. These are the extraordinary animals of the Burgess shales in British Columbia, and in *Wonderful Life* (1989) Stephen Jay Gould reappraises the importance of this incredible array, and makes an unfamiliar model of the way living things have evolved and died out. He goes on to write 'The maximum range of anatomical possibilities arises with the rush of diversification. Later history is

Top
Many animals, like this fossil trilobite, lived over 500 million years ago.

Bottom
Tyrannosaurus is probably the most famous of the dinosaurs. Birds evolved from a kind of early reptile stock.

a tale of restriction as most of these early experiments succumb and life settles down to generate endless variants upon a few surviving models'. We will meet a similar situation with the evolution of birds.

FOSSILISED RECORDS

GOULD'S MODELS ARE evolutionary trees. There is nothing new about that, for Darwin had just such a tree in *The Origin of Species*. We need to be able to find out about the organisms that go to make up these trees, and the dates at which they were alive. Fossils are certainly the surest way to tell us about the past, but there are plenty of other clues to be picked up from the comparative anatomy of different animals, from their geographical distribution and from a growing armoury of biochemical methods, often involving neucleic acids.

We have seen that the Cambrian period, which was also the start of the Palaeozoic era, began with an apparent evolutionary explosion. The Palaeozoic ended 345 million years later in disaster, as the fossil record indicated that 96 per cent of marine species became extinct at a time of great earth movements and mountain-building. The survivors had the opportunity for rapid evolution in the absence of competition, and reptiles flourished and diversified during the Mesozoic era. At the end of that time disaster struck again and the dinosaurs were gone, but by then there were feathered animals to carry on the dinosaur line. It is still often easier to say that an event happened during the Jurassic period than that it happened 160

GEOLOGICAL TIME SCALE IN RELATION TO THE EVOLUTION OF BIRDS

ERA	PERIOD	EPOCH	MILLIONS OF YEARS BEFORE PRESENT	BIRD EVENTS
Cainozoic	Quaternary	Recent		Ice age influences migration patterns
		Pleistocene	2	
	Tertiary	Pliocene	6	
		Miocene	22	Much bird diversification
		Oligocene	36	Origin of song birds
		Eocene	45	
		Palaeocene	65	Origin of modern birds
Mesozoic	Cretaceous		135	Extinct toothed sea birds
	Jurassic		200	*Archaeopteryx* and
	Triassic		225	*Protoarchaeopteryx*
Palaeozoic	Cambrian (earliest)		570	
Proterozoic	Precambrian			

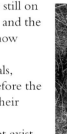

BIRD FACT:
Birds sometimes store food when it is good supply, for use later in the season. Hoarders include several species of tit, and jays. Birds can remember exactly where they hid their food for several weeks.

million years ago, for, despite modern techniques, dating can be controversial. One method, carbon dating, involves the fact that radioactive carbon decays at a steady rate. However, virtually all the carbon has gone after 50,000 years so this technique can only be used to date geologically recent fossils, like those of Neanderthal man. For older fossils, the decay of potassium and the changing magnetic field in associated rocks can be used, but rare fossils, like those of birds, will often be assigned to a geological epoch by their association with animals that have left a clearer record, as they change gradually through the different geological strata or layers of rock.

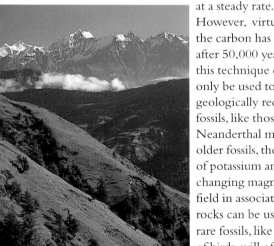

THE ORIGINS OF BIRD SPECIES

THINKING ABOUT ANIMAL evolution must be linked to an awareness of geological change. The world is far from stable, the Himalayas and the Andes are of recent origin and continents are still on the move. The Himalayas and the world's great oceans are now effective barriers to the movement of most animals, including birds, and therefore the different regions evolve their different faunas.

The Atlantic did not exist until the continental land masses of North America and Eurasia separated. At that stage, Antarctica was warm, and linked Australia and Africa. Australia has been on its own for a relatively long time and has had time to evolve its very special fauna. New Zealand's two islands have completely different origins. North America and Europe still share far more bird groups than north or south America because of their shared past geological history.

Top left
The Himalayas form an effective barrier to bird movement.

Top right
The isolation of New Zealand has resulted in the evolution of many strange birds, such as this brown kiwi.

Bottom right
Another formidable barrier to birds is provided by the high Andes of South America.

ARCHEOPTERYX

FINDING OUT ABOUT the origins of birds presents some of the same difficulties as discovering the details of human origins. Fossils are not common, the interpretation of fossil evidence is open to different opinions, and periodically new evidence is found to throw everything into confusion. I will mention doubts about the exact position of *Archeopteryx* in the story of bird evolution, but a fossil makes a good starting point.

This bird, of magpie size, was an anomaly, for its skeleton was that of a reptile, with reptilian jaws and teeth, a reptilian tail with 20 vertebrae and solid bones, without the air spaces characteristic of birds. We therefore look to reptiles for the origins of birds and, for reasons of comparable skull structure, look to the ancestors of pterodactyls, crocodiles and dinosaurs. Birds and reptiles also share nucleated red blood corpuscles and their eggs develop in a similar way.

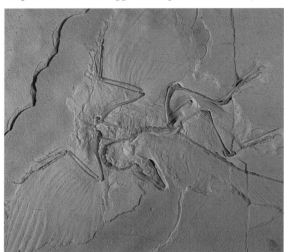

Competition is a driving force for evolutionary change and a long held-theory believed it may have forced some of these ancestral reptiles into the trees, where insects would form a likely diet. The demands of life in the trees, in pursuit of insects, could have led to a reduction of teeth and jaw muscles, and to an association between limbs and eyes to judge distance, which could have led in turn to an increase in the visual areas of the brain. This life-style could also have led to feathers, for tree-jumping would be more effective for any reptile which had slightly larger scales along the hind edge of the forearm. Alternatively, feathers arose initially for protection, and later for insulation, as suggested by Gill (1995).

FORMATION OF FEATHERS

REPTILES SCALES GIVE protection, and Gill's hypothetical steps in their evolution towards feathers starts with the elongation of scales to promote colour reflection. Splits in the elongated scales could provide flexibility and allow greater size. If the long flexible scales became frayed and pigmented they could have dual use for insulation and display. Elongation of the feathered forelimbs and tail could then allow balance and flight and later, secondary splitting, together with the appearance of hooklets, leads to the modern feather with its varied functions.

Archaeopteryx certainly had feathers very similar to those of modern birds, and had the same arrangement of primary feathers on the hand and secondaries on the equivalent of the forearm. Other features of its skeleton that were bird-like included a big toe of the sort that could grasp or perch, and clavicles which were fused to form a wishbone. By contrast, we have seen that it had reptilian teeth and tail, reptilian joints between the bones of its back, and claws on its fingers.

FOSSILISED FEATHERS

INSTEAD OF AN origin in the trees, Futuyma (1988) maintains that a sure requisite for flight is the ability to generate lift by moving the forearms down and forward. *Coelurosaur* dinosaurs had long

Top

Fossil Archeopteryx, with the feathers clearly visible.

Bottom right

Although the specialised grass snake looks far from bird-like, birds and reptiles are closely related.

Bottom left

This reconstruction shows how Archeopteryx may have looked in life.

forelimbs capable of just these movements for, equipped with claws, the forelimbs of these bipedal, running carnivores were used to grasp prey. Incidentally, there were plenty of *coelurosaurs* in the book and film, *Jurassic Park*. Into these muddied and hypothetical waters comes a new fossil. Two specimens from China are of short-armed dinosaurs, which had feathers. The arms were too short for flight, so the feathers seem even more likely to have evolved for insulation purposes, with flight coming later. One of the fossils, called *Protoarcheopteryx*, is actually more recent than *Archaeopteryx*, so we are still far from a totally clear picture.

Another early bird from China, found in 1987, is *Sinornis santensis*, toothed and sparrow-sized and sharing many features with theropod dinosaurs and with *Archaeopteryx*. It was more advanced, in having stronger 'hands', forearms and pectoral girdle and in having a larger pygostyle for the support of the tail fan.

PERCHING BIRDS EVOLVE

BY 6.5 MILLION years ago there had been a great radiation of bird species, producing most of the major groups or orders of birds that we have today. The Miocene, some 20 million years ago, was the time of another phase of diversification in which the passerines, or perching birds, mainly adapted for life in dry environments, probably evolved.

A more recent diversification, which demonstrates this principle of adaptive radiation is shown by the honey-creepers on Hawaii. They apparently evolved from a flock of small finches from Asia or North America millions of years ago. Having landed on one island they did well and spread through the archipelago. Small changes in bill shape and size led to a proliferation of bill types and related feeding behaviours. Some had heavy bills for cracking large legume seeds, in total contrast to the long sickle-like bills of others. These are for sipping nectar from flowers or probing bark crevices for insects. On the island at that time there were all sorts of opportunities available and the honey-creepers were able to make use of these in the absence of competition.

Top
Winged and swimming reptiles – a scene from the Cretaceous period.

Bottom
Hawaiian honey-creepers, showing variation in bill shape.

Evolution by Region

> *'Almost all aspects of life are engineered at the molecular level, and without understanding molecules we can only have a very sketchy understanding of life itself.'*
> Francis Crick WHAT MAD PURSUIT (1988)

I T IS CONVENIENT, if simplistic, to think of evolution as taking place in six major faunal regions, each, to a degree, with its own characteristic birds.

The Nearctic (essentially North America) and the Palearctic (including Britain and extending to Japan) form the Holarctic, with endemic orders like divers and auks. European 'warblers' are different from American 'warblers' or wood warblers. The latter are usually small, brightly coloured insectivores which rarely warble, and which have a different number of primary wing feathers. The Palearctic ends to the south with the Sahara desert, not the Mediterranean, and this desert is the northern boundary of the Ethiopian region, with its unique ostriches and secretary birds – 95 per cent of Madagascar's birds come from here, but five per cent have Indian origins, coming from the Oriental region of tropical Asia. Australasia has cockatoos and kiwis, and the Neotropical region of Central and South America has toucans and rheas.

SOME DIFFICULTIES WITH CLASSIFICATION

AS LONG AS YOU watch birds in Europe it is relatively easy to assign any bird to its family: 'That is a crow, that is one of the finches and that is a wagtail'. As you do this you are classifying, dividing birds into sub-groups on the evidence of their appearance and behaviour. Wagtails have long claws and tail, are insectivorous, have relatively simple songs and wag their tails.

If you travel to Guyana you could find long-toed, short-billed black and white birds which run and wag their tails. These are not wagtails, but have come to look like them because of convergent evolution. Birds may look alike not because they share an ancestor, but because they play the same sort of role in nature.

Above
Icterine warbler – a typical European species.

Right
The huge ostrich is at home in the dry grasslands of Africa.

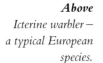

with dull green backs and yellow bellies, but vary in size, depth of colour and bill size. Further afield, in the Eastern Palearctic, in Japan and Manchuria, the birds are green-backed and white-bellied, while, over the Himalayas, in the Oriental region they are grey- backed and white-bellied.

There are also areas of hybridisation between the races, and areas of overlap where the races do not interbreed and therefore appear like separate species. Where this type of variation exists in a more or less continuous way, say with birds getting larger further north, we talk of a cline, but where the populations are more definitely separated, as on islands, we are more likely to refer to races or subspecies. Both forms of variation remind us that species are not fixed entities, nor would we expect them to be so if we think in evolutionary terms.

With some 10,000 species, however defined, there must be some way of dividing them into smaller groups, either for convenience, or because we want to work out their present relationship and past history. The basis of modern bird classification dates from 1892 and the work of Gadow who made an assessment of 40 anatomical characteristics using 'conservative' ones which he believed did not change easily in the course of ecological adaptation. T. H. Huxley had pioneered this approach with a study of bones of the palate, the partition between the nasal cavities and the mouth. Other 'conservative' features may appear equally trivial, like the structure of the leg muscles, the tendons of the feet, the number of scales on the tarsus or the presence or absence of a fifth secondary feather on the wings.

VARIETIES OF THE SAME SPECIES

CONVERGENCE IS ONLY one difficulty in classification. Many species have very extensive ranges but are not, as individuals, very mobile. These species may show great variation throughout their range. The familiar great tit breeds in most of the Western Palearctic with enough variation for ten races to have been described. These are all recognisable as great tits,

BIRD FACT:
When they drink, most birds take a little water at a time, then tilt their heads back, allowing the water to trickle down the throat. Pigeons and doves however can suck larger amounts straight into their crop.

Above left
The red-bellied toucan is a fruit-eating forest bird from Brazil.

Left
Grey wagtail, showing the characteristic long tail of members of this family.

Using Science to Classify Birds

THE NEW systematics, or approaches to classification, used in the 1940s and 1950s, accepted all the difficulties associated with geographical variation and replaced the species defined by anatomical features, by the species defined by its ability to interbreed and produce fertile offspring.

DNA IS USED

THE BIOCHEMICAL APPROACH, which started in the 1950s, gave no perfect answers, It involved the analyses blood group genes, egg white proteins and, later, enzymes, gave no perfect answers. Later DNA became the most useful classification tool, and Sibley and Ahlquist, who compared the DNA of 1,700 species, made only minor changes to the relationships suggested previously. Molecular biology is a more precise tool than comparative anatomy, and it did show that many Australian birds, not surprisingly, share an ancestor, just as marsupial mammals do. Australian nuthatches, warblers, flycatchers and wrens are not closely related to their European look-alikes. More surprisingly the technique of DNA-DNA hybridisation suggested that all crows originated from an Australian song bird that colonised Asia 35 million years ago. The two workers hoped to measure the true 'genetic distance' between species and thence to draw an evolutionary tree showing when they diverged from common ancestors.

Top right
Young great tit – a common European songbird.

Top left
Red-breasted flycatcher at its nest. This species is a rare vagrant to Britain.

Bottom
The hooded crow replaces the all-black carrion crow in the north and west, but they sometimes interbreed where they meet.

GROUPING BIRDS

IN THE PAST there have certainly been difficulties in making evolutionary trees which also try to show which birds are 'primitive' and which 'advanced'. Part of the trouble stems from the fact that mosaic evolution occurs, with one part evolving rapidly (like beaks or feet) while other parts are conservative. These can include plumage, and the sort of anatomical features mentioned earlier.

To make these trees, by whatever method, any group of similar birds, believed to be related, are put in the same taxon. This may be a large group, like an order, or a small one like a genus, which provides the first word of each name in the Linnean binomial nomenclature. Related taxa form a lineage, and there are 29 major lineages or orders, as described later. With a poor fossil record it is difficult to do more than theorise about the relationships of the orders or the times at which they separated, but the hope of the molecular biologists was that they would solve this.

The double-stranded DNA, extracted from birds' red blood cells, can be separated by heat before the resulting single strands from different species are combined to give a double

hybrid strand. This is not as firmly held together as the original, and therefore separates at a lower temperature than pure DNA from either species. This temperature difference can, hopefully, be translated into the date when the two species diverged from a common ancestor

THE WAY NEW SPECIES EVOLVE

THE ESSENTIAL IDEA when explaining the way new species evolve is that populations need to be separated from each other and to remain isolated. Among flowering plants this can happen rapidly when, as sometimes occurs, the chromosome number changes, perhaps doubling, making the new plant separate from its parents, and others of their species, because it cannot cross-pollinate with them. If it can itself reproduce asexually, without pollination, it can perpetuate its new gene combination in isolation.

Among animals, the isolation depends on some physical barrier between the populations. The sea is the most obvious barrier, hence the number of species that have evolved on remote islands and even more on archipelagos. Mountain ranges and deserts, and even relatively dry areas separating forests, and therefore forest species, are other types of barrier. Once separated, the birds will live in slightly different habitats subject to slightly different climates, predation levels and food supplies and will therefore change gradually as different gene combinations are favoured by natural selection. The ability of this natural selection to bring about rapid change is discussed later in relation to recent work on the beaks of ground finches in the Galapagos.

When the two populations are sufficiently different and unable to interbreed they are regarded as new species. It may be that the original barrier still remains, so that there is no way that the possibility of their interbreeding can be tested, but it may be that the ice melts or the desert

retreats and the reproductive isolation of the birds can be proved. Reproductive termination means that birds cannot interbreed for a variety of reasons. Courtship behaviour may have changed in terms of display, plumage or voice, so that members of one species will not be able to attract a mate from the other. If breeding times have altered or preferred breeding habitat changed the species may still not meet, despite an overlapping breeding area, and no interbreeding can occur.

It is as well to remember that in the last million years the ice has advanced and retreated ten times. Ice barriers at times of cold and higher sea-levels during warmer periods have separated populations in our latitudes. These have evolved along their own lines, as with certain closely related sibling species. The movements of ice will also have had momentous effects on bird movements as behaviour evolves as well as structure. Arctic waders have migration patterns that developed as the ice retreated. If global warming continues, a species like the knot will face all sorts of new challenges.

SOME POSSIBLE ORIGIN DATES USING DNA

60 million years ago: Divers, petrels, herons, gannets
40 million years ago: Gamebirds, waterfowl, woodpeckers
25 million years ago: Songbirds
20 million years ago: Swifts, pigeons, rails

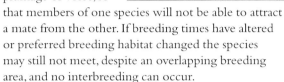

BIRD FACT:
When birds sleep they often open their eyes at regular intervals, to check out their environment for danger. It has been claimed that some birds, such as swifts, which spend much of their time on the wing, actually sleep while flying – but this is difficult to prove.

Top left
The medium ground finch of the Galapagos has quite a heavy bill.

Top right
Green woodpeckers often visit sandy lawns to search for ants.

Bottom
The sharp claws of the swift enable it to cling to cliffs and buildings with ease.

Anatomy of the Bird

M Y FEELING ON first looking at a feather under the microscope was much the same as when I first saw blood corpuscles moving along living capillaries; a feeling of total wonder that is not provided by most routine microscope work. Perhaps a head louse, climbing along a hair, or the massed ranks of ciliates and rotifers in stagnant water aroused something of the same feeling about the dynamic nature of life.

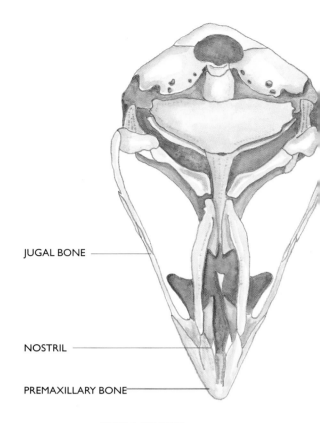

JUGAL BONE

NOSTRIL

PREMAXILLARY BONE

SKULL OF BIRD

SKELETON

Top left
This pigeon skeleton shows clearly the structure of a typical bird's wing.

Top right
Bird skull – note the spaces for the large eyes, and the nasal cavity.

Bottom
Part of a bird's skeleton (goose), showing the rib region and the wing bones.

ALTHOUGH FEATHERS PROVIDE the essence of birds and are the single feature that separates them from all other living things, birds would not be able to show their versatility but for the skeleton that moves and supports them.

Bird bones are hollow and often fused together, gaining their strength from their shape rather than their weight. The skull bones are indivisibly united in the adult, forming a structure with large eye sockets and a large nostril. This leads into a nasal cavity, with projecting cartilage all covered in moist membranes, housed inside the bones of the bill. Five bones are joined to form the lower mandible and these are covered with a hardened, cornified 'skin' to give that typical, but not unique, feature, a beak.

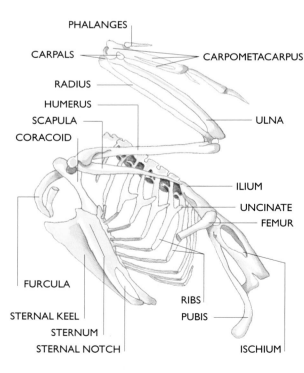

PHALANGES

CARPALS

RADIUS

HUMERUS

SCAPULA

CORACOID

CARPOMETACARPUS

ULNA

ILIUM

UNCINATE

FEMUR

FURCULA

RIBS

STERNAL KEEL

PUBIS

STERNUM

STERNAL NOTCH

ISCHIUM

SKELETON OF BIRD

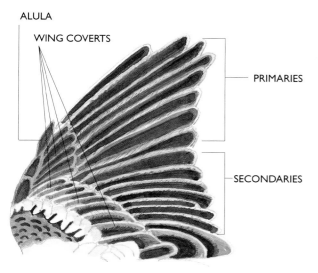

ALULA

WING COVERTS

PRIMARIES

SECONDARIES

THE WING

THE BONES OF the wing are identifiable as being the same as those of a land mammal. There is a short humerus, two longer parallel bones, the radius and ulna, two carpal or wrist bones existing free, with the others fused to form a carpometacarpus. Indications of three fingers remain.

These bones, as the foundation of the wing, are obviously vital for flight, but other skeletal features, and muscles, are also needed. The ribs have large processes for the attachment of muscles, but the more powerful ones for flight are attached, in a very clever way, with appropriate tendon pulley systems when needed, to the sternum or breast bone. To keep this part of the body firm, the vertebrae of the thorax and sacrum, at the base of the back, are nearly all joined together, but the neck, with a variable number of bones, 23 in the mute swan, is very flexible.

REMARKABLE STRUCTURE

THE WINGS ARE supported by a tripod forming the pectoral girdle: the bones involved are the scapula, coracoid and clavicle. The long scapula, our shoulder-blade, is attached to the ribs by ligaments, and the heavy coracoid, in front of the scapula, joins the sternum. Where the scapula and coracoid join, a shallow cavity fits the head of the humerus bone, allowing free wing movement. You will know the two clavicles as the wishbone which you pull apart to get your wish. Strong fliers have their clavicles spread wide to form a strut to keep the wings apart.

Just as the pectoral girdle must be strong to support the bird in flight, so the pelvic girdle is rigidly attached to the backbone to support the walking or hopping bird. Of the three bones that make up the vertebrate pelvis, the pubis is most unusual for it lies parallel to the ischium, as in some dinosaurs, and the two pubic bones do not unite in the front to form a protected pelvic outlet: perhaps because of the size of eggs.

Our foot has a series of small bones, the tarsals, between the ankle joint and what might be called the true bones of the foot, the metatarsals. In birds, some of the tarsals appear to have fused with the tibia, while others have joined the already fused and lengthened metatarsals to provide, in effect, an extra joint in the bird's leg. The fused nature of this tarsometatarsus can be seen at its lower end where there are three individual processes joining with the second, third and fourth toes. The first toe or hallux, corresponding with our big toe, has only two bones and tends to be reduced in birds that do not use it for perching. Some of the many variations in the arrangement of toes will be mentioned in the section on the orders of birds. Most birds have lost their fifth toe.

Altogether the skeleton has evolved a remarkable series of features that adapt the vast majority of bird species for flight, most for effective movement on land and many for swimming. The main features are essentially conservative, not changing much with time, so that bird skeletons are comparatively uniform, except that natural selection acts quickly and effectively on beaks, wings and legs, enabling different species to colonise a wide variety of habitats and to adapt to changing conditions.

Top right
Great skua, with wings spread in flight.

Top left
Sparrow's wing, showing the main groups of flight feathers.

Legs and Feet

LEGS AND FEET are usually covered by scales and these are moulted in much the same way as feathers. The claws, vital for gripping, digging, fighting and scratching are, like scales, made of the protein keratin.

NECESSARY MODIFICATIONS

WE TALK OF perching birds, the Passerine order, which perch by virtue of their toes and associated muscles and tendons. The term 'opposable', as with our thumb which can meet our other fingers to grip, is used for their first toe.

Some of the most obvious modifications are for swimming, where three toes are often linked by a web which can displace water backwards. This feature has evolved several times and does not indicate a relationship between ducks, gulls and auks, any more than the lobed toes of moorhens, grebes and phalaropes indicates that they are related.

The position of the legs and feet is also important, and in grebes and divers they are so placed, well to the rear, that swimming and diving is perfected at the expense of walking. High degrees of specialisation of this type have their evolutionary dangers, and there are plenty of advantages in being generalists like the gulls which can fly, walk and swim with no extreme adaptations.

SPECIALISED FEET

PREDATORS ARE ANOTHER group to show specialised feet and the osprey provides a classic example. It has a reversible outer toe and large spicules on its soles to grip slippery fish prey. The sparrowhawk has wide spreading toes, harriers long legs, golden eagles really heavy, sharp claws, while the peregrine's leg is short, presumably because of the risk of damage as it strikes large birds to kill in flight.

Woodpeckers have two toes facing forwards and two back, which helps them climb, while ptarmigan, often walking on soft snow, need a good spread of broad toes helped by their feathering.

FIBULA

TIBIA

BONES OF THE LEG

TARSOMETER TARSUS

DIGITS

BIRD FACT:
It is now known that many birds (perhaps all) can detect and 'read' the Earth's magnetic field, which helps them find their way, even in the dark, and on cloudy days.

Top left
Right leg of hen, showing the main bone structure.

Top right
Black-headed gull – note the webbed feet.

Bottom
Song thrush with berries. Its feet have sharp claws for grasping firmly onto branches.

TENDONS AND JOINTS

TENDONS ARE THE strong bands of protein, largely collagen, that link muscles to bones, and in birds, with the muscles of necessity concentrated in the upper leg, the tendons are long. In an isolated foot their upper end can be pulled to make the toes close around some object.

What a leg and its toes can do will also depend on the nature of the joints, be they simple hinges or allowing the greater range of movement needed for preening. Although a bird's legs may seen rather thin and fragile, they need to absorb the shock of landing, and in swimming species the legs are equipped with strong muscles. The rather short legs of most hawks, eagles and other birds of prey end in sturdy talons.

> 'The strangest thing about the Coot
> Must surely be its funny foot.
> Can there be anyone who knows
> Why it has long, lobate toes?
> Presumably, the Coot has found
> They help him over soggy ground,
> While, as he swims, being quite long legged,
> They're much more useful than if webbed.'
> Robert S. Morrison WORDS ON BIRDS

Legs vary just as much, with birds that wade, whatever their origin, having long legs. The avocet combines long legs with webbed feet, while divers add to their adaptations by having their lower leg, the tarsus, compressed from side to side for minimum resistance when the swimming foot is brought forward. Swifts have four toes which all point forward to help them grip on vertical surfaces.

REDUCING HEAT LOSS

ANOTHER FEATURE, NOT anatomical but physiological, is characteristic of birds' legs. As most of the leg and foot is usually unfeathered, it is going, under many conditions, to lose heat. To reduce heat loss, arteries can be deeper, but in a narrow leg that still leaves them exposed to cold. If, however, they are surrounded by, and intertwine with, the veins which are returning blood from the feet, the heat from the arteries can be transferred to the cooler blood returning in the veins, rather than being lost to the surroundings.

Top left
Female lesser-spotted woodpecker at nest-hole. Woodpeckers use their claws and stiff tails to help them cling to tree trunks.

Bottom left
Mallard drake – a typical duck, with well webbed feet.

Bottom right
The long legs of the black-winged stilt allow it to wade easily in mud and shallow water.

Beaks

I T WAS THE beaks of the ground finches in the Galapagos Islands that started Darwin along the path to his theory of natural selection. It is the beaks of certain ground finches on Daphne Major that have given Peter and Rosemary Grant, and their team, as good an insight as anyone into the power of natural selection, and its ability to bring about evolutionary change. They have studied the birds for 20 generations.

BEAKS

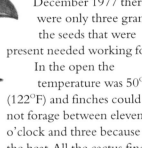

PEREGRINE

SHOVELER

GREEN
WOODPECKER

BULLFINCH

SPOONBILL

Top right
Head of fulmar, showing the characteristic tube-nose of this group.

Right
Five designs of bill. From top: peregrine, shoveler, green woodpecker, bullfinch, spoonbill.

Bottom right
The lesser black-backed gull has a tough, all-purpose bill, enabling it to eat a variety of foods.

A CASE HISTORY

IN THE FIFTH year of their study, in 1977, a drought began to develop, the crops of the young cactus finches were empty, the leaves shrivelled and there were few flies and moths. In June 1976 there had been ten grams of seeds per square metre of volcanic lava but by December 1977 there were only three grams; the seeds that were present needed working for. In the open the temperature was 50°C (122°F) and finches could not forage between eleven o'clock and three because of the heat. All the cactus finch fledglings died before they were three months old, not a single medium ground finch laid an egg or built a nest. Just as seed numbers fell and their hardness increased so the finch populations declined. From 1,500 in March 1976 to 1,300 in January 1977 and down to 300 in December.

Almost every finch was ringed and had had its tarsus, wing and beak length measured as well as the depth of the bill. Later every bird would be individually known. Looking at the beak data after the drought, the Grants found that the average medium ground finch beak had been 10.68 mm long and 9.42 mm deep before the drought while survivors averaged 11.07 mm by 9.96 mm. Of the 600 males, which are about 5 per cent larger with correspondingly larger beaks, more than a quarter were still alive, but of the 600 females, with smaller beaks, fewer than 30 survived.

SURPRISING RESULTS

THE NEXT SURPRISE was that young, big, deep-beaked birds had been dying during the drought. If a beak was 9.45 mm at 8 weeks that would be its adult size. It was found that if the average at 8 weeks was 9.45 mm, a bit later it was 8.73 mm not by shrinkage but by the death of big-billed birds. A big beak in a young bird is useless for cracking big seeds because its skull is not strong enough. Big birds need more food but are not very good at getting it; that was one of the reasons why young birds had been dying even if big-billed.

With few finches left, the males had to compete even more fiercely for mates. Some succeeded, while others failed. It turned out that the males that were most successful were the larger individuals, with the biggest bills, and these birds were winning the most mates. It was now time for the bills to get larger once more. In December 1982, more rain came than at any time since 1960, with stupendous thunderstorms as El Niño brought in warm water. Instead of dry lava everything grew to record size but it was too wet for cactus. By June, after a breeding frenzy, there were 2,000 finches on Daphne Major and young birds were breeding earlier than ever before.

NATURAL SELECTION

BECAUSE OF THE cactus failure most of the seeds were small but they were everywhere, even when another drought started. Natural selection began to operate strongly again as the huge finch population looked for food. Later analysis of results from that time showed that now the big finches were dying, and the big males were dying most. With less cactus the cactus finches, too, were low in numbers.

All this, and much more, demonstrates beautifully how natural selection operates, with tiny differences of fractions of a millimetre making the difference between life and death, and how its effects can oscillate so that there is, here, no overall trend. The plant life on the island and the seed supply also changed. A complicating factor was that hybridisation between species also occurred. Before El Niño, hybrids did not survive, but a cross later between a small finch, or a cactus finch, with *G. fortis*, does the genes of *G. fortis* a favour. In an oscillating environment, hybridisation and new gene combinations can flourish for a while, but when stability returns, the sharing of genes will slow again. Briefly, the second of Gould's evolutionary trees, the standard model, or the tree of survivors in the first, stops being a tree and becomes a tangled, interweaving creeper.

BEAKS OF BRITISH BIRDS

BRITISH FINCHES CONCENTRATE on whatever size of seed they can deal with most effectively. Thus a hawfinch, with massive conical beak, can split exceptionally hard fruits. Linnets and greenfinches, both with short, broad beaks, pick seeds from the ground or off plant stems, while the goldfinch and siskin avoid competition by having different bill lengths, although both have long, narrow ones. The goldfinch with its longer beak can probe more deeply into thistle or teazel.

Later in this book the distinctive beaks of birds like shoveler, razorbill, spoonbill and waders, which avoid direct competition by having bills that can probe to different depths and select different food items, will be used to help identification. More subtle differences, like those of different divers or grebes, are vital to help identification of different species in winter. No doubt the variations in colour found in geese, ducks and gulls have their own significance, perhaps helping intraspecific recognition; they certainly help us with recognition.

> **BIRD FACT:**
> Wilson's petrel is probably the world's most numerous seabird, with an estimated global population of a staggering 50 million pairs.

Above left
The tough bill of the greylag goose is used for grubbing and grazing.

Above right
The greenfinch has a typical seed-eater's bill – a bit like a pair of pliers.

Left
The smaller siskin has a more delicate bill, often used for extracting seeds from cones.

Breeding patterns

AMONG ANIMALS THERE is a variety of mating systems and which one is favoured by a particular bird species will depend on factors like the resources available, the level of predation, whether female breeding behaviour is synchronised, and how well the young are able to look after themselves.

MONOGAMOUS PAIRS

MOST BIRDS are monogamous, with both parents working together to raise their young. About 10 per cent are polygamous, which means they have more than one mate. When a male mates with more than one female, this is termed polygyny (as in some harriers); when a female mates with more than one male it is termed polyandry; when more than one male mates with more than one female it is termed polygynandry (as in the dunnock). A final category, promiscuous, is the term used for a free arrangement with no fixed pair-bonds (as in some hummingbirds).

Monogamy tends to evolve where the male's help is needed for successful chick-rearing. He might need to protect the nest, or to help gather sufficient food. In colonial gulls, for example, one parent needs to be constantly at the nest to protect the eggs or chicks, while the other gathers food.

REARING THE CHICKS

IF RESOURCES ARE abundant however, a single parent is able to raise a family alone, and the other parent, usually the male, can obtain further matings (polygyny). If the young are able to look after themselves quickly, then polygamy may again be favoured, but on the whole birds are monogamous, perhaps because both eggs and chicks need heavy parental involvement. Even so, DNA analysis of, for instance, dunnocks and reed buntings, often shows that offspring do not share genes with their supposed fathers. Where predation is a major risk as it often is females may come into breeding condition together, as they do in colonial birds. An advantage of this is shown in colonial nesting kittiwakes, where a stable pair-bond is maintained for years, and reproductive success increases with age.

Herring gulls, sharing incubation, defence and food collection, have fairly equal roles, whereas male mallards and pheasants are not the most attentive of mates. In fact mallards are monogamous, perhaps because the males have to defend their mates from other males.

In most birds of prey the female is larger, sometimes, as in sparrowhawks and goshawks, markedly so.

BIRD FACT:
Numbers of many birds of prey – notably peregrine and sparrowhawk – declined sharply in the 1950s and 1960s due to poisoning by organochlorine insecticides. Happily, numbers have recovered following a ban on these chemicals.

Top right
Many marsh harriers are polygamous, with one male mating with two or more females.

Right
Arctic terns are fiercely defensive at their nest-sites.

The female initiates most territorial and courtship behaviour but, perhaps unexpectedly, she is also the main incubator and protector of her young brood.

DIFFERENT BREEDING STRATEGIES

AMONG HARRIERS, POLYGYNY is common, with a male defending a large territory, and attracting more than one female to nest within the defended area. Another form of polygyny is the lek system, seen in birds as varied as black grouse and ruff. In this system, the males gather to display in small territories, and the females visit these leks to select a mate and then bring up the young on their own. This has tended to evolve in species in which the young are born well formed and almost independent (i.e. easy to rear), as in grouse and some waders.

The fact that within a single order, the waders, there are a number of breeding strategies, shows the difficulties of generalising. Although woodcocks maintain their pair-bond for a time, the males may successively mate with four females, polygyny again, but there is no plumage difference. In the dotterel, females are brighter plumaged than males, initiate the courtship and leave the males to incubate, before mating with another male (polyandry). Similarly, in phalaropes the female is brighter and more clearly patterned, and will often leave the male to incubate after a period of pair-bonding and lay a repeat clutch with another male. Lapwings and curlews are essentially monogamous, but the ruff is decidedly polygynous, with certain dominant males having far more matings than the less successful and less distinctively ruffed males; this has led to a growing differentiation between the sexes, with male plumage and behaviour becoming progressively more exotic.

There are always advantages and disadvantages in different patterns of reproductive behaviour, but whatever tends to leave most parental genes in future generations will be favoured. In red-legged partridges, as with other ground-nesters vulnerable to predators, both sexes may mate with more than one partner during one breeding season. Each sex incubates eggs in

separate 'scrapes' and if rearing the nidifugous young is successful, the pair are soon ready to mate again with the original or a different partner. If one nest fails, the incubator goes on the search for a new mate.

Some birds, like the well-studied dunnock, may show a range of different mating strategies, from monogamy, to polygyny and polyandry, and this may depend on many factors, including the nature of the habitat.

Top left
Like most species, adult reed warblers work hard to satisfy their hungry offspring.

Top right
Young coot are vulnerable and stick close to their parents.

Bottom left
Snow buntings often nest amongst boulders on high mountain plateaux.

Bottom right
Newly-hatched gulls, like this herring gull chick, have soft, downy plumage.

The Breeding Process

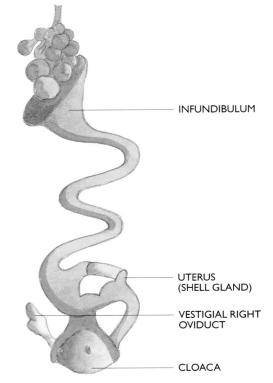

INFUNDIBULUM

UTERUS
(SHELL GLAND)

VESTIGIAL RIGHT
OVIDUCT

CLOACA

FEMALE REPRODUCTIVE SYSTEM

MUCH IS KNOWN about the factors that initiate seasonal behavioural changes in birds, and these are mainly linked with growth and recession of the reproductive organs.

FACTORS AFFECTING BREEDING

ALTHOUGH SECONDARY FACTORS, like sudden cold or warm spells which may slow down or speed up, the rate of gonadal development, there is no experimental evidence that these factors can initiate gonad growth in the absence of appropriate light regimes. The ratio of hours of daylight to darkness is the main cue which changes as spring develops. Most birds have both breeding and migrating behaviour suppressed in the absence of appropriate light stimulation.

Research workers have been helped by a behavioural peculiarity of caged migrant birds, which develop a marked nocturnal restlessness as they came into the migratory state. This provides a measurable quantity, the amount of hopping, to test experimentally the effectiveness of environmental and physiological factors in releasing the urge to migrate; this, of course, is a preliminary to breeding behaviour. Activity patterns are generally recorded by means of a spring perch attached to a micro-switch incorporated into an electrical circuit.

Gonads do not only produce eggs and sperm, but also sex hormones, and it is the level of these that determine territorial and courtship behaviour. There is an interplay of factors for final ovarian development. Egg laying may not occur unless there are other appropriate stimuli, such as the appearance of a breeding mate, or of fellow colonial nesters, or of courtship itself. As usual, there are species differences, with some birds being ready to have two breeding seasons in a year, following appropriate light stimuli, but others retaining an autonomous rhythm of gonad size according to the season, even if kept in complete darkness.

PHYSIOLOGY OF REPRODUCTION

UNDER THE RIGHT conditions, ovaries and testes can increase in weight by up to five hundred times. Except in ducks and the ostrich, which have a penis, sperm released from the testes are moved to a cloaca which, following courtship, can be brought close to the female cloaca. Fertilisation of the egg takes place in the females in the infundibulum (see diagram). As the fertilised egg travels down the oviduct, it gains food from the uterus or shell gland, and the egg, now surrounded by membranes, gains water and salts before being covered by a shell.

Top right
The reproductive system of a female bird, showing the developing eggs at the opening to the infundibulum.

Bottom left
Cross-section of egg with developing embryo.

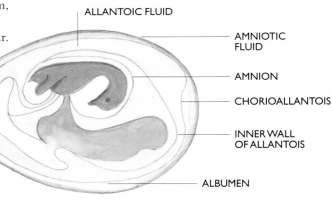

ALLANTOIC FLUID

AMNIOTIC
FLUID

AMNION

CHORIOALLANTOIS

INNER WALL
OF ALLANTOIS

ALBUMEN

FERTILISED EGG WITH EMBRYO

The large enclosed eggs of birds and reptiles are devices to allow the processes of feeding, respiration and excretion to continue as development proceeds from single cell to complex chick. Initially the actual living matter is only a thousandth of the mass of the egg, with the rest being devoted to protection and storage.

FORMATION OF THE EGG

CELL DIVISION STARTS before the egg is laid, and the growing cluster of cells moves to the tip of the egg where it will be nearest to the warmth of the brooding mother. By the tenth day, in the hen, embryonic membranes, delicate sheets of tissue, extend from the blastoderm, which can now be called the embryo. The yolk and albumen, the egg white, act as food supplies, in the form of fat and protein, and water which is steadily lost through the porous shell.

MATING

MATING CAN APPEAR very haphazard in birds, but certain behavioural techniques help to make it more efficient than it looks. One explanation, even if a rather special one, is provided by work on dunnocks. Females have a precopulatory display, involving crouching, ruffling body feathers, shivering the wings, and raising the tail to expose the cloaca for up to two minutes. Copulation is extraordinarily brief, with the male appearing to jump over the female as cloacal contact lasts only a fraction of a second.

Stuart Smith (1950) describes an 'invitation' display by the female yellow wagtail when she is ready for mating: 'The cock bird may be pirouetting around the hen ... when she suddenly crouches on the ground, puffs out her feathers, half opens and depresses her wings and elevates her tail until it is vertical. When in this position, she begins to twirl round and round on the ground ... After gyrating thus for several complete turns she stops, and the cock, if he is ready, will mount the hen and copulate.'

Above
A cock linnet displays his breeding plumage.

Bottom left
Mallard's nest with eggs and newly-hatched ducklings.

Bottom right
Mating, as in this pair of shags, is a brief and seemingly haphazard affair.

25

Feathers

THERE ARE SEVERAL generations of feathers, from the fluffy, simple, heat-retaining feathers of the very young, through various juvenile types, to those of the adult.

CONTOUR FEATHERS, including the primaries and secondaries of the wing, the tail feathers and those that cover the ears, form the visible cover. Down feathers, hidden below, have vital insulation functions, while others are specialised, such as the rictal bristles around the beak of a nightjar that help it to catch the moths of the late evening as it flies.

In his book *Life on Earth* (1979) David Attenborough gives a clear and straightforward description of feathers: 'The feather is an extraordinary device. Few substances can equal it as an insulator, and none, weight for weight, whether man-made or animal-grown, can excel it as an aerofoil. Its substance is keratin. The same horny material forms a reptile's scales and our own nails, but the exceptional qualities of a feather come from its intricate construction. A central shaft carries on either side a hundred or so filaments; each filament is similarly fringed with about a hundred smaller filaments or barbules. Flight feathers have an additional feature. Their barbules overlap those of neighbouring filaments and hook them on to one another so that they are united into a continuous vane. There are several hundred such hooks on a single barbule, a million or so in a single feather.'

Top right
Feathers are very light, but their surfaces are kept rigid by an intricate system of interlocking barbules, as shown in the close-up.

Middle left
This young redshank is covered in soft down feathers.

Bottom right
Replacement of feathers during the moult may change the plumage from winter (behind) to summer (foreground), as in this dunlin.

OBSERVING FEATHERS

AMONG THOSE WHO observe feathers most closely are artists. Charles Tunnicliffe drew a lot of dead birds, measured to exact life size, and depicted in a variety of media to achieve an accurate impression of feather texture. His *Sketches of Bird Life* (1981) include a series of nightjar paintings of this type, but when drawing and painting from life, artists still observe in a way that most of us do not. I love watching a redshank pair but I do not notice the 'very marked difference of size and plumage in these two birds. Female larger and with neck and breast much more striped than male. Her scapulars much more patterned. Male breast had a ground colour almost vinous. The female lacked this colour on upper front of breast.'

FEATHER COLOUR

THE COLOUR OF THE feathers can be vital, sometimes obviously so, but at other times in ways that are yet to be explained. Because birds live in a largely visual world, we can understand their behaviour more easily than we can the behaviour of the scent-dominated and often nocturnal mammals. Much courtship is visual, with the movements evolving to show off bright colours, like those forming the speculum on the wings of ducks. The elaborate movements of male black grouse and ruffs at their leks are further examples. Movements linked with coloured feathers serve as signals which may warn off a rival male, attract a mate or maintain a pair bond. Moorhens for instance show quite complex behaviour, but the flicking of their tails, to show the white feathers beneath, seems an obvious enough cue for the young birds to follow.

By contrast, cryptic coloration, most common among female ground-nesters like the ducks and game birds, conceals the birds. Good examples are nightjar and woodcock, which rest and incubate among the bracken fronds and dead leaves on the ground during the day, before feeding at dusk.

The way that the colour is produced is either through pigmentation or through the structure of the feather. The commonest pigment is melanin, which appears either black or brown. Carotenoid pigments show red or orange, and porphyrins and other pigments lead to some of the other colours. Feather structure can cause scattering of light waves to give iridescent colours like those of magpies and starlings. The intensity of a flamingo's pink feathers depends on the shrimps they have eaten.

Another group who also looked closely at plumage were those who used to identify their varieties after shooting them. Harting, who wrote the *Birds of Middlesex* (1866) was not responsible for the spoonbills that were shot at Kingsbury, now Brent, reservoir in October 1865, but he did trace them 'to the birdstuffer with whom they had been left'. He found that they were birds of the year and 'all the quill feathers with black shafts presenting a curious and very pretty appearance when expanded. The first four quill

feathers white with dark brown tips as follows — first with dark brown stripe on outer web; second first half of outer web brown then white; third and fourth outer webs nearly all white. The first quill shortest; the second largest in the wing.' Museum workers and some ringers will observe feathers with the same precision, but most of us operate more on impression, except in special circumstances. However there is much beauty to be seen in little details.

Top left
This blue tit clearly shows the outspread flight feathers.

Middle left
The brown plumage of a female eider helps conceal it during incubation.

Bottom right
Moorhens flash their white under-tail feathers as they display to each other.

Preening

When not a strain is heard through all the woods
I've seen the shilfa Chaffinch light from off his perch
And hop into a shallow of the stream
Then, half afraid, flit to shore, then in
Again alight and dip his rosy breast,
And fluttering wings, while dew like globules coursed
The plumage of his brown empurpled back.
William Graham (1918–86)

FEATHERS NEED regular maintenance, hence much elaborate preening to remove dirt, parasites and old preen oil and to zip the feather barbules back into place, thereby repairing the vane. Bathing is usually the first stage in feather maintenance, and most will have watched the whole-hearted activities of robins and blackbirds in bird-baths. The object would seem to be to wet as much of the body as possible without wetting it so much that damage results.

BIRD FACT:
Research has shown that male sedge warblers with the most elaborate songs are more successful in attracting a mate than those with simpler songs. This has led to the evolution of a long and varied song in this species.

BATHING

WATERBIRDS ALSO NEED to bathe, but they must also dry afterwards, and have their wing flapping movements to help them. Cormorants, as is well known, follow this up by holding their wings out for a period after bathing. But cormorants get wetter than most birds, for by driving the air from between their feathers when they dive, they can swim deeper and faster in pursuit of food. They also lack the oil which keeps most bird feathers from getting really wet — another adaptation to diving. Having dried, it is finally time for an application of oil from the preen gland at the base of the tail. Most species stimulate preen oil with their beaks, twisting their heads round to meet their twisting tails; it helps to have a long neck. A dust bath or a dose of formic acid from ants, placed strategically under the wing, or wherever, can also help parasite control.

Top
This blackbird has fluffed out its feathers during a preening session.

Bottom
Even the sleek kingfisher may look a little scruffy during the moult.

PARASITES

FEATHER LICE ARE the only parasites that feed primarily on the keratin of feathers. They are flattened from above downwards, so they can run fast enough to escape some preening; if they settle on the head or neck they can avoid the beak. Rothschild and Clay in their delightful book on an undelightful subject (1952) mention that lice have been taken from chicken dust-baths, so dust bathing does seem to help with parasite control. The fact that birds tend to be more heavily infested if they are sick also suggests that their bathing, oiling and preening activity does keep the lice in check.

A robin with most of the upper mandible missing was infected with 127 lice, but numbers rarely exceed 15 in normal robins.

Feather lice usually feed on the downy parts of larger feathers, using their legs to direct feather barbules towards their mandibles. Once the ancestors of lice had moved onto birds, or moved from scaly reptiles onto the evolving birds, their evolutionary potential was considerable. Not surprisingly, blood from any site may be part of the diet, but more exciting moves took them inside the throat-pouches of cormorants for blood and, for

part of the life cycle of one species, into the inside of the shaft of the flight feathers of curlew, to feed on dried feather cores.

Mites can also damage the plumage, while plenty of fleas will move between the feathers, if only to get to a new blood source. Luckily for birds, however, fleas have never done so well on them, as they have on mammals.

MOULT

DESPITE ALL THE dusting, bathing and preening, feathers are subject to wear. Sometimes a degree of wear can bring a bird to its conspicuous best, as when the pale edges of feathers wear off as a linnet develops its red breast before breeding.

Eventually though, replacement is needed, making for a period of difficulty, when birds may even become flightless if all flight

feathers are lost at once, as happens to ducks entering eclipse plumage. More often, moulting begins with the primaries of the wing, followed by the secondaries and tail feathers, with symmetrical loss on the two sides of the body, thus reducing, but not eliminating flight. The coot is another species which becomes flightless during the moult, and on the Ukrainian coast of the Black Sea for example, the August moulting flocks may extend for several kilometres.

Moult occurs when the new feather follicle is stimulated to grow. As the new feather begins to form, the old one is pushed out. Being an actively growing structure, the new one needs blood, but this is withdrawn as the feather matures and hardens. The stimulus for follicle growth in temperate regions seems to be changes in day length, with the thyroid gland also involved, but as there is a variety of moult patterns and as the stimulus in the tropics must be different, with little variation in day length, the regulating factors may well vary.

Garden birds become much less obvious at the time of their moult, as is suggested by many of the observation frequency curves in the *Garden Bird Watch Handbook*. Some seabirds disappear out to sea, away from their main predators, where they can swim in relative safety. Many northern waders moult in two phases; if there is not time to complete a moult as the short arctic summer draws to an end, the moult is completed after the migratory flight when hopefully there is plenty of food for the energy-demanding process.

Top left
Many birds, such as this house sparrow, take regular dust baths, probably to discourage parasites.

Middle left
Water birds, such as this Canada goose, need to preen regularly to keep their feathers in good condition.

Middle right
Kingfisher preening its wing feathers.

Bottom
Some water birds, like this shag, need to spread their wings out to dry between bouts of diving.

Flight

WHETHER WATCHING FULMARS around the cliffs of Hebridean Mingulay, whooper swans leaving Irish Tory Island for Iceland, or a spotted flycatcher over the village pond in Combpyne, Devon, bird flight can always amaze. The fulmar glides apparently effortlessly and it is gliding flight that is easier to explain.

MECHANICS AND WING STRUCTURE

IN CROSS-SECTION, the part of the wing nearest the body is shaped so that air movement leads to a build up of pressure below and reduced pressure above. The resulting force is lift, and it is this which enables a bird to stay in the air. To get more lift, in a model, one can increase its surface area, or its speed relative to the air. Alternatively, the angle of attack or the camber of the wing section can be changed. Eventually, increasing the angle of attack leads to stalling, but in birds the wing slots of the bastard wing and the emarginated primaries act as effective antistalling devices. On the cliffs where fulmars

breed, the air rises as sea winds reach the cliff face, while at sea level the air is in constant motion above the waves: in either case the long-winged fulmar needs only a minimum of flapping. Around the cliff it often uses a foot to help it to steer.

Having a long, narrow wing, the fulmar's aspect ratio is high. Another important ratio gives the wing loading, the bird's weight divided by the wing area. A heavy bird with a relatively small wing area will have to do a lot of rapid flapping. With their great weight, swans will always have to flap.

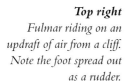

Top right
Fulmar riding on an updraft of air from a cliff. Note the foot spread out as a rudder.

Bottom right
Vertical sea-cliffs such as these are ideal habitats for fulmars and gulls.

PHOTOGRAPHING FLIGHT

AT THE TIME when Gray gave the Royal Institution Christmas Lectures in 1959 the technology of photography was already able to allow the wing movements of pigeons to be followed, as they flew towards a camera or past it, along a corridor. More recent photographs give an even more remarkable image of the movements of birds' wings. They are constantly altering, due both to the suppleness of the feathers and to the birds own internal muscular movements. The main muscles are the breast or pectoral ones, attached to the sternum. The *pectoralis major*, which pulls the wing down, is a large muscle, but those that move the wrist and raise the wing are smaller.

Perhaps the peak of flying is the ability to hover in still air. A kestrel, searching for voles, will sometimes have an almost vertical body, so that wings go backwards and forwards rather than up and down. The powering of the back-stroke demands a great deal of the smaller pectoral muscle. Although most auks, like puffins, can fly fast and direct, it is the use of their wings in swimming that is their speciality.

ADAPTING FOR FLIGHT

WHATEVER THE METHOD of flight, the lightness of the bones and other adaptations of the skeleton and feathers are vital, but so are the physiological

features. A large heart is important for long flights, and a bird's high temperature (40°C/104°F) links with their high metabolic rate and this, in turn, is linked with the respiratory system. Although the lungs are small, the air sacs connected to them may form 15–20 per cent of the body volume. The air sacs are not directly involved in gas exchange, but act as bellows for the lungs which operate, not on an in and out system, but with a through flow of air. Schmidt-Nielsen (1988) points out that the finest branches of the bronchi do not end in sacs like the mammalian alveoli, but are open at both ends and gas exchange takes place in air capillaries which surround these bronchi.

Water levels need to be regulated. As birds excrete uric acid as a paste, rather than urea dissolved to form liquid urine, they do not lose so much water. If, however, they spend time at sea, as many do, they need to drink sea water but do not have kidneys efficient enough to get rid of salt. As Schmidt-Nielsen says: 'all marine birds – gulls, albatrosses, penguins and so on – have a gland in the head that can excrete a highly concentrated solution of sodium chloride. This gland, which has a structure entirely different from the kidney, can excrete a salt solution up to twice the concentration of sea water. When the birds ingest food with a high salt content or drink sea water, the gland secretes the excess salt; the secretion flows through the salt gland ducts into the nasal cavity and drips off from the tip of the beak.'

Without these physiological adaptations, life at sea or birds' extensive migratory flights would simply not be possible.

Top right
The barn owl uses its soft, broad wings in silent, hovering flight.

Top left
The streamlined wing of a duck – in this case a smew.

Middle
The long, broad wing of an eagle.

Bottom left
Pheasants are reluctant fliers, usually coming down to land again after a short distance.

Migration

AMONG ALL THE aspects of bird life, their ability to orientate themselves accurately, to fly huge distances without stopping and to return to their identical nest site has perhaps aroused the most wonder. The fact that many of the best places to study migration and see migrants are spectacular in their own right, makes migration study even more obviously exciting, while for some, the unexpected appearance of rare migrants is the very essence of birdwatching.

PATTERNS OF BIRD MOVEMENT

A CLOSE WATCH in your own garden or familiar patch of woodland, heath or estuary will reveal the ever-changing pattern of bird movement. Pied wagtails that nested on the front of the house may

soon be down on the marshes, and many woods which have song thrushes in summer, lose them to coastal areas in the winter. Almost all birds move, but it is the spectacular long-distance flights that excite the imagination, and the two way movement, there and back, that is true migration.

REASONS FOR MIGRATION

DESPITE THE HAZARDS of these long flights, the bird population concerned must survive better by moving than by staying put, or such behaviour would not have evolved. When conditions get hard, with shorter days in which to search for more elusive food, there are two options for any bird that is going to stay for the winter.

The first option is to specialise, as the treecreeper does, with its long fine beak for reaching invertebrates dormant in crevices in the bark. The second is to change diet, as for example the change in

the digestive system of the bearded tit as it switches from summer invertebrates to winter reed seeds. From late September, the gizzard grows more muscular so that seeds can be crushed.

Alternatively, a species can migrate, as the whinchat does, unlike the closely-related stonechat that makes only local movements. Analysis of the BTO nest record cards shows that the stonechat has time for three broods, rather than the whinchat's two, and that twice as many stonechat nests produce young, giving stonechats a three to one advantage in productivity. Despite this, and the whinchat's extensive migration across the Sahara, whinchat populations are not subject to the violent fluctuations that cold weather can produce in stonechats. Avoiding food shortage can be more successful than facing the risks that cold weather brings.

Top right
Male bearded tit, feeding on a reed head, its main source of food during the winter.

Middle left
Most stonechats (female shown here) move only short distances during the winter, rather than migrating.

Bottom right
The migratory urges of the starling have been closely studied.

FINDING THEIR WAY

PRESUMABLY MIGRATION STARTED as small-scale movements, perhaps as the last ice age lifted, though no doubt there had been different patterns earlier. As the ice retreated, a bird moving further north to breed would have longer days and less competition for food. As the distances grew greater, knowledge of a familiar area, and known visual cues, would no longer be adequate for orientation. Movement in relation to the sun, particularly perhaps at dawn and dusk, and the stars, would become more important. Experiments confirm this type of orientation and link it to a bird's time clock. There is also evidence that birds can obtain directional information from the earth's magnetic field. Salmon certainly use the smell of their home river as a navigational guide, and birds, particularly hole-nesting petrels, may well use this sense in the final stages for finding their own burrows.

Smell would not however be sufficient for a breeding Welsh shearwater to find its way home from long distance. G. V. T. Matthews showed the powers of these migrants by releasing them far from home and timing their return. From relatively featureless landscapes the birds circled and set off in the right direction. Some birds were able to return at rates of 402 km (250 miles) a day, coming back to their own burrow.

In the case of shearwaters, individual birds could be traced, but another approach was to trap, ring and re-locate large numbers of a common bird whose normal migratory movements were known.

A. C. Perdeck trapped 11,000 starlings in Holland, transported them to Switzerland, and released separate flocks of adults and young. The young continued on a course parallel to their original line of migration and ended up in the South of France and in Spain. Those ringed adults which were later re-trapped had re-orientated, and were found in their normal wintering areas of northern France and Britain. There must be an inherited tendency to orientate in a given direction, but experience can modify this instinct so that they can find a particular area.

Another approach, having accepted the fact of orientation, is to experiment with birds under controlled conditions. Again using starlings, Kramer had observed that captive birds were more restless at migration times, and that this restlessness was not random. This led him to design special cages in which he could alter the sun's position, as seen by the birds, with mirrors. The restless starlings maintained the same angle to the sun's rays whether receiving them directly or reflected by the mirrors. Obscuring the sun, whether naturally by cloud or artificially, led to the birds being disorientated, just as migrants get lost when cloud or mist suddenly descends.

Top
Even in winter the treecreeper can still winkle out dormant insects from crevices in the bark.

Bottom
Some birds, like this Manx shearwater, may use smell to help them find their own burrow in the dark.

Migration Heights and Speed

MIGRATION IS DETERMINED by internal rhythmicity linked with light, and by an internal physiological clock. We have seen too that migrants in captivity show restlessness and there is a clear positive correlation between the distance of migratory flight and the degree of restlessness. Longer migratory journeys involve longer-lasting restlessness, and the migrant halts when the restlessness fades out.

BIRD FACT:
The grey heron has one of the slowest wingbeats of any bird – just 2 beats per second.

OBSERVING MIGRATING BIRDS

Top
The lesser whitethroat is an unobtrusive summer visitor to our woods and hedgerows.

Middle
Every few years large numbers of waxwings invade from Scandinavia.

Bottom
The house martin migrates mainly to tropical Africa.

IT IS THE SPEED of the bird relative to the air that determines its energy costs, but the speed and direction of the wind determine the absolute speed of the bird, and therefore the distance that it can fly. Radar observations have contributed to our understanding of these speeds, with warblers flying at 30–40 km/h (20–30 mph), larger songbirds 50 km/h (30 mph) and waders and ducks at 60–80 km/h (40–50 mph). The height of flying birds can be linked to wind speeds, and again radar has helped to find this out. Birds often start at 1,000–2,000 m (3,280–6,561 ft) over land, but move up to 6,000 m (19,658 ft) on long flights over water. Apart from there being different wind patterns at different altitudes, high flight is also useful in that heat is dissipated at height without any loss of water; if cooling involved any water loss there could be dangerous dehydration.

Another way of looking at speed is to plot the rate at which a wave of migrants crosses a land mass. Conder (1954) illustrates the progress of two waves of wheatears in relation to British and Irish Observatories in 1952. The first wave reached Lundy and Dungeness on 3 April, Bardsey and Cley on the 4 April and Monk's House (Northumberland) on the 5 April. By 7 April they were past the Isle of May in the Firth of Forth. The second wave were seen at Saltee (Wexford) and Skokholm on the 9 April, Monk's House on the 10 April, and were clear of the Scottish mainland by 11 April.

MIGRATION PATTERNS

MIGRATION TAKES MANY forms. Long distance migration to Africa or Asia, or rather lesser distances within the northern hemisphere, special seabird movements for those which are mobile whenever they are not at their breeding sites, partial migrants when some move and others do not, altitudinal migrants and irruptive species which only move distances when food shortages force them on. If these do not move back it is not a true migration.

DIFFERENT DESTINATIONS

THE HOUSE MARTIN goes to Africa, the lesser whitethroat stays in the northern hemisphere and the arctic tern is always quoted as one of the longest bird migrants. Redwings are typical winter visitors to this country, and although a ten-year-old chaffinch may be ringed within 180 m (600 ft) of its birthplace, others move into the country from Scandinavia. The stonechat and song thrush have been mentioned as moving locally, whereas waxwing and common crossbill may irrupt over large distances. The movements of some of these selected species are illustrated.

The migration of the lesser whitethroat involve weight changes during their complex movements. Birds leave their overwintering areas and pass through Ethiopia as early as January, but only put on substantial weight in preparation for their move to Asia at the end of February. There they put on weight again before moving on, but lose it all as they fly across Europe, before flying into the south of England in mid to late April.

Their summer is busy and short with two broods characterised by weight fluctuations and a moult to be fitted into some 15 weeks. Then they start their return migration, with associated weight loss, to Italy before moving on to Egypt, where more feeding provides the energy for a final flight into winter quarters elsewhere in the warmth of the north and east of Africa.

UNEXPECTED ARRIVALS

HOWEVER EFFICIENT MIGRANTS may be at reaching their destinations, they often turn up unexpectedly elsewhere. Post breeding dispersal of young birds may mean they move in a direction away from their winter quarters. Reverse migration, for whatever reason, sends migrants off at 180∞ to their normal course, while overshooting, particularly in spring and sometimes with a following wind, can bring a bird, on the right bearing, to a land fall far beyond its breeding range, as when Iberian migrants reach Devon or Cornwall.

'Migration study, complex though it is, still depends – and always will depend – on the observatory and field man, the island lover, the cape haunter, the bunk sleeper and the sandwich eater.'
James Fisher SEA BIRDS

Top
Arctic terns are famed for one of the longest migration routes of all birds – from northern Europe and the Arctic right down to the Southern Ocean.

Bottom
Redwings are regular winter visitors from northern Europe.

Bird Observatories and Migration

THE BIRD OBSERVATORY in Britain stems from R. M. Lockley who, in the 1930s, combined farming with birdwatching on the small Welsh island of Skokholm, where he built traps for catching and ringing birds. Then in the late 1940s a surge of interest was shown, and a chain of observatories developed, providing what Williamson (1965) considered one of Britain's major contributions to ornithology.

FAIR ISLE

DR WILLIAM EAGLE CLARKE, in the early 1900s, visited Fair Isle, The Flannans and St Kilda, and his thinking about bird movements led to his *Studies in Bird Migration*, a standard work for many years. He believed that migrants followed great 'trunk routes' along prominent geographical features such as escarpments, river valleys and the coast. The east coast of England could have been one of these routes. Later came the contrasting idea that the birds set out on a broad front, in a preferred direction towards their goal, but they might be diverted by mountains or the sea and so be concentrated along leading lines.

After Eagle Clarke, others kept a watch on Fair Isle, which is 40 km (25 miles) from both Orkney and Shetland. When Kenneth Williamson arrived as the first warden in 1948, its position on migration routes had already allowed it to gain ten new species for Britain. There was no addition to these until 1953 when Williamson 'thought the world had gone mad' when, opening a bag in which a trapped bird had been kept, he saw 'a dwarf thrush no bigger than a skylark with a uniformly brown back and tail and heavily spotted whitish underparts'. It proved to be a North American species, found once before in Europe, a young grey-cheeked thrush. That autumn also brought Siberian newcomers, citrine wagtails and a Baikal teal, at a time when other rare eastern birds turned up at Fair Isle.

Much has changed at observatories over the years, but perhaps nothing indicates change so much as the fact that Williamson shot his first rarity, to prove identification. Identification skills developed quickly, and have continued to do so, as is indicated by a letter from R. F. Ruttledge to Williamson after they, and others, had identified a Pallas's warbler. 'Perhaps the thing that struck me most of all, was the wonderful opportunity one gets to practice making field identifications and the chance of making rapid notes of essential characters.' That Pallas's warbler avoided not only the fate of being shot, but also that of being trapped, for it was far from any of Fair Isle's permanent traps, and mist-nets had not been developed.

Top
The tiny Pallas' warbler is a rare, though regular, visitor to our shores from Siberia, usually in late autumn.

Bottom
Birds, like this song thrush, are weighed as well as being ringed at observatories.

RINGING BIRDS

TRAPPING, TO ALLOW ringing and laboratory studies, is a major activity at observatories. Heligoland traps, first used on the North Sea island of that name, are large, permanent wire-netting cages, usually set among shrubby cover. They have a

wide, 20 m (65 ft), opening between wings, and the wire narrows to a covered funnel, perhaps 4 m (13 ft) high. The birds are then driven through a swing-door to an ever-narrowing lock up and, finally, to a windowed catching box.

In the mid 1950s, trapping birds for ringing was revolutionised by the introduction of mist-nets from Japan, where peasant farmers had used them for catching birds for eating. These nets, stretched upright between supporting poles, are so fine as to be almost invisible. Birds flying into them pocket themselves over taut nylon strands threaded through the loose panels of the net. Given appropriate dexterity the birds can be extracted unharmed, and the great advantage of these mist-nets is their lightness and therefore mobility.

Williamson mentions that the justification for trapping birds is to learn more about them. One way is by attaching a numbered metal ring to the bird's leg before freeing it, and hoping that someone else will find it later, perhaps brought in by the cat, trapped for eating or recovered by another ringer. From such recoveries, details of life expectancy, migration routes, and cause of death, can be accumulated. Captured birds are also measured and weighed and variations, state of moult and external parasites are examined.

IMPORTANCE OF OBSERVATORIES

IT BECAME CLEAR to Williamson that knowledge of weather and the movements of air masses was central to migrants, as adverse winds was what brought migrants to Fair Isle and other observatories. Impressive 'falls' of migrants, both in spring and autumn, took place when the wind was easterly. All the observatory observations supported the importance of wind, and this was particularly so for isolated Fair Isle. Bird movement there is accidental, due either to lateral deflection from the migrant's true heading, or to a down wind displacement in mist, when orientation is not possible, and in fine weather when birds are dispersing at random from their breeding haunts. These wind orientated dispersal movements are sometimes phenomenal.

Williamson left Fair Isle in 1957 to become Migration Research Officer for the BTO, and by the time he wrote Fair Isle and its Birds there were 26 observatories on islands and peninsulas around Britain and Ireland.

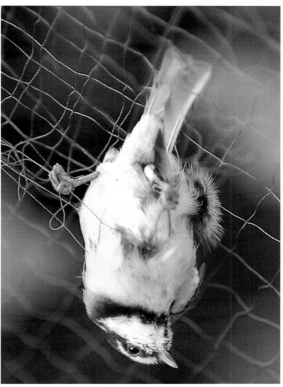

Top left
A heligoland trap on Lundy Island.

Bottom left
Ring on leg of house martin

Bottom right
Mist nets are efficient devices for catching birds – like this blue tit.

> *Bird ringing in Britain and Ireland is co-ordinated by the British Trust for Ornithology (BTO). It takes two years for volunteers to train to ring on their own and interested parties should write directly to the BTO for information.*

A TRIP TO CAPE CLEAR

IN THE SPRING of 1959 I was asked to join Garth Pettitt who wanted to explore the possibilities of Tory Island off the Donegal coast as an observatory. It was there that I had my only experience of mist-netting and my only chance to climb around a lighthouse at night, catching birds attracted to the beams.

IRISH RARITIES

IN THE AUTUMN of that year J. T. R. Sharrock and four others turned up at Cape Clear at another corner of Ireland. Sharrock (1973) describes how in 11 weeks the five of them found 17 species regarded as major rarities in Ireland, sea passage on an unsuspected scale and massive diurnal migration. If Fair Isle was associated with rare birds and the concept of drift, Cape Clear came to be associated with seabird movements. These were very poorly understood, and the only real gain in knowledge from early observatory work was the demonstration that the Balearic race of the Manx shearwater made a remarkable migration up the west coast of Europe to moult in late summer.

The Cape Clear observations began systematically in 1959, and by the time that Bourne (in Sharrock 1973) wrote *Cape Clear and Sea Bird Studies* he could base his analysis on 11 years and 2,952 hours of sea watching. This systematic work, together with the frequent recording of supposedly rarer species, stimulated interest in other sites, and co-operative observations along the length of the west coast of Europe were organised by Garth Pettitt, when the seabird group was formed in 1965.

Top
Great skuas may often be seen on passage during a seawatch from a vantage point.

Bottom
Redstarts breed in western woods, but often turn up in coastal scrub on migration.

BIRDS SEEN FROM CAPE CLEAR

AFTER FOUR YEARS it was possible to set Cape Clear in a wider context. Because they fly low, seabirds are particularly likely to be diverted by any barrier and to be concentrated along 'guiding lines', but much of the time, away from breeding areas and in good weather, they stay out at sea, which is a very uniform and featureless habitat. At the Cape, with onshore

winds and poor visibility, birds approach the shore. Passage is much more marked in a westerly direction, with the Blananarra headland concentrating the birds.

Easterly movement, except for Manx shearwaters and auks on feeding flights from Kerry colonies, is less frequent, as birds moving south along the west coast of Ireland can be seen from Erris or Brandon heads but then stay out at sea. Gannets, kittiwakes and fulmars tend to occur with onshore winds and poor visibility, local Manx shearwaters move east in the morning and west in the afternoon when they return to Kerry, and rarer shearwaters move into the area when shoaling fish reach their peak in late summer.

Skuas are only seen moving west, as are storm petrels. There may be up to 1,000 of these in an hour when there are south-westerlies with rain in late summer. Arctic and American breeders, including Sabine's gull, phalaropes, Leach's petrel and most skuas, migrate in the central Atlantic and normally have little trouble avoiding lee shores.

Rarer shearwaters, sometimes in large numbers and occasionally feeding, mainly occur between August and October. More than 1,000 great shearwaters may move west during a long seawatch, and sooty, little and Cory's shearwaters also occur, with the last species being seen earlier than the others, often in June.

VARIETY OF SPECIES

EARLY APRIL IS an exciting time on the island, with summer migrants and weather to show that spring has really arrived. It needs only the lightest of easterly or south-easterly winds to bring a rush of migrants to the island. Such movements bring the largest

numbers of sand martins hawking over the bogs, ring ouzels and wheatears, together with the first whimbrels, arctic terns and grasshopper warblers. This is the most likely time to see peregrines, jack snipe and hoopoes. Rarities have included little crake and white-throated sparrow, and choughs are very obvious, indulging in their delightful communal acrobatics.

Later in the year, no time can compare with early October, when some of the largest movements occur, and wind direction becomes everyone's obsessional interest. After evening log-writing someone is bound to look outside the Observatory and on his return a chorus of voices chants 'Where's the wind?'

A touch of easterly wind, or a calm day following a blustery day may be enough. Each clump of bushes in turn is surrounded by ornithologists twitching with excitement. Redstarts, lesser whitethroats, yellow-browed warblers, goldcrests, firecrests and red-breasted flycatchers are all in their highest numbers in October. It is almost impossible to stay on the island at the time and not see one rarity such as a spotted crake, bluethroat, Blythe's reed warbler, greenish warbler or a rare pipit. If the wind is in the west there should be few complaints, as American birds can appear, and Sharrock listed dowitcher, white-rumped sandpiper, yellow-billed cuckoo, olive-backed thrush, red-eyed vireo, American redstart and rose-breasted grosbeak.

Middle left
Whimbrels are regular on migration, especially in early spring.

Top right
Leach's petrel nests in Shetland and St Kilda, but spends most of its time out in the open Atlantic.

Bottom
The dainty yellow-browed warbler is a regular autumn visitor to Cape Clear.

BARDSLEY

SOME OF THE BIRDS flying west past Cape Clear could well have passed Bardsey, Ynys Enlli, on their way. It is a smaller island, under 200 ha (494 acres) compared with Cape Clear's 630ha (1,556 acres), but the stone walls, salt-sprayed cliffs and small fields are similar.

VARIETY OF BIRDS RECORDED

I FIRST VISITED Bardsey in 1947, and remember the puffins flying to and from Ynys Gwylan. Since 1954 there has been regular recording of all migrant and breeding birds within the main observatory season of March to November. When Peter Roberts wrote Birds of Bardsey (1985), 276 species had been recorded and over 100,000 birds ringed, and these totals are now more than 300 and over 200,000. It is interesting to compare the occurrence of some passerine migrants on Cape Clear and Bardsey.

Modern organisations are fond of quoting their aims and objectives, and the monitoring objectives of Bardsey were described in the 1996 observatory report (Adroddioid Gwylfa Ynys Enlli). Peter Hope-Jones, for long associated with the island, asks 'what precisely is the objective behind the observatory's collection of data?'

LOOKING AT BIRD MIGRATION

TO SAY 'the study of bird migration' is, he thinks, too unfocussed. Monitoring has sometimes been viewed like ringing as a 'good thing to do', but without clarifying reasons for doing it. He suggests that a major reason is that 'habitat managers, landowners, biologists and politicians can have quantified data on which to base further action.' Another outline of his objectives, accepted by the Observatory Council at its meeting in November 1996, indicates a little more of the scientific running of a modern observatory.

The aim is to carry out monitoring studies on the breeding and migrant birds at Bardsey.

Objective 1: To record numbers and biology of breeding species
Regular census of breeding birds
Productivity of breeding birds
Habitat usage by breeding landbirds
Regular habitat monitoring
Ringing as a support tool

Objective 2 : To record numbers and phenology of migrant species
Regular census of migrant birds
Standard sample – ringing of migrants
Stopover ecology of migrant land birds
Lighthouse attractions

Objective 3 : To ensure the competent documentation and storage of records
Collection of records
Collation of records
Production of Annual Report
Storage

VALUABLE REPORTS

THIS MAY SEEM a bit arid, but it is good to know what one is trying to do. Looking at a single report, no 39 for 1995, there are special reports on aspects of the ecology of choughs, herring gulls and Manx shearwaters, as well as detailed notes on landbird nesting habitats and the breeding birds of Welsh islands. Every year there is a ringing report, an account of birds at Bardsey lighthouse, and decisions from the Rarity Committee. The breadth of interest of visitors is indicated by further accounts of non-avian animals, butterflies and moths, the vegetation of two grazing areas and a botanical survey of ploughed fields to see whether arable

Bottom
The puffin is one of our most attractive seabirds. It nests mainly on offshore islands.

weeds would appear in fields which had not been ploughed for several decades. Archeological studies and a brief account of one of my favourites, an

enormously under-recorded woodlouse, *Platyarthrus hoffmannseggi*, complete the diverse diet, except of the systematic bird list and warden's report.

The warden, Andrew Silcocks, reported exciting changes, including the relaxation of grazing on the heathland which was showing wonderful regeneration, and a return to mixed farming with some arable fields to enhance plants and wildlife. He reports a heartening increase in landbirds, with three pairs of stonechats having good breeding success, and choughs fledging 18 chicks from five nests.

ARRAY OF SPECIES

CONCENTRATING ON ONE month, September, he reports reasonable sea watching, with Sabine's gull, a spate of Mediterranean gulls and two Leach's petrels, these at the lighthouse, as well as three Risso's dolphins passing close. Raptors included excellent views of an osprey and a red kite

which was watched for several hours. Dotterel and Lapland bunting, short-eared owl and little stint indicate the variety, and although there was no heavy passerine migration, there was a day of 15 redstarts, 100 goldcrests, 18 pied and 20 spotted flycatchers. Multiply that by eight, for the observatory is not usually manned in winter, and you have plenty of birds.

Observatories on islands are not only about science, or even only about birds, for their magic is linked with the sea, an ancient way of life and shared experience. Sitting among the sea pinks and vernal squills at the south end of Bardsey, admiring the evening sun on the Rhinog mountains behind Harlech, is as valued a memory as the tumultuous seas, generosity of islanders and views towards Muckish and Errigal from Tory Island.

Top left
The ringing cries of herring gulls punctuate any visit to the British coast.

Top right
Sabine's gull is a beautiful, if rare visitor – though not often seen, as here, in breeding plumage.

Middle left
Lapland buntings may be spotted on passage at sites such as Bardsey.

Bottom
Spotted flycatchers are regular migrants, in spring and autumn.

Songs and Calls

BIRDS LIVE IN a highly visual world, but however much colour, shape and visual signals matter, there is also vital communication by songs and calls. Krebs (1976) attempts to answer the question why some songs are so complex, describing some of his experiments with great tits.

Middle left
The chaffinch is one of our commonest birds; its song is a pretty sequence of descending notes, ending in a flourish.

Top right
The silvery song of the willow warbler can be heard in many of our woods and heaths in the summer.

Bottom
The song thrush has a loud, bold song, with short, repeated phrases.

SONG BIRDS

TRUE SONG IS restricted to the perching birds, about half of the world's species. In Britain, these are particularly well represented in gardens, woods and farms. In contrast to more simple calls, song is largely produced by males. Song is seasonal, and the great tits' 'teacher, teacher, teacher' song can be heard from January to May. Because of time correlations, most people associate song with claiming territory or attracting a mate, but there is little direct evidence for the attraction claim.

If woodland territory-holders are removed, new arrivals appear within hours from less desirable territories or from non territory-holders who are probably younger birds. This speedy appearance suggests they had been monitoring the woodland, listening for empty spaces. To test this, Krebs trapped and removed eight pairs from a six ha (14.8 acre) copse in Wytham Wood, Oxford. He had previously plotted the territories, well established by February. Loudspeakers playing great tit song for eight minutes per hour all day were placed in three territories, tin-whistle song substituted in two territories, while three were left silent. After eight hours of daylight, the areas without loudspeakers had been occupied by four newcomers, but it was 20 daylight hours before the loudspeaker areas were colonised. If song carries the simple 'keep out' message why is it so complex?

RANGE OF SONGS

EACH GREAT TIT or chaffinch has a small repertoire of songs, while a song thrush has a complex range. Perhaps by singing a repertoire of songs, the territory-holder causes the potential new arrivals to overestimate the density of singing males, or perhaps a big repertoire does not only mean there is a great tit here, but also that there is a dominant great tit here.

Whatever the exact function, each bird will have its own time for singing. In the dawn chorus of early summer, different species start at different times, and as Simms (1978) illustrates, each species will sing at its appropriate time of year. The early singing mistle thrush, as is well known, will sing almost regardless of weather, but territory-holders are usually most vocal on calm, bright days. There is often another burst of song as dusk approaches, with robins and thrushes being particularly active. It is not only nightingales that sing at night, sedge warblers often do so, and, where there are street-lights, robins and blackbirds may sing at any time.

CALLING

CALL NOTES, BY contrast with song, are produced by almost all birds, and are significantly simpler, although sometimes, as with the curlew, complex enough to be hard to distinguish from song. The complex versions, and some non-vocal sounds like 'drumming' of woodpeckers using their beaks, or of snipe letting air whistle through their tail feathers as they descend, serve the same function as song. Curlews, like many birds of open spaces, will advertise their territory by making themselves conspicuous in the air, as do larks and pipits, while woodland birds are more likely to rely on song alone.

ALARM CALLS

RETURNING TO THE simple calls: they are usually intraspecific signals, but sometimes involve other species as well. The alarm notes of many woodland birds – warblers, redstart, chaffinch and tits – can be very similar, with any bird that spots danger signalling to a wide range of species. This interpretation can be challenged as being too altruistic: genes are selfish. Perhaps the calls have come to resemble each other since all have evolved to be clearly audible, but difficult for a predator to locate. Similarly, wandering tit flocks, so common in autumn and winter, communicate about food supplies as no doubt do many of the waders, so busily calling as they move about the estuary at different stages of the tidal cycle.

DESCRIBING BIRD SONG

TRADITIONALLY, SONGS HAVE been described in prose. Thus Peterson, Mountfort and Hollom (1954) describe the blackcap's as a 'remarkably rich warbling more varied but less sustained than the garden warbler's, often louder at the end'. Writers attempt to describe calls so that the same book calls the voice of the green sandpiper a ringing 'tluitt, weet wet' and the greenshank's a ringing 'tew–tew–tew'.

Varied attempts to get over the lack of precision in such descriptions have been made. Harting (1866) writes how 'wherever it has been practicable I have reduced the notes to a key by means of a small whistle. The musical expression thus obtained I have introduced into the text, but the reader must not attempt to interpret these notes by the piano; for by this means he will not obtain the faintest notion of the sounds which they are intended to convey. A flute or flageolet will give a proper sound, but the most perfect expression will be obtained with a small whistle, two and a half inches long and having three perforations, similar to the whistle used by the Sardinian Picco who performed so wonderfully in London some years since.'

THE SONOGRAM

MORE MODERN AND more precise is the sonogram, by analysis of which direct comparisons can be made between the songs of subspecies, the alarm calls of birds which sound similar, the local dialects of chaffinches, or different versions in the repertoire of song thrushes. For those who want to listen and learn about songs, a large range of tapes and CDs is now, of course, available. Although some like to listen to them purely for pleasure, the real pleasure is to have birds in their natural surroundings and to try to become familiar with as many as possible. I have heard it said that a great tit has 92 separate vocalisations, and no doubt each of them has a clear meaning to other great tits.

BIRD FACT:
The bones which make up the skeleton of a bird are rigid, but they are also very light. They achieve this by having cavities inside them which are filled with air.

Top
The rock pipit's song resembles that of meadow pipit, but with a stronger trill at the end.

Middle left
The mistle thrush starts singing early in the year, usually from high up in a tree.

Bottom
The great tit is another early songster – often starting as soon as the days begin to lengthen.

Display

IN MEMORIES (1970), Julian Huxley mentions that 'scientific bird watching' was of much greater importance to his career than 'stupidly wading through Butschli's enormous German work on Protozoa'.

REDSHANKS

HE WAS STUDYING redshanks, and the male's remarkable display 'in which the wings were opened to show the white undersides and the head

advanced slowly towards the female, his conspicuous red legs repeatedly raised, while he emitted a continuous rattling note. Finally he vibrated his wings even more rapidly, until he raised himself into the air, settled on her back and, still fluttering, succeeded in copulation. I also repeatedly saw the conspicuous display flight, warning rival males off the chosen nesting area, in which the male indulges in a series of switch backs, giving vent meanwhile to a loud and melodious song.'

That was in 1910 when he published his first paper on bird courtship in relation to Darwin's theory of sexual selection. He was proud of himself for using the word 'formalised' for some of the male's actions, for we now know that much courtship behaviour is indeed stereotyped. He was much prouder of having made field natural history scientifically respectable.

GREAT CRESTED GREBES

HE PUBLISHED HIS paper on great crested grebe courtship in 1914, and was the first to apply the term 'ritualisation' to their formalised ceremonies, and to record what is now called a 'displacement activity'. Towards the end of a long spell of head-shaking the birds would make as if to free their wings, not actually preening, but just raising the tip of the wing with their beaks. This meaningless activity was also ritualised when the urges to continue displaying or to break away were in conflict.

Top
Great crested grebes have an elaborate head-shaking display in the breeding season.

Middle
A pair of gannets greet each other with ritualised gestures.

Bottom
Black-headed gulls signal to each other using a variety of different postures.

 44

GULL BEHAVIOUR

NIKO TINBERGEN UNDERTOOK pioneering work on gull behaviour and published *The Study of Instinct* (1951), the manuscript for which had been completed in 1948. Bryan Nelson, whose gannet studies are quoted later, suggests that one reason Niko Tinbergen is held in such high esteem among ethologists, students of behaviour, and ornithologists in general is that he really let us see how birds behave, and made convincing sense of what caused the behaviour and what it meant. Tinbergen's implicit dictum that natural selection is all pervasive is in contrast with an earlier gannet-watcher who wrote 'the gannet may work off surplus energy in harmless posturing'. Gannets behave in particular ways, at particular times, because a complex set of internal and external events make them do so. It would be wrong, says Nelson, to conclude that gannets know what they are doing.

Tinbergen's films of gull behaviour, black and white and rather jerky in the style of the time, showed how the 'ritualised' and 'formalised' movements Huxley had described in courtship behaviour permeated all sorts of activities, and were evident whenever there were interactions between individuals. With black-headed gulls, the various postures act as symbols, each conveying a message of some kind to fellow black-headed gulls.

DEFENDING ITS TERRITORY

A BLACKBIRD WILL defend territory by stretching its neck up, fluffing out its feathers, except those of the head which are smoothed, and raising the beak above the horizontal. Blackbirds are one of the few species which will actually fight regularly, but it seems to me they do it more at the meeting points of densely-packed garden territories than they do in woods. Because song is such an important aspect of territorial advertising, song-posts, be they television aerials, lamp-posts or rooftops are another focal point for blackbirds, and for young ones, may be more important for a time than a nest site.

For a blackbird, song and aggressive gestures are part of territorial behaviour, and time and again a characteristic movement is linked with a characteristic sound. This is so when lapwings tumble and call, when peregrines dive and shriek, or when a moorhen makes 'crake' calls with vertical neck. Any call, or display, or combination, must give an increased chance of gene survival, even when it appears to make a bird more vulnerable. Some therefore have argued that an alarm call given in a flock of unrelated individuals may manipulate these into a position of danger when the caller itself has made its getaway.

> **BIRD FACT:**
> The beaks of birds tell us a lot about their favourite food. The range of beak shape is huge – from the sharp, hooked bill of birds of prey, to thin, narrow bill of many waders.

Top left
Blackbirds are highly territorial and often squabble over a patch of garden.

Top right
Chaffinch showing an aggressive posture at a territorial boundry. This is linked with side to side movements.

Bottom
The spring displays of lapwings are a delight, involving tumbling flights and cat-like mewing calls.

Nests

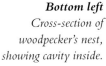

ONCE THE HOURS of daylight increase, and the anterior pituitary gland sends the appropriate stimulating hormones to the sex glands, all sorts of bird behaviour starts to change. Eventually after migration, territorial defence and courtship, comes nest-building and egg-laying, and in many ways a species' success will depend on the outcome of the events that are now set in train. How many eggs will be laid, will the nest be destroyed, and if it survives how many young will survive to fledging and become independent individuals ready for their own reproduction next year or in future years?

TYPES OF NEST

SOME BIRDS MAKE no real nest, while others make nests that are large or complex or beautifully constructed. It is usually the passerines which make the most elaborate ones based on a basic cup shape. With the long-tailed tit this is elaborated to form an enclosed dome, and the different behaviour patterns that are necessary to build so complex a structure have been analysed. This building is summarised by Perrins (1979): 'After the birds have chosen a site for their nest, they start to put pieces of moss there; although much of this may fall off, they continue until some pieces stay. When sufficient moss has adhered to the site, the birds switch to collecting spiders' webs which they pass back and forth across the moss until it sticks, when they bind it to the branch.'

Once a platform has been built they sit in the middle of it and tuck new moss around

themselves, weaving moss and web into the sides of the nest, turning as they weave so as to produce a circular nest. This is only the start, for another seven or eight different movements and the incorporation of lichens and feathers are still needed.

CHAFFINCH'S NEST

THE CHAFFINCH MAKES a compact and neat nest, with a deep cup. It is so well made that it is pliable, so well lichened that it is almost invisible, and so well sited that it is firmly held in the fork of a tree or bush. All sorts of things are brought together to achieve this, a mix of bark and fibre, spiders' webs and hair, rootlets and grass.

Another cup, with the added creativity of being woven round the supporting stalks, is produced by reed

Bottom left
Cross-section of woodpecker's nest, showing cavity inside.

Top right
The nest of the reed warbler is carefully woven around the surrounding stems.

Bottom left
Though quite small, the reed warbler's nest has quite a deep cup.

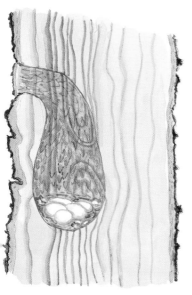

warblers and, in one form or another by other passerine reed dwellers. The non-passerines may get nearer the water, with grebes having accumulations of vegetation floating on the water, water rails adapting their cup of plant stems according to rising water levels, and bitterns adding reeds to their platform nest as the young grow.

WOODPECKER'S NEST

IN CONTRAST TO the soft and wet, could be the hard, dry heavily-worked woodpecker nests made in firm trees, or those of tits, crested and willow for instance, in softer rotten tree stumps. Even harder, but not necessarily dry, are those of guillemots which lay on bare rocks, or perhaps a bit of loose gravel, on a ledge of a vertical cliff. Most of the other cliff-breeders do make some attempt at a nest, with kittiwakes, for instance, using mud, grass and seaweed to make an elaborate cup. The steepness of the cliffs on which these birds are found gives good protection, except against skuas, but holes can be even better, and many other seabirds, Manx shearwaters and puffins for example, use rabbit-holes, and storm petrels may do the same, or use natural crevices or those in dry-stone buildings.

> 'Birds I beheld building nests in the bushes
> Which no man had the wit even to begin to work
> I wondered where and from whom the pie could have learned
> To put together the sticks in which she lays and broods,
> For there is no craftsman, I know, who could construct her nest'
> William Longland PIERS THE PLOWMAN

Top left
Woodpecker's nest from the side, showing how the entrance hole connects with the nest cavity.

Top right
The chaffinch builds a neat, soft nest, often sited close to the trunk of a tree.

Bottom
Puffins usually nest in abandoned rabbit burrows.

Eggs

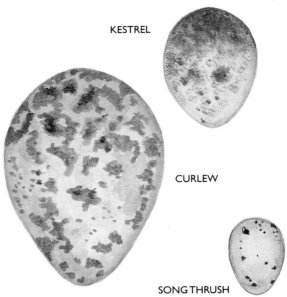

KESTREL

CURLEW

SONG THRUSH

EGGS, OF COURSE, vary in size, shape and colour. Bigger birds not surprisingly lay bigger eggs, particularly if the young are nidifugous and have to be active as soon as they hatch. A cuckoo, which is considerably larger than any of its hosts, lays relatively small eggs, and a bird that lays lots of eggs, like a partridge, also cannot produce very large ones.

VARIETY OF SHAPES

WITHIN ANY TAXONOMIC group, the shape of eggs will be basically similar, so that gulls and waders produce eggs which narrow abruptly towards the smaller end, while grebe eggs are pointed and similar at both ends. Where four eggs are laid, the narrow ends converge towards the clutch centre to form a compact group for brooding.

COLOURS OF EGGS

TWO MAIN PIGMENTS are responsible for the range of egg colour: blue-greens, perhaps derived from bile pigments, and red-browns from haemoglobin of the blood. Apart from background colour, often white in hole-nesting birds, there are bands, mottlings and scribblings due to varying pressure in the oviduct. The white of woodpecker eggs is enhanced by their gloss, and the surface texture of other eggs can have as wide a range as paints – matt, vinyl silk or gloss.

Top left
Mallard's nest with clutch of six eggs.

Top right
Eggs of (from left to right) curlew, kestrel and song thrush.

Bottom
Skylark's nest with clutch of four eggs.

NEST RECORD SCHEME

IN A BOOK CELEBRATING 50 years of the BTO, P. G. Davis in Hickling (1983) describes this scheme, the brainchild of Julian Huxley and James Fisher, which started slowly but became so successful that it has been the basis of many studies of breeding biology. As early as 1943, working on single-species studies of the robin and the wren, David Lack and E. A. Armstrong were using the material available. It was also one of many areas where computer analysis has made information much more easy to extract; as 40,000 cards were completed in 1997 alone, the accumulated number since 1939 can be appreciated.

By 1970, enough cards had been completed to achieve much of the original objective 'the collection of information on the dates of the various stages, and on incubation and fledging periods', and it was time for Henry Mayer-Gross to produce a guide to the Nest Record Scheme, which explained the instructions and requirements which appear on the cards. The guide included charts to show the length

of the breeding season from the first egg date to the last record of a young bird still in the nest. From those facts we see that two single-brooded species, the marsh warbler and nightingale, have the shortest breeding seasons, of nine and 11 weeks respectively. By contrast, whitethroats, also migrants, have a breeding season spread over 16 weeks, sometimes giving time for two broods, while stonechats, back on their breeding grounds by late February, may have time for three broods, spread over 21 weeks.

When Davis wrote, the emphasis was changing, as computing came in, and he hoped the nest record scheme would take on the role of a barometer in measuring the success or failure of each season, and would help to explain some of the reasons for the fluctuations that the Common Birds Census was demonstrating.

That this had been achieved can be seen by a look for example at *Nest Record News* (April 1998). A few examples show the sort of detail involved. April 'spanned a remarkably mild and dry spell in most districts with temperatures reaching 24/25°C. At first, fair conditions helped many birds, notably sawbills, mallard, moorhen, stonechat, siskin, pied and grey wagtails, to raise early large broods.' Later persistent downpours, in June, saturated the downy bodies of young waterbirds, leading to local heavy losses through hypothermia and drowning. Similarly, these torrential downpours, together with deliberate human interference, accounted for losses among the exciting raptor trio, merlin, hobby and goshawk.

> 'A hen's egg is, quite simply, a work of art, a masterpiece of design and construction with, it has to be said, brilliant packaging.'
> Delia Smith 1998

RESULTS OF THE RECORDS

AS A FINAL EXAMPLE, the hot weather throughout much of August coupled with damp soils, high water tables and good sources of aerial insect and soil invertebrate food supplies, triggered off late nesting attempts. Great crested grebe, stone curlew, nightjar, dunnock, wren, woodlark, house martin, linnet, yellowhammer and corn bunting often raised twin sets of young.

The vital thing is that these reports are not based on anecdotal reports from a couple of sites, but from standardised observations of many nests throughout the breeding season. After analysis, the government's Joint Nature Conservation Committee can be alerted to worrying declines in breeding

performance. The hen harrier decline is mentioned and explained elsewhere, but reed bunting nest survival has fallen by 33 per cent in the last 25 years. Sadly, there have also been significantly increased losses in lapwing nest contents, moorhen brood size has declined by nearly one nestling, and such different birds as red-throated diver and greenfinch continue to have increasing nest failure rates.

BIRD FACT:
Eider ducks line their nests with hundreds of soft down feathers. These were once collected to fill mattresses and bed coverings – the original eiderdowns.

Top
The eggs of the dunnock are a clear blue.

Middle
The tapered egg of the guillemot makes it less likely to roll off the cliff.

Bottom
Nest of common gull with clutch of two eggs.

A Bird's Year

THERE ARE MANY books about single species, and the number of individual studies of mammals and birds has grown steadily since the early New Naturalist monographs on the badger by Ernest Neal in 1948, and on the yellow wagtail by Stuart Smith in 1950.

LIFE OF BIRDS

HERE, THREE BIRDS and their activities throughout the year will be looked at, in more detail than the very brief outline sometimes provided in the species sections. The lesser whitethroat is a long-distance migrant whose weight changes in relation to migratory movements were summarised earlier. By contrast the chaffinch is an example of a familiar resident which rarely moves far from its birthplace. More detail of the chaffinch can be found in Ian Newton's *Finches* (1972), and Eric Simms in *British Warblers* (1985) gives more detail of the lesser whitethroat's life and breeding activities. Colonial nesters provide another contrast, and the huge gannet, in its vast nesting masses, has a completely different set of behaviour patterns.

Top
Lesser whitethroat on bare branch.

Bottom
More typically, lesser whitethroats skulk about in the bushes.

LESSER WHITETHROAT

EVIDENCE FROM OBSERVATORIES show that lesser whitethroats arrive in the south and south-east during a ten-day peak after 26 April, when Dungeness and Portland notice a good passage. Fair Isle's much later birds are overshooting their target areas in Germany, Denmark and Scandinavia.

Within 12 days of arrival, eggs may be laid, so that the establishment of territories, the necessary courtship, and the building of the nest are rapid events. The male's rattling song, from tall hedgerows, often with ash trees, is often our only indication of his presence, but Simms has observed courtship, when the male 'swells out his breast and the feathers thereon, raises the feathers on his crown, and fans and beats his wings, lowering the bill at the same time. There is an even greater state of ecstasy in which he tumbles and falls about, often with a leaf or grass stem in his bill.'

THE NEST

THE MALE USUALLY starts the nest, which is completed by the female. It is frequently in bramble, built from dry grasses, stalks and roots, and lined with finer roots, horsehair and catkins, and is often decorated with spiders' cocoons. Once the eggs are laid, the male helps with incubation and later helps with feeding the young, on small insects. Within a

month of arrival, by early June, the young will be able to flutter from the nest. If danger threatens, the female will often try to distract a potential predator with an injury-feigning display. At this time, the repeated 'tac-tac' call is often heard. By the middle of July, some birds may begin to moult. Some first-year birds seem to wait until they are wintering in Africa to change their tail feathers, but wings are moulted before migration, which peaks at the end of August.

PATTERNS OF POPULATIONS

DUNGENESS HAS FAR more birds passing through in the autumn than in spring, and there are other indications that departure is from the south-east on the first stage of movement, via Switzerland and Israel, to areas east of the Nile, which it reaches in mid-October. Eastern European populations end up in India, Sri Lanka and Iran; both populations move south-east. As early as late January some will have begun to return.

Judging by the pattern of singing in the thick bramble and blackthorn of my garden, and surrounding hedges, some of the birds in east Devon, on the fringes of the bird's range, are unsuccessful in finding mates. Having failed in one place, they move on after a few days, to sing somewhere else, leading to possible over-recording of singing males. However, being inconspicuous and often poorly known, there are also plenty of reasons for under-recording.

BIRD FACT:
The mute swan, weighing up to 18 kg, is one of the heaviest of all flying birds. It can only take off and land safely if it has a long stretch of water.

Top
Lesser whitethroat with hungry brood.

Bottom
A female lesser whitethroat brings food to her nestlings.

Chaffinch

A N OLD COCK chaffinch will return to its territory in mid-February, advertising his arrival with his 'chink' call and by song. The same territory may well be occupied for several years, with little change in its boundaries if neighbours also survive.

THE SONG OF THE CHAFFINCH

A YOUNG BIRD will have a different approach, moving in quietly and using his subsong, which will only develop into the typical adult song with its three parts when the bird is ten months old. Male aggression is shown by flight towards any definite intruder, exposing the white wing-patches. Recognisable postures and vigorous display are shown at territorial boundaries. If a male is joined by a female, she gives a 'tupe' call. With body sleeked and horizontal he tilts it and raises the wing nearest to her to expose his red flank. If, after his 'moth flight', which involves rapid beats of small amplitude, she wanders away, he then resumes singing. If she remains, they indulge in sexual chases and ground feeding.

ESTABLISHING TERRITORY

THROUGHOUT MARCH, WITH territory and mate established, activity, involving feeding and preening, is all confined to the territory. Courtship intensifies and the hen becomes dominant, with priority at any food.

Mild weather in April leads to a frenzy of sexual chases, and the female starts to build the nest, which has four concentric layers. The outer shell is of lichen and spider silk, ideal for concealment, and the next two layers are of moss and grass, and of grass alone. The lining is made up of thin roots and feathers. Nest building takes about seven days, with up to 1,300 visits. The male follows her very persistently, even if she attacks him near the nest tree. He also attempts to mate, but is unsuccessful until she adopts the crouching, soliciting position.

Top
The hen chaffinch is duller than the male, but still shows the white wing-bar.

Bottom right
Juvenile chaffinch

Bottom left
Female chaffinch, showing almost sparrow-like plumage.

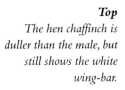

When the young do start to feed themselves they have little success, and when they attempt song it is a rambling subsong. They will hear adults and experiments suggest that this is part of the learning that will eventually lead them to a full adult repertoire when they are ten months old. By 50 days they are independent, collect into groups, and begin to moult.

RANGE OF THE CHAFFINCH

YOUNG BRITISH CHAFFINCHES rarely stray more than 5 km (3 miles) from the nest site, but a few first-year birds may wander up to 50 km (30 miles). The adults, free of young in late June or July, stop any reproductive behaviour but they may, briefly, attack other adults in their territory. When the moult begins, even this stops, and they skulk inconspicuously.

From a taxonomic point of view it is interesting that the chaffinch and its relative the brambling (both fringilline finches) have a very different pattern of territorial behaviour from the cardueline finches, like the goldfinch and linnet.

Fringillines have large territories, spreading themselves evenly over suitable habitat, while the carduelines nest in loose colonies, within which each pair defends a small territory. Compared with chaffinches, spread through the ash woods, it is very hard to count linnet territories among the shrubby blackthorn for example.

LAYING EGGS

IN LATE APRIL or May she starts laying at daily intervals, and begins regular incubation when the penultimate egg is laid. The nidicolous young are born blind, helpless and naked, but can just raise their heads. They are soon arranged with hind ends out and heads inwards, always ready to make begging calls. Eighty five per cent of feeding is done by the hen, with six to nine feeds of insects per hour; faeces are removed after each visit.

In mid to late May, the young leave the nest and continue to be fed in scattered positions.

Top
Male chaffinch in full breeding plumage, visiting a pool.

Bottom
A female chaffinch brings food to her young.

Gannet

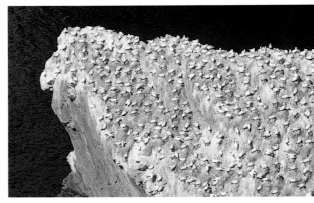

ONE CANNOT SAY that gannets are either poorly known or inconspicuous, but most people have only seen them at sea and not at their spectacular breeding colonies. Bryan Nelson, introducing the gannet, describes the stuff of a gannet's life as 'rock, wind, waves, seaweed, guano and fish together with constant interaction with its fellows'.

RETURNING HOME

YOUNG GANNETS, coming up to their second birthday, return to home waters but are unlikely to find space to settle on the island cliffs where they were born. At first they sail around in the busy air traffic, learning about cliff winds and fishing grounds. They may join a club of non adults, using a ledge near the breeding birds and interacting with other club members, with low-intensity territorial and sexual behaviour.

Years later, perhaps in his fourth, fifth or sixth year, a male begins to look seriously for a breeding site. After many flights over the potential plot he will settle uncertainly, often well within pecking distance of other birds, but the real challenge for the site will come from the air, particularly if the site was only vacant because the owner was away fishing. If our male survives without challenge for two or three days, the site becomes his and the confidence with which he flies in with loud calls, or performs an aggressive display on landing, increases. If there is still no serious challenge, he may spend three quarters of the daylight hours guarding and displaying, with much 'jabbing' by means of vigorous forward lunges at neighbours, and 'menacing' with exaggerated forward thrusts with an open beak.

A gannet 'bows' thousands of times a year, and each performance uses energy. The fact that evolution has produced such a complex and polished display also indicates that it is an important signal, but why does the gannet do it? It does not appear aggressive, but the author can assert, with a high degree of certainty, that 'bowing' is an aggressively motivated display, signalling ownership of the site.

ATTRACTING A MATE

RELATED TO THE bow, but with aggressive components greatly suppressed, is 'sexual advertising' for our bird has not got a mate yet. A female approaching will initially trigger the response for any gannet approaching, but once seen as a female the bow is changed to an inconspicuous 'headshake and reach' of the greatest importance. Although a variety of responses may follow, the female will often respond by approaching, followed by mutual bill-touching

Top
Aerial view of a gannetry in the Shetlands – note even spacing of birds.

Bottom
A gannet calls from its nest.

and by her 'facing away' – an appeasement gesture to reduce the risk of wasteful fighting. There are so many display signals in a complex gannetry that we will assume further pair-bonding with 'meeting ceremonies', 'sky pointing' and 'mutual fencing' leads onto copulation, which is closely linked with nest building. This is an important activity, adding flotsam and weed to a pre-existing 'drum' raised above the muddy mire of the colony.

LAYING EGGS

WHEN THE EGG is laid it is, extraordinarily, incubated beneath the webs of the feet which overlap above the egg. Both parents share incubation, with average stints of over 30 hours, which shorten as hatching approaches. As the embryo grows and the chick gets nearer to hatching, the parents' behaviour changes towards shorter incubating stints, and therefore shorter feeding trips, which is adaptive, in that when the chick does hatch it will not have to wait long for food. It is vital that the egg is transferred onto the tops of the webs at the right time before hatching, but some young breeders may not have developed the appropriate neural mechanisms for this innate action and so crush the hatching chick.

CARE OF THE YOUNG BIRD

THE ADULTS BROOD, preen and feed the young bird. Initially, as with our previous species, the newly-hatched gannet is too weak and wobbly to influence the parents, but soon the intensity of its begging manipulates the parents to produce the required amount of food. To get its regurgitated, semi-digested food, the chick gropes in the trough of the parent's lower mandible. Brooding becomes impossible after three weeks of growth and therefore in bad weather three to six week old chicks are at risk of chilling.

The parents maintain their care for 13 weeks and it is no lack of care on their part that ends this phase of life. After days of wing-flapping and looking out to sea, the chick makes the decision and reaches the traumatic moment when it rushes headlong to the cliff-edge and jumps, topples or is pushed over, and despite no practice is usually quickly airborne. For some the cliff-edge is far away, and these birds will be attacked by adults on their way to the edge and may well crash among other nesting birds, to be attacked again, but once in the air the young gannet flaps and wobbles and soars and may even fly as far as 3 km (1.8 miles) at its first attempt.

Landing on the sea is rarely a success, and if the landing is among adults it may be attacked again. Because it is so fat and the wings are not yet fully developed, it cannot fly up from the water but must swim away from the colony for two weeks, plunge-diving inefficiently for food. Once weight is lost, flight is again possible and in two weeks the young birds may have reached Morocco.

Top left
Gannets are majestic in soaring flight as they scan the sea for shoals of fish.

Top right
This close-up shows the dagger-like bill.

Middle left
Adult gannet with down-covered young.

Bottom
Young gannets gradually lose their down and take on a grey plumage.

Ecology of Habitats

ECOLOGY IS THE study of populations, communities and ecosystems. Eco-systems include not only the living components of a habitat, but also the non-living ones like climate and soil and, nowadays, the endless combinations of chemicals we add to the environment.

ECOLOGICAL NICHES

WITHIN AN ECOSYSTEM each bird has its own niche, which is what it does, rather than where it is; its place in the natural grand scheme of things. If one thinks of a dunnock's niche, it is everything included within

the job of 'dunnocking'. A garden or woodland or hedge is needed for a modern, British dunnock, and the right climate, roughly like that in which ancestral dunnocks grew up. It will need enough small insects and seeds on the ground to feed on, and not too many enemies. They need to be good at 'dunnocking' to survive, and the fact that wrens are also good at 'wrenning' does not matter, because they have a different, if fairly similar, niche.

Within one habitat, niches will be limited, so the number of birds in that habitat will be limited, but habitats are often isolated from each other by distance, mountain ranges or the sea. Some birds can overcome these barriers, but many small ones, or weak fliers like rails, are limited to a special niche in an isolated habitat somewhere in the world, so there are lots of different rails. Where there are lots of niches, for instance in woodlands or coral reefs, there are lots of animal species, but in the arctic tundra or in a paved city, species are less numerous.

Top left
Fulmar's egg on its rocky sea-cliff habitat.

Top right
Introduced Canada geese have adapted to a wide range of wetlands and parks.

Bottom
Juvenile dunnock.

ROLE OF NATURAL SELECTION

EACH SPECIES HAS its niche fixed by natural selection, and, once fixed, its numbers are also relatively fixed. Surprising though it may seem, the way an animal breeds has very little to do with how many of it there are. If circumstances change, or gene frequency changes within a population, then the size of that population may change, but the reproductive effort makes no difference to the size of the eventual population. Slowly reproducing fulmars, laying one egg a year, with the first when they are six to 12, have been able to increase their British population, from the original stronghold of St Kilda, by 12 times in the last 50 years, and this after an earlier period of prolonged increase. The fulmar's niche has changed, with more food being available. Calculations suggest the availability of an extra 200,000 tonnes of offal and whitefish remains every year from the fishing industry, but it may also be that fulmar genes have changed, with immigration into Britain from Icelandic populations, rather than from St Kilda.

Birds have evolved what some ecologists call the 'large young gambit' as opposed to the 'small egg gambit' favoured for example by flies, mosquitoes and salmon. So dunnocks lay their eggs and try to raise their young until they are big and strong, but however efficient the parents are, there is a limit to the dunnock population because there are limits set by the opportunities within the dunnock niche. Every parent must still make every effort to ensure its genes are represented in the next generation.

FOOD CHAINS AND WEBS

BECAUSE A BIRD spends much of its life feeding, a niche can often be defined in terms of what a bird eats and how it sets about getting its food. Food and who eats what is at the centre of a study of ecosystems. Some birds are plant-eaters, with seeds as a favourite food because of their high energy content. These birds and the grazing ducks, geese and swans, are herbivores, like those you may feed with peanuts and sunflower seeds.

Having fed their favourites, many people resent the sparrowhawk which also occasionally visits the bird table, but carnivores, flesh-eaters, are just animals that feed differently, and are higher up the food chain. In the breeding season your bird table tits will become carnivores, synchronising their breeding with the emergence of woodland caterpillars. A song thrush eating snails is just as much a carnivore as a sparrowhawk. Sparrowhawks eat lots of different birds, and blue tits, even in the best supplied garden, do not live on peanuts alone, so a food web, showing feeding alternatives, is a better way of representing who eats what.

BIRD FACT:
Many migrating birds travel at altitudes of 2000m or more, probably because they find higher following winds at this height. If they encounter strong headwinds or bad weather systems they may fly at a very low level. The bar-headed goose has been spotted at 9000m when flying over the Himalaya Mountains.

Top left
A female sparrowhawk keeps a wary watch in the woods.

Top right
Great tits are regular visitors to bird tables.

Bottom
The oystercatcher is most at home along rocky shores.

Top left
Juvenile great crested grebe, showing dagger-like bill used for catching fish and invertebrates.

Bottom left
A blackbird gathering up worms.

Bottom right
Healthy clear lowland stream in southern England.

DIFFERENT PREY FOR DIFFERENT BIRDS

DIFFERENT WADING BIRDS feed on different prey, with a few extremely numerous invertebrates being important food for many estuary birds, but most prey items being selected by only a few birds. A short-billed dunlin cannot catch a lugworm unless it is on the surface, but a curlew can reach it in its deep burrow. A stout-billed bird like a turnstone can turn over stones to find crabs, while a bird with a sensitive bill-tip, like a curlew, can rely on probing for its prey, but an oystercatcher, hammering on cockles, would do any sensitive nerve endings no good and feeds in a very different manner.

IMPORTANCE OF THE FOOD WEB

FOOD WEBS ALSO show the flow of energy through the ecosystem; a flow because there must always be new energy inputs from the sun to keep the system going. These inputs may however come rather indirectly, or in a delayed manner. The great tits and chaffinches in a winter beech wood are using last summer's energy when they pick up beech nuts, while a blackbird, scattering the beech leaves, may be

using energy from the summer before that as it searches for invertebrates feeding in the decomposing litter. On a river bed, particularly in an estuary, sediments, inorganic and organic, will be deposited from elsewhere. The organic sediments supporting the ragworms and lugworms are not obviously sun-

related but they can be traced back in time and place to earlier solar inputs, somewhere upstream. Often what goes on underground, in the so-called decomposer food chain, involves a greater flow of energy than in the green world above.

NUTRIENT CYCLES

IN CONTRAST TO the flow of energy is the cycling of elements like carbon and nitrogen. The carbon dioxide of the air, through photosynthesis, becomes the carbohydrate, sugar or starch of a plant, which, when eaten, becomes the fat or glycogen reserve of a bird.

The leaves and roots of the plant, like the bird, will eventually die and decompose. This decay depends on scavenging animals and decomposer fungi and bacteria. As they and other organisms respire, the carbon dioxide is released back into the air. We fear now about an excess of carbon dioxide in the air, and the probability of global warming, but we also fear the results of other cycles which no longer 'balance' so that surplus nitrogen and phosphate appear, for instance, in aquatic ecosystems.

NUTRIENTS AND THE NORFOLK BROADS

THE EFFECT OF a surplus of these nutrients is demonstrated by a consideration of the Norfolk Broads. When E. A. Ellis wrote *The Broads* in 1965, he

started a chapter on flowering plants by saying: 'One does not have to be a botanist to enjoy the peculiar beauty and diversity of plant life throughout this wilderness of swamps and waterways ...Thus the blue waters of Hickling, bounded by the great belts of reed

reveal in their depths a fantastic water garden of crisp leaved stoneworts ....' Elsewhere he wrote frequently of the Broads 'which abound in submerged water weeds', and of herds of wild swans. He was a most unfortunate author, for much of his book was out of date in less than ten years, as pollution changed the Broads.

Before the 1970s, there were relatively low inputs of nutrients, with more nitrate than phosphate. This kept fertility low, which in turn meant that plant plankton, drifting algae in the water, was not dense, nor did it form a cover over the leaves of the large plants below the water. With a low algal density, there were few toxic ones of the type that can kill fish. Fish could therefore thrive, and so could the great crested grebes that feed off them. The large plants provided safe fish spawning sites and cover for large numbers of large invertebrates such as nymphs and beetles.

Young fish particularly favoured the opossum shrimp *(Neomysis)* in their diet, and by keeping its population down allowed its chief food source, water fleas *(Daphnia)*, to remain common and to graze effectively on the algae that were there. When winter came there was plenty of underwater plant material for the coots and pochards and swans to eat. However much they ate, enough remained next spring to act as an 'inoculum' to set off next spring's growth. Overall there was clear water, and an abundance of attractive water plants – water milfoil, bladderwort and yellow waterlilie – these provided cover for fish, and food for birds so the whole healthy ecosystem was in balance.

BIRD FACT:
Most songbirds reach a speed of about 35 k/h (20 mph) when migrating, but waders and ducks fly faster, reaching a maximum of 80 km/h (50 mph). They often fly non-stop for several days and nights, losing weight as they go.

Above left
Pochard (this is a male) are an important part of the ecosystem at sites such as the Norfolk Broads.

Above right
Winter floods at Slimbridge – ideal for wildfowl such as Bewick's and whooper swans.

Bottom
Coot's nest in a reedy lake.

changing nutrient levels due to sewage from boats, agricultural run-off and droppings from the increasing numbers of roosting gulls had set the Broads on a sudden downward spiral.

SUCCESSION AND ZONATION

TWO OTHER ECOLOGICAL concepts are those of succession and zonation. Both could be illustrated by the Broads, but anyone with a garden is familiar enough with succession. Bare ground, carefully dug over for your flowering plants or vegetables is soon colonised by weeds, and in a year some of the short-lived annual ones will be replaced by deep-rooted docks and thistles. This is primary succession, the colonisation of bare ground, but your lawn fares little better. Unmown, it soon changes, not only because the grass is longer, but because plants that would not survive being cut are now able to thrive, and first one sort then another will colonise; a succession of different plant communities with each species competing for its own niche in the new conditions. In time your neglected lawn, or the lawn of the unsold house next door, becomes scrub, and scrub develops by steps towards woodland, which in most of Britain would be the climax vegetation.

Suddenly everything changed when the nutrient levels went up and the phosphate to nutrient ratio reached a critical point. Algae flourished, and included some toxic ones which periodically killed fish. The algae covered the water plants so that their photosynthetic rates fell, and there was less plant cover in which the remaining fish could spawn and the invertebrates feed and shelter. With fewer fish, *Neomysis* populations rose and ate more water fleas, which grazed less effectively on the rising levels of algae. These made the water a 'scummy' green, reducing light to the underwater plants still further. When the birds returned there was less food, and they left too little to get the spring growth effectively under way. Within a year a broad like Hickling had become visually less attractive, had lost many of its characteristic flowering plants and stoneworts, and was able to support fewer fish and birds. The

In nature, bare land, ready for primary succession, is unusual, and most of our abundant weeds were themselves presumably rarer, surviving for example on shingle-beds exposed by a river flood or on recently wind-blown sand. In nature too, unless there are herds of large grazing animals, grasslands are rare, but on farms, in gardens and on nature reserves we often attempt to stop the successional processes for our own purposes. In the conservation context we often want to do this to establish a particular ecosystem, by coppicing hazel, removing bramble or brush-cutting rank vegetation which we hope will create the habitats and diversity that we want.

CREATING DIVERSITY

ZONES ALSO INCREASE diversity, with different plants flourishing at different heights up a mountain for example, or different distances into a sand-dune system or at different levels below the high-tide

Top
Redshank preening
on rocky shore.

Middle
Oystercatcher in flight,
making alarm calls.

Bottom
Woodpigeons are common
birds of open country, and
are increasingly found in
parks and gardens.

Top
*Heathland is a threatened
habitat which provides
a home for many
interesting birds.*

Bottom left
*Hundreds of thousands
of knots visit Britain in
the winter, returning to
the high Arctic to breed.*

Bottom right
*Brent geese like to feed
in flocks, particularly on
saltmarshes and adjacent
mudflats*

mark. If mussels can only exist low on the beach they
are not available to many birds, except at certain
stages of the tide. A wading bird that fancies mussels
may feed a bit in a higher zone, waiting its time for
the mussel meal, while a worm-eater may have its
priority zone higher up the shore.

Redshank and knot have been shown to favour
the upper and middle shores, but when only the
upper shore is available, curlew and oystercatchers

may look for
alternative food in
fields. Levels of
salinity may also be
zoned, determining
which invertebrates
survive in the fresh,
brackish or salt
water of an estuary.
A successional
change may
introduce new
zones, as when
Spartina, a genus of
cord-grass spreads, oris introduced, onto estuarine
mud at a certain tidal level. In Strangford Lough, the
12,000 light-bellied brent geese from the Canadian
arctic, which refuel there every autumn before
dispersing across Ireland, may be in danger as their
main food, the eel-grass, is being replaced by *Spartina*.

Birds at the top of food webs will tend to be
rarer because energy is lost at each stage up the web
as animals burn up fuel to do the work of living. Birds
higher up food webs will tend also to be larger
because, in general, animals need to be larger than the
things they eat, particularly if they eat other animals.
There is not as much energy available for as many
peregrine falcons as pigeons, or for as many redshanks
as marine worms. As to why they do such peculiar
things, anything that help them to feed helps the
individual to survive, and anything that helps them to
mate helps the species to survive. Courtship
behaviour is usually the most peculiar.

BIRD FACT:
Migration takes up
huge amounts of
energy. For this reason
birds feed voraciously
before setting off and
build up large reserves
of fat. A small songbird
may weigh twice as
much as normal just
before migration.

Bird Habitats

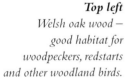

A HABITAT IS THE place where an organism lives. A cowpat can be a dung beetle's habitat, while a broad swathe of Arctic tundra is the breeding habitat of many northern waders. Within any habitat there will be a community of living things made up of flowering plants and invertebrates as well as the populations of birds with which we are concerned.

DIVISION OF HABITATS

A HABITAT, IN the broad sense of a heath or wood, will vary according to where it is, but the woodland habitat varies more than the heathland, for woods, dominated by different tree species, can grow on almost any soil and to considerable altitude. A heath, by contrast, as defined by Webb (1986) is 'an area of ericaceous dwarf shrubs growing at lower altitudes, below 250 m, in acidic nutrient-poor, mineral soils'.

Most habitats can be subdivided: apart from different types of woods, there are different layers in any wood, with different bird communities in the canopy and in the shrub layer. Similarly, with lakes, unproductive, oligotrophic lakes are very different from productive, eutrophic lakes.

DIFFERENCES IN HABITATS

AQUATIC HABITATS ARE clearly different from terrestrial ones. Among the latter, the woodlands are the most complex, with their structure separating them from more open habitats. Urban areas can be highly structured, with high-rise buildings and wooded parks, but their artificiality separates them from all others. The simpler open areas can be divided into the more natural uplands, moors and heaths, and the agricultural land which has been modified to greater or lesser extent by farming and other human activities. There are, of course, plenty of overlaps, with lakes and reservoirs in towns, sheep on the moors and open areas in the middle of a wood.

ADAPTING TO HABITATS

SOME OF THE adaptations of birds to their habitats are obvious: the webbed feet of ducks, the long legs of wading birds and the powerful beaks of woodpeckers. It is not so obvious that woodland birds tend to have short wings, that each seed-eater will have a slightly different bill, or that a number of our species have adapted to local conditions that are different from those they meet in the rest of their range. The merlin on a world scale is a bird of open forest, forest edge and low-shrub tundra, but has adapted to our heather moors derived from the forest (Ratcliffe 1990).

The classic book on plant ecology, A G Tansley's *The British Isles and their Vegetation* was written in 1939, but not until Fuller (1982) were the habitats of birds the subject of a book. This was based on information gathered during the BTO's project The Register of Ornithological Sites. Because the aim of the project was to provide conservation bodies with

Top left
Welsh oak wood – good habitat for woodpeckers, redstarts and other woodland birds.

Bottom left
Grazed, wooded landscape – ideal for rooks and buzzards.

Bottom right
Young great spotted woodpecker.

particularly in the breeding season, may in itself make a site valuable. Rarity can be judged objectively, perhaps being defined by there being fewer than 1,000 pairs in Britain, but there are also points of subjective interest. Would one prefer a few curlew, dunlin and snipe in the bogs with merlin and grouse in the heather, or sitka spruce with lots of coal tits and goldcrests and, perhaps, some siskins and crossbills? It cannot be denied that afforestation has sometimes brought more birds to the hills.

A few ecosystems are so localised that it is reasonable to mention them separately from the major habitats described later. Machair, the Gaelic word for the grassland ecosystem that has developed on wind-blown sand, typically in the Hebrides, is one such, and limestone pavement, found mainly in the north of England and the west of Ireland, another. The limestone of the Burren of County Clare and the Aran Isles of Galway Bay form a very special ecosystem. Shingle beaches, often extending into banks like Chesil Beach and Orford Ness, reach their extreme, perhaps, at Dungeness, the largest expanse of shingle in Britain. While machair and limestone are famous for their beauty and their flowers, Dungeness has long been known for its birds.

information about sites, there was a bias towards 'good' ones, and a concentration on natural and semi-natural habitats.

GOOD OR BAD SITE?

A 'GOOD' SITE can gain its status in several ways. The sheer number of birds may make a site have conservation value, whether the birds are breeding reed warblers, chattering in the *Phragmites*, or wintering knot on an estuary. The species richness of the habitat, indicated by the now much used word biodiversity, is also a valuable guide to habitat quality. Examples are given in the sections on woodland and upland habitats. The presence of rare birds,

> **BIRD FACT:**
> Several northern species appear in huge numbers every few years. These events are known as irruptions, and the species concerned include waxwings, crossbills, short-eared owls and rough-legged buzzards.

Top left
Heron patiently stalking fish.

Top right
Female merlin amongst upland heather.

Bottom
Coastal shingle – the nesting habitat of little tern and ringed plover.

DUNGENESS AND SHINGLE

BETWEEN WINCHELSEA AND Hythe the shingle forms a great triangular projection into the English Channel. It is made up of a complex of ridges where shingle has piled up at different times. It seems that all the stones have arrived from the west, but whatever its origins Dungeness has always been a convenient arrival point for migrants and is now a surprisingly wet place.

Despite a nuclear power station and a long history of gravel digging, it is man's activities that have increased the biodiversity here, not just of birds, and the gravel-pit restoration, both of old, steep-sided pits and the more rewarding shallow-sided ones, that have brought in the water birds. David Tomlinson (1988) writes about the chance of seeing all five species of grebe, of groups of wintering smew and of up to 500 shoveler. Recent winters have brought penduline tits, while breeding birds include Mediterranean gull, garganey and that gravel favourite, little ringed plover. David also maintains that 'familiarity soon starts to engender an affection for its unusual landscape for there is nothing else remotely like it in Europe. There is genuine beauty in its bleakness. If you don't believe me go and see for yourself. You are unlikely to be disappointed.'

MACHAIR AND SAND

WHILE DUNGENESS RESULTS from moving gravel, machair develops from moving sand; white shell-sand, blowing over coastal peat, has influenced land-use and culture on many Scottish islands. Tiree has a third of its land surface covered with sand dunes or machair, sometimes tilled and sometimes not, partly dry and partly wet, and ranging from the alkaline influence of the sand to the acidity of the peat. The western coasts of South Uist, Barra, Oronsay and Coll among others demonstrate the ecological principle of

zonation to perfection and, like other ecosystems, the interplay of human and other influences on the plants and animals.

Boyd and Boyd (1990) describe the Monach Isles in summer as a 'blaze of flowers; daisies, bird's foot trefoil, white clover, buttercups, eyebright, sea pansies and many others', and as being 'alive with birds; gulls, terns, shelducks, eiders, red-breasted mergansers, oystercatchers, ringed plovers, rock pipits, pied wagtails and starlings'. The typical machair zones start with sand dunes before, on the landward side, the 'plain' at the start of true machair.

As with other grasslands, the right grazing regime is vital, for few plants flower or seed when pressures are high, but too much neglect soon leads to the suppression of the attractive flowers by more aggressive grasses. Lapwing, oystercatcher and ringed plover are the breeding waders of the 'plain' and are

replaced by dunlin, snipe and redshank, nesting on grassy tussocks, when wetter grasslands appear further from the sea. In the lochs, little grebes, ducks and the rarer red-necked phalaropes, with common terns on islands, provide a different bird community. Inland again, where the buildings of the crofts are found, starlings and sparrows and wall-nesting twite occur.

Top
Little ringed plover may be seen breeding on sandy river banks and at gravel pits.

Middle
Redshank at its nest in a damp meadow.

Bottom
The red-necked phalarope is a rare breeding bird, mainly in N and NW Scotland.

more birds, with the lake system along the east being good for winter wildfowl, having almost 5,000 wigeon and plenty of teal, and with whooper and Bewick's swans outnumbering the mutes. At the north west extremity of the Burren is Black Head, where seabirds come in close during periods of westerly winds. Some are local birds, but there are shearwaters from the Mediterranean and South Atlantic, phalaropes from the Arctic, storm petrels and skuas.

In winter it is a fine place for great northern and other divers. Like much of Ireland's west coast this, like the cliffs of Moher, further south, is also chough country. These cliffs are of shales and flagstones, and therefore not truly Burren, but their precipitous ledges are full of guillemots and kittiwakes, and the lower levels have their shags, puffins and black guillemots. The Burren and surrounding area

is not full of rare birds, but its landscape is unique, and to see the abundance of mountain avens and spring gentians, mocking the efforts of most rock gardeners, makes one hate even more the destruction of much of England's limestone so that rock gardens can be built.

Apart from corncrakes, who arrive to shelter among the iris and breed among the crops that are not mown until late July, the waders are the conservation speciality of the machair, with 25 per cent of Britain's dunlin. The RSPB report that these ground-nesting birds are now at risk from what many would think an unlikely source – introduced hedgehogs. By 1995, dunlin, snipe, redshank and ringed plover had declined by 50 per cent since the 1970s through egg predation by hedgehogs .

THE BURREN AND LIMESTONE

IF THE CRAVEN district of West Yorkshire is the botanist's best limestone in northern England, then the Burren in County Clare and the Aran Isles in Galway Bay offer the finest limestone of Ireland. Perhaps the most impressive feature is the vast extent of exposed limestone rock, on which there appears to be very little vegetation. In deep frost-free crevices, sheltered from the winds, there is however a fascinatingly diverse flora.

Gordon D'Arcy (1992) admits that the open limestone has few birds; plenty of wheatears and stonechats, and a scattering of whinchats. The edges of the area provide

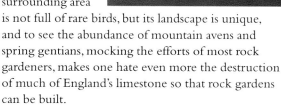

Top
Hedgehogs are unlikely predators of birds' eggs in some areas.

Middle
Cliffs of Moher, Co. Clare, Ireland. Ideal breeding cliffs for a multitude of seabirds.

Bottom
Limestone formation in the Burren, Co. Clare, Ireland.

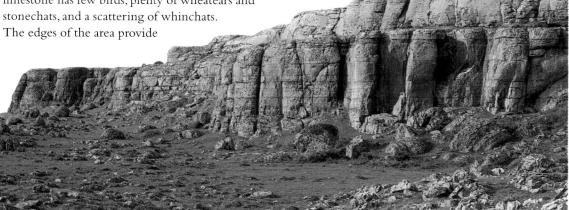

Bird Populations

DARWIN STRESSES THAT populations are capable of rapid increase and makes calculations, based on simple assumptions, as figures for animal population changes were not available to him. He also pointed out that the fulmar, that only lays one egg, was perhaps the commonest bird in the world, illustrating the fact that even slow breeders would be very abundant if there were not checks to their natural rate of increase.

COUNTING BIRDS

POPULATION FIGURES are frequently quoted, and we need to know how the figures are arrived at and still want to know what are the factors that affect populations. We may read that a species has decreased by 68 per cent in the last 25 years, or that another species is extending its range. It is relatively easy to see how the evidence for the second statement is gathered, but much less easy to see how a precise statement like the first one can be justified. Similarly, we often hear from one person that there are more swallows around this year, while another laments that she never sees any swallows these days.

Impressions about populations, like memories of the weather, are notoriously unreliable, and there are those who might maintain that figures about populations, quoted as facts, are equally uncertain. This is often so if figures for the absolute numbers of a species are quoted, but more often we need to know the relationship numbers — is a species commoner or rarer than it was, and by how much? Several methods of monitoring population levels have stood the test of time, and frequently the results of different methods can be compared, to produce an 'integrated population index'.

COUNTING LARGER BIRDS

EVEN LARGE, CONSPICUOUS birds like grebes and herons, with restricted habitat, are not as easy to count as you might expect. To be certain how many heron nests are occupied in a small local heronry, set in two rather leafless trees, is virtually impossible. Other large birds can present different difficulties, with many raptors occurring at very low densities and in remote areas. At their nesting colonies, gannets are so mobile, so densely packed and in such large numbers, that estimates without photographic support can be very misleading. For each bird, one can refer to a counting unit, and for fulmar pairs a breeding site is 'an apparently occupied nest-site, defined as an individual sitting tightly on a reasonably horizontal area large enough to hold an egg'.

Top
Densely packed gannets at a colony in the Shetlands.

Bottom
Assessing populations of some inconspicuous species, like reed warbler, may be best done through ringing schemes.

> '*Although some species may be now increasing, more or less rapidly, in numbers, all cannot do so for the world would not hold them.*'
> Darwin ORIGIN OF SPECIES

Woodcock are fairly large, but sit very tight. Those out on a pheasant shoot will see, and perhaps shoot, even more, and their shooting bags may indicate that woodcock populations are much higher than birdwatchers would believe. The increase in numbers of woodcock shot through the 1970s and 1980s may however be misleading, and due to an increase in pheasant shooting rather than a genuine increase in woodcock winter populations.

COUNTING METHODS

IN THEIR BOOK *Bird Census Techniques* (1992) Bibby, Burgess and Hill summarise these various counting techniques, and the assumptions and possible inaccuracies inherent in them all, and stress that some sort of sampling is always needed. Sometimes the sample may originally have had a different objective, as when ringing totals are used to reflect changing population levels. The ringing was done to find out about migration patterns, moult and longevity, but if twice as many mistle thrushes, allowing for changing numbers of birds caught, were ringed in one decade compared with another, it suggests twice as large a population.

Some inconspicuous birds may be best estimated by the constant effort scheme, which involves catching and ringing birds, using the same type and size of net at the same site, on a year-by-year basis. This not only monitors a population level, the number of adults trapped, but breeding success, the ratio of juveniles to adults in late season, and survival, birds re-trapped in subsequent years. As always, standardisation is vital, and other aspects of this are that no other netting is carried out within 400 m (1,312 ft), no baits are used to attract birds and 12 ringing visits are carried out between May and August. On this scheme, reed warbler populations stayed steady throughout the 1980s, while chiffchaffs started and finished high, but had a decline in between.

SAMPLING AN AREA

A VERY SIMPLE sampling method involves standing at one place and counting all birds seen or heard. If point counts like this are repeated, the birds of an area can be sampled. The limitations of the method are obvious, as soon as one tries it in the garden, with wrens singing loudly and often, being far more noticeable than the secretive bullfinches. Even with the bullfinches there would be difficulties in comparing their populations at different times of year, because of moult, tree leaves and frequency of calling for instance, but it could be perfectly adequate for comparing populations from one year to the next.

In woodland, of course, the need to be able to recognise every call and song variation, is important. Point counts might be thought to be more accurate in open country, where birds are more visible, but they are not all equally visible. On grassland in northern England, noisy and conspicuous golden plover can be located up to 500 m (1,640 ft) away. They react to the observer and may flee quietly and unnoticed from close to a transect line, but dunlin sit tight and are not detected more than 100 m (330 ft) from the transect.

Top
Chiffchaffs are usually first located by their song.

Middle
Bullfinches, despite the bright plumage of the male, can be hard to locate.

Bottom
Golden plover are noisy and easily spotted on their breeding grounds.

Population Change

UNTIL THE LAST 30 years, population changes could only be indicated by range changes, and these, particularly in Ireland and the remoter parts of Scotland, were often little known. In areas with larger populations, and more birdwatchers, local or county bird reports would have records of interesting birds.

ACCURACY OF REPORTS

JUST AS THE CBC index could be misleading about meadow pipits, as most of these breed in areas with few census plots, so county bird reports could be misleading because few people bothered to submit records about meadow pipits. *The London Bird Report* for 1950 has no mention of them, but has a page on the 17 breeding pairs of woodlarks, and almost a page giving all records of stonechats. By 1996, with increasing attention to common birds, the *Devon Report* has records of meadow pipits from 122 locations, a large increase over 1995. This increase probably means nothing at all, although the breeding records given, and the size of flocks reported, might be used to compare with something written in 1950.

Top
The meadow pipit is a common species, especially on heath and moorland.

Bottom
Grasshopper warbler – one of several species whose range has contracted in recent years.

IMPORTANT PUBLICATIONS

FOLLOWING PILOT STUDIES like the *Atlas of Breeding of Breeding Birds of the West Midlands* (1970, the *Atlas of Breeding Birds in Britain and Ireland* (1976),) 'represented a giant step forward in our knowledge of the distribution of British and Irish birds' and was 'by far the biggest co-operative effort ever undertaken by field ornithologists in these islands, indeed, probably, anywhere in the world'. It was followed by a *Winter Atlas*, which was ambitious enough to attempt to bring numbers into the mapping work, and the *New Atlas* (1993), took this a step further, using 'innovative colour cartography techniques' with the colour representing regional variation in relative abundance.

Although only 20 years after the original atlas, it also revealed the speed with which distributions can change, emphasising, as Humphrey Sitters said in the preface, that 'bird distribution patterns are dynamic, changing more rapidly than was previously thought'. Among other changes he mentions are the spread of the hobby, the goosander's extension into Wales and the south west, and the worrying contractions of black grouse, nightingale, grasshopper warbler and corn bunting.

FACTORS INFLUENCING POPULATION LEVELS

WITH ALL THE changes, in both range and abundance, it is even more vital to understand the factors that control bird populations. A possible starting point, highlighted by the *Winter Atlas's* attempts to estimate numbers, is that a breeding population of 50 pairs could lead to an autumn population of 300.

Early in Ian Newton's *Population Limitation in Birds* (1998) he quotes some old great tit figures to illustrate population levels at different times of the year over a five year period. Sometimes the adult population was only a quarter of the total adults plus fledged young. Taking these sorts of thing into account A. G. Gosler writes in the *Winter Atlas* 'The *Breeding Atlas* estimated the British and Irish population at something over 3,000,000 pairs, since then the population has risen about 11 per cent, based on CBC counts. Assuming that five chicks fledge per pair, some 15,000,000 first year birds might be included in the winter population.' After a couple of other assumptions and calculations he comes to a mean winter population of about 10,000,000 birds.

After mentioning Lack's earlier books, Newton describes his work as another attempt at a synthesis, incorporating the vast recent literature on bird populations and some new ideas. A number of the figures he quotes will appear under the species headings, but some are needed here to give a better idea of why numbers vary and what limits population growth. He lists the limiting factors as resources, interspecific competition, predators, parasites and the interactions between these factors, as when a bird weakened by food shortage dies of disease.

In addition, the weather impacts, and human influence might be thought to affect the whole population rather than being selective.

RESOURCES INCLUDING FOOD

ONE INDICATION OF the effect of food, the most obvious resource, is the variation in breeding success in rodent-eating raptors; another is the sudden catastrophic collapse in seabird breeding success, linked with a collapse in fish stocks. Because of the shortage of corpses, finding out about the cause of death of adult birds is not easy, but if autopsy reveals low weight, absence of body fat and emaciated muscle, starvation can be accepted. Kestrels and barn owls often seem to die of starvation, with 35 per cent and 40 per cent of birds analysed having died in that way.

Starvation linked with cold weather is familiar, and is marked by population declines of small insectivorous birds, including wrens, long-tailed tits, stonechats and Dartford warblers. Aquatic birds also suffer losses. When corpses, often of the larger birds, can be analysed, deaths are often found not to be random. An oystercatcher study in the Netherlands showed that 61 per cent of those that died in cold weather were handicapped by anatomical abnormalities, particularly of the mandible. Some of the others that died were still in moult two months later than usual.

Top
Barn owls often die of starvation in cold weather.

Middle
Long-tailed tits and wrens may also suffer losses in hard winters, when their insect food becomes hard to find.

Bottom
The great tit is one of our commoner breeding birds.

Predation

PREDATION WOULD appear an obvious limiting factor, but it is not always that simple. Predation in autumn could lead to a smaller winter population which survived better on a fixed and limited food supply.

EFFECTS OF PREDATORS

THOSE WHO DISLIKE sparrowhawks for 'killing all the little birds' are reluctant to accept evidence that sparrowhawks actually have little effect on the populations of their prey. Long-term population monitoring can become of value in unexpected ways. In one study, where blue and great tits have been counted each year for 50 years, their numbers were known before the sudden sparrowhawk decrease of the 1960s, known during the period of sparrowhawk absence and known for the 20 years since sparrowhawks have reappeared. Even if the peak great tit population was in a year of sparrowhawk absence, neither tit did significantly better in the absence of the hawks.

A fascinating insight into the effect of predators also involves sparrowhawks and great tits. It might be thought that a great tit at the top of the pecking order would gain most weight, to give it the best chance of surviving the winter. This was so when sparrowhawks were absent, but on their return, dominant tits, averaged over the years, were lighter and therefore more mobile and better able to escape. Being dominant they had more chance of gaining food whenever they needed it, but subordinate birds had to stock up when it was easy to get, gained weight and became at risk from predation.

Magpies are even less popular than sparrowhawks, and as versatile food gatherers they eat all sorts of young birds and eggs. Studies indicate that they actually have little influence on bird populations. However, an obsession with neat gardens can make hedge-nesting birds vulnerable to excess predation of their eggs and young.

Top
The numbers of garden and woodland birds, like this blue tit, have been little affected by increases in the sparrowhawk population.

Bottom
Female sparrowhawk with its woodpigeon prey.

There are also other factors operating; predators eat plenty of other things, and grouse depend very much on heather. For years, the grouse 'bags' have been going down, and the heather cover has decreased, as sheep grazing has favoured grass at heather's expense. This in turn encourages pipits and voles, good predator food, so their population can increase, in the absence of illegal killing and nest destruction. What is needed is better management of moorland, so that heather, grouse and predators can flourish together, perhaps with the economic benefits that shooting can bring.

Grouse are highly territorial, and if population levels are higher than the heather can support, the dominant birds gain all the territories. This in turn means that subordinate birds are forced out, and if there is not suitable heather habitat available they will die by being shot, by being predated or through eventual starvation.

RELATIONSHIPS BETWEEN PREDATORS

A CONTROVERSIAL AREA involving predators is the relationship between red grouse and raptors such as hen harriers and peregrines. The *Joint Raptor Report* (1998), a five year study in Scotland, had been widely quoted as saying that high predator levels reduce grouse populations. On one moor, predator levels went up when no illegal killing was carried out, and the autumn grouse 'bag' went down, so much that driven grouse shooting was no longer viable. There is no doubt that predators eat grouse and grouse chicks, but the breeding grouse population did not actually fall during the study period. In effect, the predators had eaten the birds that would have been shot.

EFFECTS OF A PARASITE

ANOTHER INFLUENCE on grouse numbers is a parasite. A virus transmitted by ticks, which also need sheep, causes louping ill, which can kill adult grouse but has more effect on the chicks. Chick survival in northern England was about half as high in areas with ticks and louping ill. Red grouse also suffer from nematode worms, and these may cause massive periodic reductions in populations, just as avian cholera can with waterfowl. Exceptionally, parasites can cause local extinctions, but more often they have little effect on populations, or at most reduce breeding success.

Top
Weighing a goldcrest after ringing on Lundy Island.

Bottom left
Magpies take a range of prey, including eggs and nestlings.

Bottom right
Young tawny owl.

Birdwatching

BIRDWATCHING IS NOT a new hobby. Over the last 70 years, it has gone from strength to stregth, gaining in popularity. Now, with better identification guides, easier travel, and the marvellous images of television, birdwatching has become popular enough to help support a series of industries.

Birds, the RSPB magazine, looking only at half-page and full-page advertisements, found the equivalent of 27 full-pages promoting binoculars, telescopes and cameras, 14 pages of bird-related supplies, and 12 pages of wildlife-related holidays. There were six pages on clothes and boots, and six more on what might loosely be called nature art. Five pages featured videos and CD-Roms, while a fascinating half-page invited you to 'Get Bittern' at the Lea Valley Bittern Watchpoint, where 4-7 bitterns, from a maximum, national winter population of 100, could be seen. This short list indicates the diversity of the wants of birdwatchers. Each type of birdwatcher, the home enthusiast, the habitat explorer, the 'twitcher' with immense identification skills, or the counter, who likes to contribute to research, will get their own satisfaction from birds.

Despite the comments about industries and money, birdwatching can be as cheap as you want it, and you can do it almost anywhere. Without

REQUIREMENTS OF THE BIRDWATCHER

THOSE WHO FEED birds can spend large sums attracting them to their gardens, and many spend more by providing nest-boxes. Most birdwatchers will have binoculars, and many will have telescopes and cameras. A quick look at advertisements will tell of the amount of clothing they may claim to need, to keep them warm, and the boots to keep their feet dry.

The 'twitcher' may be ready to travel anywhere, at a moment's notice, when he hears that a new 'tick' is to be had, and helps the travel industry on the way. A superficial search through three recent issues of

Middle
Pied flycatcher at nestbox; Wales.

Bottom
A robin nesting in old piping might be found in your own garden – an ideal place to start birdwatching.

binoculars you can identify birds that come to feed, and also enjoy their songs and calls. On holidays you meet new and unfamiliar species; then you will need the help that binoculars bring. I remember the excitement of my first sea and mountain birds, my early longing for rarities, and my compulsion to make lists. Many enthusiasts remain collectors; of birds seen, of photographs, of places visited or of numbers counted. Others develop special interests in behaviour or conservation, in ringing, or the study of a single bird or a bird group like owls. The choices are endless, but at some stage you will need to decide where you are going to watch your birds.

WHERE AND WHEN TO WATCH

THE SIMPLE ANSWER is at anytime and anywhere. I have seen curlew and common tern over Lords cricket ground, plotted the movements of gulls as I walked into lectures, and had redwing pointed out to me in a maths lesson, and hawfinch during biology. Another simple answer is near your home, satisfied, at least initially, with getting to know the local birds.

Many people will use birds as an opportunity to visit new places. The north Norfolk coast is a magnet at any time of year, but particularly during migration, while mountains and islands have a different lure. A week on Bardsey or Cape Clear, Fair Isle or the Scillies is unique, not only for any birds you may see, but for exposure to a special way of life.

The series of *Where to Watch Birds* books provides another set of answers. For any particular area there may be a brief habitat description, a sample of the main species to be seen at different times of year, a section on timing your watching, and details of access. In the Devon and Cornwall book (Norman and Tucker 1997) for example, the timing section directs you to dawn or dusk for migrating passerines at Prawle Point and tells you that overcast days with cool easterlies can produce rarer species in late autumn.

BIRD FACT:
There are about 9000 species of bird, and these are classified into some 28 different orders, based mainly on differences in their anatomy.

Above
Some birdwatchers get a thrill from spotting rarities, like this white stork.

Below
Birdwatchers at a seabird colony at the Cliffs of Moher, Ireland.

HIDES AND THE RSPB

GUIDE BOOKS TELL YOU where to find birds but the RSPB can make it easier still. Hides, and a dedicated and skilful management, guarantee that you can see birds well. At the RSPB reserve of Leighton Moss in Lancashire, four out of seven hides are accessible by wheelchair, and the reserve centre has a tea room, shop and live video link – 1618 ha (4,000 acres) with bitterns and marsh harriers, bearded tits and a pair of Mediterranean gulls attract 80,000 visitors a year. A carpeted hide with soft seats is only a hundred metres from the car park.

Coastal National Nature Reserves looked after by English Nature include the Farne Islands and Lindisfarne in Northumberland, the Ribble marshes in Lancashire and east coast reserves further south on the Colne estuary and at Scolt Head. Separate national agencies manage scenically dramatic National Nature Reserves in Snowdonia, the Cairngorms and around Beinn Eighe in Ross and Cromarty.

A new and growing set of ventures aim to see more seabirds; the RSPB had trips this year from Torquay out into Lyme Bay. Steve Dudley in the Birdwatcher's Year Book (Ed Pemberton 1998) writes of how sea-birding can be a supplement to the sea-watch. His description of this in the past is evocative for 'to see shearwaters, skuas and petrels you glued your eyes to your telescope and your backside to some godforsaken, windswept, sea-sprayed headland. After hours of misery you might be lucky enough to see an "auk sp" shooting past.' Some of the best sea-birding he mentions

seems equally unattractive, as we will see in the seabirds section, but comfortable trips, although at sea one can never tell, take 300 birders from the Scillies to see ten or more seabird species that would never be more than distant images from land. Other trips take watchers from Bempton to see a seabird colony from the sea.

FINDING SUITABLE SUBJECTS TO WATCH

PERSONALLY I LIKE to find my own birds and, usually, to find them near home. Many lovely but mainly smaller reserves are managed by the County Wildlife Trusts which do such vital work for conservation, but you do not need to rely on the reserves when there are town parks, reservoirs, gravel pits, woods and estuaries. Watchable birds are everywhere, but do remember that you will not see many at all, if you do not watch when the sun is in the right place.

BIRDWATCHING FOR ALL

THE FACT THAT you can watch birds anywhere is exemplified by a note from David Glue in a recent *BTO News*. He has been a wheelchair-bound since 1971, but has seen 321 species in Britain since his accident. He offers a number of tips to those who cannot get

Top
Hides are excellent for birdwatching and photography.

Bottom
A well-stocked table brings the birds in to your garden where you can watch them up close.

about much, including the elderly and housebound. His first two suggestions might seem obvious, but by adding well-placed nest-boxes to the bird table by the window, the range of activities to be watched is increased. He then advocates the use of pishing and squeaking techniques to draw secretive species like goldcrests, warblers and flycatchers into the open. Before leaving home, if you can, study maps closely to

> Sanderlings are pretty birds, quite small and very neat,
> They move about incessantly on little clockwork feet.
> They run before advancing waves then back when they recede,
> And there they find the tiny things on which they like to feed.
> They never get their feet wet, their movements are so fast.
> You stand and watch to see if they will get them wet at last.
> They never do. And then with one accord they take to flight,
> They fly a hundred yards or so and then they all alight
> And start to feed again before a different set of waves.
> It's fascinating watching how this little bird behaves.'
>
> R. S. Morrison WORDS ON BIRDS

find the best spots from where you can gain easy access to lakes or estuaries, and when there make full use of the car as a mobile hide, improved by using telescope accessories and other devices to clamp optics firmly to the car window. The essence of his message is be bold, take the risk of a seabird trip, make a personal approach to landowners and consult RADAR (Royal Association for Disability and Rehabilitation). He also has a message for me; overactive able-bodied watchers often miss much, and for all of us – 'use birds to help keep your mind and body active and provide enjoyment while contributing to science in a useful way.'

Top right
Herring gulls will sometimes take food from passengers on a ship.

Middle left
Seabird colony with guillemots; Farne Islands.

Bottom
The small, active sanderling is a common shorebird.

75

Birdwatching Equipment

'Binoculars are the instruments that define birding – like the functional equivalent of the first baseman's glove, the musician's instrument, the plough in the hands of the frontier farmer.'
Peter Dunne OPTICS FOR BIRDING

BINOCULARS REALLY ARE needed. The fact that two of the pairs I use have been in action for 50 years is a reminder that once you have them they can last a long time, but in those years lenses and design have completely changed. Many people think that magnification is the important thing, but light-gathering and weight can matter just as much.

BIRD FACT:
BTO Garden BirdWatch Scheme
This scheme depends on people keeping records of the birds that visit their gardens. Through it, the BTO keeps a track of increases or decreases in our garden birds.

TYPE OF BINOCULAR

POOR LIGHT IS hardly rare in Britain, while heavy binoculars can be tiring and hard to keep still. Another problem is that high magnification can make for difficulties with close viewing. I tend to use heavier 10 x 50 binoculars on an estuary, and 8 x 30s in woodland. The first figure gives the magnification, and the second the objective lens diameter in mm. This, usually a complex of lenses, is at the opposite end from the eye-piece. If you divide the objective lens diameter by the magnification you get an indication of light-gathering power, with a higher figure making for greater usefulness in poor light.

Having said that, the modern multicoated lenses and phase coated roof prisms, both expensive, have changed the old perspectives. If you pay the price you will get the superior brightness. Before coating, 5 per cent of light striking polished glass was reflected away. With 10–16 glass surfaces inside the binocular, the net result was dark images. Coating reduces the 5 per cent to 1 per cent, and multiple coating, in thin layers,

further reduces light reflection to a fraction of 1per cent. 'Fully coated' or 'multicoated' means all surfaces, lenses and prisms, inside and out, are coated.

FEATURES TO LOOK FOR

TRADITIONALLY WIDE-BODIED parroprism binoculars, the prisms turning inverted images the right way up again and giving the glasses their 'kink', have fewer internal surfaces and therefore transmit more light, but newer roof-prism binoculars are very tough. Their objective and ocular lenses are in line, making for a streamlined shape which some find easier to hold. Comfortable holding is important, but fast and easy focusing is vital, and central focusing with a well-positioned wheel that can move you from close to distant quickly and easily, is invaluable.

If you have limited arm strength or finger movement investigate these new lightweight binoculars, as David Glue suggests, and if you select a pair with great depth of field you will not have to alter the focus so often. Glasses wearers have different problems, but with high 'eye

Top
A telescope is essential for successful identification of seabirds and waders.

Bottom
Binoculars and telescope – the best of both worlds.

As with binoculars, the higher the magnification the narrower the field of view, and with greater weight a support system needs to be very rigid. In most cases, unless used from a car, the telescope and tripod will need to be carried so weight is significant. Always try and test out a 'scope' before buying it. Special optical field days, advertised in birdwatching magazines, give you a good opportunity to check for possible good and bad points.

CHECK LIST FOR TELESCOPES

Image brightness: dependent on lens size and coating quality, where coating is a covering of the lens by non-reflecting material

Colour coats: yellow, green or blue

Chromatic aberration: giving coloured fringes to your bird

Image sharpness: which may easily be judged by trying to read a distant poster

Field of view: a wide-angled eye-piece may make it easier to find your bird.

relief', the distance between ocular lens and eye, they can keep their glasses on. Rubber cups or 'twist in' eye cups may help.

Apart from quoted figures like magnification and objective lens diameter, there are a range of features which are often not quoted, but which determine the quality of a pair of binoculars and therefore the quality of the image you will see. You need to use the binoculars under trial conditions to test their resolving power, alignment and transmission and the absence of colour fringes and distortions. In addition you may want to pay for protection features that may make your purchase dust-, water- or fog-proof.

BENEFITS OF A TELESCOPE

UNTIL VERY RECENTLY I have not owned a telescope – not very convenient or useful in Welsh mountains or woodlands. Furthermore I had memories of the difficulties using the old tubular ones, propped on the railings of the causeway at Staines Reservoir or on an unsteady shoulder peering out to sea and hoping for skuas or shearwaters at Blakeney. While binoculars have improved, telescopes are unrecognisably better and easier to use, and even on a small estuary I am already gaining the benefit of extra detail to sort out identification and give extra pleasure with even the commonest waders.

OTHER EQUIPMENT REQUIRED

YOU WILL ALSO need to have a field notebook as well as a larger one in which you keep your permanent records. In the field I like little waterproof ones in which you really can write in pencil, even when it is wet. Avoid the more brightly coloured of modern waterproofs, and make sure your feet stay dry in the wet places that birds love. In all aspects of your birding equipment you will need to resist at least some of the heavy advertising aimed at you.

Top
Good bird artists work from detailed field notes and sketches.

Bottom
A birdwatcher's field notebook.

Whether this advertising is on behalf of the birds or their watchers it becomes more colourful, imaginative and persistent year by year. Seed storage feeders, squirrel-proof feeders, stainless-steel feeders, those that take 3.5 kilos of sunflower seeds or even one ready to take 6.4 kilos and feed 16 birds at a time! Many of these are in polycarbonate tubes which are tough, see-through and provide feeding points with perches.

New foods like sunflower hearts, foods for swans and ducks developed with help from the Wildfowl and Wetlands Trust with minerals, trace elements and vitamins, together with mealworms and earthworms full of good protein. With the emphasis now on summer feeding as well, your budget can be well stretched, but the resulting pleasure is enormous and the value to the birds incalculable. If you try to estimate, making your own assumptions, how may weed and cereal seeds used to be left in a 2-ha (five-acre) arable field, or how many berries might be available along half a mile of hedge that was not cut back so often, you will see that the way you manage your garden can have as much influence on food supplies as a number of new feeders. They are wonderful but only part of the story of bird survival.

NEST BOXES

NEST-BOXES ARE a great addition to garden or woodland, but try to develop natural sites and cover as well. There is no doubt the expensive 'woodcrete' boxes do last well and are alleged to 'breathe',

reducing condensation and humidity: tits certainly love the ones I use but I am still waiting for a nuthatch to move in. Do not forget that you can make your own boxes, that pallets can often be found for free, while cheap offcuts of wood may also be available. Some details of nest-boxes will appear later, mainly in the town and garden section.

Booklets on bird guides are equally rich in choice and special offers – the latest, most exciting CD-Roms, videos and books, David Attenborough's marvellous *Life of Birds* on video, CD-Roms allowing you to compare plumage and calls, and with video-clips and freeze frames. Birdwatchers have never had so much on offer, but do remember that you do not need it all, or even any of it, to enjoy your birds, and that a pocket identification guide that can go everywhere with you may cost relatively little to purchase.

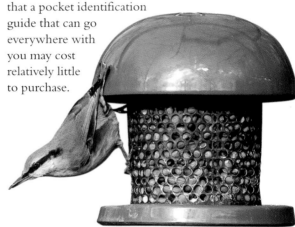

RECORDING

ONCE YOU START identifying the more unusual birds or monitoring numbers of common ones on your patch, you will need to share your records by

Top
Blue tits are usually amongst the first to appear at the feeder.

Middle
A more unusual sight – a nuthatch attracted by peanuts.

Bottom
Redwings often come into gardens to feed on holly berries, especially in cold winter weather.

everything and report everything and that, therefore, their observations are not needed.

As county recorders, they see their job getting more difficult in that, 'with the advent of commercialisation, through colourful, professionally designed magazines, telephone bird lines and pagers, there has been a drift away from the local bird club, as old and new birdwatchers have realised they have up-to-date information from other sources'. The clubs need to 'think about demographic trends and gender imbalance in their membership and about youth policies, in particular working with the RSPB's YOC and Phoenix groups. These, after all, are the birders of tomorrow.'

The authors would like to see the profile of county recorders raised, and an organisation to take overall responsibility for bird recording in the country as well as a total refusal to accept hearsay

records. Many, like me, are against the growing standardisation of many aspects of life but, if recording is to be effective, some sort of standard approach will have to be adopted. There are many like me who have accumulated personal knowledge of an area but have submitted few records. In my case, years of counts at different times of the year in conifer plantations and oak woods in Wales, together with estimates of grassland breeding populations at different altitudes have been lost, and only the results of BTO surveys submitted. This sort of approach does not help the conservation cause, however much pleasure it may bring. All information about nationally important sites, widespread but threatened habitats, and your local patch, need to be shared if the hard facts that influence decision makers are to be available.

Bowey and Smith hope that computerisation of county databases, hopefully to become universal if the National Biodiversity Network takes off, will create a powerful tool for conservation.

passing them on to someone who holds a file of local or county records. County recorders have never had an easy time. There would be a great deal of work even if every record was genuine, and every birder punctilious in the presentation and punctuality of their submissions, but Bowey and Smith (1998) write of new difficulties. They wonder how a system can be devised in which all watchers submit records which can be used nationally in the interests of conservation. They mention 'black sheep' who may be competent rarity-seekers but who never pass on their records except by hearsay, and local societies who are too insular and only think about their local area with no regard to the national scene. They also mention visitors to reserves who assume that a warden or ranger will see

Top
A bird-friendly garden, with varied shrubs, lawn and a pond.

Middle
Birdwatcher consulting his field guide.

Bottom
Nestboxes can help boost the bird numbers in your garden.

Bird Identification

CROWN

NAPE

BREAST

RUMP

WHEN PEOPLE DESCRIBE to me a bird they have seen I often have to tell them, somewhat unhelpfully, that it must be new to science as their description fits no bird I know. When a more experienced watcher describes a bird, there is more chance of helping, for they include the details that are needed for identification.

CORRECT IDENTIFICATION

THE USE OF THE correct terms for the parts of the body, the observational ability to notice inconspicuous features, an awareness of comparable species and their size and some method of recalling sounds, all help in making a good description. There is great merit in this methodical approach, but how do you actually recognise your friends? Do you know all the details of their nose profile and ear lobes? I doubt it. You spot something distinctive about the way they move or they have some special feature and you know it is them even if they are a long way off. It is the same with birds, and when we refer to their JIZZ we mean distinctive shape and movement. 'Little brown jobs' can always cause difficulties, but even with tree, rock and meadow pipits their gestures, calls and habitat tell you which is which although they look so similar.

QUICK IDENTIFICATION

RECENTLY, IN SOME flooded fields I had an immediate 'feel' that three small waders by a muddy pool were little ringed plovers. I had not seen the species for years, but something about their jizz alerted me. Confirmation was needed and it would have been easy to make a proper field sketch, including details of plumage, leg and bill colour and features of the eye. Idly I only jotted brief notes about pale legs and back, bobbing action, the horribly vague 'ring extending downwards' and the not at all helpful 'black through eye'. Luckily the birds flew, had no wing bar and gave their distinctive call, so my 'feel' had been right.

LEARNING FROM EXPERIENCE

WATCHING WITH SOMEONE who knows more than you is the best way to learn. You may have a friend to teach you or you may decide to join a local group who watch the likely localities. If it is easier to learn the appearance of birds with help, it is even more useful to have someone to teach you the calls and songs, but ultimately you will have to develop the confidence to make your own decisions.

Top
This standard bird (thrush) shows some of the features to watch out for when identifying a bird.

Bottom
A trio of winter-plumage grebes – red-necked, black-necked and Slavonian (left to right).

Some of the sounds are clearly distinctive, but many, alarm-calls for instance, are very similar, and among flocks of waders it is hard to tell which calls are associated with which birds. To many people, one warbler singing in the brambles is much like another. Finding the garden warbler that is lurking there and seeing it well enough to identify it may require great patience. Whatever the difficulties, sounds are vital for identification and surveys. Once the leaf cover has developed on the ash trees of the Lyme Regis Undercliff, where I do a Common Bird Census, I rarely see a bird, never use binoculars, but record some 150 individuals in a three-hour count.

Knowing what species are likely to be around can also be a great help. A booklet on the local area, particularly when you go somewhere new, can indicate likely birds, and more or less rule out others. Last year in Menorca a little guide by Hearl (1996) told me about good sites and Balearic specialities. Nearer home Stan Davies (1987) has provided a useful guide to the Exe.

WHAT TO LOOK FOR

KNOWING WHAT TO look for can have a different meaning. The classic *Handbook of British Birds* was, and is, valued for many things, but the field character section was the most notable feature for most bird watchers. Later Peterson introduced the judicious use of arrows in highlighting fieldmarks in his American guides, and contributed the same with his illustrations for the *Field Guide to the Birds of Britain and Europe* (1954). An arrow to the black axillaries, arm-pits, of the winter grey plover, to the long bill of a spotted

redshank or to the light edge of a willow tit's wing ensure you know what to look for.

Some field marks are more reliable for identification than others, there are three categories of field mark. There is the diagnostic feature that is absolute, like those highlighted by Peterson and in many guides since. Peterson might also use an arrow to indicate that species A has longer wings or a darker back than species B, but there is another sort of field mark where we get into greater difficulties. There are percentage differences, where A usually has a dark iris (but not always) while B usually does not, but sometimes does. This is the sort of area where the gull experts are happy mentioning that herring gulls sometimes have yellow legs or this, that or the other wing feather.

Top
Spotted redshank – note the rather long, narrow bill compared with common redshank.

Bottom
Herring gull overhead – note the black wing tips, with white flecks, and the heavy bill.

Identifying Rare Birds

THE FACT REMAINS that identification experts, describing rare birds which they cannot identify by jizz, need to observe and record with precision if their records are to be accepted by the Rarities Committee of British Birds.

DIFFICULTY OF CORRECT IDENTIFICATION

REPORTING ON RARE birds in Great Britain in 1996, M.J. Rogers and members of the Rarities Committee say how 'it grieves us to receive a report of a really "good bird" that is clearly unacceptable on the skimpy details provided, or to hear of something rare and special that never sees the light of day of a submitted report'. Commenting later on the photographs that are now so often taken to support rare bird identification he continues 'some twitching episodes resemble a car boot sale and many observers can buy a photograph of a particular rarity on their way to see it: little wonder, perhaps, that field notes and drawings seem to some people to be superfluous.' However, they indicate the level of accurate observation needed by the good field worker who is really interested in identification.

PERSONAL OBSERVATIONS

BECAUSE OF THE sort of birdwatcher I am I have hardly added to the repertoire of two hundred or so birds I can identify easily for 40 years. A trip to Kenya gave me a mass of new birds, but they did not help my identification skills in Britain, and while a series of holidays, not primarily birdwatching, to southern Europe and its islands have given me chances to see hoopoes and woodchat shrikes, bee-eaters and black-winged stilts, rock thrushes and vultures, assorted eagles and wheatears, most of these are easy birds or are not likely to turn up here. I have had to try to get to grips with the skulking *Sylvia* warblers, of which there are so many, but have not grappled with most of the volumes of song that come from reedbeds, or with the larks that are often everywhere. If I really did want to improve my identification, then travel and hard work would be the way to do it, and many of our best birdwatchers, writers, recorders and members of Rarities Committee have continually extended the range of birds with which they are familiar in the field.

'Look at them turkeys in the water' said Olive
'Those aren't turkeys,' said her father. 'They're ducks. You can tell by the bill. India-runner ducks, that's what they are.'
They weren't. They were Canada geese.
Oh, Lord! I do hope I don't seem unkind. We all make such fat headed mistakes that we can all afford to smile at others.

Robert Gibbings
SWEET THAMES RUN SOFTLY

Top
Black-winged stilt – showing its remarkably long legs in flight.

Bottom
Canada goose – escaped or feral birds sometimes confuse the unwary.

DEVOTED TO RARE BIRDS

THEY WOULD ALSO be regular readers of *British Birds*, a monthly magazine devoted, among other things, to the identification and recording of rare birds. This publication is being revamped, with more colour and new design, for the bird magazine world is highly competitive and all have good coverage of rarities. I have a photocopy of a couple of pages from

BB, as it is always known, for February 1996, with an article about the identification of little and Baillon's crakes by three authors (Christie, Shirihae and Harris) who have gathered material over many years observations of hundreds of individuals of both species, as well as extensive examination of skins.

With that sort of background it is possible to be a real expert. After dealing with habitat, general features and structural differences, including a detailed look at wing structure, they move on to separate adult males, with details of how to distinguish little crake from Baillon's for example. But despite all the sophistication of the modern birdwatcher, identification remains an art as well as a science and it is still possible for different interpretations of the same bird to take years to resolve.

Above left
This is the fleeting glimpse a lucky birdwatcher might have of the rare hoopoe.

Above right
It is worth checking out wheatears during migration – this is the standard model!

Below
The tiny Baillon's crake is a rare and secretive bird – seldom seen, let alone photographed.

Bird Classification and Names

NAMES, AS CAIN (1954) says, are arbitrary, and there tend to be a great many of them. Peter Conder's book on the wheatear (1989) lists almost a hundred local names, many in the chacker, chicker, chatchock line, because of the wheatear's call, but including coney sucker, underground jobler and whitestart.

MOST OF THESE seem perfectly applicable, in one way or another, and perhaps more reasonable than wheatear. But 'wheatear' itself can be analysed, and Conder tells us that 'wheat' is a corruption of the Anglo Saxon 'hwit' meaning white, and 'ears' is a corruption, or Bowdlerisation, of 'aers', meaning rump – hence an old English name of 'white arse'.

VARIETY OF NAMES

BRYAN NELSON (1978) writes of the range of gannet names, stressing that the gannet is essentially a Scottish bird and that 'Solan goose' was for a long time the proper name. Variants of solem, solen, solan, soland, solent and sollem existed, and all may derive from the Gaelic 'suil' or eye, linked with the gannet's keen sight. A vernacular Welsh name was Gwydd Lygadlon (clear-eyed goose), and a lovely Gaelic name 'Ian ban an Sgadon' (the white bird of the herring). Gannet, with its obvious links to gander, is a modification of the ancient British 'gan' or 'gans', corresponding with modern German 'Gans', Latin 'anser' and Sanskrit 'hansa'. Many birds have

fascinating local or regional names, some quite different from the modern English name, and this provides a rich field for research. The most productive sources for the such names are Greenoak (1997), Boyd (1951) for Cheshire names, Berry and Johnston (1980) for Shetland, Kearton (1908), and the poems of John Clare (1793–1864) for traditional Northamptonshire names.

SCIENTIFIC NAMES

THE ARBITRARY AND often local nature of bird names has caused difficulties for those attempting classification and, while Latin was the language of the educated, attempts were made to produce brief, accepted, Latinised descriptions as names. No coherent system emerged until Linnaeus, and our accepted animal nomenclature stems from the date of the publication of the tenth edition of his *Systema Naturae*, effectively the first of January 1758. Previous names, even involving two words like his, had no standing. The 'Law of Priority' states that the correct name for any form is that which conforms to the binomial systerm and is the first validly published in, or since, *Systema Naturae*. In the binomial system, the generic name is written first, using an initial capital, thus *Morus* for a gannet, and the specific or trivial name follows without an initial capital, in this case *bassanus*, to complete the gannet's species name or binomial.

Top left

Common gull – something of a misnomer, as this species is usually less common than black-headed and herring gull.

Top right

The wheatear takes its English name from its white rump, not its ear.

Bottom

The name 'dunnock' has widely ousted the somewhat misleading name 'hedge sparrow'.

AMERICAN NAMES

THIS BRINGS US to another problem for birds found on both sides of the Atlantic are often given different names. In America 'divers' are 'loons', their sparrowhawk is a falcon, and a sand martin is a bank swallow. Another common situation is that the American name has an added adjective, to separate different species found there, where we only have a single one. Many Australasian birds have been given English names, even when the birds concerned are not related to any in Europe.

We have only one wren, but *Peterson's Field Guide to Western Birds* illustrates nine species. Our wren, *Troglodytes troglodytes*, is known there as the winter wren, while others in the same genus are the house wren and brown-throated wren. Marsh wrens, rock wrens and short-billed marsh wrens are in a different genus, but still within the wren family. The American dipper is a different species from ours, but is sometimes referred to simply as 'dipper'. A classic cause of confusion is the American robin, which is actually a species of thrush.

Although most modern bird guides agree on the English names, there are still some variations, and in an attempt to deal with these difficulties, the Records Committee of the British Ornithologists' Union has drawn up a list of new English names to meet the need for international acceptance. Some changes are minor, thus the wheatear becomes the northern wheatear, but others are greater and likely to meet more popular resistance – winter wren, black-billed magpie and willow ptarmigan may be among these.

CHANGING ENGLISH NAMES

MOST OF US do not use either local names or binomials, but call birds by their English names, which we see as part of the language. As such they change with time under the influence of both books and people. E.M. Nicholson in *Birds and Men* (1951) was keen to change several of the names that had been used in the *Handbook of British Birds*. He preferred dunnock to hedge sparrow, throstle to song thrush and pied and barred woodpecker as names for our two spotted woodpeckers. The preference for dunnock seems to have been widespread, partly because it was certainly never a sparrow. Interestingly, in the light of recent events, Nicholson wanted to replace common gull, which is certainly rarely common, with mew gull which is the accepted American name.

Top
The gannet's name involves a complex history. It is sometimes known as 'Solan goose'.

Bottom
Our wren is called the winter wren in North America.

The Orders of British Birds

THIS SECTION SUMMARISES the main orders of birds found on the British list. It also includes a short summary of the features of the different orders, and includes a few examples.

GAVIIFORMES

Red- and black-throated Diver, Great Northern Diver
SPEAR-SHAPED BILLS, stocky necks, streamlined bodies and can dive down to 75 m (250 ft), staying under water for a possible eight minutes. The male and female are similar, the young have a second coat of down, before developing their adult feathers. The loud calls of these long-lived birds are often regarded as evil omens in northern cultures.

> **BIRD FACT:**
> Most of our warblers are summer visitors, and migrate south for the winter. However, recently it has been shown that some blackcaps migrate west from central Europe (where the winters are hard) to spend the winter in Britain (where the winters are milder).

Top
Red-throated diver in winter – note upturned bill-tip.

Bottom
Fulmar – note the tube-shaped nostrils on top of the bill.

PODICIPEDIFORMES

Dabchick, Great Crested Grebe, Red-necked Grebe, Black-necked Grebe, Slavonian Grebe
SMALL TO MEDIUM-LARGE swimming and diving birds. They have a short tail tuft, flattened tarsi, and three of the toes are broadly lobed. Many have display markings on the head. An unusual behaviour feature is that the young are initially carried by the parents and have downy plumage, usually with stripes.

PROCELLARIIFORMES

Fulmar, Manx Shearwater, Storm Petrel
PELAGIC SEA BIRDS with long, narrow wings, fly more than they swim and are very vulnerable on land. Sometimes known as 'tubenoses', referring to the nostrils being in dorsal tubes in the hooked beak.

They are colonial breeders, making a minimal nest and laying white eggs. Petrels are much smaller, with short, rounded wings and black plumage; they are long-distance migrants.

PELECANIFORMES

Gannet, Cormorant, Shag
FISH- AND SQUID-EATING aquatic birds which are usually colonial nesters. The toes are unique in that all four are joined by webs. The group have a more or less distensible pouch of bare skin between the branches of the lower mandible. Cormorants and gannets have closed external nostrils and breathe through their mouths. The members of the group have diverse feeding methods.

CICONIIFORMES

Grey Heron, Bittern, Little Egret

LONG-LEGGED, long-necked wading birds like herons, bitterns, egrets and spoonbills which are often colonial nesters. Different families are often separated by their bill structure. Herons have modifications to the bones of the neck, allowing a spearing mechanism and letting it fold into an S-shaped curve.

ANSERIFORMES

Mallard, Mute Swan, Greylag Goose

WEB-FOOTED, LONG-NECKED swimming birds. The feet are webbed in a different way from the previous order, with the fourth, hind, toe being somewhat elevated and not, therefore involved in the web. The flattened, blunt-tipped bill has fine lamellae along the margins of the maxilla and mandible. The feathers are in distinct tracts, with down underneath.

FALCONIFORMES

Sparrowhawk, Buzzard, Golden Eagle, Kestrel, Peregrine, Merlin

BIRDS OF PREY, with sharp, curved talons and hooked beaks and highly adapted sight and flight. They have unfeathered skin, the cere, at the base of the bill. They often soar in flight.

GALLIFORMES

Red Grouse, Grey Partridge, Pheasant

GAMEBIRDS, WITH SHORT, rounded wings, a well developed keel and sturdy legs with four toes. In pheasants the hind toe is not in contact with the ground. The tip of the upper mandible overlaps the lower mandible. Two other characteristics, not unique, are a large muscular gizzard and the laying of large clutches.

Top left
Cormorant in typical silhouette.

Top right
The pure white little egret is typically heron-shaped. Note the yellow feet.

Bottom
This buzzard shows the classic bird of prey features of hooked bill and heavy talons.

GRUIFORMES

Water Rail, Coot, Moorhen, Crane

THIS IS AN OLD, widely dispersed order, with few unifying characters. Most of our members, the crakes and rails, have slightly webbed toes and tend to be highly secretive; something that can hardly be said of the large bustards and cranes which also belong here.

CHARADRIIFORMES

Curlew, Black-headed Gull, Guillemot

THE WADERS, GULLS and auks are clearly waterbirds or, if not, like the lapwing, derived from water birds. They are united by characteristics of skull, vertebral column and syrinx. Of the three sub-orders, the waders rarely have webbed toes but usually have a good hind toe, the gulls either lack a hind toe or have a small one, are web-footed and have a salt-gland above the eye. Auks are stocky marine birds with webbed feet and no hind toe, and a distinctive upright stance.

COLUMBIFORMES

Woodpigeon, Stock Dove, Collared Dove

DOVES AND PIGEONS have small heads, short legs with small scales and a fleshly cere at the base of the bill. They have a muscular gizzard and large crop, the lining of which secretes a unique 'milk' to feed the young. The two eggs hatch into nearly naked young. As pigeons can drink by sucking, they do not have to tilt the head back to swallow.

PSITTACIFORMES

Ring-necked Parakeet

AN ORDER WITH a single large family, the parrots, mainly confined to the tropics, except for some introductions. Mainly vegetable feeders with a stout, strongly hooked bill with a woodpecker-like arrangement of their toes, they are good climbers and despite a large range in size are an extremely uniform group. Gregarious, noisy and intelligent.

Top
Water rail in typical habitat.

Bottom
Auks, such as these guillemots, are rather penguin-like in shape – but they can fly.

CUCULIFORMES

Cuckoo

USUALLY LONG-TAILED and long-billed. Many, including the European species, are brood-parasites. Cuckoos have a slightly decurved bill and are insectivorous, favouring hairy caterpillars. This order also contains the peculiar hoatzin of South America, whose young have two functional claws on their wings to help clamber in the trees, and the turacos of tropical Africa.

STRIGIFORMES

Barn Owl, Tawny Owl, Little Owl

MAINLY NOCTURNAL, with large, rounded heads and big eyes. Most can turn their heads to look sideways or over their shoulder. The eye is strengthened and lengthened by a cylinder of bony plates that help provide telescopic vision. The large facial disc of feathers concentrates sound. Owls have hooked bills, with the base covered in bristles.

CAPRIMULGIFORMES

Nightjar

NOCTURNAL, FAVOURING DUSK and dawn. Small weak feet, a short bill but with a large gape, surrounded by long bristles. Eggs are laid on bare ground. The highly specialised oilbird of South America also belongs here, as do the frogmouths, owlet-nightjars and potoos.

APODIFORMES

Swift

THE RELATIONSHIP BETWEEN swifts and the mainly tropical hummingbirds (also classified in this order) is uncertain, but they share a specialised wing structure and a unique egg-white protein. They have tiny feet, short humerus bones, but long bones in the outer portion of the wing. The crop is lacking in swifts.

CORACIIFORMES

Kingfisher, Bee-eater, Hoopoe

ALTHOUGH THIS APPARENTLY diverse group, which includes rollers, kingfishers and hoopoes, share peculiarities of the palate and leg muscles and have their front toes fused at the base, they may not be monophyletic, that is they may stem from more than one ancestral form.

PICIFORMES

Green Woodpecker, Great Spotted Woodpecker, Wryneck

WE HAVE NO honeyguides or toucans (also included in this order), but woodpeckers also have unique feet, with two toes pointing forwards and two back. True

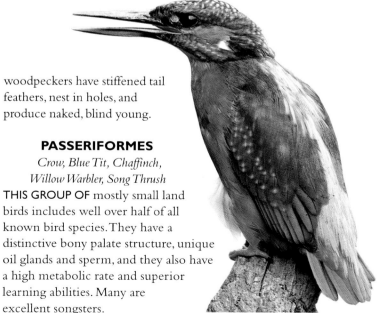

woodpeckers have stiffened tail feathers, nest in holes, and produce naked, blind young.

PASSERIFORMES

Crow, Blue Tit, Chaffinch, Willow Warbler, Song Thrush

THIS GROUP OF mostly small land birds includes well over half of all known bird species. They have a distinctive bony palate structure, unique oil glands and sperm, and they also have a high metabolic rate and superior learning abilities. Many are excellent songsters.

Top
Pigeons and doves are all very similar in general shape. The collared dove is common in towns and farmland.

Bottom left
Tawny owls are more often heard than seen. Owls have a rounded head and large eyes.

Bottom right
Many a birder's favourite, the kingfisher redefines the term brilliant.

Town and Garden Birds

NINE OUT OF TEN people in Britain live in towns. The idea of the concrete jungle is however something of a myth, and in most towns and cities private gardens and parks provide large areas of green space. In the Black Country of the West Midlands, for example, woodland doubled between 1977 and 1989 as neglected 'derelict' land was colonised. Such 'brownfield' sites are under heavy threat from further housing, but for all of us, wherever we live, it is important that the urban majority have greenery, and birds, within reach. In many newly planned urban areas, wildlife corridors provide relatively unbroken green links between the countryside and the centre of the city.

BIRDS FOUND IN CITIES

SUBURBAN NORTH LONDON has changed somewhat since Harting was able to write of 'whinchats in every grassfield; willow wrens and whitethroats in the green lanes; and the handsome Butcher-bird in the tall tangled hedges'. Nevertheless the variety of urban habitats still yields enough birds to interest most birdwatchers today.

The *Birds of the London Area* (1957) includes 245 species seen within 32 km (20 miles) of St Paul's Cathedral. Fitter dealt with a smaller, almost wholly built-up area, the administrative county of London, but still listed 45 residents, 13 summer visitors and 34 regular winter visitors and passage migrants. Red-backed shrikes sadly are now gone, grey partridge and hawfinch are rarer, and not everyone would see the gain of magpies and collared doves as fair exchange. The opportunist magpie is ready to 'tidy up' dog litter, clear roads of the victims of cars, and take away food leftovers and the contents of fragile plastic bags. The collared dove, another versatile feeder, is now one of the top ten garden birds; it had only reached the southern Balkans at the turn of the century, and it was only in 1952 that it reached Britain.

A quick look at some regional Bird Reports shows that London is not alone. Greater Manchester, stretching from Wigan to Oldham and Rochdale to Trafford, reported its usual clutch of rare birds in 1996.

Working through the year these included Iceland gull, red-necked grebe, bittern, Mediterranean gull, osprey, garganey, firecrest, dotterel, Savi's warbler, marsh harrier, bee-eater, Arctic skua, purple sandpiper, blue-winged teal, hoopoe, hen harrier, snow bunting and twite. On the other side of the Pennines the 1993/1994 report of the Barnsley and District Bird Study Group had records of great northern diver, bittern, eider, crane, pomarine skua, long-tailed skua and yellow-browed warbler in one year, and purple heron, great white egret, honey buzzard and Temminck's Stint in the next.

Top
The smart black-and-white plumage of the magpie is seen increasingly in both towns and gardens.

Middle
The blackbird is now one of the most common garden birds in Britain.

Bottom
The number of collared doves has increased rapidly over the last 30 years.

GARDEN INHABITANTS

BUT FOR MOST of those who love birds it is the ones found in town gardens that are most important.

Recent BTO research reports that the blackbird tops the list of visitors to gardens large and small, with 96.4 per cent of gardens being visited. The other most commonly seen birds are blue tit, robin, great tit, chaffinch, house sparrow (decreasing), collared dove, dunnock, starling and greenfinch. The *Bird Table*, newsletter of the Garden Bird Watch scheme, reports seasonal fluctuations among birds which would have been thought rare in gardens until a few years ago. Goldfinches come in twice as much in late spring, a time of seed shortage, blackcaps turn up in winter in up to 40 per cent of town gardens, and the appearance of wandering winter siskins, redwings and bramblings depends on such remote events as the scarcity of food in Scandinavia. These facts, together with a host of others from the first three years of the scheme are brought together by Andrew Cannon in the *Garden Bird Watch Handbook* (1998). This book, based on weekly observations by over 10,000 garden birdwatchers will be much quoted in the species section.

TOWN BIRDS

TITS AND ROBINS are probably the garden favourites. With four million pairs in Britain and Ireland, for a time they replaced the blackbird as the top garden bird. blackbirds' panic alarm calls at breeding times are a headache for anyone worried about the survival of young birds, but their beautiful song produces no such headache, unless it is too early in the morning and too loud, when densely-packed suburban blackbirds defend their territories in the dawn chorus.

House sparrows used to be thought of as the typical urban bird, and at times the noisy flocks of roosting starlings have taken over city centres, as well as the chimney pots of suburbia. Perhaps feral pigeons are now the true urban birds. These are descended from the rock doves of wild coastal cliffs, and they are well able to use the year-round food supply of towns to help prolong their extensive breeding season. They may have five broods a year, and attempts to reduce numbers and the damage caused to buildings have met with little success.

The black redstart is also urban. This rather secretive and local species chooses derelict industrial sites, gas works, power stations and other places with little normal appeal to birdwatchers. Equally unexpected, until recently, would have been the noisy screeching of a gorgeously coloured parrot, but ring-necked parakeets have settled well, notably in south-east London, and the 1997 *Surbiton Bird Report* has the extraordinary record of 1,507 Parakeets roosting at Esher Rugby Club.

Top
Robins are very adaptable and will happily nest in an abandoned pot or kettle.

Middle
The once ubiquitous house sparrow has suffered a steep decline in numbers over recent years.

Bottom
The distinctive plumage of the great tit makes the species easily recognisable among garden birds.

THE GARDEN VISITOR

APART FROM FEEDING birds, many people put up nest–boxes and it is not difficult to make your own. Humble garden nest–boxes are important, as gardens now cover more land area than nature reserves. There are various reference books, including, *Nest boxes*, that contain practical details about construction, siting, maintenance and protection against predators.

Gardeners can also help by not being too tidy; by leaving some shrubs to grow, by leaving dead flower-heads to provide seeds, saving piles of wood for invertebrate food and sheltering wrens, and cutting down on or abandoning pesticide use. If

gardeners can help, so too can councils, who can save money by not mowing all their parks, and by some healthy neglect of odd corners, providing shelter and food sources. Do not leave it to others, if you are an urban enthusiast you will want to work, preferably as part of a group, to protect valued oases so that birds can continue to adapt to town and city life.

Top
Most garden birds enjoy the provision of clean water for bathing in as well as drinking.

Middle
Blue tits will look in garden beds and on lawns for caterpillars with which to feed their hungry brood.

Bottom
All birds enjoy the provision of nuts and other scraps in the garden, especially in winter.

GARDEN BIRD WATCH 'TOP TEN TIPS'

1. Only put out as food that will be consumed in a day or two. Never allow food to accumulate; reduce it at quiet times.

2. Keep feeders reasonably clean and move them around the garden periodically, to avoid infectious droppings building up.

3. In the nesting season avoid presenting whole peanuts. Chop them, or use a mesh feeder from which adult birds can only take small fragments.

4. Try to have reasonably clean water available at all times for bathing as well as drinking – never add salt or any chemicals in winter.

5. Do not put out salted snacks, highly-flavoured foods, uncooked rice, whole bacon rinds or unsoaked, desiccated coconut which can be fatal to birds.

6. Keep food away from any cover where cats might lurk and consider electronic scarers, which need relocating weekly for best results.

7. If sparrowhawks are present, place feeders next to shrubs to allow birds to escape. Clip the shrubs back so cats cannot hide.

8. Provide a variety of foods in different positions and types of feeder. Offer unmixed foods in different positions and types of feeder. Offer unmixed foods separately rather than mixtures.

9. Cereal grain attracts pigeons. Use better quality, pure foods – black sunflower seeds or peanuts – if pigeons are a problem.

10. Stick to natural foods, rather than chemically altered or processed foods like margarine.

like protein-rich caterpillars, is available for the young. Coal tits occur in over 50 per cent of gardens in the survey at peak times, usually just before New Year; the period of highest attendance, depending on weather conditions in January and February. Our long-tailed tits, which do breed in the garden, start visiting the sunflower seeds, and any available fat, in November.

With an equally small body, wrens are also extremely vulnerable to the weather. A low level seems to occur at the time of moult, when birds are very wary and hard to see, but this is much more evident in the song thrush population.

THE GARDEN BIRD WATCH SCHEME

THIS GARDEN BIRD recording project, running all year round, aims to record changes that may occur among the birds visiting our gardens. Each observer fills in two lists weekly. For ten very common species there are four levels of abundance, and each week one of these levels is marked. The second list, of less frequent visitors, includes 31 species. Clear patterns have emerged after only three years of the scheme but good numbers of participants in any project make for meaningful results.

Some surprising patterns have emerged. The great spotted woodpecker, which might be expected to turn up most in winter, actually occurs most often in early June. Then the base rate of 20 per cent of gardens increases slightly, as young woodpeckers, as part of their apprenticeship, are shown how to peck at peanuts; another good reason to keep feeding through the summer, for they are spectacular birds to see at close quarters.

Tits are in almost every garden, with blue tits the most abundant. If adult birds have a good supply of food made available, from artificial sources, any natural food,

With the threats hanging over song thrush populations it will be interesting to see how the recording frequency, at present peaking at nearly 60 per cent of gardens, changes in the future.

Two final birds, which would not have been expected in gardens 30 years ago, are the magpie and the collared dove. The very consistent levels of both suggest how suitable the garden environment is for them. If 50 per cent of gardens have magpies then 50 per cent do not, and, in those gardens, it cannot be the magpies that are damaging eggs and young!

The whole of this scheme is organised by the BTO – more participants are always welcome, and interested parties should write directly to the the BTO address in the Further Information section.

Top
Long-tailed tits are seen mostly in gardens during the autumn and winter months.

Middle
Wrens will search out dense vegetation in which to hide their nests, which are built mainly of moss.

Bottom
Great spotted woodpeckers can often be seen in gardens, especially when there is woodland nearby.

Feral Pigeon

33 cm (13 in)

SPECIES INFORMATION	
SCIENTIFIC NAME	Columba livia
RELATED SPECIES	Rock Dove (the wild ancestor), Stock Dove
CALL	Cooing courtship call 'doo-roo-dooo'
HABITAT	Found in towns and cities; originally rocky sites and sea-cliffs (rock dove)
STATUS	Resident, some wild colonies on cliffs of north-west England

SIZE

IDENTIFICATION

HABITAT

POPULATION

MAP

A VERY FAMILIAR BIRD of towns and cities, with very variable plumage, from blue-grey to rusty-brown, or even very dark, or pure white; double black wing-bar. The wild rock dove always has white patch on rump.

FERAL PIGEONS HAVE come to substitute city ledges and shop-fronts for their ancestral cliffs. Accumulated droppings at nesting sites or roosts can cause serious economic problems as they have a corrosive action on stonework, particularly limestone. Pavements and ledges fouled by droppings are slippery and dangerous to pedestrians and workmen, and feathers and nest material may block gutters and drains.

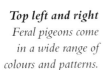

Top left and right
Feral pigeons come in a wide range of colours and patterns.

Bottom
The pigeons are so common in some cities that they may constitute a health hazard.

Collared Dove

32 cm (12.5 in)

SPECIES INFORMATION

SCIENTIFIC NAME	Streptopelia decaocto
RELATED SPECIES	Turtle Dove
CALL	Flight-call a nasal 'shvair-shvair'. Courtship song a monotonous tri-syllabic 'coo-cooo, coo', accented on the second syllable (sometimes causes confusion with cuckoo, if third syllable omitted)
HABITAT	Towns and villages, especially where there is an abundance of food, as in parks, zoos, grain stores, farmyards. Often visits bird tables
STATUS	Most of Europe, except far north-east (rather patchy in south-west Europe). In BI about 230,000 pairs

SOME PEOPLE MISTAKE the persistent trisyllabic calls of collared doves for the previous species, but many more try to turn them into cuckoos. These elegant, long-tailed doves with black half collars in contrast to their pale greyish buff, pale pink and subtle blue grey are now familiar in gardens.

SIZE

IDENTIFICATION

HABITAT

POPULATION

MAP

THE COLLARED DOVE'S colonisation of Britain, such a success since 1952, may have been helped by the chicken runs and feeding on house balconies, which were too close to human activities for woodpigeons to use. The collared dove now seems very much a bird of the bird table and less a bird of the farmyard.

In its Indian heartland it favours open, dry, cultivated country, even semi-desert, so it has adapted well to new habitats. In his note Goodwin mentioned changes in colonial roosting in response to sparrowhawk predation, so the bird seems adaptable in every way.

As well as adaptability, a long breeding season helps it to flourish, with eggs being laid from March to October. Courtship involves a steep upward flight, followed by slow descent, accompanied by the nasal flight-call. The nest is a flimsy platform, usually in a tree, but sometimes on a building, and once the young have fledged they soon seem to be on their way so that a new brood can be produced.

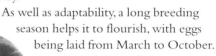

Top left and right
Collared doves are commonly seen in gardens and public parks.

Bottom
The preening bird spreads its tail into a fan shape and shows the white tips to the tail feathers.

Swift
16–17 cm (6.5 in)

SPECIES INFORMATION	
SCIENTIFIC NAME	Apus apus
RELATED SPECIES	Alpine Swift
CALL	High-pitched shrill squeals; very vocal in breeding season
HABITAT	Originally a cliff-nester, but now breeds mainly in buildings such as church towers, chimneys and tower blocks; also under the eaves of houses. Common, especially in towns, but declining
STATUS	Summer visitor; most of Europe. In BI about 100,000 pairs

SIZE

IDENTIFICATION

HABITAT

POPULATION

MAP

BLACKISH PLUMAGE WITH pale chin and neck, and long, sickle-shaped wings. Juveniles have pale brow and paler markings on head. Swifts spends most of their lives in the air, often for weeks at a time outside breeding season. They are also very sociable, often flying fast in tightly knit flocks. In summer they may circle to a great height in the evening, even apparently sleeping on the wing.

THE FIRST BIRD BOOK in the main New Naturalist series was *Birds and Men* (1951) by E. M. Nicholson. In his preface he said that he 'tried in each case to bring out the different character and way of life of each species'.

'No other British bird is so aerial as the swift, a species which not many people can claim ever to have seen at rest. Except at the nest the swift's life is spent flying in a layer of air which stretches from just above the ground to fully 1,000 ft above it. This layer is rather deeper than a swallow's but is more briefly tenanted because to support the type of insect life on which the swift depends it must not normally drop to a temperature below a critical level.'

I changed my views on a swift's life when I found a grounded swift in the Close in Salisbury. It

did not take much to make a diagnosis for darting among its feathers were louse flies. Closer examination found 12 of these 6 mm (0.25 in) blood-sucking parasites. Rothschild and Clay (1952) compare two of these insects creeping about the feathers 'to a man with a couple of large shore crabs scuttling about in his underclothes'.

I have never fancied being a swift quite so much since, but still admire and love them screaming around a church or large Victorian house. When the sun is out the dark birds cover a wide area on swept back wings, but when it is damp and cold they may find it hard to feed their young which become almost torpid as they reduce their metabolic needs to survive.

Top
Swifts are often found nesting under the roofs and eaves of buildings.

Bottom
Because of their agility, swifts find it easy to cling to the side of vertical buildings.

House Martin

12.5 cm (5 in)

SPECIES INFORMATION	
SCIENTIFIC NAME	*Delichon urbica*
RELATED SPECIES	Swallow, Sand Martin
CALL	Flight-call 'prrt, trr-trr'. Song a simple twitter
HABITAT	Towns and villages. Also in quarries and in mountains to 2,000 m (6,500 ft). Builds mud nest with entrance hole
STATUS	Summer visitor, wintering in tropical Africa. Throughout Europe. In BI about 400,000 pairs

METALLIC BLUE-BLACK above, with white rump and pure white underside. Smaller and more compact than swallow, with short, only weakly forked tail, and flight is more fluttering; often glides. Usually feeds at a higher level than swallow.

GILBERT WHITE WROTE of house martins, 'House martins are distinguished from their congeners by having their legs covered with soft downy feathers down to their toes. They are no songsters; but twitter in a pretty soft manner in their nests. During the time of breeding they are often greatly molested with fleas.'

House martins have moved nearer city centres since the Clean Air Acts encouraged the return of aerial insects. Their white rumps are the clearest features to distinguish them from other insectivores who spend time in flight, but the blue back and slightly forked tail are also characteristic.

House martins are summer visitors to most of Europe, and across central and northern Asia to southern China. The European birds are almost totally linked with man's buildings and with the need for mud. Martin lovers may make muddy pools or

brew up their own mud mixes and leave them on an appropriate flat roof, but do beware of cats if you do this to encourage martins.

Mud, building sites and insects can all be limiting factors, and in cold, wet summers the last broods may still be in the nest in September. When insects are around the house martins will search at higher altitudes than the swallow, but below the swift, picking off flies and aphids which are often drawn up high. Our birds arrive in mid April and the male selects the nest site and starts to build. There is no doubt that the birds produce plenty of mess from the nest, and that many nests are destroyed because of this, but as far as I am concerned the martins deserve every bit of help as they share their lives with us.

SIZE

IDENTIFICATION

HABITAT

POPULATION

MAP

Top right
House martins have a distinctive white chest and are plumper than swifts.

Top left and bottom
House martins gather damp mud with which to make their adhesive nests.

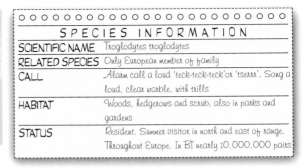

Wren

9–10 cm (3.75 in)

SPECIES INFORMATION	
SCIENTIFIC NAME	Troglodytes troglodytes
RELATED SPECIES	Only European member of family
CALL	Alarm call a loud 'teck-teck-teck' or 'tserrr'. Song a loud, clear warble, with trills
HABITAT	Woods, hedgerows and scrub; also in parks and gardens
STATUS	Resident. Summer visitor in north and east of range. Throughout Europe. In BI nearly 10,000,000 pairs

SIZE

IDENTIFICATION

HABITAT

POPULATION

MAP

O NE OF OUR commonest (and smallest) species. Tiny, with short tail (often cocked). Creeps mouse-like close to the ground or in vegetation or among tree roots. Flight is direct, with rapid wing-beats.

ITS TINY SIZE and cocked tail are unmistakable, despite the fact that its colour could make it one of 'the little brown jobs'. In fact the rufous brown and fine barring are attractive when seen at close quarters. Wrens often search among dense cover for insects and spiders. The long thin bill enables it to probe in crevices in bark, rocks and walls and only in hard weather, when much heat is lost from its tiny body, does the death rate rise. One of their strategies for coping with winter cold is for lots of them to pack into a confined space, often nowadays a bird box, and share the generated heat.

Despite the small wings and their normally short, low flights wrens can move extensively away from winter cold, with Swedish birds moving up to 2,500 km (1,550 miles). It is not so surprising then that it has become a good

coloniser of islands, but presumably this colonisation is not that frequent as a complex of island races has evolved. Fair Isle, St Kilda and Shetland birds form a cline, with wing, tail, bill, tarsus and foot found to be longer as one moves north.

Apart from the vehement rattling territorial song, wrens have a softer courtship song and a series of loud 'ticks' and 'churrs', for almost any situation, but particularly threat from predators.

It seems that wherever one goes there are wrens; on plenty of my woodland surveys among conifers or in all sorts of deciduous woodland they are among the commonest, often the commonest, birds. High in the mountains, as long as there is cover, from boulders or heather, or on precipitous Hebridean cliffs there are wrens. They rattle away in the garden, love heathery heaths and do as well as any bird in farmland hedges.

Edward Armstrong, who wrote both about wrens and folklore, described annual wren hunts, often to coincide with twelfth night and the tradition of Lord of Misrule when all the usual order of things was set topsy-turvey. Armstrong reckoned there was a cult of the wren from pagan times and its ritual slaughter was a sign of the death of the old year and ensured the fertility of the new.

In most circumstances however it has been seen as bad to harm a wren; it was the Druidic bird of augury, and in Cornwall they say 'hunt a robin or a wren, never prosper man or boy'.

Top right
The wren often nests on heathland but is just as happy in a hedgerow.

Top left and bottom
The dainty, rather mouse-like wren gathers spiders' webs to incorporate in its nest; it also includes spiders in its diet.

Dunnock

14 cm (5.5 in)

```
○○○○○○○○○○○○○○○○○○○○○○○○○○○○○○○
```

SPECIES INFORMATION

SCIENTIFIC NAME	Prunella modularis
	Alternative Names: Hedge Sparrow, Hedge Accentor
RELATED SPECIES	Alpine accentor
CALL	Alarm-call is a thin 'tseeh'. Song a pleasant warble, gently rising and falling
HABITAT	Woodland, parks and gardens
STATUS	Resident. Most of Europe, except the far south. In B about 2,800,000 pairs

UNOBTRUSIVE, rather nondescript, with sparrow-like plumage but robin-like shape. Head and breast are slate grey, the flanks with darker streaks. Bill thinner than house sparrow's.

DUNNOCKS MAY BE unobtrusive birds, but they have real character as they peck for almost invisible food items under the bird table or half hidden in garden shrubbery. The slim bill shows that it is no sparrow, and the uniform pale blue-grey face and underparts contrast with delicate streaks elsewhere.

After all the extraordinary colours and peculiar antics filmed with such breathtaking patience and skill by David

Attenborough's photographic team for the 'World of Birds', it was good to see the Dunnock. It may have taken almost equal patience to record their peculiar breeding behaviour, for it is only in recent years that it has been recorded, despite the Dunnock's readiness to show itself, at times, in almost every garden.

As Andrew Cannon reports in the *Garden Birdwatch Handbook*, 'Many dunnocks are polyandrous, which means the females lay eggs fertilised by more than one male. Professor Nick Davies of Cambridge University showed that even more complex "mating systems" are quite common, in fact, only about a third of female dunnocks are monogamous. This partly depends on how cold the winter has been. More females die in cold winters as males tend to monopolise the available food, so there are often extra males in the spring population. It was generally thought that male birds set up territories and females chose between them, but studying dunnocks revealed that in this species the females compete amongst themselves for territory without reference to the males, which then have to compete with each other to "move in" A dominant (alpha) and subordinate (beta) male whose territories overlap the larger territory of a female, often both join forces with her and cease to compete, defending the single territory as a trio.'

SIZE

IDENTIFICATION

HABITAT

POPULATION

MAP

Top left and right
Dunnocks are familiar birds in parks and gardens, especially those with plenty of cover.

Bottom
The Dunnock has a pale blue-grey face and a slim bill, which distinguish it from the house sparrow.

Robin

14 cm (5.5 in)

○○○○○○○○○○○○○○○○○○○○○○○○○

SPECIES INFORMATION

SCIENTIFIC NAME	Erithacus rubecula
RELATED SPECIES	No close relatives in BI
CALL	Sharp 'tick', often rapidly repeated; also a high-pitched 'tsee'. Tuneful song, heard from autumn, is a clear descending series of rippling notes
HABITAT	Woodland, especially broadleaved woods with rich undergrowth. Also in parks and gardens
STATUS	Resident and partial migrant. Throughout Europe. In BI about 6,000,000 pairs

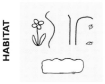

SIZE

IDENTIFICATION

HABITAT

POPULATION

MAP

THIS FAMILIAR GARDEN bird has a rather rounded shape, relatively long legs, and obvious red breast (sexes similar). The juvenile lacks the red, and is mainly mottled brown.

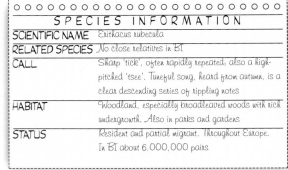

BECAUSE THEY SING so close to us as we dig or tidy up the garden most people know the song, with its melodic warble. Fewer people spot the sharp 'tick' or high-pitched 'tsee' which indicates territorial defence or alarm.

We are lucky that we can see our individuals at close quarters, but most continental birds are noticeably less tame and inclined to skulk. As well as this difference in behaviour, other races are usually paler, have different intensities of rufous on the upper

Robins traditionally covered the dead with leaves, linking up with the legends of the babes in the wood. The first postmen who wore red waistcoats, were called robins, and so we get robins on Christmas cards, often with letters in their beak.

'In the first mild day of March:
Each minute sweeter than before,
The red-breast sings from the tall larch
That stands beside my door.'
William Wordsworth

tail coverts, and vary in size. Further afield there are populations in Tunisia, the Urals and the Caucasus, as well as a more isolated one in the Canaries which is more distinctly different. Wherever they are they like a good deal of cover, some patches of open ground, and a song post or two.

Because we have a mild, oceanic climate, many of us are surprised by the amount of movement of northern and eastern populations, but some of our robins move as far as Iberia. When all goes well, a high-flying, nocturnal migrant gives little away.

Top and middle
Perhaps our best-loved and most famous garden bird, the robin is fiercely territorial and may be quite violent against its own kind.

Bottom
The male robin does not gain its famous red breast until it reaches maturity.

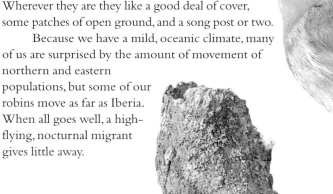

Starling
21 cm (8.25 in)

SPECIES INFORMATION	
SCIENTIFIC NAME	*Sturnus vulgaris*
RELATED SPECIES	Spotless Starling replaces Starling (both present in winter) in Spain, Portugal, Corsica, Sardinia and Sicily. It lacks spots in breeding plumage
CALL	Shrill 'rrairr' or 'shrii'; alarm-call 'vett-vett'. Song is very varied, with whistles, interspersed with crackling, snapping and rattling calls, and many imitations of other birds and sounds
HABITAT	Broadleaved and mixed woodland, cultivated areas, urban areas, parks and gardens
STATUS	Resident and partial migrant. Most of Europe, except extreme south and south-west. In BI about 3,000,000 pairs

FAMILIAR DUMPY GARDEN bird with rather long, pointed yellow bill. In winter heavily spotted with white and with dark bill. Breeding plumage has glossy green-violet sheen. Juvenile grey-brown. Flight direct, showing pointed, triangular wings. Roosts in large flocks, in trees or reedbeds. Often visits bird tables.

STARLINGS APPEAR BLACKISH whether searching grassland for leather-jackets or flying to roost. In flight the pointed wings and short tail make for a triangular silhouette. When well seen all sorts of spots and shiny speckles and reflections appear, and even if you did not like them before you briefly have to admit to admiration.

Starlings have done very well by taking advantage of human settlements and they have been spreading in the north of their range for more than 100 years. The possible peak winter British population was in 1967, with some 37 million birds. The significant decrease since could be because of the reduction in permanent pasture. The starling is one of the birds that has been successfully introduced elsewhere, so that it is now familiar in America, Southern Africa, Australia and New Zealand, as well as natural homes east of the Urals, and from Iran to Pakistan. With this extensive range, variation is not surprising, with differences in gloss, juvenile plumage, foot and bill structure, and size.

The nest can be bulky if in a big cavity, and is situated as far as possible from the cavity opening. Almost anything can go to make up the lining if it is not too coarse but the base contains tougher grasses and twigs.

Although they are hole nesters they do not like low, dense vegetation except for where they roost in reedbeds. Seasonality of habitat has already been suggested and the same applies to diet, with animal food dominating in the spring and being fed to nestlings when the adults yellow bills may have legs of insects and spiders sticking out in all directions. They also take a lot of plant foods, including soft fruits and seeds.

Why people do not like starlings is not clear. Some call them reptilian, and some blame their apparent greed and bossiness at the bird table. Others may find that their noisy nesting not far from a bedroom window makes for little summer sleep, while the mess their roosts can cause in cities or in country copses make further causes for unpopularity.

Nicholson in his *Birds and Men* emphasised not only their sociability with their own kind but their readiness to mix with other species. He reckoned that the closest attachment is to lapwings, whether in the fields or less convincingly in the air where the different styles of flight cause comic awkwardness. Starlings are happy with rooks and jackdaws and redwings in fields, and with oystercatchers and turnstones foraging on the sea shore, and they do not limit themselves to birds, for a quick parasite grazing on a sheep's back is always in order.

SIZE

IDENTIFICATION

HABITAT

POPULATION

MAP

Top left and right
Starlings are seldom far away from house or garden. They sometimes gather at large communal roosts in the winter.

Bottom
Starlings have a bright yellow bill and, in the winter months, a distinctive spotted chest.

Blackbird

25 cm (10 in)

SPECIES INFORMATION

SCIENTIFIC NAME	*Turdus merula*
RELATED SPECIES	Song Thrush, Mistle Thrush, Fieldfare, Redwing, Ring Ouzel
CALL	Alarm-call a metallic 'tsink-tsink' and a shrill chatter. Song loud, melodious and fluting, with rather slow phrases (not repeated as in song thrush)
HABITAT	Woods, hedgerows, parks and gardens
STATUS	Resident and partial migrant. In BI over 5,000,000 pairs

SIZE

IDENTIFICATION

HABITAT

POPULATION

MAP

VERY COMMON GARDEN bird, with all black (male) or all brown (female) plumage. Bill and eye-ring of male orange-yellow. Female has weakly speckled breast. Juveniles reddish-brown and strongly speckled beneath.

THE RICH BLACKBIRD song, and equally rich orange bill, setting off the glossy plumage of the male are well known but the brown female may be less so. The alarm note when a cat or other predator is around, and the mess they make as they search for food make blackbirds among the most noticeable of birds.

As usual Nicholson has apposite comments based on his own observations. 'The alarm of the blackbird is much more than a note, having the length and pattern of a song, but not the function or the music. Beginning with two or three throaty chuckling protests, it suddenly rises in pitch and accelerates into a shrill excited chatter, to which as an anti-climax two or three more chuckles are often added. The chuckle is also used by itself as a note of caution, and the familiar "mik-mik-mik" expresses suspicion and emotional tension on such occasions as going to roost in winter or mobbing an owl or cat.'

Blackbirds are very suburban birds, and Garden BirdWatch reports a comparison with blackbirds in more natural woodland habitat. 'Woodland nests suffered a high predation rate of around 80 per cent with corvids (magpies, jays etc) mainly responsible, but wild mammals such as weasels also very active. In gardens, the rate of predation was much lower, at around 50 per cent, which might be expected, as there are generally fewer wild predators in inhabited areas, cats and magpies being the chief culprits.'

> *'Sing a song of blackbirds,*
> *Who will not let me keep*
> *Orange peel or tea bags*
> *On my compost heap.*
> *When the heap is opened,*
> *Upon the worms they sup.*
> *I wouldn't mind the mess they make*
> *If they would clear things up.'*
> Robert S Morrison WORDS ON BIRDS

Top and bottom left
Blackbirds enjoy gardens with lawns, as they spend quite a lot of time searching for earthworms.

Bottom right
The male blackbird, with its yellow beak, has become a familiar sight in suburban areas.

Song Thrush

23 cm (9 in)

SCIENTIFIC NAME	*Turdus philomelos*
RELATED SPECIES	Mistle Thrush, Blackbird, Fieldfare, Redwing, Ring Ouzel
CALL	Alarm-call a sharp 'tick-tick-tick-tick'. Song loud and variable, with fluting phrases, each repeated two or three times (often more). Sings for long periods from tree-top perch in spring
HABITAT	Woodland, copses, parks and gardens
STATUS	Resident. Most of Europe, except the extreme South. In BI about 1,380,000 pairs

SMALL THRUSH WITH brown upperparts and large, dark eyes. Underside covered with small dark spots. Often feeds on fields close to woodland. Also eats snails, sometimes using a stone as an 'anvil' to break the shell.

A VERY POPULAR species. A vote in 1997 made the song of this thrush the favourite one in Britain. Snow (1998) describes it as 'a loud, clear, vigorous succession of simple but mainly musical phrases distinguished by their repetitive character, great variety and clear enunciation; more penetrating and less rich than Blackbird, lacking wild skirling quality of Mistle Thrush. Unmusical, harsh, or chattering sounds regularly intermixed with pure notes, also mimicry of other species.'

'With shorter bill and slighter build than the blackbirds', Cannon writes in the *Garden BirdWatch Handbook*, 'Song thrushes take a more limited range of prey than their bigger relative, extracting smaller worms from lawns and generally only from January to June, whereas stronger blackbirds can manage to pull them out of even quite dry summer grass.' The one resource which song thrushes do have available that blackbirds do not is snails, and many will have heard the cracking shell with relish as another garden pest is destroyed. How many who hate the snails and slugs have used pellets which are not safe for other wildlife, and have therefore contributed to the song thrush decline?

Many people remember song thrushes as being more common than blackbirds. Part of the change has been an increase in blackbirds, but since the mid 1970s the song thrush has suffered more than a 50 per cent decline, so that the BTO and RSPB have it among those birds on the red list of conservation importance. Even in woodlands, numbers are down by 45 per cent.

The song thrush has a special place in history for 'On the tenth day of April, eighteen hundred and ninety two' wrote Richard Kearton in 1908, 'my brother photographed the nest and eggs of a song thrush in the neighbourhood of London, and the result appeared to me to be so full of promise that I at once determined to write a book on British birds' nests and get him to illustrate it from beginning to end by photographs taken in situ.' He was writing then in a new and revised edition of *British Birds Nests*, the first book of its kind to be illustrated throughout by means of photographs taken direct from nature and showing things 'as they are and not as they are supposed to be'. A letter about 'this truly sporting method of studying Nature' emphasises one result. 'I consider that the birds ought to be extremely grateful to you for inventing bird photography. I never knew anything that has done so much for their protection during the nesting season as your example. I myself have for several years given up egg collecting entirely, and know many others who have done the same.'

SIZE

IDENTIFICATION

HABITAT

POPULATION

MAP

One of our finest songbirds, the song thrush has suffered a puzzling decline in recent years.

Blue Tit

12 cm (4.75 in)

SPECIES INFORMATION	
SCIENTIFIC NAME	*Parus caeruleus*
RELATED SPECIES	Great Tit, Coal Tit, Marsh Tit, Willow Tit
CALL	Call a nasal 'tsee-tsee-tsee'. Song is a rather pure-toned 'tseet-see-sirrrr'
HABITAT	Broadleaved and mixed woodland, especially oak, parks and gardens. In winter often feeds among reeds
STATUS	Resident. In BI about 4,500,000 pairs

SIZE

IDENTIFICATION

HABITAT

POPULATION

MAP

SMALL, COMPACT TIT with blue and yellow plumage. Female slightly less colourful than male. Juvenile much paler, with greenish-brown upperparts and yellow cheeks. Blue tits have blue crown, wings and tails and yellow underparts. The bill is short, the wings round and short, and the tail short, so not surprisingly it is a small bird which is vulnerable to cold weather. Its song is not as loud or distinctive as the 'teacher, teacher, teacher' of the great tit, and its wide range of calls is not quite so extensive. Scolding or churring alarm calls followed by a 'tsee', a high-pitched contact call, and a special alarm call for flying predators are among these.

'NATURE IS CRUEL — but not so cruel as the Book of Genesis' wrote Robert Gibbings (1940) thinking about the great flood. 'What harm had a wren or a blue tit ever done that they should be destroyed. I mentioned this once to a man who engaged me in religious conversation. His reply was that probably God was human like the rest of us, and that after all it was the first world He had ever made, and that it was only natural that there should have been a few mistakes.'

Whatever one's views on that, there is no doubt that we make plenty of mistakes and that we have only one world to damage. The decrease of so many species, the destruction of so many habitats, and the belief that nature is to be conquered, all tell us that we, and our government and the leaders of the world have got to learn and to change.

Luckily, despite all, 'the bluecap' still 'tootles in its glee' (John Clare) and a garden reporting rate of nearly 100 per cent, in winter, of this abundant and still increasing species, is an encouraging sign. We are learning too. Chris Perrins has studied tits in nest-boxes for many years and discovered a great deal about the biology of these common birds. Each tit species illustrates basic ecological principles mentioned earlier — each has its own ecological niche. The average size of insect and the height at which tits feed differ, with blue tits foraging in winter among twigs, but great tits often feeding on the ground.

Top
Blue tits are frequently the first to appear at the bird table, and often scare off larger birds.

Bottom left and right
The blue tit is a small compact bird with a colourful plumage.

Great Tit

14 cm (5.5 in)

SPECIES INFORMATION	
SCIENTIFIC NAME	Parus major
RELATED SPECIES	Blue Tit, Coal Tit, Marsh Tit, Willow Tit
CALL	Wide repertoire. Chaffinch-like 'pink' or 'tsi-pink', alarm-call 'tsher-r-r-r'. Song (variable) is a loud simple phrase such as 'tee-cher, tee-cher'. Starts singing as early as January
HABITAT	Woodland, parks and gardens
STATUS	Resident. In BI about 2,000,000 pairs

THE LARGEST EUROPEAN tit, with black and white head, yellow underparts, and a broad (male) or narrow (female) black stripe down centre of belly. Juvenile paler, with yellowish cheeks.

examples of birds from all round the world, were about great tits in Oxford's Wytham Woods, and Newton's recent *Population Limitation in Birds* has 67 page references to great tits.

All this erudition is fascinating, but has little to do with most people's appreciation of the bird. The yellow underparts with black central stripe, wider in males, is as familiar as the white cheeked black head and essentially green back. Variation in the black breast stripe one of the features which other great tits use to assess the dominance of competitors.

Birds maintain a dominance hierarchy in which those at the top of the 'pecking order' have preferential access to food. The hierarchy is continuously being challenged, especially in winter when the flocks of great tits that form in the autumn often aggregate together at food resources such as beech mast or in gardens with feeding stations.

LIKE BLUE TITS, great tits like nest-boxes as long as the opening is of adequate size. Whether nesting there, in a natural tree hole, or in a man-made drainpipe or crevice, great tits make a mossy nest thickly lined with hair, wool and feathers. This is much the same as the blue tit's in structure and contains a similarly large number of eggs, usually in the 6–11 range.

The great tit has given rise to a voluminous literature, much of it based on British nesting birds, many of them living near Oxford. Three of the 15 chapters in Lack's *Population Studies of Birds* which used

SIZE

IDENTIFICATION

HABITAT

POPULATION

MAP

Top
Great tits will often happily use nesting boxes in which to rear their broods.

Bottom left and right
The handsome great tit, with its striking colouring, is the largest of the European tit family.

House Sparrow

14.5 cm (5.75 in)

○○○○○○○○○○○○○○○○○○○○○○○○○○○○
SPECIES INFORMATION

SCIENTIFIC NAME	Passer domesticus
RELATED SPECIES	Tree Sparrow, Spanish Sparrow (parts of Spain, S. Italy, Greece and Turkey)
CALL	Chirps – repeated as song
HABITAT	Houses: villages, towns and farmyards
STATUS	Resident. In BI about 6,000,000 pairs

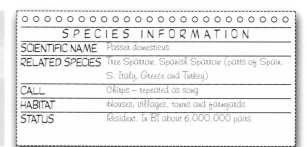

SIZE

IDENTIFICATION

HABITAT

POPULATION

MAP

A VERY FAMILIAR SMALL bird of towns. The male has grey cap and black bib; the female and juvenile are a drab grey-brown. House Sparrows, as seed eaters, have heavy bills, and they are tubby birds with broad wings and square-ended tails. On close inspection, the male is boldly patterned, with a grey crown and black eye-stripe and bib, dull white cheeks, dark streaks on the back, grey rump and greyish underparts. Females are, admittedly a little featureless and in Spain are hard to tell from Spanish sparrows.

IT IS ALWAYS THOUGHT that sparrows were everywhere, whether in London gardens and streets or in farm stackyards. The stackyards are mainly gone, and whereas 1950 counts, in Bloomsbury and Lambeth, gave densities of 4.3 and 4.0 birds per acre,

Formerly, this species was so common that it was widely regarded as a pest. In one Suffolk village 2,587 dozen sparrows earned a reward of 2d per dozen over 15 years, and in the 1860s the Sussex Express reported 'The thirteenth anniversary of the Sparrow Club, Rudgwick, was celebrated with a dinner at the Cricketers' Inn, on Tuesday last. On reference to the books it was ascertained that 5,321 birds' heads had been sent in by members during the year, 1,363 being contributed by Mr W. Wooberry, to whom was awarded the first prize.'

Turning from Man and Birds to *Birds and Men*, Nicholson as usual has a sparrow's eye view of sparrows. 'Free of the drains on time and energy represented by territory holding, competitive song and migration, and being intelligent enough to live where living is easy, the sparrow has a different daily timetable from almost any other small bird. His great outlet is social activity of many kinds. Nesting, roosting, feeding, bathing, dusting, quarrelling and even pairing are, for the sparrow, naturally social occasions; wanting to be alone, or to be out of the gang, are foreign to sparrow temperament.'

there were signs that London populations were already on the way down. House sparrow populations have not been effectively monitored by woodland or farmland common bird census work but the New Atlas showed a retraction in range in Scotland, Ireland and North Wales. Although still a numerous bird, the once ubiquitous house sparrow is now a bird of high conservation concern.

Top

The male sparrow is a boldly patterned, tubby little bird with a square tail.

Middle and bottom

House sparrows are still common in many towns and on farmland, but they have declined markedly in recent years.

Chaffinch
15 cm (6 in)

○ ○

SPECIES INFORMATION

SCIENTIFIC NAME	*Fringilla coelebs*
RELATED SPECIES	Brambling
CALL	Call a loud, short 'pink'. Song is a pleasant, descending phrase, accelerating towards the end
HABITAT	Woodland, gardens, parks and scrub; in winter flocks to farmland
STATUS	Resident and winter visitor. In BI about 7,000,000 pairs

OUR COMMONEST finch. Breeding male has blue-grey crown, brown back and pinkish breast. Female is olive-brown above and grey-brown below. In flight shows white wing-patch and wing-bar, and white outer tail feathers (rump not white).

Chaffinches are primarily woodland birds, but they are found in a wide range of habitats and have adapted well to farm hedges, orchards, parks and gardens.

Although widespread through Europe and the East into Russia, the chaffinch is replaced by the brambling to the north. In winter flocks the two are often together, feeding off seeds on the ground in woods or open fields and flying up with a flurry of white wing bars (chaffinch) and white rumps (bramblings).

> 'While the chaffinch sings on the orchard bough
> In England - now!'
> Robert Browning
> HOME THOUGHTS
> FROM ABROAD

SIZE

IDENTIFICATION

HABITAT

POPULATION

MAP

DOMINANT FEATURES OF chaffinch appearance, demonstrated in the section on a bird's year, are the white panels on the wing coverts and other bars on the secondaries and primaries. While outer tail feathers are also conspicuous. There is plenty of additional colour in males with blue-grey crown, pale red to pink face and underparts and dark back-ground to the white wing and tail marks.

Top left and right
Chaffinches are one of our most cosmopolitan species — at home in most habitats, including parks, gardens, orchards and woodland.

Bottom
The striking little male birds have a pinkish breast and brown back with black and white striping on the wing.

Greenfinch

15 cm (6 in)

SPECIES INFORMATION	
SCIENTIFIC NAME	Carduelis chloris
RELATED SPECIES	Goldfinch, Linnet, Twite, Redpoll, Siskin
CALL	Include 'chup-chup-chup', and a nasal 'dzveee'. Song consists of canary-like trills, with whistles and wheezing notes, often in slow song-flight
HABITAT	Mixed woodland, farmland, hedges, parks, orchards and gardens. Common at bird tables in winter
STATUS	Resident (and winter visitor). In BI about 700,000 pairs

SIZE

IDENTIFICATION

HABITAT

POPULATION

MAP

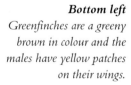

A LARGE, YELLOW-GREEN or brownish finch. Shows yellow wing patches, especially in flight. Female mainly grey-green with less yellow on wings and tail. Juvenile heavily streaked. The plump shape and cleft tail with yellow patches are always distinctive in flight.

IN SPRING, GREENFINCHES indulge in the so-called 'bat flight' with deep, slow wing beats. The body rolls from side to side and the bird weaves around the breeding area singing and calling. Hollom, wisely, avoids any attempt at description of the song saying just it is based mainly on calls, but *Birds of the Western Palearctic* (BWP) is braver: 'Song consists of groups of rolling tremolos ... punctuated by more slowly delivered repetition of tonal and more noisy units also by single longer and rather nasal "chew lee" and the familiar nasal or buzzing wheeze.'

In winter, hungry flocks move into gardens to feed on peanuts or sunflower seeds.

Hedge flailing does not leave many tough seeds on wild shrubs in later winter, so garden feeding then can lure them to breed if you have a stout hedge, creeper or dense conifer available. The nest, like the bird, is robust, made with grass, moss and lichen, with a lining of hair, feathers and fine grasses.

Bottom left
Greenfinches are a greeny brown in colour and the males have yellow patches on their wings.

Top right and bottom right
Greenfinches often make their presence known by their nasal, wheezing calls.

> 'Thou linnet! In thy green array
> Presiding Spirit here to-day
> Dost lead the revels of the May
> And this is thy dominion'
> William Wordsworth THE LINNET

Bullfinch

15 cm (5.75 in)

```
○ ○ ○ ○ ○ ○ ○ ○ ○ ○ ○ ○ ○ ○ ○ ○ ○ ○ ○ ○ ○ ○ ○ ○
```

SPECIES INFORMATION

SCIENTIFIC NAME	*Pyrrhula pyrrhula*
RELATED SPECIES	*No close relatives in BI*
CALL	*A quiet, rather plaintive 'dyuh'. Song is a soft, whistling twitter*
HABITAT	*Forest, scrub, plantations, mixed woodland, parks, gardens and orchards*
STATUS	*Resident and winter visitor. In BI about 200,000 pairs*

MALE UNMISTAKABLE, WITH bright, salmon-pink underparts, blue-grey back, black head and white rump. The female is brown-grey; the juvenile brownish, without black cap. Often looks plump, especially in cold weather. White rump prominent in flight.

THE BULLFINCH IS THE only finch of economic importance in Britain and Newton wonders why it has never become a major pest. It takes a greater proportion and variety of buds and for a longer period than any European bird and it does so with a beak, feeding technique and digestive system that have evolved for the job. A single Bullfinch can remove the buds of fruit trees at a rate of 30 per

minute, and it can be remarkably systematic in the way that it does it. Bullfinches enter orchards from nearby woods and hedgerows, attack the nearest trees first and penetrate by stages into the orchard, stripping every tree in turn.

In the late 1950s Newton started a six-year study of bullfinch biology near Oxford. He found that six plants formed the basis of bullfinch winter diet – dock, nettle and bramble were consistent seed producers in late summer, whereas privet, birch and ash varied their production. This was particularly so for ash. Inevitably, seed supplies dwindled during the winter, and buds became increasingly important, with a preference for hawthorn.

During short days the birds could not eat enough buds to maintain their weight so some seeds were essential and it was necessary, both for Newton and for bullfinches, to know how many there were. He therefore measured the decline in seed stocks during a winter when the ash crop was good. By the end of the winter, 99 per cent of ash remained, together with some bramble and dock, but the next winter the ash crop was poor and few seeds, except 7 per cent of the bramble, remained at the end of that winter. In the first year no buds of native trees were eaten before March, and damage to fruit farms was negligible, but in the second winter tree buds were stripped from mid-December and fruit farm damage was severe. Ash tends to fruit in alternate years, and national enquiries about fruit damage indicated alternate year problems.

SIZE

IDENTIFICATION

HABITAT

POPULATION

MAP

Bottom right
The male bullfinch is a very attractive bird with a salmon-pink under-carriage and contrasting dark blue back.

Top and bottom left
Bullfinches adapt well to a variety of environments but are known to be voracious eaters.

Pied Wagtail

18 cm (7 in)

SPECIES INFORMATION	
SCIENTIFIC NAME	Motacilla alba
RELATED SPECIES	Yellow Wagtail, Grey Wagtail
CALL	'Tsick', 'tsilipp', often repeated. Song is a rapid twitter
HABITAT	Open country, especially near water. Towns and villages, farms and gravel pits. Also seen on lakes, rivers, meadows, fields and wet areas
STATUS	Resident and partial migrant. In BI about 430,000 pairs

SIZE

IDENTIFICATION

HABITAT

POPULATION

MAP

LONG, BLACK TAIL with white outer feathers, and long black legs. The continental race, sometimes known as white wagtail (*M. alba alba*), has light grey back and rump. The British race (*M. alba yarrellii*), has a black back. Female less contrasty, and with less black on head. In winter has white chin and dark breast-band. Juveniles brown-grey above, without black. Overhead their call is as distinctive as their looping flight – a few flaps followed by a descending glide.

PIED WAGTAILS really live up to their name, with black upper parts, throat and breast and white forehead, face and chest. The long tail is in constant motion. The female has a slate grey back which is not as pale as the back of the white wagtail, the European subspecies counterpart of our bird.

These fine birds often visit gardens, especially to pick flies and other insects from lawns, or to take scraps fallen from the bird table. In the winter, they often gather at communal roosts, which may number many hundreds of birds. These may be in a reedbed, copse, or even in built-up areas. Pied wagtails make local movements, often dispersing after breeding, to wet meadows or riverside marshes. With so much food there, they can indulge in aerial flycatching, quick darts after insects, often among the legs of the cattle or in searches among the vegetation in shallow pools.

Top right and left
Pied wagtails are often found near water, but they also like to feed on garden lawns.

Bottom
Pied wagtails are opportunist, feeding their young with a combination of insects and scraps from gardens.

SPECIES INFORMATION

SCIENTIFIC NAME	Pica pica
RELATED SPECIES	Carrion Crow, Jay, Rook
CALL	A chattering 'shak-shak-shak'. Song is a low, babbling chatter, with rattling calls and whistles
HABITAT	Open country with hedges and fields, villages, parks and gardens with trees, even in urban areas; avoids dense woodland
STATUS	Resident. In BI about 800,000 pairs

Magpie
46 cm (18 in)

A LARGE, RATHER SHOWY bird with shiny black and white plumage and a long, graduated tail. Rather sociable and often seen in small groups. The adult is a handsome bird indeed, with its very long green and bronze purple tail and black and white wings and body. In flight there is an almost African impressiveness about the outline, the spectacular silhouette and the noisy chattering. Young birds have shorter tails and duller black plumage with little gloss. The most frequently used adjectives applied to magpies: aggressive, noisy, intelligent and adaptable could be used about many of the crow family, but the long tail is less typical. It has to be said that many would use less restrained adjectives about them and, while many garden birds are almost universally loved, magpies are widely disliked.

MAGPIES PREFER OPEN woodland or scrub and their complex domed nests can easily be seen in winter when not hidden by leaves. Mud, twigs, roots, hair, feathers and leaves may all be part of the core of the nest, while sticks, often thorny, protrude in a bulky mass around the underlying bowl. There are often two entrances.

Magpies are very successful birds, and this is in part due to their opportunistic feeding, taking a range of prey, from worms and insects, to nestlings, eggs and scraps. They are now enjoying the extension of free-range pig farming.

Magpies have been blamed by many for the widespread decreases in farmland birds, but this is not supported by the latest evidence. Does their opportunism bring about the decline of smaller species? Tree sparrows are declining fast, on red-alert, but nesting in holes their eggs and nestlings are usually safe from magpies so magpies are probably not to blame. Bird prey for magpies is mainly at the egg and nestling stage and the nest record cards, completed by BTO volunteers, provide a great deal of data on the success rates of nesting songbirds over a long period of time. This information is vital if we are to understand the cause of change in bird populations. For a number of declining songbirds, including the song thrush, nest records show us that breeding success has not really changed, so other factors, not nest predation, must have caused the declines.

SIZE

IDENTIFICATION

HABITAT

POPULATION

MAP

Bottom
Magpies are noisy, conspicuous birds; they are also rather clever, like other members of the crow family.

Top
Magpies are showy birds with a smart black and white plumage.

Jackdaw

33 cm 13 (in)

○○○○○○○○○○○○○○○○○○○○○○○○○○○○○

SPECIES INFORMATION

SCIENTIFIC NAME	*Corvus monedula*
RELATED SPECIES	Carrion Crow, Rook, Raven
CALL	Very vocal. Short, loud 'kya' or 'kyak', often repeated. Song (seldom heard) is a quiet warble with crackling and miaowing calls
HABITAT	Old, broadleaved woodland, cliffs, quarries, isolated trees in fields, parks with old trees, churches, castles and ruined buildings. Also breeds on houses, especially in chimneys
STATUS	Resident and partial migrant. In BI about 600,000 pairs

SIZE

IDENTIFICATION

HABITAT

POPULATION

MAP

SMALL AND CROW-LIKE, with mainly black plumage, grey nape and back of head, and pale eye. Its small size, pale eyes, ash grey nape and distinctive call at once distinguish the jackdaw from other crows. In winter they often form mixed flocks on fields with rooks.

THE JACKDAW IS a familiar species of towns, especially those with plenty of old buildings, such as a ruined castle or old church. Half the feeding time is on grassland, where invertebrates are an important part of the diet, with seeds also significant. When feeding their young they may move to trees in search of defoliating caterpillars and, later, for pupae. If adequate food is in short supply at that time nest sites are also often limiting and competition leads to typical noisy, jackdaw squabbling.

These sites are nearly always holes, but these may be in buildings or trees, nest boxes, or even rabbit burrows. The *Garden Bird Watch Handbook* reports research which shows how hard it is for a pair of jackdaws to find enough food to raise all their brood. Urban jackdaws are fairly frequent visitors to bird tables or to gardens where scraps are available. They also scavenge readily at rubbish dumps.

Top left and right
Birds of town and country, jackdaws are particularly fond of chimneys, church towers and similar sites, as well as cliffs and quarries.

Bottom
Jackdaws have a distinctive grey hood over the nape of their necks.

'There is a bird who,
by his coat
And by the hoarseness of his note,
Might be supposed a crow,
A great frequenter of the church,
Where, bishop like,
he finds a perch
And dormitory too'
William Couper THE JACKDAW

Carrion Crow

47 cm (18.5 in)

SPECIES INFORMATION

SCIENTIFIC NAME	Corvus corone corone
RELATED SPECIES	Hooded Crow, Rook, Jackdaw, Raven
CALL	Hoarse monotonous cawing, often repeated three times, sometimes more
HABITAT	Open country
STATUS	Resident. In B about 800,000 pairs (absent from most of Ireland)

CARRION CROWS LIVE up to their name by including some carrion in their diet, helping for example to clear the corpses of birds or mammals killed on the roads. But they will eat almost anything, from seeds and fruit to insects and worms.

Although the hooded crow is a race of this species, it is included in the uplands section, despite its occurrence at all altitudes in Ireland.

In England people say of the magpie 'one for sorrow, two for joy', in Wales the same is said of the crow. There is also a Saxon tradition that deemed seeing a crow on your left was a portent of disaster:

ALL BLACK, WITH rather powerful bill. Lacks 'trousers' of rook. Not colonial, and less sociable than rook. Some say a crow-bar is so called because of the power of a Crow's bill, which is not quite up to a raven's. This bill, coupled with the all black plumage and harsh call, is usually sufficient to identify a crow. In flight the wing fingers are less spread than those of a rook, and the tail much squarer than a raven's. The flight silhouette shows a distinct bulge to the rear edge of the wing.

'The carrion crow, that loathsome beast,
Which cries against the rain,
Both for her hue and for the rest
The Devil resembleth plain'
George Gascoigne 1573

SIZE

IDENTIFICATION

HABITAT

POPULATION

MAP

Top and bottom right
The carrion crow is all black, with a harsh call and a square tail.

Bottom left
The rather featureless carrion crow is an opportunist feeder, taking a wide range of food, including small dead animals.

113 🍃

Woodland Birds

WHEN BRITAIN SEPARATED from the main continent, much of it was covered with deciduous forest, although pine was probably common in Scotland. Four thousand years later Neolithic man had opened up large areas on Breckland and on the chalk, and by Domesday the country was only sparsely wooded. Today woodland is even more patchy, following further deforestation for industrial charcoal and for building. Such woodland as has been replanted, particularly since 1920, has been largely coniferous.

MORE RECENTLY, AMBITIOUS plans for replanting with native trees have been drawn up, adding a welcome diversity to the newer forests. Many woodland birds also visit gardens, and there is much

DIVERSITY OF WOODLAND BIRDS

IN ANY ONE 'plot' in Chaddesley Woods NNR in Worcestershire I never met more than 30 species during a year of sampling by transect. To the 30 found along woodland edge adjacent to an old meadow, different species could be added from a plot of denser oak, others from a damp plot with alders, and more from spruce and pine. The diversity was greatest along the woodland edge, and least in the conifers. Different types of wood have their own distinctive bird communities. This is illustrated in the following table compiled by Simms shows the relative abundance, expressed as the number of contacts with a species per 100 birds seen, for different woodlands.

RELATIVE ABUNDANCE OF BIRDS IN DIFFERENT WOODLANDS

PEDUNCULATE OAK (ENGLAND)	SESSILE OAK (ENGLAND AND WALES)	SPRUCE (SCOTLAND)	BEECH (IRELAND)
Chaffinch 13	Chaffinch 17	Woodpigeon 38	Chaffinch 16
Robin 11	Pied flycatcher 7	Goldcrest 15	Blackbird 11
Wren 10	Willow warbler 7	Chaffinch 8	Woodpigeon 11
Blackbird 8	Wood warbler 6	Wren 6	Robin 8
Willow warbler 7	Wren 6	Crow 5	Song thrush 7
Woodpigeon 6	Robin 5	Coal tit 4	Starling 7

Top
The willow warbler is a common summer visitor to broadleaved and mixed woodland.

Bottom left
Woods with plenty of old timber are attractive to great spotted woodpeckers.

Bottom right
Oakwoods such as this support healthy populations of woodland birds.

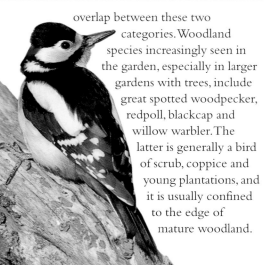

overlap between these two categories. Woodland species increasingly seen in the garden, especially in larger gardens with trees, include great spotted woodpecker, redpoll, blackcap and willow warbler. The latter is generally a bird of scrub, coppice and young plantations, and it is usually confined to the edge of mature woodland.

SUPPORTING A RANGE OF SPECIES

REGARDLESS OF GEOGRAPHY and tree type, woods also differ in size, altitude and structure. The amount of undergrowth, the nature of the field layer (such as bluebells or mosses) and the density of the canopy, are all aspects of the structure. Management can affect some of these variables, and the ideal is to maintain wildlife-rich open spaces, in effect to increase the edge effect, and to keep a full range of age-classes of trees within a wood.

In some of Snowdonia's sessile oak woods, which are full of pied flycatchers and redstarts in summer, there are no young trees because of grazing by sheep. Such woods cannot survive in the long term unless regeneration occurs. Many woods have a very different problem: there is not enough dead wood to provide a habitat for the beetle larvae which are food for woodpeckers and other birds, and not enough holes for the very many species which could nest in them.

CONIFER PLANTATIONS

CONIFER PLANTATIONS HAVE aroused strong feelings over the years, partly because of the earlier tradition of planting in straight rows, regardless of contour and landscape, and of clear-felling when the trees were needed, leaving almost a battlefield scene of desolation. Plantations do however demonstrate beautifully the ecological principle of succession, whereby as one aspect of an ecosystem changes with time, it causes other associated changes.

A recently established plantation, with sheep excluded, develops thick ground vegetation regardless of the young trees. Here insects flourish, small mammals can thrive along with birds such as meadow pipits. The mammals may in turn encourage predators like short-eared owls and hen harriers. After ten years or so the trees are pushing through the vegetation and will soon

begin to suppress it, by claiming most of the light. Until they do, there are still plenty of invertebrates associated with the ground vegetation and others linked with the growing trees, so insectivorous birds can flourish. Whinchats and the rare woodlark may do well at this stage, using the young conifers as perches and song posts, but they in turn will be replaced by willow warblers, chaffinches and eventually, after 30 years or so, by coal tits and goldcrests. Many moan that nothing except coal tits and goldcrests are there but, in Wales, siskins and crossbills have moved in. Bird diversity in winter is actually comparable with the oakwoods, and in cleared areas grasshopper warblers and black grouse provide a contrasting pair of species.

A high proportion of British woodlarks and nightjars are now found in young plantations. For the woodlarks this is mainly an East Anglian phenomenon ,with Breckland larks having abandoned their normal heathland habitat. Both species like some bare ground – woodlarks for feeding as they walk, and nightjars for nesting.

Left
The beautiful redstart is a relatively rare speciality bird, found mainly in oak woods.

Top right
Dead or decaying trees provide huge numbers of insects and other invertebrates, in turn supporting bird populations.

Bottom
Crossbills are mainly associated with pinewoods. They sometimes come down to drink at woodland pools.

Woodland Management

ENGLISH NATURE WOULD like to see at least 5,000 ha (12,355 acres) of ancient woodland restored over the next 10–20 years, and members of the Woodland Trust believe that conservation of ancient woodland is a top priority. Ancient woodland is land that has been continuously wooded since 1600, but it may well have been replanted, even with conifers.

which allows flowering plants to flourish to the benefit of woodland butterflies and other wildlife.

The most likely sequence of bird communities that will form the succession following coppicing will be as follows. Initially, as regrowth starts, and before ground vegetation thickens, conditions favour whitethroat and tree pipit, dunnock and yellowhammer. As the canopy of shrubs begins to close, after some three to seven years, optimum conditions for a host of migrants develop. Nightingale, garden warbler, blackcap and willow warbler all thrive, but if the coppice is left to mature, conditions change again, becoming more suitable for tits and robins. The age and density of standard trees also influence the bird life – old trees have more holes, and dense trees cast more shade. A possible ideal would have old, sparse standards, set among coppice shrubs which are cut back every seven to ten years, and with different areas of the wood being cut in different years, so that a mosaic of habitats is maintained.

RENEWING WOODLAND

WHILE SOME WOODS, and dependent organisations such as fungi, mosses and leaf-litter spiders can thrive on minimum interference, most woodland needs active management. Coppicing is one management technique, historically widely used, which, while not ideal for wildlife in all circumstances, can maintain a high density of trees and shrubs, a spectacular array of spring flowers and a succession of conditions suitable for breeding birds. Large single-trunked trees, standards, are left to mature, with a probable eventual use as timber, while the woodland shrubs, such as hazel and sweet chestnut are cut to near ground level, every few years, to produce wood for burning, hurdles or fences. These coppiced shrubs regenerate with multiple stems, but, before they do, light has been let in,

Top

The pied flycatcher is one of the prettiest woodland birds native to Britain.

Middle

The male blackcap lives up to its name, whereas the female's cap is brown.

Bottom

Green woodpeckers have started to increase in numbers since woodland conservation began.

A WOODLAND NATIONAL NATURE RESERVE

WOODLAND NEAR TO towns has many attractions, one of which is its ability to 'lose' people. There may be lots of people there, but they are much less visible

than on the beach or in open parkland. Wyre Forest, close to the towns of the Black Country and only 32 km (20 miles) from the centre of Birmingham, has 25,000 visitors a year, but little damage is caused by disturbance or trampling. It is hard to say what we mean by 'natural'. For centuries the oaks of Wyre Forest were coppiced to produce charcoal for iron smelting, which meant that few of those standing today grew directly from acorns, but have sprouted from the stumps of felled trees. The use of scrubby oak for charcoal had its compensations for wildlife, as open clearings and broad rides, together with sheltered pastures and hayfields to supply fodder for horses, created a fine mosaic of habitats.

Wyre Forest has the added benefit of the Dowles Brook, whose valley divides the forest, and which is home to dipper, grey wagtail and kingfisher, while the steep slopes and acidic soil make conditions ideal for sessile oak woodland, with redstarts and pied flycatchers. Since the mid 1960s, pied flycatchers have increasingly made use of nest-boxes here. Also found here are nightjars, woodcock, long-eared owls, woodpeckers and warblers.

SESSILE OAKWOODS

WELSH SESSILE OAK woods have a special attraction, with their interestingly shaped trees, carpets of moss and abundance of lichens. Those in the Vale of Ffestiniog for example have a long-standing reputation. One of these, Coed-y-Maentwrog, was declared a National Nature Reserve in 1966, and is one of a series of oak woodland reserves designated by the then Nature Conservancy Council to represent the range of woodland types that occur in the variety of conditions to be found in North Wales.

Transects of this reserve to find about the age structure of the oaks showed that most were well over 100 years old, reflecting past management practices and the all-pervasive effects of grazing. Boulders and tree roots beneath the canopy are well covered with woodland mosses. The numerous crevices and knot holes in the mature trees provide an abundance of nest sites for tits, nuthatches, great spotted woodpeckers, redstarts and pied flycatchers. Wood warblers and tree pipits are other summer visitors, while goldeneye and pochard visit Llyn Mair in winter. Early studies showed that a good acorn crop, perhaps every four years, could give 40 acorns per square metre, often distributed and buried by jays. As in many woods, effective fencing and the destruction of alien rhododendrons have been vital management priorities.

Top
Damp woods may develop a rich ground flora, rich in mosses.

Middle
The spreading branches of an oak tree provide a multitude of cracks and crevices.

Bottom
Nuthatches are unusual in being able to clamber down tree trunks as well as upwards.

Red Kite

60–70 cm (24–28 in)

○○○○○○○○○○○○○○○○○○○○○○○○○○○○

SPECIES INFORMATION	
SCIENTIFIC NAME	*Milvus milvus*
RELATED SPECIES	Black Kite (not I)
CALL	Whistling cries, often heard in spring; also single 'deeair' or 'yeee' calls
HABITAT	Hilly, wooded landscape, with open areas such as small wetlands and clearings
STATUS	Resident in Wales, where there are some 80 pairs. Currently being re-introduced to Scotland and England

SIZE

IDENTIFICATION

HABITAT

POPULATION

MAP

LONG WINGS AND long, deeply forked tail. Light grey head, pale patches towards ends of wings, and red-brown body. Soars with slightly raised wings; sometimes hovers with deep, relatively slow wingbeats; often twists tail in flight

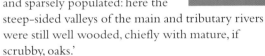

WHILE BREEDING DIVERS and Slavonian grebes are Scottish specialities, the kite has for long been associated with Wales, although in earlier days it was abundant everywhere. Recent re-introductions, in Scotland and England, are making the bird more familiar once more.

In 1970, Colonel H. Marrey Salmon reviewed the story of the kite's preservation in Wales. First he described why, within half a century after 1800, a widespread and relatively common bird had ceased to exist throughout almost the whole of Britain. 'Those who brought this about were the game preserving landowners and their indiscriminate and destructive agents, the gamekeepers, who pursued their calling with a callous indifference for anything but game, and an appalling amount of cruelty exercised with the connivance and, in some cases, the active participation of their masters.

By the middle of the second half of the nineteenth century the last remaining kites were confined to central Wales, which was wild, mountainous and rugged, remote and sparsely populated: here the steep-sided valleys of the main and tributary rivers were still well wooded, chiefly with mature, if scrubby, oaks.'

By 1889, kites were increasing around Brecon but then Scottish gamekeepers were brought into local estates and nine or ten kites were killed in the spring of that year. Some landowners were horrified for they had been trying to protect the birds. Around that time J. H. Salter, Professor of Botany at Aberystwyth took steps to bring into being an organisation for the protection of Welsh kites which has continued in one form or another up to the present.

In the 1976 *Atlas* there were only 26 pairs and some young seemed to emigrate to the south-east. By the 1993 *Atlas* figures of 77 proven pairs in 1991 could be quoted, but birds were still being killed by illegal poisons spread for crows and foxes.

These Welsh haunts are essentially upland, but kites could well flourish, as they used to, elsewhere and the Welsh birds hunt over low intensity farmland, rough grassland and heath. Red kites fly magnificently, with buoyant wing action, soaring gracefully with their long, broad wings and deeply forked tails. It is a wonderful thought that all the dedicated work of kite enthusiasts is making this one of the pleasures of British birding.

Top left and right
The red kite is an elegant bird, with agile flight, aided by its long, deeply forked tail.

Bottom
Red Kites have recently been reintroduced into England and Scotland from Wales.

SPECIES INFORMATION

SCIENTIFIC NAME	Buteo buteo
RELATED SPECIES	Rough-legged Buzzard
CALL	Almost cat-like mewing, especially in spring
HABITAT	Wooded regions with fields, marshes and hedges. Hunts over open country, nesting mostly at woodland edges
STATUS	Resident and partial migrant. Absent from most of Ireland (except north), and much of south and east England (but gradually spreading eastwards)

Buzzard

43–55 cm (17–22 in)

SIZE

IDENTIFICATION

HABITAT

POPULATION

MAP

MEDIUM-SIZED BIRD of prey with short neck and large, rounded head. Wings are broad, and the tail is rounded when spread. Very variable in plumage, from almost white to uniform dark brown, but usually brownish, with paler breast-band. Eye dark brown to yellow. Rather compact in flight with wings held somewhat stiffly, and wingtips noticeably upturned when soaring. Occasionally hovers.

BUZZARDS WILL TAKE a wide variety of prey. In many parts of the British Isles rabbits and other smaller mammals form the major part of their diet but birds are also taken, especially newly fledged young in the summer. Their diet also includes worms, larvae and beetles. Buzzards often grub about in fields in wet or misty weather but one thinks of them soaring, with the 'fingers' of their broad wings extended. Those who live in Devon often think that they are 'home' when they start seeing plenty of buzzards but visitors to the south-west are now more frequently saying 'we see buzzards too', whether they live in Basingstoke or Midhurst, Worcester or Shrewsbury. The *New Atlas*

shows gains as well in Scotland, and a good foothold has been established in Ireland. Despite their varied plumage buzzards are easy to identify as medium-sized soaring raptors with broad wings, short head and relatively short tail. When perched the tail only protrudes slightly beyond the wing tips. The yellow base to beak and yellow feet may show as it sits, paying little attention to cars, on a roadside telegraph pole. When soaring, the dark border to the two-toned underwing is clear, however dark or light the plumage, and the dark almost terminal tail-band is another feature.

Buzzards are territorial when breeding, often displaying in interlocking spirals, but group soaring of nearby territory holders also occurs in spring and if all birds are making their far reaching 'meow' calls the sky can seem to be full of buzzards. When the young are calling later in the year a valley may again seem buzzard-saturated, but the birds may be harder to find at that time.

Nest are bulky affairs, usually in trees, and made of tree or heather twigs in which a shallow cup is lined with green foliage.

From September to February Dartmoor buzzards hunt mainly from perches. Later they hover more than they perch, except when visibility is poor, but in the New Forest they seldom do. These sort of details, painstakingly gleaned by ardent buzzard watchers show the difficulties of totally valid generalisations, but a buzzard soaring is unlikely to be hunting. Even if a buzzard can see a rabbit from a mile away it is not conspicuously successful and has to spend a lot of time hunting to get sufficient food.

Top and middle
Buzzards often hunt by soaring, but may also be seen watching the ground from a low perch, or even grubbing for worms.

Bottom
The tail of a buzzard is only just visible beyond the wing tips when the bird is perching.

Sparrowhawk

30–40 cm (12–16 in)

SPECIES INFORMATION	
SCIENTIFIC NAME	*Accipiter nisus*
RELATED SPECIES	*Goshawk*
CALL	*Alarm call (usually near nest) a high-pitched 'kyikyikyi'*
HABITAT	*Mainly wooded country, but increasingly suburban*
STATUS	*Resident. In BI common and increasing (about 45,000 pairs)*

SIZE

IDENTIFICATION

HABITAT

POPULATION

MAP

MALE SMALLER THAN female. Wings rounded, tail long, narrow and square-ended. Underparts narrowly banded, rust-brown in male. Female brownish-grey above, male blue-grey. Juveniles dark brown above, barred below.

THERE ARE MIXED views about sparrowhawks but I love their sudden appearance and silent flight. When overhead their barred underparts are clear and the short blunt wings most unlike a kestrel's; they are seen at their best when they soar as they often do. The sexes differ markedly in size, with the grey-brown backed female larger than the male with his bluish back. After severe decreases when organochlorine pesticides were passed along the food chain, sparrowhawks are now very successful.

Leslie Brown (1978) quotes figures which indicate the amount of food a sparrowhawk pair and their brood need during the year. To achieve the 30 kg (66 lb) of food killed per adult per year and the 20 kg (44 lb) eaten, getting on for 800 average sized or 1,600 small birds need to be killed each year. For the three months that a brood of two is fed another 400 small birds are needed. It might well be thought that the 3,600 birds taken would make serious inroads into local populations, but the evidence quoted in the population section indicates that great and blue tits are no less common when sparrowhawks are about than when they are absent. Many of the birds fed to the young are young themselves, and tits have large broods, and many of those caught at any time will be older, less fit or less well fed than those they miss.

Top

A female sparrowhawk crouches over her prey – a male chaffinch. Female sparrowhawks are capable of catching prey up to the size of a pigeon.

Bottom

A woodland ride in the New Forest, which is classic sparrowhawk habitat.

Housemartins and long-tailed tits most often warn of sparrowhawks, but the house martins fly too well and the long-tailed tits stay too close to cover for either to be major prey items.

Sparrowhawks often pass within a couple of feet of my head, which brings them very close to bird rich cover. A local watcher here saw one kill a bird as large and apparently well protected as a kestrel, but only a large female would have any chance of this. In one study Newton found that 85 per cent by weight of prey items was made up of finches, thrushes, starlings and pigeons but more tits (10 per cent of diet by number) than pigeons (6 per cent by number) would be caught.

Top
A juvenile sparrowhawk perches on a tree branch in woodland.

Bottom
The adult male sparrowhawk is much smaller than the female and feeds on smaller prey, such as tits and finches.

Tawny Owl

38 cm (15 in)

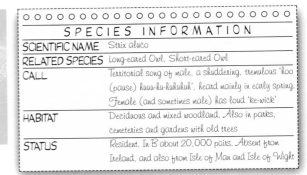

SPECIES INFORMATION	
SCIENTIFIC NAME	Strix aluco
RELATED SPECIES	Long-eared Owl, Short-eared Owl
CALL	Territorial song of male, a shuddering, tremulous 'hoo (pause) huuu-hu-huhuhuh', heard mainly in early spring. Female (and sometimes male) has loud 'ke-wick'
HABITAT	Deciduous and mixed woodland. Also in parks, cemeteries and gardens with old trees
STATUS	Resident. In B about 20,000 pairs. Absent from Ireland, and also from Isle of Man and Isle of Wight

SIZE

IDENTIFICATION

HABITAT

POPULATION

MAP

TAWNY OWLS ARE dark eyed, medium-sized, relatively broad-winged owls with rather uniform mottled brown plumage. There are two colour forms: a bark-coloured grey form and a red-brown form (the latter commoner in BI). More often heard than seen. Our commonest woodland owl. In many views the shape is critical, and the large, rounded head, compact body and long flat glides on broad wings are identifying features. They like plenty of lookout posts for hunting, and favour woodland with clearings, hedges and mature trees.

WELL KNOWN IN children's stories and familiar for its hooting in gardens and parks, it is the most spectacular bird that will actually nest in a suburban garden. Woodland owls take mainly small mammals, but in parks and gardens they will catch small birds as they roost and will even forage on the lawn at night looking for earthworms. They listen alertly, then hop forward like a gigantic but not very skilful blackbird, breaking most of the worms pulled from the ground. In damp weather half the owls' pellets may be brown, fibrous worm remains rather then the normal grey fur and bones.

'Sweet Suffolk owl, so trimly dight
With feathers like a lady bright.
Thou singest alone sitting by night
Te whit, te whoo, te wit, te wit.
The note, that forth so freely rolls
With shrill command the mouse controls
A sings a song for dying souls.'
Thomas Vanter (1616)

Top and bottom right
Tawny owls are more often seen than heard, preferring to stay under cover until dark.

Bottom left
These owls have large, rounded heads and are either bark-grey or reddy-brown in colour.

Long-eared Owl

36 cm (14 in)

SPECIES INFORMATION

SCIENTIFIC NAME	*Asio otus*
RELATED SPECIES	Short-eared Owl, Tawny Owl
CALL	Male has low 'huh', heard as early as February. Alarm call a barking 'wick', repeated. Contact call of young birds is a high-pitched 'tsee'
HABITAT	Breeds in coniferous forests and plantations, also in light woodland. In winter often in communal roosts of over 20 birds
STATUS	Resident. In BI about 5,000 pairs

SLIM, MEDIUM-SIZED long-winged owl with orange eyes and long 'ear' tufts. Plumage with tree-bark pattern. Nocturnal and rarely seen. In flight, the wings are longer and the head narrower than the tawny while, when perched, its shape alters markedly with posture. It is long and slender when alarmed but fluffed out when relaxed. The long ears, buff facial disc and white divide between orange eyes are fine if seen well but the ear tufts may be invisible. The song has been described as similar to the sound made by blowing across the top of an empty bottle, but for much of the year the birds are silent.

LONG-EARED OWLS, particularly favouring conifer plantations, are one of the least familiar woodland birds, and the scattered distribution shown in the Atlases might reflect under-recording for they sit very still by day, often close to a tree trunk with which their cryptic plumage merges, and they favour dense conifer woodland. How many of us go searching for owls in plantations soon after the New Year when they start to call?

They have two alternative habitats: shelterbelts and small mature woodlands in northern Britain, and broad-leaved fen woodland, including sallow and thorn scrub in the south. In Scotland they favour deep heather in open hilly sites and they are obviously versatile in choice of habitat. In Ireland, Ruttledge (1966) found long-eared owls breeding in every county, being thinly distributed where suitable woodlands exist. More recently it seems to have thinned out in the west.

In most ways their biology is similar to the tawny owl with competition over food and nest sites likely. Voles are important but birds and shrews are also taken. Both owls often use old magpie nests but tawny owls favour holes in trees and long-eared will nest on the ground, so the two can, and do, co-exist.

SIZE

IDENTIFICATION

HABITAT

POPULATION

MAP

Bottom
Few birdwatchers have had a good view of a long-eared owl – this species is even more elusive than the tawny owl. Dense conifer woodland is one preferred habitat.

123

Woodcock

34 cm (13 in)

SIZE

IDENTIFICATION

HABITAT

POPULATION

MAP

SPECIES INFORMATION	
SCIENTIFIC NAME	Scolopax rusticola
RELATED SPECIES	Snipe
CALL	Occasional high-pitched 'tsveet' when disturbed. Roding male alternates deep 'kvorr-kvorr-kvorr' with very high-pitched sharp 'pitsick'
HABITAT	Mixed woodland with clearings, rich herb- and shrub-layer, and damp areas
STATUS	Resident and winter migrant. Estimates of BI population around 25,000 pairs

SHORT-LEGGED, LARGE-HEADED wader with long, straight bill and highly camouflaged plumage. Flight soft and usually silent, almost owl-like. In display flight ('roding') male describes low circuits in weak zig-zag curves, grunting and clicking as he flies. Wings broad and rounded, bill held angled towards ground. Crepuscular and nocturnal.

THE RUFOUS, MARBLED plumage cannot really be appreciated at distance, but the dumpy shape and bat-like evening flight are so distinctive that description is superfluous. A snipe like 'schaap' is characteristic of night-time disturbance, but the roding 'song' of two to five growling sounds, followed by a sneeze is more exciting but again not easily described.

'Despite the brilliance of its plumage a woodcock is wonderfully difficult to see on the nest. The markings so brilliant when seen at close quarters form one of the very best examples of camouflage in the world of nature, and a sitting woodcock is to all intents and purposes invisible at a distance of only a few feet. She knows it, too,' writes Brian Vesey Fitzgerald (1946) 'and generally sits so close that you can pass her day after day and be unaware of her presence.' Like many of those interested in country sports (he was editor of the Field) Vesey Fitzgerald was obviously a very good and persistent observer and knew his game. 'It is very unusual to see a woodcock feeding in the daytime, but I have watched them feeding at midday in very frosty weather.

Woodcock walk like snipe with the neck drawn in and the bill inclined downwards, but the walk is not nearly so easy and they seldom walk very far. When flushed from cover during the day they rise with a great swish of wings, but generally they do no more than dodge through the trees to come down again at a safe distance.'

Woodcock like moist woods, with oak, birch, larch and spruce, and woods with open glades and rides, a good cover of bracken and bramble and evergreen bushes. The abundance map in the *Breeding Atlas* shows a very scattered distribution of breeding birds but the *Winter Atlas* shows a wider distribution as birds from Scandinavia move in. At that time extensive conifer plantations can suit woodcock and they will also turn up on bracken and heather covered hillsides, parks and large gardens.

Top
Woodcock favour woodland with clearings as their natural habitat, especially if there are damp areas under the trees.

Bottom
The woodcock has remarkable camouflaged plumage which makes it hard to spot against the woodland floor.

Green Woodpecker
32 cm (12 in)

```
○ ○ ○ ○ ○ ○ ○ ○ ○ ○ ○ ○ ○ ○ ○ ○ ○ ○ ○ ○ ○ ○
        SPECIES  INFORMATION
```

SCIENTIFIC NAME	*Picus viridis*
RELATED SPECIES	Great Spotted / Lesser Spotted Woodpecker
CALL	Flight-call (and near nest) a hard 'kjek' or 'kjook'. Laughing territorial song, 'klee-klee-klee-klee-klee', carrying over long distance. Drums only very rarely, and then weakly
HABITAT	Broadleaved and mixed woodland, in copses in fields, orchards, parks and gardens with old trees. Fondness for ant-rich pasture. Sometimes visits garden lawns
STATUS	Resident. In B about 15,000 pairs (absent from Ireland)

A LARGE WOODPECKER with green and yellow plumage and a bright red crown. Male has red moustache with black edging, black in female. Juveniles are heavily barred below, with less intense red on head. Shows conspicuous yellow rump in flight. The crimson crown and black face are as striking as the green back and yellow rump. The male had red below the black eye patch, but the female lacks this.

WOODPECKERS ARE HIGHLY specialised for life in the trees and for extracting insects from crevices with their long tongues with barbed tips. The arrangement of toes, with two pointing up and two pointing down, when climbing, is another adaptation, as is the structure, and pattern of moult, of the tail feathers; these help to stabilise upward movement.

The green woodpecker can stretch its tongue out 10 cm (4 in) beyond the tip of its beak. Using its tongue, it can probe deep into the galleries of an ants

nest. Ants adhere to the sticky saliva which coats the tongue as it wriggles, worm-like into the underground chambers. The most mobile part of the tongue is the extreme tip which has developed into a wide, flat sort of lip, and which can be moved about independently of the rest. The spoon-like lip feels the location of the ant pupae and then scoops the prey up.

In a garden with ants and ant-hills, or in old grassland, green woodpeckers find rich pickings, often making a blackbird seem a tidy gardener. But its beauty compensates for any damage caused.

On tree trunks it will spiral upwards with jerky hops, pausing to chip at the bark or peep over its shoulder.

'*But most the hewel's wonders are,
Who here has the Holt – festers
(Forester's) care,
He walks still upright from the root.
Meas'ting the timber with his foot;
And all the way, to keep it clean
Doth from the bark of wood moths glean
He with his beak; examines well
Which fit to stand and which to fell.*'

Andrew Marvel (1621–78)

Top
Green woodpeckers excavate their nest holes in old and rotting timber, and rear their brood in the holes.

Bottom
Like all woodpeckers, they use their stiff tails as balance to help prop themselves upright when climbing.

Great Spotted Woodpecker

22 cm (9 in)

○○○○○○○○○○○○○○○○○○○○○○○○○○○○○○

SPECIES INFORMATION

SCIENTIFIC NAME	Dendrocopus major
RELATED SPECIES	Lesser Spotted Woodpecker, Green Woodpecker
CALL	Metallic 'kick', repeated as alarm-call. Most rapid drumming of all our woodpeckers. Drums on hollow trees, dry branches, posts
HABITAT	Woodland, copses, parks and gardens
STATUS	Resident. In B about 28,000 pairs (absent from Ireland)

SIZE

IDENTIFICATION

HABITAT

POPULATION

MAP

OUR COMMONEST woodpecker. Black and white plumage, with white shoulder patches; lower tail coverts bright red, flanks unstreaked. Male has red patch at back of head; juveniles have red crown. Flight undulating.

IN FLIGHT, FIVE or six flapping wingbeats alternate with closure of the wings to give the typically undulating performance, which demonstrates well the pied pattern of the wings. It has the typically broad wings of a woodland bird. On a tree trunk it is less chequered but equally black and white, with black crown and upper parts and bold white ovals on the scapulars. The black bar from bill to nape distinguishes it from other pied European woodpeckers. The female lacks the male's small red nape patch. Both have a bright red patch under the tail, while young birds have more red on the head.

Great spotted woodpeckers drum much more than green woodpeckers in advertising territory, usually from mid-January through to the end of June.

The great spotted woodpecker's tongue has its own adaptations for spearing insect larvae and pupae

inside their chambers. The end of the tongue is like a hardened stiletto with a great number of small barbs at its horny tip. This species uses its beak more than the last, hacking and pecking at bark and wood, knocking off loose material in the search for insects. In winter, conifer seeds become an alternative diet, as do nuts and other foods supplied in gardens.

Apart from their drumming, these are noisy woodpeckers which often utter their sharp alarm or flight call. Harsh chattering court-ship chases are much more noisy, but the young in the nest make most noise of all.

Top and bottom right
The thrush-sized great spotted woodpecker can often be seen in British woods and, increasingly, in parks and gardens as well.

Bottom right
The male of the species has a red patch at the back of its neck.

Lesser Spotted Woodpecker

15 cm (6 in)

SPECIES INFORMATION	
SCIENTIFIC NAME	Dendrocopus minor
RELATED SPECIES	Great Spotted Woodpecker, Green Woodpecker
CALL	Song is a soft 'kee-kee-kee', usually heard in spring. Male and female drum (rather long, yet weak)
HABITAT	Broadleaved and mixed woodland, often damp woods and riverside trees; also parks with old willows or poplars, and orchards
STATUS	Resident. In B about 5,000 pairs (absent from Ireland).

SMALLEST EUROPEAN woodpecker, sparrow-sized. Back is black, with horizontal white bands; no red on underside. Male has red cap with black margin, female has no red colour at all.

THIS SPECIES IS much more retiring than great spotted, but again its call is often the first sign of its presence. Having heard the high-pitched call, it is worth searching small branches for a woodpecker-shape with barred back and, depending on gender, a crimson or a pale crown. There is no red on the underparts. This is as much a bird of parkland, old hedgerow trees and riverside alders as of true woods. When near these habitats in the spring listen for its drumming which is a much less aggressive sound than that of its larger relative.

Lesser spotted woodpeckers are essentially birds of England and Wales, with a markedly south-eastern preference. There are far fewer in the Midlands or Devon than around London, and there is a marked decrease in a band from the Wash to Lands End which might correlate with the death of hedgerow elms. When elms were first diseased, the abundance of beetles and beetle larvae helped raise the BTO's Common Bird's Census index, but once substantial elm felling had taken place the woodpecker lost not only food but also a favourite nesting tree.

Just as these little birds often feed in the smaller branches, very largely on insects, their holes are often not in the trunk but in a rotten side branch. This emphasises again the need to leave some rotten wood in situ in any woodland management plan. As with so many other hole nesters, the eggs, usually four to six, are white, and the chicks hatch in a nest some 15 cm (6 in) below the nest hole.

Both the spotted woodpeckers are associated with rain, and for some reason legends abound about woodpeckers disobeying God or Gods.

> 'Zeus won't in a hurry restore to the woodpecker tapping the oak, In times prehistoric 'tis easily proved, by evidence weighty and ample
>   That birds and not Gods were the rulers of men
>   And the lords of the world.'
> Aristophanes THE BIRDS

SIZE

IDENTIFICATION

HABITAT

POPULATION

MAP

Top
Lesser spotted woodpeckers are surprisingly small, being only sparrow-sized. They drum quietly in the spring.

Bottom
Since the advent of Dutch elm disease, the lesser spotted woodpecker has fallen in number.

Nuthatch

14 cm (5.5 in)

○○○○○○○○○○○○○○○○○○○○○○○○○○○○
SPECIES INFORMATION

SCIENTIFIC NAME	*Sitta europaea*
RELATED SPECIES	No close relatives in British Isles
CALL	Call a liquid 'tvit-tvit-tvit'. Song a whistling 'vivivivivi...' or 'peeu-peeu-peeu'
HABITAT	Broadleaved and mixed woodland, parks and gardens. Shows fondness for old oaks
STATUS	Resident. In B about 50,000 pairs (absent from Ireland)

SIZE

IDENTIFICATION

HABITAT

POPULATION

MAP

DUMPY, WOODPECKER-LIKE with short tail and powerful bill. Blue-grey above, creamy yellow or rusty below. Scandinavian race has white breast and belly. Climbs well, up, across and down trees.

WITH ITS POWERFUL bill, short tail, long claws and sturdy legs, the Nuthatch is well adapted for climbing up and down large trees. The blue-grey upperparts and salmon pink underparts are very smart, but often no colour is to be seen, only a distinctive silhouette, going about its business, usually noisily, searching the branches or flying from tree to tree in parkland. In flight the round wings, sharply pointed head and the short square tail aid identification.

Top
Nuthatches apply mud around the edges of natural holes to make the entrance to the nest just the right size.

Bottom
The agile, beautifully balanced nuthatch can climb along, up or even down branches with equal ease.

Nuthatches are among the most exciting garden visitors, but are equally welcome calling all year round as they maintain their territory in lowland woods or parks with well grown or mature trees; if there is a bit of decay then so much the better. Oak tends to be favoured but they are happy with ash. The territorial trilling 'song', and a series of whistles intergrade with each other, but the excitement call is clearly separate as is a tit-like contact call which is very clear and loud.

The nesting hole is often that used before by a woodpecker, but may be natural or even a nest-box, the hole often plastered with mud to narrow it to the required specifications, and the nest itself is largely loose flakes of bark, preferably from Scots pine. A happy nuthatch will therefore need an old deciduous tree, a barky pine and a supply of mud within its territory.

SPECIES INFORMATION	
SCIENTIFIC NAME	Certhia familiaris
RELATED SPECIES	Short-toed Treecreeper (central and southern Europe)
CALL	High-pitched 'srii'. Song is rather scratchy, ending in a trill
HABITAT	Broadleaved woodland, mixed woodland, also coniferous woods (especially in south), parks and gardens
STATUS	Resident. In BI about 245,000 pairs

Treecreeper
12.5 cm (5 in)

HEARING A HIGH pitched call was enough to make me glance up and see a treecreeper moving to the base of another tree as dusk fell one chilly December evening. By the time I got home I had made a few calculations, based on assumptions that I fear are pure guesswork, to concentrate my mind on the difficulties for small insect eaters facing a winter night. Such a small bird probably needs to eat thousands of tiny insects and spiders each day.

Whatever the realities, the treecreeper, like the coal tit and every other small bird is hard pressed in winter. Commenting on BTO Common Bird Census trends, Marchant points out that treecreepers suffer particularly when freezing rain or persistent freezing fog leads to pronged ice coating of tree trunks. These conditions caused a major decline for example in the winter of 1978–79.

WOODPECKER-LIKE BIRD with long, distinctively decurved bill. Plumage brown above and white below, with rust-brown rump. Creeps in spirals up tree trunks. Treecreepers use their lengthy stiff graduated tail as a support. Mouse-like in appearance and movement they need vertical trunks, preferably with loose bark as, like a mouse, they can use the smallest crevice beneath for nesting. Assorted debris in a crevice or behind bark forms the nest into which the bird fits tightly. The song is reminiscent of the goldcrest, but louder.

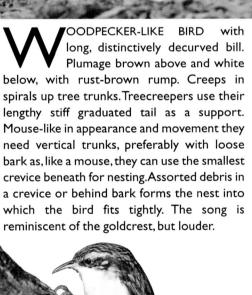

 SIZE
 IDENTIFICATION
 HABITAT
 POPULATION

 MAP

Top
The treecreeper climbs in a steady spiral up a tree trunk, flits down to the base of an adjacent tree and starts again.

Bottom
The treecreeper has a curved bill and white and brown plumage.

129

Jay

34 cm (13 in)

○○○○○○○○○○○○○○○○○○○○○○○○○○○○○
SPECIES INFORMATION

SCIENTIFIC NAME	Garrulus glandarius
RELATED SPECIES	Magpie and other members of crow family
CALL	Loud, raw screaming calls. Song a varied, low chatter
HABITAT	Mixed woodland, wooded parks and gardens
STATUS	Resident. In BI about 170,000 pairs

SIZE

IDENTIFICATION

HABITAT

POPULATION

MAP

L ARGE COLOURFUL crow-relative. Very conspicuous in flight, with black tail, white rump, and white and blue wing-patches. Body buff, with black moustache.

DESPITE THEIR COLOURFUL plumage, jays behave in such a way that they can often be missed, being heard more than seen during the breeding season. The most typical sound is the harsh screeching call, but jays make a range of other mewings and clickings, sometimes augmented by mimicry.

It is a southern bird, in as much as it is mainly English and Welsh; it is expanding its range in the Great Glen but declining in Ireland, despite a build up in county Kerry. Although never abundant, in Fuller's analysis of woodland birds it occurs in over 80 per cent of the woodland sites investigated.

Jays also now use parks and gardens, perhaps most frequently in autumn when, particularly in irruption years they can be seen overhead with undulating flight and broad wings. Jays everywhere arouse contrasting feelings, with some disliking their predatory cunning and nest-robbing, while others admire the pinkish plumage and intense blue patch on the wing. For recognition the white rump is crucial for they are shy birds often seen flying away.

An important interaction with human activities is the jay as oak planter. When acorns are freely available the birds spend much time hoarding them and carry up to six at a time with one in the bill and the remainder in the oesophagus, to hiding places in the forest floor. Many of these are later recovered, but many are not and germinate instead. By April or May only a few buried acorns can be found, and the proportion of these in the birds' diet falls from more than three quarters in January to less than a fifth.

At first, adults feed their young on larvae, but as jays breed later than many woodland birds the next lot of acorns will be on their way before the young jays are grown. Jays also act as a dispersal agent for beech, and so have a major impact on the regeneration of natural European forests.

Top right and left
For such a large, brightly-coloured bird, the jay is surprisingly hard to spot; it can occasionally be seen burying acorns in a lawn.

Bottom
Jays come in for some adverse criticism for their nest-robbing ways, but others admire their showy looks.

'From bush to bush slow sweeps the screaming jay
With one harsh note of pleasure all the day.'
John Clare SELECTED POEMS

Nightingale
16.5 cm (6.5 in)

WOODLAND BIRDS

SPECIES INFORMATION

SCIENTIFIC NAME	Luscinia megarhynchos
RELATED SPECIES	Bluethroat (same genus) and other members of thrush family
CALL	'Huit'; alarm-call a grating 'karrr'. Song loud and very varied, with warbling and clear fluting phrases, interspersed with deep 'tjook-tjook-tjook', and chirps. Also long crescendo sections, such as 'hiu-hiu-hiu'
HABITAT	Broadleaved or mixed woodland with thick undergrowth, river-valley woodland and fen
STATUS	Summer visitor, wintering in tropical Africa. In B about 5,500 pairs (absent from Ireland)

INCONSPICUOUS PLUMAGE and retiring habits make it hard to spot. Uniform brown above, except for red-brown tail. Underside slightly paler. Juveniles resemble young robins, but are larger and have russet tail. The nightingale is famed for its wonderful song.

THE BTO HAVE had a good initial response to their Nightingale Appeal, which is aimed not only towards nightingale research and conservation, but to all woodland birds in decline, such as spotted flycatcher, dunnock, bullfinch and marsh tit. More management guidelines are needed for enhancing the quality of scrub and woodland habitat.

Fuller looks at some of the peculiarities of nightingale requirements. 'Its occurrence in coppiced woods is extremely patchy even where underwood of a suitable age is available. Not only does the bird eschew chestnut but it is absent from a high proportion of woods with apparently suitable mixed coppice. It is a mystery why particular sites with high density are so favoured. It is possible that the reasons lie not so much with current habitat quality but with the behaviour of the birds themselves.' His hypothesis is that individual birds may show strong fidelity to particular sites or be attracted to sites already holding birds and therefore the species is slow to recolonise even when the habitat is right.

Despite the owl's words in the poem below, nightingales are not without beauty once you can see them. The rounded, rusty tail is rich and when seen in full song, for they sing by day as well as by night, the white throat vibrates as if with enthusiasm. Their wintering grounds in the African tropics are not well known, but spring movement along the north African coast and on Mediterranean islands is on a broad front.

'... besides you're filthy, dark and small
Like a sort of sooty ball
You have no loveliness or strength
And lack harmonious breadth and length,
Beauty somehow passed you by
Your virtue, too, is in short supply.'

John of Guildford
THE OWL AND THE NIGHTINGALE (1225)

SIZE

IDENTIFICATION

HABITAT

POPULATION

MAP

Top left and right
Nightingales prefer woodland with a rich undergrowth, and are only found in the south and east of Britain.

Bottom
The nightingale is probably our most famous songbird, and is more often heard than seen.

Redstart

14 cm (5.5 in)

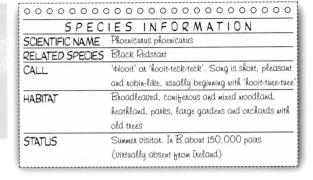

SPECIES INFORMATION	
SCIENTIFIC NAME	*Phoenicurus phoenicurus*
RELATED SPECIES	Black Redstart
CALL	'Hooit' or 'hooit-teck-teck'. Song is short, pleasant and robin-like, usually beginning with 'hooit-tuee-tuee'
HABITAT	Broadleaved, coniferous and mixed woodland, heathland, parks, large gardens and orchards with old trees
STATUS	Summer visitor. In B about 150,000 pairs (virtually absent from Ireland)

SIZE

IDENTIFICATION

HABITAT

POPULATION

MAP

BREEDING MALE HAS blue-grey crown and back, black face and throat, and orange-chestnut breast, flanks, tail and rump. Female has paler underside and is grey-brown above. Juveniles strongly mottled below.

OUR BIRDS WINTER in tropical Africa north of the equator, and another race, with variable white areas on the wings, winters to the east, in Sudan and Ethiopia and moves up to breed around the Black and Caspian Seas.

On passage, the warbler-like 'hweet' call is less likely to give it away than its tail and on arrival in breeding woods, parkland or among the drystone walls of the Pennines, the distinctive but undistinguished song marks out the breeding territories. Redstarts often sing from perches, some favoured throughout the breeding season, but later there is a quicker song as part of a nest-showing display involving both his ends, the white forehead as he looks out and the red tail as he looks in.

A feeding bird likes some bare areas among the trees, flitting down to pick up small beetles and spiders and returning with its prey to the branch it came from. At other times birds will make aerial sallies or search the trunks or leaves for invertebrates.

Since my first searches for one in Richmond Park, through landfalls of drifted migrants on the Norfolk coast, to years of summer companionship in the sessile oaks of Eryri's valleys I have loved redstarts. A pair even nested in a hole in our kitchen wall one year. Few commentators from the past, mythologists or poets, seem to have celebrated the ever-quivering red tail, the black face set off by a white forehead and orange underparts. Even the grey back, which sounds dull, has a perfect texture to contrast with the darker wings. Females have the same pert and lively posture and like the mottled young have the diagnostic red tail.

Bottom
The male redstart has a characteristic, ever-quivering red tail and a black face.

Middle and Top
Redstarts thrive in woodland, heathland and increasingly in parks and gardens.

Mistle Thrush
27 cm (10.5 in)

SPECIES INFORMATION

SCIENTIFIC NAME	*Turdus viscivorus*
RELATED SPECIES	Song Thrush, Blackbird, Fieldfare, Redwing, Ring Ouzel
CALL	Flight-call a dry, rattling 'tzrrr'. Song reminiscent of blackbird's but more melancholy and less variable, and in shorter, similarly-pitched phrases. Often sings as early as January
HABITAT	Broadleaved and coniferous woodland, wooded pasture, also in parks and gardens in some areas
STATUS	Resident. In BI about 320,000 pairs

LARGEST EUROPEAN THRUSH, greyer than song thrush and with longer wings and tail. Grey-brown above with large spots below; outer tail feathers tipped white. Juveniles spotted above with pale markings and whitish neck.

THE WILD CHALLENGING song is its most spectacular feature, but when looked at closely the combination of confident posture, large clear breast spots, grey back and, in flight, white underwing make it an attractive bird. Even though the nest is large, with sticks, mud and fine grasses, it is easily missed high in a tree fork.

Mistle thrushes have large territories in open woodland. They are very conspicuous in the breeding season, singing loudly from visible positions and making endless noisy complaints about magpies and other potential dangers. A little later they often seem to disappear, but in some areas, where bilberries grow among the heather, late summer is when they appear.

Mistle thrushes have gradually spread, becoming more tolerant of people, and also more suburban, being found in towns as well as plantations.

All sorts of people have said all sorts of things about mistle thrushes. In the fourth century Aristotle was already writing about its fondness for mistletoe, and there is an old belief that mistle thrushes could speak seven languages. In the west country local names often associate it with holly, and the berries on our tree are certainly often defended in winter. Holen is the Old English for holly and holm thrush, holm cock or holm screech were local Devonshire names.

'In early March, before the lark
Dare start, beside the huge oak tree
Close fixed agen the powdered bark,
The mains' nest I often see;
And mark, as wont, the bits of wool
Hang round about its early bed;
She lays six eggs in colours dull,
Blotched thick with spots of burning red'

John Clare SELECTED POEMS

SIZE

IDENTIFICATION

HABITAT

POPULATION

MAP

Larger and more wary than the songthrush, the mistle thrush is less often seen in gardens. In winter, they are partial to ripe berries, such as crabapples.

Spotted Flycatcher

14 cm (5.5 in)

SIZE

IDENTIFICATION

HABITAT

POPULATION

MAP

S LIM AND INCONSPICUOUS, with large, dark eyes and streaked crown. Grey-brown above, whitish and streaked below. Juveniles spotted above. Makes repeated agile forays from perch to catch insects in the air.

SPOTTED FLYCATCHERS ARE perhaps more typical of large gardens than of woodlands (or at least more often seen there) but, if there are good gaps among the trees, if it is a warm day and if you listen as well as look, you may easily find them. On colder days, rather than making their typical aerial flights, they have to make do with smaller insects or spiders in the trees. Perhaps it is a shortage of larger insects that has caused their population to fall to a quarter of its former level.

When Nicholson wrote in 1951 they were far more common, and he contrasted their style with that of other birds that lived off aerial insects. 'Instead of cruising about to seek the flies, midges, gnats, butterflies, moths or other insects on which it preys, the

Spotted flycatchers were once much commoner, and have certainly declined in recent years – possibly due to problems encountered in their winter quarters.

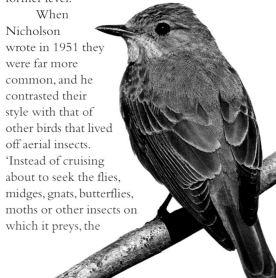

flycatcher picks some commanding perch and waits for its food to come along. Its design for living is only less economical than the spiders; its plumage, its posture, its haunts and its migrations are all determined by that design.'

The nest is a loosely built cup of twigs, rootlets, lichens, hair and feathers, sometimes in creepers or on top of a flat branch and sometimes in an open-fronted nest-box. As Nicholson points out, they are exceptional among strongly territorial birds in not having developed a territorial song, but they do spend a lot of time patrolling in their food search and can therefore chase off any intruders. They do have a contact alarm call but unless you know it well, it can seem much like a myriad of other bird sounds; if you do know it you will see many more spotted flycatchers.

Spotted flycatchers are long-distance migrants, wintering south of the equator and being one of the last of our summer migrants to arrive back in Britain. Their breeding area spreads over much of Europe, with the usual passerine gap in Iceland, and well into Asia. There seems to be a migratory divide, with birds from western Europe moving south-west towards Iberia, while Central European birds have a more easterly route through Italy and the Aegean.

Possibly habitat degradation or more plausibly a widespread use of insecticides have had their impacts on decreasing flycatcher populations. They also have to cross the Sahara twice a year. Anything that could stem the decline of this much-loved visitor would be welcome, and we can hope that the Nightingale Appeal helps us to find out more.

Pied Flycatcher
13 cm (5 in)

SPECIES INFORMATION

SCIENTIFIC NAME	*Ficedula hypoleuca*
RELATED SPECIES	Spotted Flycatcher, Collared Flycatcher and Red-breasted Flycatcher (both rare vagrants)
CALL	Alarm-call a sharp 'bit'. Song is an ascending and descending 'voo-ti-voo-ti-voo-ti', rather reminiscent of the Redstart's
HABITAT	Broadleaved, coniferous and mixed woodlands, parks and gardens (uses nest boxes in woodland)
STATUS	Summer visitor, wintering to West Africa. In B about 40,000 pairs, locally in north and west (virtually absent from Ireland)

MALE BLACK OR grey-brown above, white below, with clear white wing-patch and white spot on forehead. Female grey-brown above, wing-patch and underside dirty white. Winter male like female but with white forehead.

SIZE

IDENTIFICATION

HABITAT

POPULATION

MAP

IN FOREST REFRESHED Norman Hickin writes how Professor Steele Elliot persuaded the pied flycatcher to nest in Wyre Forest by providing suitable but artificial nesting sites. 'In 1963, two pairs nested in an old overgrown orchard, their nearest neighbours being in the Forest of Dean. As we stood immobile against an old damson tree in the hedge, a cock, in his black and white, delighted us by fluttering down from a moss-covered crabapple and, hovering like a humming bird, picked a fly from a buttercup and then returned to his perch. The beauty of this little action was most exhilarating and I find myself recalling it to mind and reliving the breathless thirty seconds.'

Soon after Hickin's book, David Lack devoted a chapter of his *Population Studies of Birds* to the breeding of the pied flycatcher, and the main study area was the Forest of Dean from which Hickin's Wyre Forest birds had come.

Because of the ease with which nesting-boxes can be examined, the pied flycatcher was one of the earliest subjects of population studies in birds, and Lack points to two advantages over the great tit. It can freely be caught at the nest without deserting, and the black and white cock is readily distinguished from the much browner hen.

In summer, the pied flycatcher feeds on both caterpillars and adult insects. It can catch the adults in the air at times, but more often hunts for caterpillars in the foliage or drops on insects on the ground from a perch above. In the Forest of Dean, caterpillars formed about half the diet of one nest studied. Despite their liking for caterpillars, they usually breed two or three weeks after the great tits, thus missing the best caterpillar time. Yarner Wood, in Devon, is another good site for this species.

Despite scattered areas of breeding in France and Spain, where it prefers damp, hilly areas with sessile oak, they are essentially northern birds, and outside the Palearctic extend to Siberia. As long-distance migrants, wintering in West Africa, they have a major fattening area in Iberia so that initial migration direction is often south-west before turning south.

Pied flycatchers are birds of the western oakwoods. Their populations have been boosted locally by the use of nest boxes.

Garden Warbler

14 cm (5.5 in)

SPECIES INFORMATION	
SCIENTIFIC NAME	Sylvia borin
RELATED SPECIES	Blackcap, Whitethroat, Lesser Whitethroat, Dartford Warbler
CALL	'Vet-vet-vet' or 'tsharr'. Song is soft and musical, with blackbird-like phrases
HABITAT	Tall scrub, damp thickets, bushy woodland margins, woods and parks with rich undergrowth, large gardens
STATUS	Summer visitor. In BI about 200,000 pairs (about 200 in Ireland)

SIZE

IDENTIFICATION

HABITAT

POPULATION

MAP

PLUMP AND RATHER drab, with no obvious markings. Head rounded, bill relatively short. Grey-brown above, somewhat paler below, with the hint of an eye-stripe, and pale eye-ring. The garden warbler really has very little distinctive about it and as it skulks more it is vital to get familiar with the song.

THE DURATION OF the garden warbler's babble (perhaps an unkind word, but brook babbles are lovely) is much more prolonged but the song is softer, and lacking the rich variation of the blackcap's.

When counting birds in Chaddesley Woods in Worcestershire there were quite as many garden warblers as blackcaps, but in north Wales and in my Devon CBC plot blackcaps were, and are, much more common. They are both sylvia warblers with songs that are easy to muddle after a winter without them. *Sylvia* warblers are very much a feature of Mediterranean scrub, where they make up a much higher proportion of the bird community than they do in temperate scrub. In the south of France they can be the commonest birds in scrub of 1–6 m (3.2–19.7 ft) tall. The species concerned are dartford, sardinian and subalpine warblers and they, together with nightingales, can reach very high densities. Most Mediterranean *sylvia* warblers are resident, but of ours, the garden warbler and the two whitethroats are trans-Saharan migrants, the blackcap is a medium-distance migrant, and only the dartford warbler is resident.

Left
The garden warbler is one of our most featureless birds, but it has a very pleasant song, rather like a muted blackbird.

Right
Garden warblers like damp woodland with rich undergrowth.

Blackcap
14 cm (5.5 in)

SPECIES INFORMATION

SCIENTIFIC NAME	Sylvia atricapilla
RELATED SPECIES	Garden Warbler, Whitethroat, Lesser Whitethroat, Dartford Warbler
CALL	Alarm-call a hard 'tack'. Song is very pretty, starting with a soft twitter, and developing into a loud, clear fluting phrase (higher-pitched towards the end)
HABITAT	Open broadleaved and coniferous woodland, river-valley woodland, plantations, parks and gardens
STATUS	Summer visitor (some overwinter). In BI about 800,000 pairs

GREY-BROWN, with cap black (male), or red-brown (female and juvenile). The blackcap's song period, as opposed to the length of the individual song, is longer than the garden warbler's, extending into July, but its loud wheatear-like 'tack' is to be heard for even longer as it searches among the blackberries in September.

BLACKCAPS TEND TO establish their territories before the arrival of garden warblers and they also choose slightly different sites. Garden warblers are more numerous in downland scrub and six- or seven-year old coppice scrub, while the blackcap is found in taller, older scrub and is more frequent in true woodland; garden warblers are often confined to woodland edge. In my CBC plot blackcaps, one of the commonest birds, are at high density in thick, high impenetrable bramble patches, and less common among the ash, with less dense bramble and hazel.

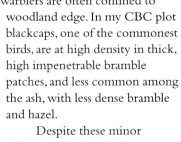

Despite these minor differences, feeding behaviour and food itself seems much the same, with insects, in the breeding season, found mainly in the shrub layer, and fruit at other times. Blackcaps are quite happy to include berries, apples and even peanuts in their winter diet. Garden warbler nests tend to be a bit lower, in bramble or nettle, than blackcap's which may be in shrubs or a low branches.

Both male and female blackcaps have good diagnostic visual features and are quite happy to show them at times. Paler below than above, the cap is the distinctive feature, reaching down to the eye; in the female it is a rich russet.

Blackcaps turn up in gardens in winter much more than they used to. A German team, using lightweight coloured rings that could easily be spotted at bird feeders, found that many of their ringed birds ended up here and it turns out our small wintering population is completely different from the summering one.

Cannon, in the *Garden Bird Watch Handbook*, writes that 'Experiments show that migration direction in Blackcaps is genetically controlled and inherited, hence subject to natural selection. West European blackcaps migrate south-west and eastern birds south-east but in central Europe there is a small intermediate population which migrates north-west and so tended not to survive. However in the last forty years wintering conditions in Britain and Ireland seem to have improved, possibly helped by garden feeding, so instead of all these blackcaps dying, more and more of our wintering birds are surviving to breed the next spring and pass this unorthodox migration to their offspring.' This then is an opportunity to witness evolution in action.

SIZE

IDENTIFICATION

HABITAT

POPULATION

MAP

Only the male blackcap has the black cap — that of the young birds and adult female is chestnut brown.

Wood Warbler

12.5 cm (5 in)

SIZE

IDENTIFICATION

HABITAT

POPULATION

MAP

SPECIES INFORMATION	
SCIENTIFIC NAME	Phylloscopus sibilatrix
RELATED SPECIES	Willow Warbler, Chiffchaff
CALL	Alarm-call a soft 'diuh' or 'vit-vit-vit'. Song a descending trill, beginning 'sip-sip-sip-sipsirrr...', often including melancholy whistling 'diuh-diuh-diuh-diuh'
HABITAT	Tall, open deciduous or mixed woodland (especially upland oak and beech)
STATUS	Summer visitor, wintering in Africa. In BI about 17,000 pairs, mainly in the west (the small Irish population of around 30 pairs is increasing)

SOMEWHAT LARGER THAN willow warbler and chiffchaff, and with longer wings. Greenish upperparts contrast with yellow neck and breast, and with white belly. Yellow stripe over eye. The legs are yellowish. Lives mainly amongst the crowns of tall trees.

WOOD WARBLERS HAVE two somewhat different songs. The most common is the trill song, one of the joys of western oak woods, which is a delicate series of similar 'sip' or 'tip' units fusing into a shorter, faster shivering trill. The piping song, a slowing series of many piping 'few' notes descending in pitch is less frequent. Although western, it rarely reaches Ireland. Wood warblers have a special song flight around conspicuous branches within its territory. The bird starts to sing as it flies with shallow wing beats, keeps singing until it lands and finishes with a trill.

The wood warbler distribution coincides largely with upland oakwoods, usually with little ground cover, although beech stands are also favoured in some parts.

If *Sylvia* warblers present their difficulties, then *Phylloscopus* or leaf warblers can be a greater challenge. Our three have fairly distinct habitat preferences, but there are several more species between the British Isles and the Bering Straits, and another 15 in the mountain forests of the Himalayas and Burma.

These include a number of vagrants which sometimes reach us, notably the Arctic, greenish and yellow-browed warblers, which are pushing into Europe from Asia. Pallas's and Radde's warblers can turn up from Siberia, although Radde's extends to lake Baikal and Korea. Another vagrant, Bonelli's warbler, is from southern Europe.

W. H. Hudson describes the song of the wood warbler as 'long and passionate ... the woodland sound that is like no other'.

Top left and right
Wood warblers spend much of their time in the treetops, where their silvery song often betrays their presence.

Bottom right
Tall beechwoods are the favoured habitat in some areas.

Goldcrest
9 cm (3.5 in)

SPECIES INFORMATION

SCIENTIFIC NAME	Regulus regulus
RELATED SPECIES	Firecrest
CALL	High-pitched 'sree-sree-sree-sree'. Song is short, very high-pitched, with a clear, somewhat deeper, end section: 'sesim-sesim-sesim-sesim-seritete'
HABITAT	Mainly coniferous forest or groups of conifers in mixed woodland, parks and gardens
STATUS	Resident and partial migrant. In BI about 860,000 pairs

TINY AND DUMPY – with firecrest, Europe's smallest bird. Olive-green above, with double white black-edged wing-bar. Head rather large, bill small and thin. Male has bright yellow crown, edged orange-red; female has light yellow crown. No stripe through or above eye. Juvenile lacks head markings.

IT IS PERHAPS odd, looking at the histograms in the Birds of Bardsey to see a clear spring peak, averaging 10–15 goldcrests a day, and an autumn one showing at least 20, from September through October. A small west coast island and yet the tiny goldcrests are moving through, sometimes in their hundreds. Most of our birds do not migrate, but an extra million goldcrests arrive in Britain in the autumn, at east coast observatories in far higher numbers than at Bardsey.

As the smallest bird in Europe, with a correspondingly high surface area to volume ratio, it loses heat very fast, and is extremely vulnerable to cold winters. Looking at BTO Common Bird Census indices the resulting fluctuations are clear, with a huge fall in 1986 so that, on farmland, the index fell to around 20, a tenth of what it had been 12 years before, and a fifth of the previous year. Farmland being a secondary habitat, its fluctuations are greater than in woodland. The effects of cold weather vary considerably according to its duration and geographical pattern. Marchant *et al.* say of the goldcrest: 'Cold periods interrupted by brief thaws are less likely to prove damaging than those of continuous freeze, and temperatures probably matter less than snow and ice conditions. Also important is whether or not an ice-coating or hoarfrost persists on trees.' After its population decimation in the 1916–17 winter T. A. Coward wrote that the goldcrest 'could have little more than an obituary notice'.

The woods it prefers are coniferous, with optimum conditions in spruce, silver fir and pine, and goldcrests make good use of the many coniferous plantations around the country.

Goldcrests often visit gardens, but not bird tables, and you have a better chance of seeing them well there than in conifer plantations. Unless the bird is below you, the yellow-orange crown can be less clear than the dark eye, set in a pale face and two white wing bars. The olive back and buff below could well suggest a tiny warbler, but its acrobatic behaviour, in its constant search for minute insects and spiders, is really more tit-like.

SIZE

IDENTIFICATION

HABITAT

POPULATION

MAP

Top
Although goldcrests are quite tame, these tiny birds are hard to see as they flit about amongst the foliage of conifers.

Bottom
Only rarely do they come down to feed on the ground, or to drink or bathe at a puddle.

Willow Warbler

11 cm (4.25 in)

SPECIES INFORMATION	
SCIENTIFIC NAME	*Phylloscopus trochilus*
RELATED SPECIES	Chiffchaff, Wood Warbler
CALL	Alarm call soft 'hoo-eet'. Song is a melancholy descending series of clear notes: 'titi-dje-djoo-dooe-dooi-djoo'
HABITAT	Broadleaved and mixed woodland, clearings, willow scrub, larger parks and gardens
STATUS	Summer visitor. In BI over 3,000,000 pairs

SIZE

IDENTIFICATION

HABITAT

POPULATION

MAP

SLIM AND DELICATE warbler; best separated from almost identical chiffchaff by its very distinct and pretty song. Somewhat yellower than chiffchaff, with clearer stripe over eye, and a less obvious eye-ring. Legs normally (but not always) light brown. Juvenile uniform yellowish below. The bill has a pinkish lower mandible and dark upper mandible. Our most numerous summer visitor.

WILLOW WARBLERS HAVE bright greenish-olive upperparts, yellow-white underparts and yellow-brown legs. Unless seen at close quarters, they are impossible to separate from chiffchaffs, except by song, and neither species is easy to observe as they flit quickly from leaf to leaf searching for insects and spiders.

Willow warblers are very adaptable, being found in heathy woodland, fen carr, and even large gardens with scattered trees. They can be very common in young conifer plantations, love birch woods and also thrive in a variety of scrub. They normally arrive in early April, leaving in late September. Most overwinter in tropical Africa, south of the Sahara.

T. A. Coward, on the willow warbler: 'a tender, delicious warbler with a dying fall – it mounts up round and full, then down the scale and expires upon the air in a gentle murmur.'

Chiffchaff

11 cm (4.25 in)

SPECIES INFORMATION	
SCIENTIFIC NAME	*Phylloscopus collybita*
RELATED SPECIES	Willow Warbler, Wood Warbler
CALL	Alarm-call 'hweet'. Song is a monotonous and somewhat irregular repetition of two notes 'chiff-chaff-chiff-chiff-chaff...'
HABITAT	Broadleaved and mixed woodland, with plenty of undergrowth, river-valley woodland, tall scrub, parks and gardens
STATUS	Summer visitor. In BI over 900,000 pairs

SIZE

IDENTIFICATION

HABITAT

POPULATION

MAP

VERY LIKE WILLOW warbler, but looks less slim, with shorter wings, and more rounded head. Legs usually dark. Olive-brown above; underside whitish. The bill is dark, with a paler base and the eye has a thin white ring around it (compare willow warbler).

THE CHIFFCHAFF IS more of a true woodland bird, liking tall deciduous trees. Occasionally seen (or heard) in larger gardens. Chiffchaffs arrive early and this is often the first visitor to be heard, as early as March. Some birds overwinter, but most migrate to the Mediterranean or Africa.

John Fowles wrote of 'newly arrived chiffchaffs and willow warblers singing in every bush and tree' in the *French Lieutenant's Woman*, but only the chiffchaff stays in any numbers in the Lyme Regis Undercliff where the book was set.

'*The uncrested wren, called in this place chif-chaf is very loud ….It does only two piercing notes.*'
Gilbert White

Marsh Tit
11.5 cm (4.5 in)

SPECIES INFORMATION	
SCIENTIFIC NAME	Parus palustris
RELATED SPECIES	Blue Tit, Great Tit, Coal Tit, Willow Tit, Crested Tit
CALL	'Pitchew' or 'psiche-che-che-che...' Song made up of rattling phrases such as 'tji-tji-tji-tji...' or 'tsivit-tsivit-tsivit...'
HABITAT	Broadleaved and mixed woodland, copses, parks and gardens
STATUS	Resident. In B about 140,000 pairs (absent from Ireland, and most of Scotland)

MARSH TITS ARE small and rather chunky, mainly a dull grey-brown, except for the extensive shiny black cap and white cheeks, and small black bib. They are best distinguished from the often similar-looking willow tit by their calls.

IN THE GARDEN Bird Watch Scheme marsh and willow tits are counted together because of their similarity but they do have rather different habitat preferences. Marsh tits tend to occur in open woodland, especially damp woods, copses, and in parks and gardens. The name marsh tit is not really suitable, for there is no need for dampness as long as it has open woodland with a rich understorey.

Marsh tits are great storers of food. They often cache seeds for a short time, generally a day or less, rather than storing them away for the winter. Their reason for hiding them thus may be to keep them from dominant great tits. Seeds are hidden among grass, moss or leaves. Marsh tits certainly take a lot of black sunflower seeds from bird tables, and are seen with them up to 200 m (656 ft) from the feeding station.

SIZE
IDENTIFICATION
HABITAT
POPULATION
MAP

Willow Tit
11.5 cm 4.5 (in)

SPECIES INFORMATION	
SCIENTIFIC NAME	Parus montanus
RELATED SPECIES	Marsh Tit, Blue Tit, Great Tit, Coal Tit, Crested Tit
CALL	Characteristic nasal, buzzing 'chay-chay-chay'.
HABITAT	Damp woodland, especially alder and birch scrub, such as fen carr. Usually in wetter sites than marsh tit.
STATUS	Resident. In B about 60,000 pairs (absent from Ireland, and most of Scotland)

VERY SIMILAR TO marsh tit, but has a duller black cap, a larger black bib, and a pale wing panel. Often has a large-headed, or bullnecked appearance.

WILLOW TITS PREFER rather damp, scrubby areas of elder, alder and birch, with plenty of dead stumps. These are short-lived trees that rot rapidly, and therefore are good for nest excavation. Both marsh and willow tits nest in holes, but willow tits usually excavate their own, in rotten wood. In the nest there is less moss than is usual among tits and a lot of wood chippings may be used.

SIZE
IDENTIFICATION
HABITAT
POPULATION
MAP

Long-tailed Tit

14 cm (5.5 in)

○ ○

S P E C I E S   I N F O R M A T I O N

SCIENTIFIC NAME	*Aegithalos caudatus*
RELATED SPECIES	No close relative in the region; bearded tit has similar shape
CALL	Flocks keep up contact calls: 'tserr, si-si-si'. Song is a thin trill
HABITAT	Woodland with rich undergrowth, often near water, parks and gardens
STATUS	Resident. In BI about 250,000 pairs

SIZE

IDENTIFICATION

HABITAT

POPULATION

MAP

VERY SMALL, BUT has long, graduated tail, making up more than half of total length. Broad, blackish stripe over eye (but note that the race found in north-east Europe has a pure white head). Juvenile has dark cheeks.

IF THEY COME, as they increasingly do, to food at a bird table, you can see, apart from a mass of tails, that they are not just black and white but have a rosy pink tinge to shoulders, flanks and belly. When they move they communicate with excited contact calls.

Chris Perrins (1979) examined studies of the preferred feeding areas for British tits. The long-tailed tit is usually found among the thinner twigs of the trees, pecking in and around the buds. It practically never comes down to the ground in its search for food. In Marley Wood, the year begins with most birds in oak and ash, but whereas oak remains popular (over 30 per cent of feeding birds) ash drops out of

favour, spindle berries become important, and both birch and hawthorn have 10–5 per cent of feeding birds. Dependence on oak drops in April when the twigs and branches of ash, and maple hold food for more than 20 per cent of birds. By June, a wide range of trees are searched, with sycamore contributing the aphids which so often cluster on their leaves. In July and August birch is favourite, with hazel, maple and elder attracting over 10 per cent of feeding birds. In autumn, hawthorn is important. The value of a range of trees and shrubs to provide a selection of invertebrate foods at all times is evident. Long-tailed tits also eat a few seeds, the flesh of fruits, and sap exuded from broken branches of birch and maple.

Long-tailed tits are most familiar as extended family parties wandering through winter woods like so many flying teaspoons with their extraordinary tails as handles. If not flying teaspoons then perhaps 'bumbarrels'.

The long-tailed tit is an active, lively bird. They build delicate, oval nests, woven from mosses, lichens and spiders' webs.

> *'And coy bumbarrels twenty in a drove*
> *Flit down the hedgrows in the frozen plain*
> *And hang on little twigs and start again.'*
> John Clare EMMON SAILS HEATH IN WINTER

Coal Tit

11.5 cm (4.5 in)

SMALLEST EUROPEAN TIT, with a relatively large head, white cheeks and large white patch on the back of its neck. Grey above and buff below. Juveniles have yellowish undersides and cheeks. The coal tit's song is sprightly, repetitive and piping, and the alarm and contact calls are essentially based on units of the song.

SIZE

IDENTIFICATION

HABITAT

POPULATION

MAP

provided a chapter in Lack. In *Coal Tits in Breckland*, breeding success appeared to have little influence on the subsequent breeding population. After breeding, the population fell by about a half each autumn as tits dispersed to other habitats even if, at that time, there was still plenty of food in the conifers.

In a nine hour day an individual may search more than a thousand trees, taking ten food items from each, at a rate of one every 2.5 seconds.

COAL TITS ARE familiar visitors to many bird tables, identified by the white patch on the nape, contrasting with the black crown. The double white wing bars are often not noticed, and the overall impression, especially in flight, is of a dull grey-brown. Although associated with conifers, they turn up anywhere, advertising themselves with noisy calls. The very narrow bill is adept at searching for insects between conifer needles, and the ability to search for food under branches is useful when twigs are frozen.

Most early work on tits and the factors regulating their numbers was done on breeding populations, so a year-round study of coal tits

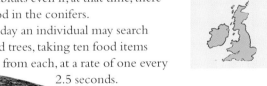

One of the best fieldmarks of the tiny coal tit is the white stripe along the back of its head.

Siskin

14 cm (4.75 in)

╔══════════════════════════════════════╗
SPECIES INFORMATION

SCIENTIFIC NAME	Carduelis spinus
RELATED SPECIES	Redpoll, Linnet, Goldfinch, Greenfinch
CALL	Melancholy 'tseelu'. Song a hurried twitter, with 'tooli' calls, and often ending in a sustained note
HABITAT	Spruce forests and mixed woods, especially in the mountains up to the tree-line and conifer plantations. In winter often feeds in birch and alder trees, and also visits bird tables (likes peanuts)
STATUS	Resident and partial migrant. In BI about 360,000 pairs

SIZE

IDENTIFICATION

HABITAT

POPULATION

MAP

V ERY SMALL, GREENISH-yellow finch, with dark wings and a yellow wing bar. Male has black crown and small black chin patch. Female is grey-green, more heavily streaked and without black on the head. Juvenile is browner above and even more heavily streaked.

A FEW DECADES ago siskins were not often seen outside their scattered breeding sites in upland coniferous woods (mainly in Scotland), but they have

increased markedly in recent years, and have now spread to many mature plantations. There have been major expansions in Wales, southern Scotland and in and around the New Forest, and increases also in Ireland and in the Breckland of East Anglia.

Another major change is that they have become garden birds, frequently coming to feed, even during the summer if the garden is near conifers, especially on peanuts. Surprisingly, they can even 'see off' greenfinches at the bird table. When feeding you may

notice their sharp beaks, very different from the greenfinch as it is adapted for feeding in conifers, extracting tiny food items from tight spaces.

Siskins are very attractive birds at close quarters, with their intricate pattern of black and yellow on the wings and tail. The male has black crown and bib, streaked green upperparts and broad yellow wing bars. The female has no cap or bib but is more streaked and has a pale lemon chest. There are even more spots and streaks on young birds. Siskins are also attractively acrobatic as they feed at the tops of birches or alders. The song is thin and high, but has a peculiar yodelling quality with a characteristic 'dluee' note and often a strange wheezing note at the ends of phrases.

> *'They fed wholly on the alder and looked beautiful, hanging like little parrots, picking at the drooping seeds of that tree.'*
> J. Thompson
> NATURAL HISTORY OF IRELAND

Siskins are often attracted to peanuts, especially in cold winter weather. They are aggressive birds, and will often keep away larger species from the bird table.

Redpoll
13 cm (5 in)

```
○ ○ ○ ○ ○ ○ ○ ○ ○ ○ ○ ○ ○ ○ ○ ○ ○ ○ ○ ○ ○ ○ ○ ○ ○ ○ ○ ○
        S P E C I E S   I N F O R M A T I O N
```

SCIENTIFIC NAME	*Carduelis flammea*
RELATED SPECIES	Siskin, Linnet, Goldfinch, Greenfinch
CALL	Flight-call is a rapid, buzzing 'dshe-dshe-dshe'. Alarm-call a nasal, drawn out 'vaiid'. Song is a twitter mixed with buzzing notes and musical whistles
HABITAT	Moorland and heath, especially with birch, alder and willow scrub, and lowland coniferous plantations. Also northern and mountain birch and coniferous woodland. Increasingly in gardens
STATUS	Resident and partial migrant. In BI about 230,000 pairs.

A VERY SMALL finch with grey-brown, streaked plumage, red forehead and black chin. Breeding male also has pink on breast. Juvenile lacks red.

REDPOLLS ARE STREAKY little brown finches with yellow bills and deeply notched tails. Breeding males have plenty of pink on breast and rump, while the female has a brownish rump and virtually no pink except for the forecrown. At times the pale wing bars become conspicuous, but very often colour is less important in identification than bouncy flight of busy feeding parties noisily calling as they move among birches or riverside alders.

further explanation. There was certainly a time when redpolls seemed everywhere if you knew their flight call, that used to fill the birchwoods or young forestry plantations.

For students of variation or collectors of records of rare subspecies, redpolls are ideal, and some of the races have even gained long-standing English names. Our race, found in Europe and Southern Sweden and Norway, is the lesser redpoll, which is smaller than a Linnet, whereas the mealy redpoll from further north is linnet-sized. The Greenland race is larger still. The Arctic redpoll, or Hornemann's redpoll, is regarded as a separate species.

Redpolls feed on seeds whose supply varies, and the birds generally concentrate wherever their food is plentiful at the time. Thus their numbers in particular localities fluctuate from year to year, partly in response to changes in local seed crops.

In recent years, redpoll levels have risen roughly four-fold from the mid 1960s through the 1970s, but after 1980 a downward trend began, and by 1990 levels were back to those of the late 1960s. The rises coincide with the age of many conifer plantations but the falls, which have continued, need

Redpolls are lively little finches, often seen in gardens as well as in woodland and heathland.

Common Crossbill

16.5 cm (6.5 in)

○○○○○○○○○○○○○○○○○○○○○○○○○○○○○

SPECIES INFORMATION

SCIENTIFIC NAME	Loxia curvirostra
RELATED SPECIES	Scottish Crossbill, Parrot Crossbill
CALL	'Gip-gip-gip', also a soft 'tjook'. Song is rather like that of Greenfinch, with repeated phrases and twitters
HABITAT	Coniferous woodland, especially spruce forests or plantations
STATUS	Resident. Occasionally shows population irruptions, after which may range widely. In BI population at least 1,000 pairs (variable)

SIZE

IDENTIFICATION

HABITAT

POPULATION

MAP

DUMPY AND RATHER large-headed finch, with short, forked tail, and crossed mandibles. Adult male is brick-red; female olive-green with yellow rump. Juvenile heavily streaked.

CROSSBILLS SHOW ONE of the most marked sexual dimorphisms, the adult male being rusty red and the female greenish-yellow. Both sexes are chunky, with a blunt-looking head and short forked tail so outline is very characteristic as they pass with bounding finch flight. A good look at a male will show a red bird with a brighter red rump, whereas the female is greener above and yellowish below, with a clear greenish-

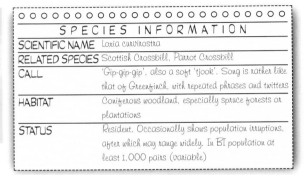

The rare Scottish crossbill of the native pine forest is our only endemic bird. Another relative, the slightly larger parrot crossbill has a heavier and deeper bill. It is an occasional visitor to Britain, and has bred.

yellow rump. Young birds are coarsely streaked above and below, without the colour of either bird. All of them have the distinctive crossed mandibles, with which they deftly extract the seeds from cones – mainly spruce in the case of the common crossbill.

At the time of the last *Atlas* there was breeding evidence of crossbills in 462 squares in Britain and Ireland, they were present in another 457 squares. There are large numbers in Scotland included plenty outside the range of the Scottish crossbill. Common crossbills also have concentrations in the developing forests of Wales, in Breckland and in the New Forest and Kielder Forest. In Ireland, common crossbills are beginning to colonise the conifer plantations.

The crossed mandibles of the crossbill enable it to probe between the scales of pine cones and extract the edible seeds.

Hawfinch
18 cm (7 in)

LARGE, HEAVY-BODIED finch with large head and very large bill. Female has slightly duller plumage. Juvenile brownish-yellow. Looks thick-set in flight, and shows pale areas on wings, and white tip to tail. Rather shy.

HAWFINCHES SEEM TO have decreased but it is not an easy bird to census, or even to see, and once again the calls, explosive tickings, must be known. The massive head and bill, bull-neck and short tail combine to give the birds a stocky, top heavy appearance. The general coloration appears orange-brown with mainly blackish wings and large white shoulder patches. In the male the head is chestnut, the nape pale grey and the back a rich brown, while the underparts are pinkish-brown shading to white beneath the tail.

The flight feathers are iridescent and close observation, in the hand, shows the four inner-primaries to be notched and curled at the ends. Like many special features, in this case shown by no other finch, these are used in courtship.

The internal structure of the hawfinch's beak is one of the secrets of its capacity to deal with hard objects. There are ridges on the palate, and behind them a pair of knobs which overlie a similar pair in the lower jaw. Large seeds are held between these four knobs and the strain of cracking the seeds is shared by the muscles on both sides. The four knobs are horny and do not develop immediately as young birds are fed on insects and softer seeds.

 SIZE
 IDENTIFICATION
 HABITAT
 POPULATION
 MAP

This largest of our finches has a truly massive bill, strong enough to crack open even cherry stones. Hawfinches are shy birds and are seldom spotted.

147

Farmland, Downland and Heathland Birds

FARMING SYSTEMS HAVE produced some of our most distinctive habitats: lowland heaths, chalk downs and upland moors have all been produced by grazing. The moors will be considered with the rest of the uplands, but downs and heaths fit in best here. On the whole, farmland means fields and their associated hedges or walls, and the farm buildings and copses which are part of the agricultural scene.

FIELDS HAVE ALWAYS been liable to change, in size and shape and in arable to pasture ratio. Modern agriculture started in earnest in the eighteenth century, with population doubling and a move to the towns creating the first need for commercial agriculture.

Top
Pheasants, though not native, are very much at home in the farmed countryside of Britain.

Bottom left
Sparrowhawks were very badly hit by the use of toxic pesticides applied to crops.

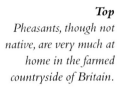

Bottom right
The sterile landscape of herbicide-treated fields.

EFFECTS OF MODERN FARMING

CHANGES IN FARMING practice have had dramatic effects on the birdlife of farmland, notable effects being the loss of permanent pasture in many regions, stubble burning and ploughing, which reduces seed and insect levels, and the disappearance of corn ricks and chaff heaps, reducing food for finches in particular. The use of chemical pesticides has also taken its toll of wildlife.

From a wildlife point of view, the declines of grain-eating birds, stock doves, pheasants and partridges, following the treatment of cereal seed with organochlorine insecticides, aimed at pests such as wireworms and wheat bulbfly, initiated public concern. Soon predators such as sparrowhawks, badgers and foxes, died, and evidence from autopsies and laboratory feeding experiments showed that dieldrin, taken by the grain-eating birds and small mammals, was being passed through the food-web with lethal effects. Population declines of peregrines, sparrowhawks and kestrels were observed.

POPULATION DECREASES

MOST FARMLAND BIRDS have decreased in the last 30 years. The birds have less food because of herbicide use which is effectively cumulative, depleting the seed bank in the soil. Seeds on the surface of newly ploughed land, as on vegetable patches, used to

number thousands per square metre, but have now almost disappeared in cereal growing regions. The best documented example of population effects through reduction of food supply concerns the grey partridge. Field trials with reduced herbicide use have led to increased weed and insect populations, better chick survival and greater partridge densities. Once again it can be demonstrated that it is possible to reverse population trends, but much depends on economics as well as effective research.

Species of open country, such as the skylark, have suffered particularly through changing land use. Thus, since 1970, the UK population of skylarks has declined by some 68 per cent. They are not alone, for 10 species monitored by the Common Bird Census decreased by more than half in the 25 years up to 1994, and were danger-listed by the conservation organisations in their leaflet *Birds of Conservation Concern* (1996). Tree sparrow, partridge, cornbunting, linnet, song thrush and lapwing populations have all halved in that time.

Hedges are of great importance for the birds of farmland, as they provide shelter, food and nesting sites for many species, and are home to insects and plant life. Old hedges, with their variety of trees and shrubs, are of particular value, though any hedge is better than none at all.

Some 289,674 km (180,000 miles) of hedges have been removed since 1940, and although 450,604 km (280,000 miles) remain, hedgerows continue to be lost at a rate of 3,218 km (2,000 miles) a year. Just as bad is the quality of many that remain, leggy, over-cut or neglected, which has contributed to significant declines of not only many farmland birds, but also plants and butterflies.

DOWNLAND AND HEATH

DOWNLAND AND HEATH are also, in the main, the creation of man; of his work long ago when chalk was the easiest land for Neolithic man to clear, and where his burial barrows and hill forts remind us of his activities. Heathland was also created by clearance, but because of its acid soil produces very different plants. It also often shows signs of stone-age man. Neither of these habitats suffered from hedgerow removal nor from the direct results of insecticides, but they have suffered other pressures, with ploughing and house building being the most widespread. Even so, our remaining fragments of these two vulnerable habitats are the most extensive in Europe, and a valuable heritage.

Top
Skylark numbers have dropped alarmingly with recent changes in land use.

Middle
A healthier landscape, with grazed fields and well-maintained hedges.

Bottom
Lapwing numbers have halved in the last 25 years.

PRESERVATION OF DOWNLANDS

SHEEP USED TO maintain much of the chalk of southern England as well-grazed grassland and extensive flower meadows. The shepherd's life involved bringing the sheep back to the farm at night, where their droppings would fertilise the fields by the house. By day, watched by the shepherd, they could drift across the extensive grasslands.

Because remaining chalk grassland is mainly on steep slopes, we tend to forget that the downs used to reach extensively across the lowlands, as they still do for example on Salisbury Plain. Army activities here

land encircled by Neolithic hill forts has often been ploughed, and on this flinty land nothing would grow without the heavy use of fertilisers. Some of downland turf, full of orchids and vetches, yellow-wort and rock-rose, may survive on the round, raised, rim of the fort, along with some butterflies, but in limited areas like this, isolation from other suitable habitat may lead to their extinction.

The magnificent great bustard (now sadly extinct in Britain) once roamed on Salisbury Plain, and that classic downland bird, the stone curlew, has sometimes seemed to be going that way too. It was

have saved the Plain from the plough and from fertilisation, just as they have on Lulworth ranges in Dorset. Similarly, Porton Down, with its restricted access, has preserved some of the best downland in Europe for flowering plants and butterflies. In most other areas, except for a few nature reserves, downland is fragmented and limited to steep slopes which the plough cannot reach. Even the enclosed

never great birding country, too dry and too uniform, but lapwings, larks and wheatears loved it. Among the shrubs which would always have been invading, corn buntings would rattle and linnets dance. Martin Down near Salisbury, Wiltshire, is still excellent for nightingales, and one can still see the occasional wintering hen harrier or short-eared owl on the Berkshire Downs.

Top
Chalk downland provides excellent habitat for a range of birds, including skylark and kestrel. Sadly, much has now been ploughed and planted with crops, as in the foreground.

Bottom left
Skylark at its nest hidden amongst ground vegetation.

Bottom right
The cock linnet is a handsome bird when seen at close quarters.

Top
Lowland heath, with clumps of heather in the foreground. Another semi-natural habitat which has sadly reduced in extent over recent decades.

DAMAGE TO HEATHLAND

THE PLOUGH HAS damaged much heathland, particularly in war at a time of food shortage, but more recently it has been seen as land for forestry or for housing – too unproductive for the farmer but still in demand. The loss of much of the Dorset heathland, largely due to the expansion of Bournemouth, has been frequently described, but now, at last, there are moves to conserve much existing heath and to restore, usually from forestry, past heathland.

Neolithic man probably started the process of heathland creation, and there must have been factors acting against trees if heath was to remain open. Human factors, fire and grazing, seem most likely, or perhaps the absence of trees led to still further deterioration and acidification of the soils.

In the nineteenth century, when transport improved, it became possible to obtain fuel, timber, animal feed and fertilisers from elsewhere, and the use of the heaths began to decline. Since then heathlands have been neglected, scrub and bracken have invaded and the vegetation composition has changed.

BIRDS OF THE HEATHLAND

IN WINTER, DEPENDING on the heath, one might find wrens, meadow pipits, stonechats and Dartford warblers and an occasional predator, while summer could be more productive with linnets and willow warblers and perhaps tree pipits, nightjars and hobbys, with a chance of woodlarks.

Oliver Rackham (1944) concludes how much more widespread heathland must have been in the past: 'Heathland was much more prominent in Anglo Saxon England than it is today. There are 14 places called Flatfield, Heathfield or Hadfield (field being Old English field, an open space), at least 15 called Hadley or Headley (heath-clearing), and others called Hatton (heath town). More than 100 place names allude to broom (Brampton, Bramley, Bromley) and 26 to gorse (or furze or whin). These show that

heathland occurred all over Anglo Saxon England and lowland Scotland.' No doubt these heaths would have had their populations of black grouse and red-backed Shrikes.

Although heathlands are not as important for birds as they are, for instance, for reptiles and for invertebrates like silver-studded blue butterflies, dragonflies, and species of grasshopper, their birdlife does have plenty of interest, and heathland has enormous amenity value as well. Management is therefore often vital to reduce bracken, with rotational burning on large sites to maintain heather plots of different ages. Hardy native ponies and certain rare sheep breeds may also be good for long term grazing regime.

Middle
The resident Dartford warbler is virtually restricted to mature lowland heath in Britain, where it is at the northern limit of its range.

Bottom
Stonechats are typical birds of scrub and heathy habitats.

151

Kestrel

28–32 cm (11–13 in)

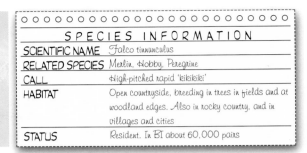

SPECIES INFORMATION	
SCIENTIFIC NAME	*Falco tinnunculus*
RELATED SPECIES	Merlin, Hobby, Peregrine
CALL	High-pitched rapid 'kikikiki'
HABITAT	Open countryside, breeding in trees in fields and at woodland edges. Also in rocky country, and in villages and cities
STATUS	Resident. In BI about 60,000 pairs

SIZE

IDENTIFICATION

HABITAT

POPULATION

MAP

COMMONEST SMALL BIRD of prey, often seen by main roads; hovers frequently. Small falcon with long tail, long, pointed wings and brown upperparts. Male has weakly speckled red-brown back, grey head, and grey tail with broad terminal band. Female uniformly red-brown, with barred upperparts.

THE STREAKED UNDERPARTS and a black band near the tip of the tail are visible when overhead, while the pointed wings help to distinguish it from sparrowhawk. The facial pattern is not striking, but a dark 'moustache' below the eye shows on all birds.

Kestrels are highly adaptable and are, perhaps, most familiar hovering over motorway verges where vole populations are high. As small mammals are widespread so are kestrels, hunting over waste ground and farmland, where they breed in old trees or outbuildings.

It is amazing to think of the levels of persecution that kestrels used to suffer in the game preserving era. Despite this, with good-sized broods and breeding in their first year they always kept their numbers up, except for a dip, in southern and eastern England, in the pesticide era of 1960–63. As they have always been ready to use railway sidings and industrial wasteland there were always safe populations even in the most intensively farmed parts of England.

Its range is widespread, including much of Asia and sub-Saharan Africa, with a large part of the northern and eastern populations moving to, for instance, Angola, Zambia and Malawi in the winter. There are areas it avoids, dense forests, precipitous mountains and treeless wetlands, but if there are small mammals that can be seen from the air kestrels are likely to be there. Attenborough (1998) reports on how some species of bird can see over a wider colour spectrum than we can and of how it is useful to a kestrel to be able to detect ultra-violet light. Voles mark their tracks through the grass with squirts of urine, which reflect ultra-violet light. This in turn, is detectable by a hunting kestrel.

Kestrels can be quite noisy, particularly when the young are exercising their wings and there is a possibility of nest disturbance.

> '… by the *Two Brewers* pub I watched them – flickering arrowheads – quartering their territory on chestnut-red, slender wings and hovering at bus roof height.'
> Kenneth Allsop SUNDAY TIMES MAGAZINE

Bottom left
This kestrel shows the long tail and pointed wings so typical of falcons.

Bottom right
By hovering into an updraft or headwind, the kestrel can keep its head perfectly still as it searches the ground below for signs of small mammals such as voles.

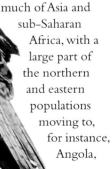

Hobby

28–35 cm (11–14 in)

SPECIES INFORMATION	
SCIENTIFIC NAME	*Falco subbuteo*
RELATED SPECIES	Kestrel, peregrine, merlin
CALL	'Kew-kew-kew' and 'ki-ki-ki-ki'
HABITAT	Wooded country with heathland, damp meadows and lakes or gravel pits. Breeds in light woodland, at forest edges and in lone trees in fields
STATUS	Summer visitor. In BI mainly in S and E England, where increased in recent years (from about 60 pairs in 1950s to over 1,000 pairs in the 1990s)

FLIGHT OUTLINE LIKE a large swift. Kestrel-sized, but with shorter tail and long, sickle-shaped wings. Upperparts blue-grey, head with conspicuous moustache. Leg feathers and under tail coverts rusty-red.

HOBBIES TOO CAN be highly vocal when greeting during courtship or warning young. The piercing call is difficult to describe.

The hobby has specialised requirements, and is a bird of heaths and farmland with scattered pine and preferably a good population of dragonflies. If more poets knew about them there would be writings on the flight of these experts who can even catch swifts and swallows after pursuit on swept-back wings; these manoeuvres can even make it look like a swift. With this diet and the odd bat and any bird rash enough to have an aerial song flight, it is not surprisingly a summer visitor, returning late to northern Europe from southern Africa. A lot of farmland breeding hobbies are probably overlooked, and populations may be higher than we think.

Hobbies are elegant and long-winged, with heavily streaked underparts, rufous under the tail and upper legs and with head markings that recall peregrine.

It has a fast and regular wing action when hunting birds, but will almost close the wings as it stoops. When hunting insects the flight pattern is different, slower and with flatter wing-beats, occasionally almost stalling to catch its prey. When perched, it has an upright posture and the wing tips reach the end of the short tail.

SIZE

IDENTIFICATION

HABITAT

POPULATION

MAP

The hobby is slimmer and more delicately built than the kestrel. It can catch dragonflies and other airborne insects in its nimble talons.

Grey Partridge

30 cm (12 in)

SPECIES INFORMATION

SCIENTIFIC NAME	Perdix perdix
RELATED SPECIES	Red-legged Partridge, Pheasant, Grouse
CALL	Alarm call a loud 'kerripriprip'. Territorial males make a hoarse, repeated 'girreck', mainly in morning and evening
HABITAT	Lowland cultivated country, with agricultural fields, pasture, hedges and overgrown field margins, also heaths
STATUS	Resident. In Britain rather rare in extreme west. Rare in Ireland. Declining due to more intensive cultivation and decrease in food and cover

SMALL AND DUMPY, with short tail. Rusty-brown stripes on flank, and dark, horseshoe-shaped patch on breast. Flight rapid. Glides with wings bowed.

GREY PARTRIDGES ARE dumpy runners and fast, noisy fliers. The vermiculated brown and grey plumage of the body contrasts with the orange head and grey neck. Males, and some females, show a dark lower breast. The absence of flank bars separate both from red-legged partridges, and in flight the grey partridge is paler on the back and wings.

Richard Jefferies writing in 1879 when partridges were abundant, adds partridges 'to the number of those birds whose call is more or less apparently ventriloquial; for when they are assembling in the evening at their roosting place their calls in the stubble often sound some way to the right or left of the real position of the bird, which presently appears emerging from the turnips ten or fifteen yards further up than was judged by the ear.' This call is a repeated metallic 'girreck' used as self advertisement or threat, with other calls to summon a mate, gather the chicks or when suspicious.

Grey partridges are widespread but declining in Europe and into central Asia; their natural distribution pattern is often confused by sporting introductions. Apart from the cover that it needs, some bare dusty ground, which can be ploughed land, is enjoyed. For most of the year the food is plant material, green leaves, cereals and clover and grain and weed seeds, particularly bistorts if available.

Nests are on the ground, often in hedge bottoms and are shallow depressions lined with grass and leaves. The clutch size is large, sometimes more then 24.

As long ago as 1951 Nicholson was able to say that partridges were 'like many other birds, increasingly troubled by the inconsiderate tendencies of farmers to mess about with their farms in spring and early summer, when complete quiet is desirable, and to seek to tidy up and bring into cultivation all sorts of rough fringes and waste patches which their forefathers were content to leave untouched from generation to generation.'

He describes the partridge as being 'the most content of all our birds to stay on the earth, and moreover to stay on that part of the earth where they first saw the light. Strong on the wing though they are, they rarely seem to fly farther than across a few fields or higher than they must to clear some ground obstacle.'

Grey Partridges were at one time so common that, had it not declined, it would now be the tenth most common species in Britain and Ireland.

Extensive research has shown that chick survival rates can be increased by the use of unsprayed 'conservation headlands' or by the traditional system of undersowing cereals with a ley pasture. This system is of great benefit to sawflies, a favourite chick food.

Top left
A partridge stretches upwards to deliver its hoarse territorial call.

Bottom
Partridges are rather shy birds which skulk close to the ground for long periods, flying reluctantly.

SPECIES INFORMATION	
SCIENTIFIC NAME	*Alectoris rufa*
RELATED SPECIES	Grey Partridge, Pheasants, Grouse
CALL	'Chuk-chuk-er', also a grating 'shreck-shreck'
HABITAT	Prefers dry, stoney fields, sandy heaths, also chalk downland
STATUS	Resident. Introduced to Britain where commonest in south and east

Red-legged Partridge

33 cm 13 (in)

ROUNDED SHAPE, BARRED flanks and distinctive white, black-bordered face mask. Flies low, with wings bowed.

THE INTRODUCED RED-LEGGED partridge, which in 1950 was outnumbered by grey-partridge by twenty to one, is now the commoner species. The first recorded introduction here was in 1673, and a successful colonisation from Sussex started in 1790. It can cope with dry mountain foothills, marginal cultivation and all kinds of arable land.

Its distinctive barred flanks, red legs and bill and rufous chest separate it from the grey partridge. It likes the drier south-east, and fields of sugar-beet, but is adaptable over its range.

The *Concise BWP* describes aspects of its behaviour as 'territorialism announced by a "steam engine call" delivered in upright posture with swollen throat. In aggressive self assertive displays, given by male to opponent or mate and by female to male or female intruders, birds stands sideways on, with head held high, drawn back, and inclined away from object of display, white bib and black borders erected and twisted towards it.' The steam engine or advertising call of the male is described as 'go chak–chak–chak go chak–go chak chak' and a rally call as a harsh, grating 'go chok–chok–chokorrr'.

SIZE

IDENTIFICATION

HABITAT

POPULATION

MAP

The handsome red-legged partridge is sometimes known as the French partridge as it was introduced to Britain from the continent.

155

Pheasant

55–85 cm (22–33 in)

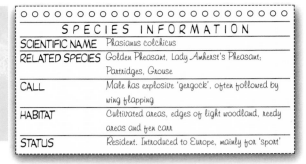

SPECIES INFORMATION	
SCIENTIFIC NAME	*Phasianus colchicus*
RELATED SPECIES	Golden Pheasant, Lady Amherst's Pheasant; Partridges, Grouse
CALL	Male has explosive 'gergock', often followed by wing flapping
HABITAT	Cultivated areas, edges of light woodland, reedy areas and fen carr
STATUS	Resident. Introduced to Europe, mainly for 'sport'

SIZE

IDENTIFICATION

HABITAT

POPULATION

MAP

MALE HAS STRIKING, bronze plumage, red face wattle, shiny green neck (sometimes with white ring) and a very long, pointed tail. Female is yellow-brown with dark speckles, and somewhat shorter tail.

It can run extremely fast, and when running carries its tail a little above the horizontal: the faster the run the more vertical the position of the tail. The flight is strong, direct and fast – but in my experience nothing like as fast as that of blackcock.'

'Feasants were brought into Europe from about the Caspian Sea. There are no feasants in Spaine, nor do I heare of any in Italy.'
John Aubrey
NATURAL HISTORY OF WILTSHIRE

EVERYONE RECOGNISES THE pheasant, a bird of arable land and woodland edge, whose numbers are maintained at a high level by breeding and release for shooting interests. Its explosive flight when disturbed, the male's green head and, usually, white neck ring, and the cryptically coloured female with shorter tail, are all well known.

Vesey Fitzgerald (1946) describes 'its normal gait as a walk, not unlike that of the domestic fowl only more stately, and it flies only on extreme provocation, much preferring to crouch in cover.

It is hard to believe that pheasants were introduced, since they are now so much a part of the country scene. Most populations are still fed food supplements to keep them going, and they are vulnerable to hard weather.

Lapwing
30 cm (12 in)

SPECIES INFORMATION

SCIENTIFIC NAME	*Vanellus vanellus*
RELATED SPECIES	Golden Plover, Grey Plover
CALL	Whiny, hoarse 'peewee' or 'kee-vit'; wings make humming noises in courtship flight
HABITAT	Damp meadows, bogs, coastal pasture, wet heath, fields and farmland
STATUS	Resident and partial migrant in BI. Commonest breeding wader in BI, about 250,000 pairs

BLACK AND WHITE plumage, with long, curved crest on head. Female has shorter crest and paler chin. Outside breeding season upperside paler and crest shorter. Tumbling courtship flight in spring. Forms large flocks in the autumn and winter (sometimes with black-headed gulls and golden plovers).

THE LAPWING IS indeed a handsome bird, whether as a black and white aerial acrobat or as a crested wader. The green and iridescent upper parts, black throat and breast-band, long crest and cinnamon under tail coverts make it a very special bird. Because of their diet of ground-living invertebrates they were much loved by farmers, who often marked the position of their nests so that they could avoid them.

Over the period of 1962 to 1982 there was a steady decline in lapwing numbers in areas of England and Wales dominated by cereals. Lapwings prefer nesting on spring-tilled land but like to be able to move their chicks to grassland for feeding; old style mixed farming thus suiting them well. As lapwings protect their eggs by aggressive defence of their nest site a need to see approaching predators is critical, which may be one reason they prefer relatively bare to well vegetated areas. With the switch from spring-sown cereals, crops are taller at breeding time and breeding densities and clutch size are both lower. Autumn sowing brings changes, with

many tractor visits using tram-lining techniques to spread autumn herbicides, early nitrogen dressings and foliar fungicides.

Adults disperse from many breeding areas as early as late May or June, moving west long before the juveniles who move west or south-west on a broad front from September to November. Many coastal areas therefore get their highest populations in early winter before colder weather has driven birds west to Ireland or south to Iberia or north Africa.

'Upon approaching the old bird flies up, circles round, and comes so near as almost to be within reach, whistling 'pee-wit, pee-wit' over your head. He seems to tumble in the air as if wounded and scarcely able to fly; and those who are not aware of his intention may be tempted to pursue, thinking to catch him. But so soon as you are leaving the nest behind he mounts higher, and wheels off to a distant corner of the field uttering an ironical 'peewit' as he goes.

Then you have a good opportunity of observing the peculiar motion of their wings, which seem to strike simply downwards and not also backwards, as with other birds; it is a quick jerking movement, the wing giving the impression of pausing the tenth of a second at the finish of the strike before it is lifted again. If you pass on a short distance and make no effort to find the nest, they recover confidence and descend. When the peewit alights he runs along a few yards rapidly, as if carried by the impetus. He is a handsome bird, with a well marked crest.' Jeffries (1879)

SIZE

IDENTIFICATION

HABITAT

POPULATION

MAP

Top
When seen at close range the lapwing is a striking bird, with its unusual upturned crest.

Middle
Lapwings have broad wing-tips and a characteristic floppy flight.

Bottom
For its nest it makes just a simple scrape on the ground.

157

Woodpigeon

41 cm (16 in)

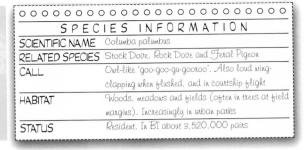
○ ○

SPECIES INFORMATION

SCIENTIFIC NAME	Columba palumbus
RELATED SPECIES	Stock Dove, Rock Dove and Feral Pigeon
CALL	Owl-like 'goo-goo-gu-goooroo'. Also loud wing-clapping when flushed, and in courtship flight
HABITAT	Woods, meadows and fields (often in trees at field margins). Increasingly in urban parks
STATUS	Resident. In BI about 3,520,000 pairs

SIZE

IDENTIFICATION

HABITAT

POPULATION

MAP

LARGE PIGEON WITH white patches on wings and neck, visible in flight. Longer-tailed than the rock dove or feral pigeon. Often form large flocks on fields outside breeding season.

ALTHOUGH WOODPIGEONS WERE originally woodland birds, they have adapted well to changes brought about by agriculture. Pigeons and doves can feed on a wholly vegetarian diet, even when they have young, for they can secrete protein-rich 'pigeon's milk' from their crops.

The major arable farming areas of Britain used to have extensive cereal stubbles which could be searched as a prelude to the winter cereal sowings. It is interesting that earlier attempts to limit Woodpigeon numbers failed, because autumn shooting, by reducing numbers, made relatively more food available for the survivors. Shortage of food between January and March is the limiting factor on population growth. Woodpigeons may be no more popular with gardeners than with farmers, being very destructive of cabbages and some other vegetables.

Woodpigeons flock to farmland and fields, but are equally at home in woodland and, increasingly, in parks and larger gardens.

Unlike other pigeons and doves they will take green leaves, even when there is a good supply of alternative foods, like seeds or acorns.

While many country folk may not like woodpigeons, many town-dwellers love them for their size, gently contrasting colours and character. In open space the flight is fast and direct and the white wing-patches show clearly. On the ground, the white neck-patches and pink chests make them attractive at close quarters.

Woodpigeons build bulky nests, usually in large trees, but in other respects they have now become birds of farmland as much as woods, with a more recent move to towns. It is interesting that urban birds, perhaps because of increased light and warmth, but also because of a ready supply of food at a time of shortage in the country, may breed somewhat earlier than rural birds.

Most people know, and many love, the assorted 'coos'. Some of these are associated with the impressive territory-holding display flight when, after a clatter of wings as the bird rises steeply, it glides down gently with tail spread.

> '*Coo – coo – coo*
> *It's as much as a pigeon can do,*
> *to bring up two;*
> *but the little wren can maintain ten*
> *and keep them all like gentlemen.*'
> TRADITIONAL

Stock Dove

33 cm (13 in)

SPECIES INFORMATION

SCIENTIFIC NAME	Columba oenas
RELATED SPECIES	Rock Dove, Feral Pigeon and Woodpigeon
CALL	Alarm call a short 'hru'. Song (heard as early as March) is a quiet, rapidly repeated 'gooo-roo, gooo-roo, gooo-roo'
HABITAT	Deciduous and mixed woodland and parks with old standard trees. Also in trees at field margins and orchards. Nests in holes in trees and needs open country nearby for feeding. Outside breeding season often flocks to fields
STATUS	Resident. In BI about 270,000 pairs

RESEMBLES GREY FERAL pigeon, but somewhat slimmer and with grey rump, and thin black wing bars (often not prominent). In flight, distinguished from the larger woodpigeon by narrower wings with black margins and tips, and lack of white wing-patches. Flight straight and rapid.

THESE BLUE-GREY doves easily escape notice and it is a negative feature, the absence of white on the wings, which is most distinctive. The small wing bars, grey rump and green sheen on the neck are positive things to look for. Some feral pigeons, always highly variable, can cause problems, but the pale-centred, dark-rimmed wings and grey (not white) rump are distinctive.

They are often gregarious, even in the breeding season, with flocks gathering on thinly vegetated patches in cereal fields where, if they had their way, there would be plenty of weed seeds, particularly bistorts. Recently, set-a-side has provided more habitat suitable for winter flocks.

Though stock doves rarely feed in trees, holes in trees are a favourite nest site, along with buildings and cliffs, and the occasional rabbit burrow.

When organochlorine seed dressings came in, stock dove numbers fell steeply because of their preference for newly-sown grain. The worst-hit habitats and regions were largely abandoned at the time. Conditions are still not ideal, with the loss of breeding sites in elm trees after elm disease, with fewer autumn stubbles, fewer weed seeds and the introduction of tram-lining techniques which make for a more even density of cereal crops and therefore fewer bare areas.

The stock dove had a period of range expansion in Europe in the nineteenth century when agricultural practices suited it. It did not breed in Ireland until 1877. They have an extensive range outside the Palearctic to include Siberia, central Asia and Iran, and not surprisingly many of those birds are migrants.

> 'They rose up in a twinkling cloud
> And wheeled about and bowed,
> To settle on the trees
> Perching like small clay images.
> Then with a noise of sudden rain
> They clattered off again.'
> Andrew Young THE STOCKDOVES

SIZE

IDENTIFICATION

HABITAT

POPULATION

MAP

Stubble-field with a line of trees nearby — ideal stock dove habitat.

Turtle Dove

26 cm (10 in)

SPECIES INFORMATION	
SCIENTIFIC NAME	Streptopelia turtur
RELATED SPECIES	Collared Dove
CALL	Song a soft, purring 'turrr-turrr'; alarm call a short 'ru'
HABITAT	Breeds in wooded country, orchards, and sometimes in well wooded parks and gardens. Prefers warm, dry lowland sites
STATUS	Summer visitor and passage migrant. Winters in Africa, south of Sahara. In BI about 75,000 pairs. Recent decline, perhaps due to droughts in winter quarters. Very common in Spain (about 1,000,000 pairs)

SIZE

IDENTIFICATION

HABITAT

POPULATION

MAP

OUR SMALLEST DOVE, with rather delicate build. Plumage rusty-brown, speckled wings and black and white markings at side of neck. Juveniles browner and lacking neck marking. Tail shows black feathers and white margin when spread. Flight rapid with slight rocking motion.

TURTLE DOVES ARE elegant birds, with long, rounded tails with white rim and dark patterned backs. There is a black and white neck patch, orange eye and grey cap. In flight, rapid and agile as befits a long-distance migrant, the blue-grey mid-wing panel and similar coloured rump are distinctive. The very clearly different tail rim, separating it from doves, is particularly well exposed on take-off or landing.

The turtle dove's contented 'purring' is heard so much less in the land now, and the rapid decrease has put the bird on the red list of birds of conservation concern because of a decrease of more than 50 per cent in the last 25 years. Decreases are also reported in Portugal, Belgium, Netherlands, Germany and Greece.

Apart from the shortage of weed seeds on a modern clean farm, turtle doves have long been shot, like many another migrant, on their way to Britain, and they have not always been safe when they reach here. Harting (1866) writes of them 'as timid and hard to approach but by sending some one round to the other side of the field to drive

them you may obtain a good shot as they pass over your head. They are very fair eating.

'For lo, the winter is past, the flowers appear on the earth; the time of the singing of birds is come, and the voice of the turtle is heard in our land'
THE SONG OF SOLOMON

The turtle dove is one of our prettiest summer visitors. Its song has a soft, purring quality — once learned, never forgotten.

Cuckoo
33 cm (13 in)

SLIM, WITH LONG wings and tail. In flight, cuckoos have kestrel-like shape, but markings more like sparrowhawk. Normally grey, but sometimes red-brown. Brood-parasite of smaller birds (commonly meadow pipit, reed warbler or dunnock).

CUCKOOS ARE MOST often seen flying quite fast and low over scrub or reedbed, when the long tail and long, narrow, pointed wings are distinctive. They fly with low wing-beats, interspersed with glides, spending as little time as possible in the open, and regaining cover as quickly as possible.

Cuckoos are found quite commonly throughout most of Britain and Ireland (and Europe, except for Iceland), but they are rare in Orkney and Shetland. Their range is determined mainly by the distribution of the host species which they parasitise, but also by the availability of their favourite food – hairy caterpillars, a food that most birds will not eat. The fat fox moth caterpillars on bilberry and heather are common most years on moorland, but are rejected by most birds except cuckoos. The last 20

years have seen a decline in numbers, especially in Ireland and in north-west Britain, perhaps reflecting a decline in meadow pipit numbers.

When on the look-out for a suitable host, the female cuckoo uses a tree or other convenient tall perch as a spying post. She is a patient and careful observer of her host's behaviour, especially during the breeding season, and may spend hours watching and waiting for the right moment. Once a nest has been located, she moves in quickly and stealthily to deposit a single egg into the nest, while the host bird is still in the process of completing her own clutch, but before incubation has started. A cuckoo can lay her egg in just a few seconds and be away again before the host has even detected her presence.

If a host does see a cuckoo at or near its nest, it will attack it and try to drive the cookoo away, and will also then be more likely to desert the clutch. It therefore pays the cuckoo to lay its egg very rapidly in the host's nest.

The adults begin to leave in mid-July, at a time when their young are still being cared for by their foster-parents. The young birds make their first migration a little later, in August or September, never having seen their own parents. The precise wintering grounds are not known, but most birds probably cross the Mediterranean Sea and the Sahara desert, to spend the winter months in equatorial Africa, where there are abundant supplies of insect food.

Although the biggest group of brood parasites are the cuckoos, with 47 parasitic species, about 80 species of bird (including some widow-birds and Cowbirds) depend on other species to rear their young. Worldwide there are 127 species of cuckoo, so about a third of all cuckoo species are in fact parasitic.

SIZE

IDENTIFICATION

HABITAT

POPULATION

MAP

Top and bottom right
With its sleek body, barred plumage and pointed wings, the cuckoo has a hawk- or falcon-like appearance. It is a threat to small birds, but only as a brood parasite.

Bottom left
A tree pipit feeds a cuckoo chick; the latter will soon be bigger than its exhausted foster parent!

Barn Owl

35 cm (14 in)

SPECIES INFORMATION	
SCIENTIFIC NAME	Tyto alba
RELATED SPECIES	No close relative in region
CALL	Very vocal at breeding site. Snarling and screeching sounds, such as 'khreehreehreeh'. Chicks make snoring noises
HABITAT	Mainly in open, cultivated areas; breeds in hollow trees or church towers, barns and derelict buildings
STATUS	Resident. In BI about 5,000 pairs (declining)

SIZE

IDENTIFICATION

HABITAT

POPULATION

MAP

MEDIUM-SIZED OWL with long legs, black eyes and no ear-tufts. Conspicuous pale, heart-shaped facial disc. In flight shows long, slim wings and very pale underparts. Usually seen when hunting over fields or ditches at dawn or dusk.

WITH FEWER BARNS to nest in and mercury from fungicides having possible toxic effects, barn owls are a species in decline. There were perhaps 12,000 pairs in an RSPB survey in 1930, but now there are only around 5,000.

Many are seen as 'white owls' in car lights, but there is plenty of buff in the plumage too. They are less frequently noisy than tawny owls but make eerie screeching calls. Being dependent on small mammals, numbers fluctuate. By dissecting owl pellets for bones (not an unpleasant activity) much can be learned

about the relative population densities of shrews, voles and mice around their habitat. I have only found occasional rat or bird, usually sparrow, bones in the pellets. The Barn Owl and Hawk and Owl Trusts works hard in support of the species, providing nest-boxes and information, and encouraging land owners to leave enough grassland suitable for the small mammals that they need.

Barn owls are among the most widely distributed birds in the world, even reaching Madagascar, South America and Australia. These birds have been considered in the section on farmland and open habitats section but these open habitats can be of almost any type as long as there are rodents and not too much snow.

Top right
Barn owl in classic location. These owls can seem almost ghost-like when suddenly spotted in the night.

Bottom left and right
The facial disc of the owl's face helps it to detect even the faintest of rustles as it flies in search of prey.

Little Owl

22 cm (9 in)

SPECIES INFORMATION	
SCIENTIFIC NAME	*Athene noctua*
RELATED SPECIES	*No close relative in region*
CALL	*Alarm call a loud 'kiu'. Male's territorial song is a drawn out, nasal 'gu&g'*
HABITAT	*Open country with trees, copses or hedgerows. Meadows and pasture with pollarded willows, orchards and the edges of small, open woods*
STATUS	*Resident. Absent from Ireland and north-west Britain. In B about 10,000 pairs*

SMALL, SHORT-TAILED owl with smooth crown and large yellow eyes. Flight is undulating, rather like woodpecker. Often active by day it can be seen sitting on fence posts or telegraph poles.

slightly more rational times emerged. Further introductions took place in Bedfordshire, Northamptonshire and elsewhere and by 1900 they were breeding regularly in the wild.

Little owls were greatly disliked by gamekeepers, although they pose little threat to gamebirds, feeding as they do mainly on insects, voles and mice. Nicholson (1951) reports: 'little owls are on the whole noisy birds, both by day and by night, calling to each other with a variety of notes which have little of the mysterious and unworldly quality of many owl voices'. In flight, they show 'a series of strong strokes alternating with long pauses producing a conspicuously up and down motion. When alarmed they bob comically up and down. They sit very upright.'

These birds of hedges, copse and orchards are plump, flat-headed and white eye-browed, with a plumage of two tints – a dark chocolate brown background with buffish white spots, bars and mottlings.

WHILE BARN OWLS are very good for whooping cough when made into a broth (Yorkshire) and their eggs, hard-boiled, charred and powdered do wonders for eyesight, salted little owl is very good for gout! Furthermore eating little owls will cure drunkenness, alcoholism, madness and epilepsy. Most of these gems of information came from Greenoak (1997), but a marvellous 'factoid' is reported by Robert Gibblings who had found the beetle ridden corpse of a mole. 'No doubt' he wrote 'the little owl who owned the larder was watching us, but we failed to see him. As is well known, the owls pounce on the moles when they are working near the surface, but instead of eating the body they leave it near their lair and feed on the beetles which congregate about the corpse.' Considering that little owls were only introduced in Yorkshire, from Italy, in 1842, it is surprising that they had built up such reputations in the fields of gout and drunkenness before

SIZE

IDENTIFICATION

HABITAT

POPULATION

MAP

Top right
Little owls eat a lot of insects. This one has caught a yellow-underwing moth.

Top left and bottom
They often sit bolt upright on a post or tree stump, and are frequently active by day.

Nightjar

28 cm (11 in)

○○○○○○○○○○○○○○○○○○○○○○○○○○○○
SPECIES INFORMATION	
SCIENTIFIC NAME	*Caprimulgus europaeus*
RELATED SPECIES	Red-necked Nightjar (Spain and north Africa)
CALL	Flight-call a liquid 'kuik', or when disturbed a raw 'vack'. Male's song is a continuous two-toned purring – 'errr…orrrr-errr', mainly heard in the evening
HABITAT	Heathland and light pinewoods on sandy soil. Also in thick forest with clearings or felled areas, and in dunes
STATUS	Summer visitor. Winters in tropical Africa. In B about 3,000 pairs (fewer than 30 in Ireland)

SIZE

IDENTIFICATION

HABITAT

POPULATION

MAP

SLIM, LONG-WINGED and long-tailed nocturnal bird, with flat head and large, dark eyes. Plumage highly camouflaged, with bark-like pattern. Small bill opens wide to reveal large gape, surrounded by bristles. Male has white spots on wing tips and tail. Rather cuckoo-like in flight.

A BIRD OF the summer night is the nightjar which, when well seen, shows its very small bill, white spots near the wing tips and on the outer tail feathers. Often, at dusk, it is just a silhouette or, more often, an evocative 'churr' in early succession woodland. It needs bare ground for its nest site and, perhaps because its exact needs are known, management is helping a recent increase after a long period of very little success.

Fuller, writing of the importance of young plantations for nightjars, says that they occupy a wider range of plantation ages than woodlarks, which are flourishing in plantations in Breckland. Nightjars will use restocks throughout the establishment and pre-felling stages. The highest densities are in three- to five-year-old pine, but they will use considerably older growth. In Thetford Forest and elsewhere, densities remain fairly high until at least ten years, with birds continuing to use some stands for up to 15 years. Being an aerial feeder, the nightjar is not as critically dependant on the vegetation structure for feeding as is the woodlark. Nonetheless it does need bare ground or sparse vegetation for nesting.

A bird that sounds and looks as strange as a nightjar has not surprisingly gained many names and been written about in many contexts. The Yorkshire name, gabble ratchet, or the Norfolk, scissors grinder, are typical, but why is it a corpse bird? It seems there was a belief in Nidderdale that the souls of unbaptised children went into nightjars.

> '*To hear the fern owl's cry, that whews aloft*
> *In circling whirls … she wakes her jarring noise*
> *To the unheeding waste.*'
> John Clare SELECTED POEMS

Centre

The nightjar's plumage is so cryptically patterned that the bird seems to blend into its background when sitting on the ground.

Below

The nightjar has a very wide gape, allowing it to scoop up flying insects such as moths.

Woodlark

15 cm (6 in)

<table>
</table>

○ ○

SPECIES INFORMATION

SCIENTIFIC NAME	Lullula arborea
RELATED SPECIES	Skylark
CALL	A soft, liquid 'did-loee'. Song is rather beautiful, made up of different melancholy phrases such as 'dleedlee-dleedlee-dleedlee', falling towards the end. Richly varied repertoire. Sings early in season (from February in Britain)
HABITAT	Woodland clearings in pine forests or on wooded heathland. Likes recently planted areas, with young pines
STATUS	Partial migrant. Distribution rather patchy. In B about 350 pairs (absent from Ireland)

SMALLER AND SHORTER-TAILED than the skylark. Has pale eye-stripes, meeting at nape, and black and white markings at the bend of wing. Crest rather small and rounded, often inconspicuous. Often nests near tree pipit.

THE JIZZ OF a woodlark may give it away when feeding with skylarks on winter seeds. Something about the fine bill, the short tail and the broad, rounded wings may say 'woodlark' even if their features are not analysed. Analyses might add the long white eye-stripe and black and white marks on the wrist or carpal feathers. The cheeks are rufous, and the streaky upper breast is clearly separated from white below. The wrist pattern is also clear in flight, while wing shape, hesitant flight and white end to short tail are distinctive. In song-flight it does not rise as high as does the skylark, but circles widely before spiralling in descent, or sings from a perch. Song-flight is often started from a tree-top.

Being confined to milder latitudes, woodlarks only reach the southern part of Scandinavia and there has been range retraction there as in Britain. Northern and eastern populations, like our Breckland ones, are migratory, moving into the breeding range of the southern and western populations. This migration is very inconspicuous with no large flocks.

While the French call the woodlark alouette lulu, the Germans call it Heidelerche, heath lark, and some of its strongholds here are certainly on heathland. The 1997 woodlark survey, showing a great upsurge in population, had 46 per cent of larks in heathland, 40 per cent in forestry plantation, a perverse Devon population on low intensity farmland, and a 'new' habitat where woodlarks bred on bare ground around old mine workings. When times were bad, heath fires helped the Surrey/Hampshire population in the 1970s by

providing bare ground, while the felling of Breckland conifers did the same, so the British populations rose to 400 pairs in 1981. Severe weather reduced this and a woodlark survey in 1986 found only 241 territories.

In 1997 the New Forest population, although increased to 183, was smaller than the Suffolk Breckland (457), the Suffolk coastal sandlings (245) and Norfolk (245). Woodlark populations have always fluctuated and I remember a lovely surge in breeding birds in the London area in the 1940s. There having been none in the area in 1940, they were up to 45 pairs in 1950, including a pair quite close to a main road on Putney Heath which is only about 10 km (6 miles) from St Paul's Cathedral.

If the occasional sight of a hoopoe is one reward for a southerly visit, then hearing the song of the woodlark is surely another. While the song is as always impossible to describe, Kightly *et al* (1998) attempts this: 'song outstanding for its clarity and sweetness, comprises short fluty phrases; dilee – dilee – , lu – lu – lu; may last several minutes but sound seems to come and go'. The 'lu lu lu' part is adapted by the French who call the bird lulu.

SIZE

IDENTIFICATION

HABITAT

POPULATION

MAP

The woodlark is a much daintier bird than the skylark, and is associated with lowland heath and forestry clearings.

Skylark

16 cm (6.5 in)

SPECIES INFORMATION

SCIENTIFIC NAME	*Alauda arvensis*
RELATED SPECIES	Woodlark
CALL	Flight-call a pleasant 'chree' or 'chreeoo'. Song, usually delivered in vertical song-flight, is a long-lasting, almost continuous mixture of trills and whistles
HABITAT	Open country, especially agricultural fields and pasture, meadows and downland
STATUS	Resident and partial migrant. In BI about 2,500,000 pairs

SIZE

IDENTIFICATION

HABITAT

POPULATION

MAP

COMMON LARGE LARK of open country, with camouflaged plumage and small crest. Trailing edges of wings and outer tail feathers white.

THE SONG AND SONG-FLIGHT of the lark seem to tempt the poets to verse more even than the song of the nightingale, but the skylark got an equally abundant press from those who have revelled in trapping and eating them.

The decline of he skylark, highlighted by surveys by BTO volunteers, has been the stimulus for

much research into the birds of farmland, especially by the BTO and RSPB. Using Common Birds Census data it was evident that declines in coastal and upland habitats had not been as great as on farmland. The timing of the farmland decline coincided with agricultural intensification, with big changes in winter feeding opportunities. A set-aside survey showed plenty of larks there, as well as on stubble and saltmarsh, but in winter-wheat the numbers of larks decreased as winter went on. The Breeding Bird Survey is beginning to produce vital habitat data for skylarks, with more larks where farms are more diverse. Recently surveys have shown worrying declines in upland areas too, and the reasons for this are still far from clear.

Nicholson (1957) writes that 'skylarks, when they are not on the wing, like to have their feet firmly on the ground, and are remarkable among passerine birds in not only refusing to perch on trees

Bottom right
Skylark atop a post. Note the obvious crest.

Top left
A skylark returns to its nest which is hidden amongst the long grass.

but in usually keeping a good distance away from them.' He goes on to mention the great flocking and migratory movements of larks. 'Their flight on such journeys is dogged but purposeful, with spasms of wing flapping interrupted by longish rests. When flying about the fields the action is quite different from either the song flight or the migratory flight and the broad triangular sail shaped wings are fluttered as if their power were an embarrassment in the short, slow, deliberate flights which often seem to serve for patrolling and looking round.'

On migration flights and in the fields they produce a constant 'chirrup' call. Their movements do not take them that far, for few winter far south of the Mediterranean, while many make no more than local movements.

'We have great plenty of larkes and very good ones especially in those parts adjoyning to Coteswold. They take them by alluring them with a dareing glass which is whirled about in a sun shining day, and the larkes are pleased at it, ass at a sheepe's eye, and at that time the net is drawn over them' writes Aubrey in 1847 in the Natural History of Wiltshire. Greenoak (1998) mentions that the song 'Allouette, gentille allouette' goes into great details about plucking the birds and the saying 'the land where larks fall ready rosted' would be equivalent of land flowing in milk and honey.

> *'And still the singing skylark soared*
> *And silent sank and soared to sing.'*
> Christina Rosetti SKYLARK

SPECIES INFORMATION

SCIENTIFIC NAME	*Anthus trivialis*
RELATED SPECIES	Meadow Pipit, Rock Pipit
CALL	When flushed 'psee' or 'tsitt', often repeated. Song louder and more musical than meadow pipit's, with long canary-like phrases. Usually sings in parachuting display-flight from and returning to a perch in a tree
HABITAT	Heath with scattered trees and bushes. Also margins of broadleaved and coniferous forest, and in clearings
STATUS	Summer visitor. In B about 120,000 pairs (virtually absent from Ireland)

Tree Pipit
15 cm (6 in)

Tree pipits breed up to the Arctic fringes and south until conditions became too dry. It is a summer visitor to Europe, wintering in Africa, west as far south as the equatorial rain forest and in the east as far south as Natal.

SLIM, WITH YELLOWISH breast and neck, streaked heavily with dark brown. Legs reddish. Slightly larger and paler than Meadow Pipit.

TREE PIPITS LIKE trees rather than woods, but woodland fringes and young forestry plantations are as acceptable as scattered birches and pines on heathland. In two of the places I have known Tree pipits best, an English railway embankment and an open field in north Wales, they have used telegraph wires as the base from which to launch themselves into their song flight which, though beautiful and distinctive, is impossible to describe. Kightley *et al* (1998) attempts it with 'cheery song is much stronger than meadow's; opens like a chaffinch and concludes with terminal flourish: seeurr – seeurr – seeurr – seeurr'.

Tree pipits have large territories, 1.5 ha (3.7 acres) in one study, within which the nest, a cup of dry grass stems, is made either on the ground or in low cover.

> '*Its a pity pipits have*
> *No diagnostic features*
> *Specifically they are the least*
> *Distinctive of God's creatures.*'
> BULLETIN OF THE BRITISH MUSEUM

SIZE

IDENTIFICATION

HABITAT

POPULATION

MAP

Top
The tree pipit is slim and graceful, with paler plumage than the meadow pipit, and a much more tuneful song.

Bottom
A tree pipit brings home a juicy grub for its brood.

Swallow

18 cm (7 in)

SPECIES INFORMATION

SCIENTIFIC NAME	Hirundo rustica
RELATED SPECIES	House Martin, Sand Martin
CALL	Flight-call 'vid-vid' or 'tsi-dit', often repeated. Song is a pleasant twittering and warbling
HABITAT	Open countryside, villages and farms. May flock in wetlands on migration
STATUS	Summer visitor, wintering in Africa. In BI about 800,000 pairs

SIZE

IDENTIFICATION

HABITAT

POPULATION

MAP

SLIM AND ELEGANT, with long tail streamers. Metallic blue above, with red-brown chin and forehead. Juveniles less brightly coloured and with shorter tail streamers. Flight rapid, and rather more direct than the house martin's and often feeds at low level. Its nest is a mud half-cup.

SWALLOWS ARE MANY people's idea of the country bird and the essence of summer. Where there is warmth, insects and somewhere to nest swallows are to be found, showing their long wings and forked tails in flight. Perched on telephone wires the chestnut-red throat and forehead, dark chest-band and pinkish belly are clear.

Swallows are extensive migrants, even if a few winter in southern Spain. Ronald Hickling (1983) says how the swallow has always been an especial favourite of ringers. Its nests in farm buildings are easy to discover and are readily accessible; large numbers of nestlings can thus be ringed with little effort. In addition, the mist-net has enabled many swallows to be ringed at their autumn roosts, when for brief periods enormous numbers gather nightly in reedbeds. By the end of 1980 over three quarters of a million had been ringed. The recovery rate of birds from their winter quarters

in southern Africa has also been gratifyingly high. Few recoveries can have caused such excitement as the first swallow found in South Africa. It was caught in a farmhouse at Utrecht, Natal, on 27 December 1911, 18 months after being ringed as a nesting adult. Autumn recoveries of British ringed swallows have ranged from western France, eastern Spain, the Straits of Gibraltar and in Nigeria, en route to South Africa.

Swallows begin their return flight in February, and by mid-April they will be back taking their flying prey after aerial pursuit in characteristic swoops and sweeps. Just as welcome will be their chattering warble of a song and 'witt witt' call in flight. By the end of April they will be laying in their cupped mud pellet and feather nests set on a beam or window ledge and as they brake, by spreading their tail, on approach to the nest they show the white spots on the tail. Usually there will be a second brood with the young birds recognisable by their shorter tail streamers, patchy breast-band and altogether duller plumage.

> 'Sister, my sister, O fleet, sweet swallow
> Thy way is long to the sun and the south.'
> Swinburne ITYLUS

Top right
Swallows build a cup nest of mud and feathers, usually inside a barn or similar outbuilding.

Bottom
A young swallow begs for food on a twig.

Yellow Wagtail

17 cm (6.5 in)

THE YELLOW WAGTAIL (1950) was the first of the *New Naturalist* monographs on birds and arose from a seven-year study of 'this attractive species, so lovely to look upon, and so full of a dainty and buoyant airiness of stance and flight' along a strip of so called green belt, the vegetable plots of the market garden country flanking the Mersey south of Manchester.

'THE COCK YELLOW wagtail is an extremely handsome bird, and when it first arrives in the spring is a joy to see. It has a bright yellow head, with crown and ear coverts more or less greenish, through there are wide variations in the plumage of the head ....There is an eye stripe which is yellow, while the chin and throat are a bright yellow which extends down and under the belly. Certain cocks however, especially those which have not completed the spring moult, may appear so poorly coloured as to resemble hens.'

This species shows some of the most marked and complex colour variations among a European species. Such variation involves the use of subspecific or trinomial names because male birds from the different areas are distinctive. Some might argue that

they should therefore be different species, but there are zones of hybridisation and therefore it is best to consider the Yellow Wagtail a polytypic species. Yellow Wagtail (*M. flava flavissima*), the British race, has yellow-green upperparts and yellow stripe above eye. Blue-headed wagtail (*M. flava flava*), the central European race, has slate-grey head and white stripe above eye; female somewhat duller with somewhat brownish head. The blue-headed occurs in a band

through temperate Europe, the grey-headed (*M. f. thunbergi*) is found to the north, and the black-headed (*M. f. feldegg*) to the south-east.

For a summer visitor with such an extensive northern range there are different winter quarters, but our birds head for African tropics and, like moving skylarks or tree pipits, can often be heard overhead as they tend to move by day, making a drawn out 'tsweep' which many find difficult to distinguish from the call of pied or grey wagtails.

All wagtails are insectivorous, and yellow wagtails collect their insect food from the ground when walking (often among cattle) or by more rapid pursuit, or by short flycatching flights. Although half yellow wagtail nests are by water, where insect food is often abundant, I have known Midland populations on sandy fields growing sugar-beet.

The reliance of yellow wagtails on insect food has made then vulnerable to the instensification of British farming, especially the improvement and reduction of pasture.

SIZE

IDENTIFICATION

HABITAT

POPULATION

MAP

Top left
The Somerset Levels – these wet meadows are good habitat for yellow wagtails.

Top right and bottom
The yellow wagtail is pure yellow underneath, greenish grey above.

BIRD SPECIES

Fieldfare

26 cm (10 in)

SIZE

IDENTIFICATION

HABITAT

POPULATION

MAP

○○○○○○○○○○○○○○○○○○○○○○○○○○○○○

SPECIES INFORMATION

SCIENTIFIC NAME	*Turdus pilaris*
RELATED SPECIES	Redwing, Blackbird, Song Thrush, Mistle Thrush
CALL	Flight-call a loud, raw chatter: 'shack-shack-shack'. Song fairly quiet warbling and twittering, often given in flight
HABITAT	Mountain forests, tundra also and tall trees in parks. In winter flocks to open fields, farmland and occasionally gardens
STATUS	Winter visitor (some breed). In B about 20 pairs, mainly in the north (absent from Ireland)

CHESTNUT BACK AND wings, grey head and rump and black tail. In flight shows contrast between black tail, light grey rump and white lower wing coverts.

FIELDFARES HAVE GREY heads and rumps and dark tails. The typical thrush speckling is darker on the upper breast. Being large and bold and constantly noisy with their 'chack chack chacking' they are part of many winter county walks. The flight can be described as 'noticeably loose and leisurely with bursts of wing beats alternating with brief glides on extended wings'.

Their Anglo Saxon name 'Felde Fare' makes them travellers over fields, and pasture and open fields are certainly their favourite winter feeding grounds.

By contrast with the noisy colonies of the northern birch and pine forests

Fieldfares are partial to apples, and they sometimes come into gardens to feed during frosty weather. Redwings take a range of berries in the winter; a flock can strip a holly tree in just a few days.

David Snow in the *New Atlas* writes that 'isolated breeding pairs, as all those recorded so far in Britain have been, are much less easy to find. The song a feeble warble interrupted by wheezes and chuckles, is of little help for it is not persistent or audible from afar. Also, in late spring, pairs tend to wander, presumably in search of a suitable nesting area.' He suggests that the breeding population over the years of the Atlas might be 25 pairs, scattered widely.

In winter there might be a million birds here, but where they will be depends on the stage of winter and the weather, with a tendency for these highly mobile and nomadic birds to move further south later and in cold weather. Ringing recoveries in Italy and Spain, of birds ringed here, show possible alternative destinations. No doubt such large numbers of a large bird make great inroads into food supplies, and it is tragic that so many hedges are flailed so frequently so that no berries have a chance to appear or to survive. As ground feeders for much of the time, however, they seek out a wide range of invertebrates, turning over small stones in their search.

Redwing

21 cm (8.5 in)

S LIGHTLY SMALLER AND darker than Song Thrush, and with whitish stripe over eye, red-brown flanks, and streaked, not spotted breast. In flight shows the red-brown under wing coverts.

THE REDWING'S VERSION of thrush plumage involves parallel rows of dark streaks on the breast. Its underwing is red in flight and this colour shows as rusty flanks as the bird devours holly berries or is tempted into gardens by fallen apples. Given the opportunity redwings are also great worm eaters. Their high pitched call as they migrate overhead at night is frequent in October but also around the hedges and fields throughout the winter, and particularly when they plunge suddenly into roosting quarters.

The winter range of redwings is from only just outside the western Palearctic to the east of the Black Sea so birds from eastern Siberian have long, 6,500 km (4,000 miles), south-westerly flights but European birds have relatively short movements. As with fieldfare ringing returns show little fidelity to one wintering area, with British-ringed birds appearing in subsequent winters in Italy and Greece.

Whereas singing fieldfares are inconspicuous, the song of the redwing is rather more distinctive and penetrating. It consists of a series of four to seven, but most commonly five, descending, fluted notes of such tone and volume as to be clearly audible at a considerable distance.

The first British nest record is from Sutherland in 1925. There were breeding records in only 17 of the next 41 years, but with 20 pairs in Wester Ross in 1968 a firm foothold was established. Fluctuations followed, with many nesting in remote parts.

SIZE

IDENTIFICATION

HABITAT

POPULATION

MAP

You will be able to sight redwings on clear October nights and hear them call as they migrate south.

Stonechat

12.5 cm (5 in)

SPECIES INFORMATION

SCIENTIFIC NAME	Saxicola torquata
RELATED SPECIES	Whinchat
CALL	Scratchy 'trat'. Song is a short, hurried phrase with coarse, rattling and whistled notes, sometimes in short, dancing song-flight
HABITAT	Open, stoney country; heaths, especially those with gorse or broom; raised bogs and pasture; to 1,400 m (4,593 ft) in mountains
STATUS	Resident and partial migrant. In BI about 20,000 pairs

SIZE

IDENTIFICATION

HABITAT

POPULATION

MAP

M ALE IS DARK above, with black throat, white half-collar and orange belly. Female and juvenile paler, but still with dark head and ruddy colour below. Often sits at top of bush. Flight low and jerky.

Scotland, which were attributed to habitat loss, disturbance on the marginal, gorse-clad land beloved of stonechats and the growing maturity of many forestry plantations, colonised when the plantations were young.

On breeding territories, where gorse and bare patches are often favoured, males make distinctive song-flights, with brief hovers, involving a dunnock-like variable rattle. The nest is sited near to the ground in thick vegetation and is a loose cup of grass and leaves. Fledging success is often remarkably high, up to 80 per cent, and with two broods and a clutch size of four to six, stonechat populations can increase rapidly. Gorse-covered cliffs on the Lleyn Peninsula of north Wales can seem delightfully alive with young stonechats.

THE WHITE WING-flash and the constant twitching of wings and tail are very distinctive. Females, and males in winter until they have worn away the brownish new feather tips, are duller, with the female's head grey-brown rather then black. Young stonechats are robin-like with a hint of rufous, and pale flecks on the back. The call, aptly and frequently likened to two stones being struck together, greets your approach, as birds move from perch to perch on rapidly whirring broad wings.

The stonechat has a markedly western and coastal distribution reflecting areas with the mildest winters and least habitat change, but even parts which rarely expect freezing conditions can suffer. The stonechat population of Cape Clear in County Cork was between 50 and 150 pairs in 1961, but was down to three pairs in 1963 after two really cold winters. Fortunately stonechats are resilient, and there were 33 pairs by 1967. By the time of the *New Atlas* the breeding range had retracted enormously, with many losses in Ireland, the south-west and southern and eastern

Stonechats like to perch in a prominent position — for example at the very top of a gorse bush.

SPECIES INFORMATION	
SCIENTIFIC NAME	*Saxicola rubetra*
RELATED SPECIES	Stonechat
CALL	Hard, very short 'tek-tek' or 'tsek-tsek'. Song is a mixture of short, hurried phrases made up of scratchy, warbling and fluting notes; includes mimicry
HABITAT	Open bushy meadows and wasteland. Often near wet habitats, but also on dry heath
STATUS	Summer visitor. In BI about 20,000 pairs

Whinchat

12.5 cm (5 in)

 SIZE

 IDENTIFICATION

 HABITAT

 POPULATION

 MAP

SQUAT AND SHORT-TAILED. Male has white stripe above eye, paler in female. Male dark above, with orangey breast.

WHINCHAT MALES WITH their streaked brown upperparts, reddish underparts and dark face are attractive. The white eye-stripe and white sides at the base of the tail are more useful in identification as they are shared by female and young. The upright posture, short tail and sharp call are typical of chats, as is its pleasant warble. Breeding whinchats perch and dart, often among bracken, in open country, while on passage they may turn up in cereal fields and coastal marshes.

Whinchats are slimmer than stonechats, with whom they often share coastal and upland habitats, and females of the two could be mistaken, but the stonechat is darker and the whinchat has the eye-stripe. Young birds, too, are paler than stonechats. The diet of the two species, mainly invertebrates, is much the same.

Unlike stonechats, whinchats are long-distance migrants, moving from a wide area of northern and central Europe to winter in Africa, with many birds crossing the Sahara to Senegal, Nigeria and Uganda.

Top
The whinchat enjoys a diet of insects and their larvae, together with spiders and worms.

Bottom
The bold eyestripe helps to distinguish the whinchat from the rather similar stonechat.

173

Whitethroat

14 cm (5.5 in)

SIZE

IDENTIFICATION

HABITAT

POPULATION

MAP

LIVELY WARBLER WITH white throat, grey head and back and chestnut wings. Relatively long tail with white outer feathers. Narrow white eye-ring. Female drabber, with brownish head.

WHITETHROATS ARE CLASSIC hedge and scrub birds. Their jerky display flight and urgent chatter can also be found in early successional stages of woodland. The male's rich rusty back and ashy head contrast with the white throat; the female is browner. The longer tail, more slender build and white outer tail feathers, which are common to both sexes, distinguish the autumn male, the females and the young from the garden warbler. During the summer the male whitethroat has a delicate pink suffusion overlaying his buffish breast and flanks, but a few females may display some pink as well. The bill is brownish-grey and the feet and legs a paler brown.

Whitethoat populations are strongly influenced by conditions in their African wintering grounds – the Sahel region to the south of the Sahara Desert. Numbers fell markedly in 1969, and have fluctuated since, but at a lower general level.

As extensive migrants, 'falls' are a feature at many bird observatories and much pioneering work on navigation was carried out on this and other *Sylvia* warblers, showing that nocturnal migrants depend partly on the stars, and establishing the concept of a 'star compass'.

> '*And after April, when May follows*
> *And the whitethroat builds, and all the*
> *swallow …*'
> Robert Browning
> HOME THOUGHTS FROM ABROAD

Top
This whitethroat, perched in the open, clearly displays its pure white throat.

Bottom
A whitethroat pours out its chattering song, throat distended.

Lesser Whitethroat

13.5 cm (5 in)

SPECIES INFORMATION

SCIENTIFIC NAME	*Sylvia curruca*
RELATED SPECIES	Whitethroat, Dartford Warbler, Blackcap, Garden Warbler
CALL	'Tjeck' and, when alarmed, an irregularly repeated 'tack'. Song is in two parts: a quiet, hurried warble, followed by a loud rattle all on one note. From a distance, only the second section is audible
HABITAT	Scrub, hedgerows and bushes and hedges in larger gardens
STATUS	Summer visitor. In B about 80,000 pairs (virtually absent from Ireland)

SLIGHTLY SMALLER THAN whitethroat, and without chestnut on wings. Has indistinct mask-like dark cheeks, contrasting with white chin, and a relatively short tail.

Naturally occurring examples of this habitat are largely confined to chalk grassland scrub. They like taller and more scrubby hedges than whitethroats, and can be found occasionally in hedges in larger gardens and parks.

LESSER WHITETHROATS ARE greyer with dark cheeks and no rusty wings. They are noticeably smaller and more compact than whitethroats and the sexes are similar, with shorter white-edged tails. Their 'tuks' and 'churrs' among a variety of scolding calls are not that different from whitethroat but their rattling song, somewhat like an unfinished yellowhammer's, is their best identification feature. Once known you will find lesser whitethroats more common than you perhaps thought.

Their habitat is overgrown railway embankments, hedgerows and scrub; they may also be found in such places as disused mineral workings, and even derelict industrial sites.

'A rare, and I think a new little bird, frequents my garden. This bird much resembles the whitethroat but has a more white silvery breast and belly; is restless and active, like the willow wrens and hops from bough to bough examining every part for food.'
Gilbert White
NATURAL HISTORY OF SELBORNE

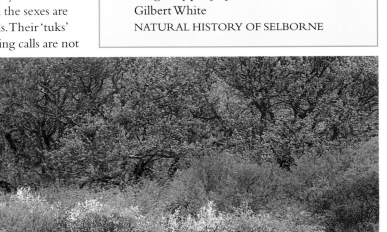

SIZE

IDENTIFICATION

HABITAT

POPULATION

MAP

Top right and left
Lesser whitethroats tend to be more secretive than whitethroats, and they often stay hidden in the foliage.

Bottom
Habitats such as this old hedge are favoured by lesser whitethroats.

Dartford Warbler

13 cm (5 in)

SPECIES INFORMATION	
SCIENTIFIC NAME	Sylvia undata
RELATED SPECIES	Whitethroat, Lesser Whitethroat, Blackcap, Garden Warbler
CALL	Call 'tchairr'. Song is a short, scratchy warble, from bush-top or flight
HABITAT	Heath and scrub, especially with gorse
STATUS	Resident. In B about 900 pairs in southern England (absent from Ireland)

SIZE

IDENTIFICATION

HABITAT

POPULATION

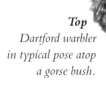

MAP

SMALL, LIVELY WARBLER, with dark plumage. Slate-blue above and brown-maroon below. Tail is long and often held cocked; wings are rather short. Red eye-ring.

FEMALES ARE PALER above and less chestnut, more buff, below. Its short scratching warble and drawn out alarm calls can often be heard when the elusive bird cannot be seen; it may even be down on the ground looking for invertebrate prey. The nest, a compact cup, will also be in deep cover and made up of grass, leaves and stems, and often some heather.

The Dartford warbler is the classic bird of southern heathland, and is therefore included here, even though it is rather rare. Such mature heath habitat is in short supply, with constant pressure to burn off this element of the vegetation at a greater rate than it is replaced. Uncontrolled burning kills individual animals, or flushes them from refuges, after which they can be picked off by predators (notably kestrels and buzzards). Grazing widely checks gorse regeneration, and trampling by livestock also damages mature heath.

Although Cetti's and a growing number of blackcaps and chiffchaffs overwinter in Britain, Dartford warblers have, historically, been the only warbler to remain in Britain throughout the winter.

Their food is mainly beetles, spiders, lepidopterous larvae and bugs, with nestlings fed on large spiders and caterpillars mainly caught among gorse.

Top
Dartford warbler in typical pose atop a gorse bush.

Bottom
Shades of maroon and blue-grey characterise the male Dartford warbler in breeding plumage. Also prominent is the bright red eye-ring.

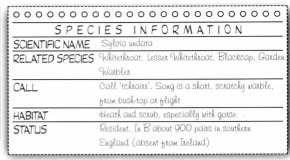

Whereas Dartford warblers breed in areas with July temperatures up to 30°C (86°F) and above, they barely survive if January temperatures fall below an average of 4°C (39°F). They are therefore limited to the maritime areas of France, as well as being on the extreme of their range in Britain.

W. H. Hudson, writing early in the century, describes the Dartford warbler: 'To some who have glanced at a little dusty, out of shape mummy of a bird, labelled "Dartford warbler", in a museum, or private collection, or under a glass shade, it may seem that I speak too warmly of the pleasure which the sight of the small furze lover can give us. He is of the type of the whitethroat, but idealised; .... A sprite-like bird in his slender exquisite shape and his beautiful fits of excitement, fantastic in his motions as he flits and flies from spray to spray, now hovering motionless in the air like the wooing goldcrest, anon dropping on a perch, to sit jerking his long tail, his crest raised, his throat swollen, chiding when he sings and singing when he chides, like a refined and lesser sedge warbler in a frenzy, his slate black and chestnut plumage showing rich and dark against the pure and luminous yellow of the massed furze blossoms. It is a sight of fairy-like bird life and of flower which cannot soon be forgotten.'

Grasshopper Warbler

13 cm (5 in)

SMALL, OLIVE-BROWN, streaked above, and with narrow, rounded tail. Underside pale, weakly striped, frequently identified by its song.

MORE OFTEN HEARD than seen, grasshopper warblers tend to skulk in thick undergrowth, except when singing, when they usually perch on the very top of a bush or thicket. Even then they can be difficult to pick out as their song is difficult to pinpoint. The ventriloquist's effect is increased as the singing bird moves its head from side to side. This serves to broadcast its territorial song and to make it less easy for a predator to locate.

Rook

45 cm (18 in)

BLACK, WITH PALE bill and bare grey bill-base, and steep, angled forehead. Belly and thigh feathers tend to be loose, giving trousered effect. Nests colonially and often flocks.

NOWADAYS ROOKS ARE most familiar to many as scavengers along motorway verges and roadsides. They will take a wide range of food, like most members of the crow family, and they often feed in open fields.

Back in 1866 Harting wrote that 'we should not be too hasty in condemning them ... for during the year they destroy innumerable quantities of slugs, snails, worms, beetles and grubs. And when we reflect upon the ravages committed by a single species, the wire-worm, which is greedily devoured by rooks, we can hardly fail to arrive at the conclusion that the amount of evil committed on the one hand is counterbalanced by the good rendered on the other.'

Rooks are real specialists at extracting invertebrates from below the soil surface, digging with the bill and probing deep in the ground. Their noisy rookeries have always fascinated the country observer.

Tree Sparrow

14 cm (5.5 in)

SIZE

IDENTIFICATION

HABITAT

POPULATION

MAP

SPECIES INFORMATION	
SCIENTIFIC NAME	Passer montanus
RELATED SPECIES	House Sparrow
CALL	Flight-call a hard 'tek-tek-tek'. Song similar to house sparrow's, but shorter
HABITAT	Less dependent on houses and people than house sparrow. Breeds in open country with hedges, copses and orchards, in parks and at edges of towns and villages
STATUS	Resident. In BI about 285,000 pairs

SOMEWHAT SMALLER and slimmer than House Sparrow, and with brighter plumage. Chestnut crown and nape, black spot on white cheek, and small black chin spot. Juvenile has grey-brown head and dark grey chin.

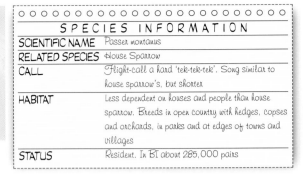

THE BROWN CROWN and black cheek spot of the tree sparrow separate it from its commoner relative, and its sharp flight note is often the first indication that it is around. Many of us have treated it like the stock dove as a bird 'that is around somewhere' in the farming landscape and, but for routine monitoring of its numbers by the band of farmland Common Birds Census workers, we might not have realised that the population has actually fallen by a staggering 89 per cent in the last 25 years.

Old orchards, willows, hedgerow trees with holes, quarries and outbuildings all provide possible nest sites. Elm disease and the subsequent death and felling of the trees may have reduced the numbers of breeding holes, but reduced food supply seems to be the main cause of their decline.

The key features of the tree sparrow are the chestnut brown crown and the black spot on a white cheek.

They mainly feed on the ground, favouring seeds of small weeds At all times feeding tends to be in groups. Colonial nesting groups may disappear suddenly for no apparent reason. Out of the breeding season, tree sparrows mix with other finches and are highly mobile in their search for suitable food. Perhaps it is this mobility, following a build–up of continental populations, that occasionally boosts our numbers.

```
○ ○ ○ ○ ○ ○ ○ ○ ○ ○ ○ ○ ○ ○ ○ ○ ○ ○ ○ ○ ○ ○
```
SPECIES INFORMATION	
SCIENTIFIC NAME	Fringilla montifringilla
RELATED SPECIES	Chaffinch
CALL	A rather wheezy 'eeekp'. Song is a soft combination of greenfinch-like calls and rattling sounds
HABITAT	Breeds in northern birch woods and coniferous forests. In winter often in large flocks to fields and under beech trees
STATUS	Irregular winter visitor. In BI a handful of pairs breed, usually in Scotland (absent from Ireland)

Brambling

15 cm (6 in)

BREEDING MALE HAS black back, head and bill, with orange breast and shoulders. In winter male loses most of black. Female has grey cheeks, black streaks on crown and brown back. Shows white rump in flight and has less obvious wing bar than chaffinch.

THE BRAMBLING IS one of the most migratory of finches, and over much of Europe is entirely a winter visitor. In a mixed flock it can be distinguished from the chaffinch by its white rump, darker patterned head, tortoiseshell shoulders and scaly black back as well as by distinctive wheezing call notes. The females are paler, with buff grey heads, and young birds are paler still. Tail is shorter and more forked than chaffinch's.

In the birch woods of northern Europe, the brambling is usually the commonest bird after the willow warbler. It is strongly territorial, but where chaffinch and brambling overlap there is not interspecific territorial aggression. Under ideal conditions bramblings may breed at densities of 50 per square kilometre. Breeding densities fluctuate, as do in turn the winter populations in Britain. If the bramblings have bred well, feeding their young on insects, and then the tree crops fail there are enormous irruptions, as opposed to the regular brambling migrations.

Wintering bramblings feed very largely on beech-mast. This is only used by chaffinches if they chance upon it, but bramblings roam in search of it. The brambling here is more of a specialist, for it can open the nuts more easily with a bill that is one tenth deeper and has sharper edges than the chaffinch's.

Bramblings have established a tenuous foothold in Britain, with ten or so proven records of breeding in Scotland, and a scattering of singing males have been heard down the east of the country.

SIZE

IDENTIFICATION

HABITAT

POPULATION

MAP

A beechwood in winter — typical brambling country, if the beechmast crop has been good.

Goldfinch

12 cm (4.75 in)

○○○○○○○○○○○○○○○○○○○○○○○○○
SPECIES INFORMATION
SCIENTIFIC NAME	Carduelis carduelis
RELATED SPECIES	Linnet, Greenfinch, Siskin, Twite, Redpoll
CALL	High-pitched 'deed-lit'. Song is a high-pitched rapid twitter
HABITAT	Parks, orchards, hedgerows, gardens and cultivated fields. Often feeds on thistles
STATUS	Resident. In BI about 300,000 pairs

SIZE

IDENTIFICATION

HABITAT

POPULATION

MAP

COLOURFUL, SMALL FINCH with black and yellow wings and red face. Juveniles lack head colours, but do have the characteristic yellow wing bars.

THE GOLD OF the name shows on birds of all ages, with the shining panel along the centre of the black wing, but the head pattern is, perhaps, even more striking with near vertical bands of red, white and black. The back and tail have three bands too; brown back, whitish rump and black tail with white spots. Young birds have plain faces and lack the white tips to the tertials and primaries that feature on the adults. The pointed bill enables the bird to feed off its favourite seeds, such as those of thistles and teasel.

Nicholson writes: 'They further recommend themselves by their fondness for feeding on the seeds of the thistle, groundsel, knapweed and other plants objectionable to both the farmer and the gardener.' It is interesting to see how he saw the future of farming:- 'Greater use of science, improved equipment and education and

The goldfinch must be one of our prettiest birds, but they seldom keep still long enough for one to appreciate their plumage.

higher prices make for more intensive farming and may be expected to involve more wholesale eradication of weeds and the diminution of waste patches, banks and even hedges on many farms. The ploughing and reseeding of grassland aims at results which will leave little food for birds such as goldfinches.'

In fact goldfinches have not done badly, perhaps because of their flexibility. As an alternative to weed seeds they join siskins and redpolls among the birch and alder seeds and recently they have become more ready to use garden feeders in time of need. In addition if conditions become difficult, particularly in response to cold, a large part of the population may move south-west.

Many European devotional paintings include goldfinches, which are apparently a symbol of fertility and healing powers.

'Who can stay indoors when the goldfinches are busy among the bloom on the apple trees? A flood of sunshine falling through a roof of rosy pink and delicate white blossom overhead; underneath, grass deeply green with the vigour of spring, dotted with yellow buttercups and strewn with bloom shaken by the wind from the trees. Listen how happy the goldfinches are in the orchard. Summer after summer they build in the same trees, bushy – headed codlings; generation and generation has been born there and gone forth to enjoy in turn the pleasures of the field.'

Linnet

14 cm (5.5 in)

MAINLY BROWN, ACTIVE finch. Breeding male has red forehead and breast; duller in winter with no red on head. Female lacks red, is streaked and dark brown above. Juvenile more heavily streaked. Often forms flocks in open country outside breeding season.

IT IS EASY TO take linnets for granted and they are often overlooked, perhaps because they are nearly always on the move. Seen close, they are attractive, especially a male in full breeding plumage.

Although linnets are found over most of lowland Britain, but more scattered in Ireland, the abundance map in the *New Atlas* shows a marked coastal bias, particularly along the east.

'Over the years' as Newton (1998) reports 'herbicide use has enormously reduced the populations of various farmland weeds, on which many seed-eating birds depend and once common arable weeds have now become rare in lowland

Britain. Each application of herbicide depletes the soil's seed bank with seeds turned to the surface being killed before producing seeds. Linnets thrive on fat-hen, persicaria and chickweed which could at one time be counted in thousands per square metre on newly turned farmland soil whereas now, after years of herbicide use, they have almost disappeared from the soil of cereal growing regions.'

SIZE

IDENTIFICATION

HABITAT

POPULATION

MAP

Top left
Cock linnet in full breeding plumage.

Top right
Gorse scrub and woodland edge in Dorset – excellent habitat for linnets.

Bottom
Feeding a nest of young linnets.

Yellowhammer

16 cm (6.5 in)

SPECIES INFORMATION	
SCIENTIFIC NAME	Emberiza citrinella
RELATED SPECIES	Cirl Bunting, Reed Bunting
CALL	Call 'tsik'. Song is a short, melancholy phrase with final syllable at lower pitch – 'tsi-tsi-tsi-tsi-tsi-tsi-tsi-tsi-duh'
HABITAT	Heath, open country with hedgerows, copses, bushy woodland margins
STATUS	Resident. In BI about 1,400,000 pairs

SIZE

IDENTIFICATION

HABITAT

POPULATION

MAP

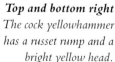

SLIM, YELLOW-HEADED bunting with long tail and cinnamon-brown rump. Female and juvenile less yellow, with dark streaks on head and throat. White outer tail feathers obvious in flight.

THE BRIGHT YELLOW head of the breeding male is what people think of in the plumage of yellowhammers, but the chestnut rump and long, white-edged tail are equally distinctive. Females and non breeding males are duller but yellow on head and streaky belly can usually identify, although some first winter females are rather nondescript.

In Gaelic, the yellowhammer is the yellow broom bird and the association between yellowhammers and gorse or broom is close, even if the development of farming with tall hedges and scruffy patches of scrub helped it to spread originally. Now its world is changing again and like the linnet it no longer has the food supply it used to have.

Nicholson (1951) writes that 'those who go about with their eyes open find themselves constantly crossing invisible lines on one side of which there are plenty of yellowhammers and on the other few or none. These lines are less distinct than those bounding the tribes of corn buntings, for the cock yellowhammer, although conspicuous in plumage, is less dominating in voice and in choice of singing posts, and is moreover sufficiently widespread and common to be easily taken for granted unless the observer takes the trouble to notice where yellowhammers are not as well as where they are.'

Top and bottom right
The cock yellowhammer has a russet rump and a bright yellow head.

Bottom left
The female, here at its nest, is much less brightly coloured.

He then gives same examples of these 'invisible lines' and is once again ahead of his time in stressing the value of negative records, and in setting up a problem for investigation. As we get to know more of the ecology of individual species we are more able to explain declines and to help to bring about recoveries.

Everyone knows the common rendering of the yellowhammer's song: 'a little bit of bread and no cheese', but in Scotland this is said to be rendered as 'may the devil take you'.

Apart from the song, the common contact call, given in flight or perched, is particularly useful to us when birds feed in mixed winter flocks.

Most populations are partial migrants, with part of the north of its range being vacated and wintering birds moving to northern Spain, Italy and Greece. British birds though are largely sedentary, few moving more than 5 km (3 miles). The few ringing recoveries indicate passage of a few Scandinavian birds along the east coast in spring and autumn.

'*In early spring when winds blow chilly cold*
The yellow hammer trailing grass will come
To fix a place and choose an early home
With yellow breast and head of solid gold.'
John Clare SELECTED POEMS

Corn Bunting

18 cm (7 in)

SPECIES INFORMATION

SCIENTIFIC NAME	*Miliaria calandra*
RELATED SPECIES	Yellowhammer, Reed Bunting, Cirl Bunting
CALL	Flight-call a sharp 'tick'. Song consists of short clicking notes which run together, ending in a tinkling final section – 'tik-tik-tik-tik-tik trilinilinee'
HABITAT	Dry, open cultivated country. Farmland with hedgerows
STATUS	In B about 20,000 pairs (rather local and decreasing). Rare in Ireland

LARGE BUNTING WITH lark-like plumage. Cream coloured below, with brown streaks on throat and flanks; no white in tail (compare larks). Is often seen sitting on telephone wires.

THE SONG OF THE corn bunting is a great deal more conspicuous than its rather drab plumage. This is usually likened to the rattling of a bunch of keys. It also has distinctive 'quit - it – it' flight-call, and a harsh 'chip' as contact call.

The corn bunting in a bulky bird, which often sits in a conspicuous position, on a wire or bush-top. It has a fluttering flight, and sometimes dangles its legs.

Although mainly associated with agriculture, any open country with song posts can be corn bunting country. As the nest is usually on the ground, little cover is needed, although protection in rank vegetation is helpful.

Food is taken on the ground, with seeds, mainly cereals, featuring importantly, together with invertebrates. Because of the importance of cereals, the range has retracted not only in Britain but in many parts of Europe.

In winter there are local movements, and information about the whereabouts of food supplies may be shared among birds at winter roosts in gorse, scrub or reedbeds. On a wider scale, the central European birds are most migratory, heading south or east, while other populations show a westerly tendency.

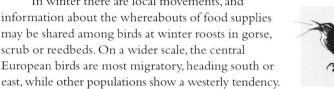

SIZE

IDENTIFICATION

HABITAT

POPULATION

MAP

Corn buntings, once ubiquitous in farmland, have decreased in recent years following changes in agriculture and in particular the decrease in barley growing.

Mountain and Moorland Birds

LOOKING TOWARDS THE Cuillins of Skye or across many a Scottish loch, the highlands and islands seem to extend for ever. Many of the islands have their hills, and even those that do not retain their upland character with moorland often reaching to sea level. In fact, hills cover a third of all Britain, while Ireland is ringed by uplands.

BIRDS OF THE REGION

MOUNTAIN BIRDS MAY be few, but they can be exciting. The calls of red-throated divers along coast evoke the lonely hills and the jingling of Snow buntings hints at the hardness of life among the summits. One of the finest of all mountain bird sounds is the whistling song of the dotterel, a wader of the high mountain summits of Scotland.

The birds at the top of the mountain and moorland food chains are the birds of prey, such as kestrel, merlin, golden eagle, buzzard and hen harrier, and the raven which is a general scavenger.

THE UPLANDS ARE made up of a variety of habitats, with zones at different altitudes, each with its characteristic birds. Species, as well as individuals, are few, even in summer, for under the dual influence of poor soil and harsh climate food is short. When winter comes, wheatears and ring ouzels will have migrated, and the meadow pipits moved down from the hills, making these habitats seem even more deserted.

Top left
Meadow pipits are common birds of mountain and moorland .

Top right
Merlins like to nest in deep heather – but you would be lucky indeed to spot one.

Bottom right
Golden plover is another species which breeds on high moorland – mainly in Scotland and the northern Pennines.

If Scotland, with its remains of post ice-age arctic tundra, has most of the gems, from ptarmigan to rare breeding waders, Wales has its choughs and kites, the pennines have golden plover and twite, and the most southerly dunlin in the world still breed on Dartmoor.

Two northern areas need special mention for their climatic peculiarities lead to bird habitats of the utmost importance. The blanket bogs and wet heaths of Shetland and the 'flow country' of Sutherland and Caithness hold a significant percentage of a number of British birds.

Shetland lies in the track of depressions that sweep westwards across the North Atlantic and is in the same latitude as southern Greenland. Not surprisingly, northern birds are the speciality here, with 95 per cent of Britain's breeding whimbrels, 70 per cent of great skuas and 60 per cent of arctic skuas. Including the coastal areas as well as the moorland, Shetland also holds a significant percentage of eiders, ringed plovers, oystercatchers and dunlins. Where the drainage is better and ling gives way to bell heather, crowberry, bilberry and cranberry, the golden plover breeds, with 5-10 per cent of the British population.

The Flow Country, where the undulating moorlands of east Sutherland gradually descend into Caithness, includes, to the west, higher peaks and ranges projecting from the peat. As on Shetland, moor and water are inseparable. The importance of this country as our nearest equivalent to the wet tundras of the Low Arctic is seen by their recognition as of 'outstanding universal value' on the UK's new tentative list of world heritage sites for submission to UNESCO.

Detailed study of the area only began in 1979, when the then Nature Conservancy Council launched a breeding bird survey of this difficult terrain. Ten species of wader were widespread, but breeding wood sandpipers, red-necked phalaropes, Temminck's stints and ruffs have also been found. Native greylag geese, red- and black-throated divers, common scoters and Arctic skua are important, with the black-throats making up some 20 per cent and the common scoter 40 per cent of the British breeding populations.

CWM IDWAL

This reserve, the first National Nature Reserve in Wales, is one of the most easily accessible mountain areas in Britain, and has some of the most exciting arctic alpine plants south of Scotland.

As soon as one starts along the path into the Cwm from April on, wheatears will 'chack' and show their white rumps. Quite soon, if one is lucky, the ringing song of ring ouzels will carry from the lower crags, and grey wagtails will flit after flies along the stream. From the rocky slopes of Tryfan or the crags of the Glyders, ravens or peregrines glide across the cwm, while in winter the occasional whooper swan or goldeneye will turn up on Llyn Idwal. A small island gives some indication of what the vegetation might be like with fewer sheep.

Apart from meadow pipits, there are birdless times as one climbs towards the botanist's mecca, Twll Du, black chasm or the Devils Kitchen. Emerging onto wet grassland above the Kitchen and turning towards the summit of Y Garn, outside the reserve, skylarks sing. In late summer choughs come to feed in the short grass, searching for insects particularly where grass meets stone and the crevices can be explored with their long, curved bills. In winter, when snow covers the slopes, snow buntings may feed on seeds on isolated rush heads jutting through.

Top
Whimbrel breed in the north of Scotland, mainly Shetland, where they are increasing.

Bottom
Red-throated divers like to nest close to small lakes.

Unless there is a great reduction in the emission of greenhouse gases, global warming is likely to be with us for some time, and although its consequences for birds can be debated, our mountain birds will probably not benefit. In Scandinavia the tree-line is already rising, and if we had a 300 m (984 ft) shift in altitude of the upland zones and a longer growing season even the Scottish mountains could well lose their mossy *Racomitrium* heath, their solifluction terraces and their snow-beds.

Des Thompson, Principal Advisor on the Uplands in Scottish National Heritage sees three likely consequences: the numbers and breeding distribution of upland species will change, upland birds will breed earlier and patterns of migration and overwintering behaviour will also be influenced.

Ravens are already breeding earlier and, as greenshank breeding is linked with soil temperature, they will probably follow suit. The upward movement of grasses will change grazing practices with consequences for dotterel, while snow bunting and the occasionally breeding purple sandpiper might be

lost. Although oystercatcher, hen harrier, lapwing and twite may benefit, the spread of arable at lower levels and of scrub at higher levels, will need imaginative conservation measures. If the threat to the uplands in the 1980s was afforestation and in the 1990s agricultural change and overgrazing, it is now climate change that could lead to a different Cairngorm bird community by 2050.

Middle left
The raven, largest of our crows, favours remote, rocky uplands.

Middle right
Moorland – typical golden plover country.

Bottom
Greenshank, here seen on migration, nest in parts of north-west Scotland.

THE HIGHLANDS

IN THE *Highlands and Islands* Fraser Darling describes the delights of the arctic-alpine grassland for the human observer. 'The high grasslands on a summer day have an idyllic quality. They are remote and quiet. They are green and kind to the eye. They are easy to the feet. The very pebbles among which the flowers grow have a sparkle and show of colour. To climb on one of these alps of grass and descend again in a few hours is not enough.'

He goes on to say, 'Take a little tent and remain in the quietness for one night at least. It is a magnificent experience to rise in the morning in such a place and feel fresh, knowing that your enjoyment of the peat-free plateaux is not to be spoiled by a gruelling climb and the necessity of going down the same day. The only sounds breaking the silence, if you can get the best of the early July weather, will be the grackle of the ptarmigan, the flute-like pipe of the ring ouzel, perhaps the plaint of a golden plover or a dotterel and the bark of the golden eagle. These are good sounds, and do not

disturb what is for the moment a place of peace. See how the deer, now bright-red-coated, lie at ease in the alpine grassland. Listen, if you have stalked near enough, to the sweet talkings of the calves who are like happy children. Here is new herbage over which no other muzzles have grazed: the very soil has been washed by fifty inches of rain since the deer were here before, in November.'

THREATS TO THE ENVIRONMENT

EVEN THOUGH MANY mountain and moorland sites are rather remote, nevertheless the threats to them are real enough. Forestry schemes have reduced the wildlife value of parts of Flow Country for example, perhaps the nearest to a unique British habitat, leading to reductions in breeding waders. Access to the summit plateaux of the Cairngorms grows ever easier, while leisure activities everywhere, together with intensive grazing, acidification of rivers, drainage and fertilisation of marginal land, have all had their effects.

The Pennine moors now lack many of the plants that normally make up the upland community, partly as a result of decades of acid rain, and the destruction of the soil through erosion. But the news is not all bad, and many mountain birds are beginning to show increases as awareness grows of the value of these marvellous upland habitats.

Top left
Golden plover – camouflaged amidst the lichens and mosses of high moorland.

Top right
Upland farmland is good curlew habitat.

Bottom
Curlews use their long bills to probe in the ground for worms and grubs.

187

Red-throated Diver

50–65 cm (21–26 in)

○○○○○○○○○○○○○○○○○○○○○○○○○○○○○
SPECIES INFORMATION	
SCIENTIFIC NAME	*Gavia stellata*
RELATED SPECIES	Black-throated Diver, Great Northern Diver
CALL	Wailing on breeding grounds, occasional ringing 'ah-oo-ah' in winter and goose-like flight call. Long like cooing of collared dove, but harsher and louder
HABITAT	Small lakes in moorland and tundra, coastal in winter
STATUS	Breeds in North Britain. Winters mostly on North Sea and Baltic coasts; rare but regular on inland lakes, reservoirs and larger rivers

SIZE

IDENTIFICATION

HABITAT

POPULATION

MAP

SOMEWHAT SMALLER THAN black-throated diver, with slimmer head, neck and bill (latter slightly upturned). Head normally tilted upwards. In breeding plumage with red-brown patch on neck, looking black from a distance. In winter very like black-throated, but back lighter. Less distinct border between dark and pale colours on the head and neck.

FOR MOST OF US, divers only occur as winter excitements around the coast, and seeing the red-throat of the one and the black of the other of our breeding divers is just a hope of pleasure to come. The red-throated diver is a bird that likes small lochs for breeding and needs to fly, often far, to collect food, whereas the black-throated, with its distinctive blacks and whites and neck streaks, prefers bigger expanses of water and therefore does not need to fly so much.

The red-throated diver only has a red throat in breeding plumage. In winter a distinctive feature is the up-turned bill-tip.

Both have similar calls, but description can do no justice to the sounds which epitomise the wild, open northern spaces. These sounds are mainly responsible for the place divers play in folklore, but not for their Shetland name of rainbird or, for red-throated diver, learga-chaol, the slender raingoose.

It is at sea that most of us will see divers, and on cold winter days with chilly fingers on the binoculars, with birds half hidden behind waves and never as close as you would like them, you need to know what to look out for.

Divers, grebes and cormorants have features in common. Cormorants swim low in water with bill pointed slightly upward, grebes of comparable size hold their thin necks quite erect and ride higher in the water, while the thicker-necked divers are longer-bodied and larger-billed. Those of red-throated divers appear uptilted because of an angled lower mandible, while black-throats are straight-billed.

There should be no such difficulty in summer, as the red-throated, appropriately, has a wine red patch on its neck and uniform grey brown upperparts, whereas the upper parts of the black throated are chequered black and white. Black and white also feature on the side of the neck bordering the black throat. At all times the bill of the black-throated is heavier and the forehead higher. In flight in winter they are hard to tell apart, but the red-throated diver has a thinner neck and pale face. In flight the black-throated has slower wing beats. Both birds are largely silent in winter.

```
○ ○ ○ ○ ○ ○ ○ ○ ○ ○ ○ ○ ○ ○ ○ ○ ○ ○ ○ ○ ○ ○ ○ ○ ○ ○
```
SPECIES INFORMATION

SCIENTIFIC NAME	*Gavia arctica*
RELATED SPECIES	Red-throated Diver, Great Northern Diver
CALL	Seldom heard in winter. Long drawn-out wail, also miaowing call when disturbed. Croaking call: long, pulsed and hoarse, like raven. Wailing call: three brief notes given in territorial encounters. Long call: resembles low-pitched whistle composed of two notes with marked pitch increase in longer second note
HABITAT	Large lakes in summer. In winter usually on coastal seas
STATUS	Breeds mainly in north-west Scotland. Winters on North Sea and Baltic, more rarely on large inland lakes

Black-throated Diver

58–73 cm (23–31 in)

DUCK-LIKE, WITH rather snake-like head. Bill held straight, head upright. In breeding plumage has grey head, black throat and striped neck. Back with striking black and white markings. In winter uniform dark above, pale underneath, with clear border on head and neck; bill black; juveniles in winter rather paler.

BLACK-THROATED DIVERS choose to breed on larger lochs which, although often nutrient deficient, have enough small trout, and a range of invertebrates such as crustaceans, molluscs and insect larvae, to feed adults and young. In the past, the link between black-throated divers and trout led to direct persecution, but now disturbance is more of a problem with birdwatchers being quite as disturbing as fishermen.

The main breeding area of both divers is Scandinavia, as well as northern Russia and across northern Asia. In winter they spread out around coasts as far south as France, Italy and the Black Sea.

 SIZE

 IDENTIFICATION

 HABITAT

 POPULATION

 MAP

The usual view of a black-throated diver is a distant bird in winter, at sea or on a reservoir.

Golden Eagle

75–89 cm (30–35 in)

SPECIES INFORMATION	
SCIENTIFIC NAME	*Aquila chrysaetos*
RELATED SPECIES	White-tailed eagle
CALL	Occasional yelps, but rarely heard
HABITAT	Mainly restricted to remote mountain areas
STATUS	Mainly resident. Young birds may wander. Mainly Scotland but occasionally breeds in Lake District. British population about 450 pairs

SIZE

IDENTIFICATION

HABITAT

POPULATION

MAP

LARGE, DARK, AND powerful, with heavy bill and strong talons. Crown and neck golden brown, wings long and relatively narrow. Tail rather long and broad. Juveniles dark with large white patches on wings; tail white with broad black tip.

GOLDEN EAGLES OUGHT to be easy to identify, but many a buzzard has been turned into an eagle when watchers in remote hills were over hopeful. With the return of white-tailed eagles there is another possible source of error, but the squarish tail of the golden sets it apart from the white-tailed, which has a wedge-shaped tail with a dark end. Apart from size, golden eagles have relatively larger heads than buzzards, and young birds have a helpful white wing patch and rounded tails.

Adult birds are uniform dark brown but with some golden on the crown and hind neck. It soars with its wings raised slightly on either side of the body, the wings narrow at their base and the body is noticeably darker than the flight feathers. Leslie Brown suggests that an average home-range might be of the order of 5000 ha. Another point he makes is that no one can give a good account of how a golden eagle spends its day, or the proportion of time spent

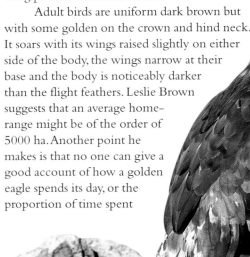

hunting, for one sees an eagle about once a day, and if lucky for one minute, when on the hill.

The Scottish birds form about per cent of the European population, which is widely spread but scattered, with Spain and Norway each having more than per cent. Although aerial displays are less developed than in some other eagles, this is a fine bird with a history of devoted supporters.

'The clinching, inter locking claw,
a living fierce gyrating wheel,
Four beating wings, two beaks,
a swirling mass tight grappling,
In tumbling turning, clustering loops,
straight downward falling.'
Walt Whitman THE DALLIANCE OF EAGLES

The golden eagle, our largest bird of prey, is truly magnificent, with a huge wingspan and massive hooked bill.

Peregrine Falcon

39–50 cm (15–20 in)

SPECIES INFORMATION

SCIENTIFIC NAME	*Falco peregrinus*
RELATED SPECIES	Kestrel, Hobby, Merlin
CALL	'Kek-kek-kek' at or near nest-site
HABITAT	Hilly and mountainous areas, and at coast. Needs steep rocks or cliffs for nest-site. Estuaries and other wetlands in winter
STATUS	Resident. In BI about 1500 pairs, mainly in north and west

CROW-SIZED, POWERFUL falcon. Pointed, broad-based wings; short, tapering tail. Broad, dark moustache. Underparts pale, with dark barring. Juveniles dark brown above, yellow-brown beneath, with heavy dark streaks. Normal flight relatively slow, with powerful, shallow wingstrokes, and periods of gliding.

APART FROM SPEED and power, the dark head and relatively short tail are characteristic, and at close quarters the head can be seen to be almost completely dark except for white on the neck up to the bill, with another white extension of the pale chest towards the rear side of the head. Between these two white areas, a distinctive curved V of black covers the side of the neck. Adults are slate-coloured above and barred below, while young birds are dark brown above with small, but noticeable, pale tip to their tails.

The peregrine is a large falcon exuding strength, and the success of its population recovery brings pleasure to all except the most ardent pigeon fancier. The problems with persistent organochlorine insecticides were outlined in the introduction to farmland birds, and peregrines were among those most affected, as the long-lived residues moved up the food chain to end in the top predator. A decline began around 1956, when southern populations had almost recovered from egg destruction and shooting, resulting from its liking for homing pigeons during the war. By 1962 it was down to 68 pairs, and was extinct over much of its former range. Now, apart form returning to many traditional and new cliff haunts, it is even using buildings such as cathedrals, churches and office blocks, as breeding sites.

Whether chasing, soaring or just flying by, peregrines are spectacular, but when they indulge in high circling or flight-play together, or when the male displays in undulating flight or with downward plunges, it is appreciated by almost everybody. The noise it makes can make it more impressive. These calls, mainly near the eyrie, are essentially a harsh chattering, repeated rapidly, and carrying far, so that the bird itself can be hard to find against a background of mountain crags. It is on record that some eyries occupied in medieval times were still being used in 1939.

As indicated by references to pigeon fanciers and homing pigeons, peregrines feed largely on birds largely taken on the wing and often over the sea. Most frequently they are caught from above, with a rapid stoop, but pigeons often need hectic pursuit, during which they too may show acrobatic ability. Breeding auks may be the target at some breeding sites but, over winter estuaries, waders and ducks are important prey and the appearance of a peregrine can cause estuarine chaos.

SIZE

IDENTIFICATION

HABITAT

POPULATION

MAP

Peregrines have made a steady recovery from the earlier effects of pesticides and persecution. They have even started to nest in some of our cities.

Merlin

25–30 cm (10–12 in)

SPECIES INFORMATION	
SCIENTIFIC NAME	*Falco columbarius*
RELATED SPECIES	Kestrel, Peregrine, Hobby
CALL	Very rapid 'kikiki', usually near nest
HABITAT	Upland birch woodland, heather moors, and dunes. In winter often at coast or washland
STATUS	Resident. Wanders in winter. In BI recent decline to about 600 pairs

SIZE

IDENTIFICATION

HABITAT

POPULATION

MAP

SMALLEST OF OUR falcons, with low, rapid flight. Male is grey above; rusty yellow underneath with long dark streaks. Female has larger streaks below, and is dark brown above, with a barred tail. Juveniles very like female.

BY CONTRAST WITH the heavy power of eagles, we have the dashing forays of merlins in pursuit of moorland birds. Merlin prey is usually caught after a short distance by surprise attack, but sometimes they may be chased to exhaustion.

Ratcliffe mentions two great difficulties with merlins. The first is the complex interplay of facts, afforestation, organochlorines, mercury, and unknowns, involved in trying to explain the decline in merlin numbers and range, and the second is the difficulty in finding out what their numbers actually are.

A pair may apparently be interested in one part of a moor and then move elsewhere, while sitting birds may sit so tight that they will not move even with a hopeful observer hand clapping or shouting from 25 m; the off-duty bird may also leave the

nesting area for hours. Why do merlin much prefer heather moor to grassmoor, when meadow pipit populations are much the same in both? The answer may be that merlins like tall heather for nesting sites, but old crow nests in bushes will do on grassmoor.

Merlins are dark, uniform-looking falcons with apparently long tails. If seen well the male has dark slate-blue back and pale streaked pinkish underparts, while the larger female has a distinct head pattern with contrasting dark and white. In flight both sexes have dark but barred underwings and pointed wing tips, but the tail of the male ends in a single subterminal bar whereas those of females and immatures are strongly barred. A typical falcon alarm call near the nest and other calls are used in courtship.

The merlin has a markedly northerly distribution, with Scandinavia and Iceland its European stronghold, so not surprisingly many birds migrate. Even among our western populations most leave the summer's heather for the coast; this is not so true of Ireland.

Top left
The sharp-eyed merlin catches mainly small birds such as meadow pipits.

Top right
A brood of merlin chicks, still covered in soft down.

Bottom
Open moorland is favoured by merlins, with tall scrub and heather for nesting.

Hen Harrier
43–50 cm (17–20 in)

SPECIES INFORMATION	
SCIENTIFIC NAME	Circus cyaneus
RELATED SPECIES	Marsh Harrier, Montagu's Harrier
CALL	Male has a high-pitched 'piuu piuu' in courtship flight; female a hoarse 'pih-e'. Alarm call 'chek-ek-ek-ek'
HABITAT	Open landscapes – heather moor, dunes, marshes and damp meadows; also in young plantations. In winter regular in open marshland and wet heath
STATUS	Resident and partial migrant. In BI mainly in N and W about 800 pairs. Ranges south in winter

SLIM AND LIGHT in flight. Male has ash-grey plumage, with contrasting black-tipped wings and white rump. Female is dark brown above, pale yellow-brown beneath, with striped wings and tail, and clear white rump. Flight buoyant and gliding.

THERE ARE BOTH Welsh and Scottish hen harriers, a good Irish population and some in northern England, on heather moor and young forestry. All harriers fly low on long wings and the female of this species, larger than the male, is not easily distinguished from the more delicate (and rarer) Montagu's, but she does have a broader white rump. The male has 'clean' grey back and upper wings with black tips. His combination of black on all primaries, decidedly broader wings with dark trailing edge below should distinguish him from male Montagu's harrier.

Like the red kite, hen harriers suffered much in the interests of game preservation, and by the turn of the century had a few refuges on Scottish islands and Irish uplands. As a rarity it suffered at the hands of egg collectors, but the Second World War reduced the gamekeepers, and increased young forestry plantations, to such an extent that in 20 years the hen harrier had again become a widespread breeder in the uplands of Britain and Ireland. Since then a decline has set in, certainly driven by illegal persecution, for it is the most hated of raptors for those with interests in grouse populations. In fact, meadow pipits and small mammals form a high percentage of its prey in upland areas.

One unusual feature is the relatively high level of polygamy, with some males pairing with more than one female.

From their summer breeding haunts hen harriers spread more widely to coasts and lowland downs and heaths, avoiding trees (except for roosting) because of their hunting method of low-level flight. Similarly, forestry plantations are used only for breeding and not for hunting. There are often smallwinter roosts, collecting birds from a wide feeding area. These roosts, often in reedbeds, are on the ground or on platforms of vegetation.

In parts of its range there are more extensive movements, and in France it is sometimes known as St Martin's bird as it passes through on or around St Martin's Day, 11 November.

 SIZE
 IDENTIFICATION
 HABITAT
 POPULATION
 MAP

Top
Downland sometimes attracts visiting hen harriers during the winter.

Bottom
Hen harriers are very buoyant in flight as they quarter the moorland for small mammals and birds.

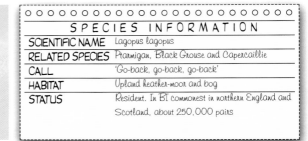

Red Grouse

38 cm (15 in)

SPECIES INFORMATION	
SCIENTIFIC NAME	Lagopus lagopus
RELATED SPECIES	Ptarmigan, Black Grouse and Capercaillie
CALL	'Go-back, go-back, go-back'
HABITAT	Upland heather-moor and bog
STATUS	Resident. In BI commonest in northern England and Scotland, about 250,000 pairs

SIZE

IDENTIFICATION

HABITAT

POPULATION

MAP

THE RED GROUSE is the British and Irish subspecies of the willow grouse of Scandinavia and North Asia. Both sexes are reddish-brown, with black barring. Flies strongly and glides on drooping wings.

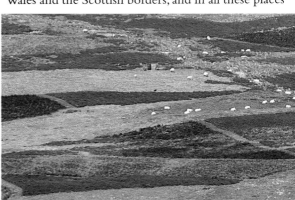

BRITISH RED GROUSE were thought to be an endemic species, but are now considered as an isolated race of the willow grouse which is found all round the arctic. Because of shooting interests grouse are among the most studied of birds, and their fluctuating populations have been well documented. It would seem that numbers are influenced by a complex of factors with the activities of predators, gamekeepers and parasites

Red grouse are at home on upland heather moor. Their call is a highly characteristic 'go-back, go-back'.

interacting with territorial behaviour of the birds and the quality of the heather. Red grouse are dependant on heather at all times, and their explosive flight and noisy 'go back, go back' calls are quite enough to identify them when disturbed.

MacGillivray in his *History of British Birds* (1837-52) wrote that 'the Celts, naturally imagining the moorcock to speak Gaelic signify it (the call) as 'co co co co mo chlaidh, mo chlaidh' i.e. who, who who goes there, my sword, my sword.'

Some of the highest densities are found in north Yorkshire, but elsewhere in England there are areas where too many grazing sheep have converted grouse moor to grassland. This has also happened in Wales and the Scottish borders, and in all these places heather has also been lost to afforestation. The greatest range retraction had been in Ireland. Paradoxically perhaps, high densities of red grouse are very dependant on shooting and the associated management of the heather.

When looking for grouse it may be only a head that is visible above the heather, when the bright red wattle in spring may be conspicuous, but the white woolly feet are less likely to be seen. Females lack the wattle and are paler and browner but most frequently grouse are only seen as they 'explode' with a clatter of wings and noisy calls, showing a characteristic profile from behind with dumpy body and wings forming a shallow inverted U during the gliding phases of their flight.

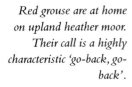

SPECIES INFORMATION	
SCIENTIFIC NAME	Lagopus mutus
RELATED SPECIES	Red Grous, Black Grouse and Capercaillie
CALL	Characteristic grating call of male 'arrr-arr-krrr-ak-ak-ak'
HABITAT	Above tree-line in rocky sites. At lower levels in winter
STATUS	Resident. Scottish highlands about 15,000 birds

Ptarmigan
36cm (14 in)

SLIGHTLY SMALLER THAN red grouse. Wings are white at all seasons. Breeding male marbled dark brown-grey on upperside and breast, otherwise white, with small red comb. Female yellow-brown, with darker crescent-shaped markings. In winter pure white, except for jet black tail, male with black stripe through eye.

VERY SUITABLY THIS peculiar name is derived from the Gaelic name 'tarmachan'. Going back somewhat further, some 10,000 years, we come to the ending of the ice-age, at which stage British ptarmigan became separated from other populations. Like many of the arctic–alpine plants, which have become isolated as relicts near the summits of the hills, the ptarmigan is a true survivor. Despite this period of isolation, Scottish birds are much like their relatives in the Alps, Pyrenees, Iceland and Scandinavia.

One might expect this bird of the high tops to be plumper and larger than the red grouse, so that it could conserve heat better, but in fact it is smaller and

slimmer, with narrower wings and a more slender bill. In summer the males can look like stones. The wings and underbody are white, and in winter the whole body becomes white, except for the black tail which is hidden until the bird flies. The male has a red comb over the eye; more prominent in spring. The female, when not white, has more obvious

dark barring than the male and a yellow rather than grey back. The calls of the two birds have a different pitch, the female's higher; both involve peculiar cyclic clicks and creaks.

Ratcliffe describes how the ptarmigan has a claim to being the hardiest bird on earth. 'It endures the appalling severity of winter throughout the high Arctic region, with mean January temperatures down as low as -40° C. Even in these inhospitable wastes the ptarmigan appears to move little in seeking to escape the terrible cold, but burrows into the snow for shelter and access to its buried food supply. Scottish haunts must be mild by comparison, for at 1,200 m, mean January temperature is only -5° C, even though the extreme windiness of the highland climate can give additional adversity in winter.'

In much of its Arctic habitat, where food webs are simplified, the ptarmigan faces further danger as the chief food of the gyr falcon which has few alternative food items in winter and even in summer targets the ptarmigan as its favourite single item of prey.

Ptarmigan populations have suffered from the rising density of sheep, whose grazing converts dwarf shrub heath to grassland. Ptarmigan need the dwarf shrubs as providers of shoots, buds, berries, twigs and seeds, and indiscriminate burning does not help their cause either. Another problem is that easier human access makes for more litter of one sort or another, which encourages crows, which then eat ptarmigan eggs. Nevertheless, this tame attractive grouse can be one of the commonest bird of the tops where it occurs.

 SIZE

 IDENTIFICATION

 HABITAT

 POPULATION

 MAP

Top and bottom left
In winter the ptarmigan change to an almost pure white, blending in with the snow and ice.

Middle right
In summer, the belly and wings remain white, but the upper parts are grey-brown.

Black Grouse

40–55 cm 16–22 (in)

SPECIES INFORMATION	
SCIENTIFIC NAME	Lyrurus Tetrao
RELATED SPECIES	Capercaillie, Red Grouse, Ptarmigan
CALL	Male song at display ground (lek) is a bubbling coo, interspersed with hissing or sneezing
HABITAT	Heather moor and bog, open wooded areas and dwarf shrub heath near tree-line
STATUS	Resident. In Britain about 10,000 breeding females (in steady decline) absent from Ireland

SIZE

IDENTIFICATION

HABITAT

POPULATION

MAP

MALE HAS SHINY blue-black plumage and lyre-shaped tail feathers, fluffed out during courtship to reveal white under tail coverts. Female is smaller, with camouflaged grey-brown plumage. Bill slightly hooked. Flight involves rapid wingbeats, interspersed with periods of gliding. Often perches in trees.

THE VERY SPECIAL tail may not be conspicuous, but the white shoulder patches of the male are. The black body is glossed with blue. Almost as distinctive as plumage, behaviour and the dove-like bubbling is the flight which may be high, gliding on stretched wings or, as with other woodland grouse, involve rapid wing-beats as the short-winged bird rises among trees. Females in flight have a whiter underwing than red grouse, a notched tail and often a whitish bar on the upperwing. On the ground her larger size and longer tail distinguish the so called 'grey hen' from a female red grouse.

The black grouse is one of our finest birds, and also sadly now rather rare. The males pirouette and spread their feathers in an elaborate lekking display.

Black grouse country has tall heather or young conifers to nest and hide in, together with patches of forest edge and rushy meadows that have not been improved for sheep grazing. These grouse like an abundance of shoots, buds and leaves, especially of heather and bilberry to keep the adults well fed. The young chicks need spiders and beetles and moth caterpillars and sawfly larvae; these are found among bog myrtle and the rushes and grasses of wet places.

In upland areas where rough grazing, moorland edge and heather have disappeared under conifers, and where fields have been 'improved', with the heather, boggy hollows and rushy fields enclosed by wire fences, black grouse have problems. They have little to eat, and few places to hide or nest. Other species such as lapwings, curlews, redshanks and snipe face similar difficulties.

Black grouse are famous for their leks in which the male birds gather to court the females. The leks are usually found in an open area of bog, marsh or forest glade; the males have their own territory within this open area, with low status young birds visiting as intruders. Those with central territories gain the majority of matings; they are usually the older birds. In display the males fan their tails wide: the white under tail converts form a circle as seen from behind. All this is accompanied by a cacophony of 'rookooing' song which carries for up to 3 km (1.8 miles) but is extremely hard to locate. There is also much rushing to and fro within the territory, and fighting at the boundary, which seems to attract the females. They have been at the periphery of the lek, perhaps in nearby trees, watching the males and sometimes preening. Successful matings also attract more females, so one success is likely to precede another.

Golden Plover

27 cm (11 in)

SPECIES INFORMATION

SCIENTIFIC NAME	*Pluvialis apricaria*
RELATED SPECIES	Grey Plover
CALL	Soft 'dui'. Alarm call a sharp 'tlie', also a plaintive, musical 'tlooi-fee'. Song consists of high, trilling whistles
HABITAT	Breeds on moorland. Moves to open fields, meadows, pasture and estuaries in winter, often in large flocks
STATUS	Resident and partial migrant. Numbers swelled by migrants from further north in winter. In BI mainly breeds in Scotland and north Pennines. British population about 23,000 pairs. Ireland about 400 pairs

IN BREEDING PLUMAGE speckled gold above, jet black neck and belly with white curving dividing line from face to tail. Amount of black on underside is variable and sometimes lacking completely. In winter plumage much duller, without black. Winter flocks on fields can look very thrush-like, both in coloration and behaviour.

As their habitat suggests, they are northern birds with large populations in Iceland, Scandinavia and Russia. All their populations are migratory, mainly moving to western maritime regions as far south as North Africa.

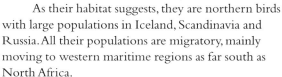

'A golden plover's golden music calls
Across the moor. A heady fragrance spills
From freshly opened peat, then silence falls.'
R. S. Morrison WORDS ON BIRDS

SIZE

IDENTIFICATION

HABITAT

POPULATION

MAP

BREEDING GOLDEN PLOVER really are golden, when seen well, but the dusky face and black belly are more noticeable from a distance, when the back looks brown rather than golden. A description of non-breeding birds would make them seem rather drab, but the upright posture, fast, jerking running and plaintive call always help with identification. In winter, large flocks gather, often with lapwings, on stubble fields, floodlands, extensive grazed grass and aerodromes. Frost prevents them getting to the earthworms which are their staple diet, although other invertebrates and even berries and seeds may be eaten.

Bottom right
The golden plover in full breeding plumage is golden-yellow above and jet black beneath.

Top right
A flock of golden plover in winter.

Curlew

50–60 cm (20–24 in)

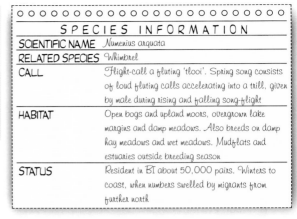

SPECIES INFORMATION	
SCIENTIFIC NAME	Numenius arquata
RELATED SPECIES	Whimbrel
CALL	Flight-call a fluting 'tlooi'. Spring song consists of loud fluting calls accelerating into a trill, given by male during rising and falling song-flight
HABITAT	Open bogs and upland moors, overgrown lake margins and damp meadows. Also breeds on damp hay meadows and wet meadows. Mudflats and estuaries outside breeding season
STATUS	Resident in BI about 50,000 pairs. Winters to coast, when numbers swelled by migrants from further north

SIZE

IDENTIFICATION

HABITAT

POPULATION

MAP

L ARGE WADER, WITH long, decurved bill. Speckled brown plumage, with white rump and lower back. Legs long and strong. Flight strong and gull-like, often in lines or formation.

CURLEWS ARE EUROPE'S largest waders, and with their size and bills they need little more description. The intricate markings at close range disappear into a general grey-brown when seen from a distance, as the long-legged wader wanders at the edge of the tide. In flight, which is slightly gull-like, the white rump and lower back is conspicuous.

Spring in the Welsh uplands, or winter by a west country estuary and the curlew calls. It may be its bubbling, rippling call or the rich whistling 'corlee corlee corlee' that enlivens the winter day, but better still is the 'song' delivered in undulating display flight with long downcurved beak open to deliver accelerating whistles which turn to bubbling.

A comparison of breeding densities on improved and unimproved hill grasslands in the north Pennines showed that snipe virtually disappeared after drainage, fertilising and, sometimes ploughing and re-seeding. Curlew showed an 82 per cent reduction, redshank 81 per cent and lapwing 74 per cent. On the unimproved grassland, with plenty of rush clumps, densities of waders of up to 140 pairs per square kilometre could be found, so the scale of the losses was considerable. Curlews like damp soil so that they can insert their bills into soil or mud to extract invertebrates.

The curlew is usually heard before it is spotted, but when seen, the long, decurved bill is distinctive.

In the last century, curlews spread north in Europe, but more recently there have been declines. They are only scattered in France and Denmark, but become more widespread in Scandinavia and Russia, and other populations extend across Siberia and into north Central Asia. Many of them are migrants, with western birds wintering on European and African coasts. Ireland has a good population wintering inland, but British wintering birds are mainly coastal, with populations of international importance in Morcambe Bay, where there may be 14,000 in March, the Wash and in the estuaries of the Solway, Severn and Dee.

E. A. Armstrong, in his *Birds of the Grey Wind* recalls the birds of Ulster: 'When scattered skeins of curlew passed over in the night their mournful calls chilled and yet thrilled me. They were the very spirit of loveliness wandering homeless through the empty spaces and trackless ways. In later years when I discovered that the Gael consider the curlew to be one of the ominous, dreaded Seven Whistlers and call him by names which signify, Wail of Sorrow, Wail of Warning, Death Cry and Wailing Music I understood and was glad; for I then realised that the wild beautiful sadness which I heard throbbing in the curlew's cry was not born of mere childish apprehension but an intuition shared by a people highly sensitive to mystical images…But if the curlew's is a lonely call, it is the Spirit of the Wild in music, as full of changeful meaning as the voice of the wind, as mysterious and fascinating as the song of the sea.'

SPECIES INFORMATION

SCIENTIFIC NAME	Numenius phaeopus
RELATED SPECIES	Curlew
CALL	Flight call a stammering trilled 'pu-hu-hu-hu'. Song rather like curlew's, but trill section harsher
HABITAT	Breeds on moorland and wet heath in coniferous forest zone and tundra. Migrates to coasts, mainly mudflats, but also to rocky coasts
STATUS	Breeds in north of Scotland, about 465 pairs, increasing. Coastal on migration

Whimbrel
40–46 cm (16–18 in)

L IKE A SMALLER version of curlew, with somewhat shorter, less smoothly curved bill. Upperparts more contrastingly patterned; head with two broad, dark brown stripes. Faster wingbeats than curlew.

Most frequently one hears the tittering call of seven notes, and looks up to see a small party of curlew-like birds with faster wing-beats than their larger relatives. You may notice the darker back or dark barring on the underwing, and sometimes the party will stay to give pleasure for a few days. Spring passage is mainly from mid April to May, and in autumn the birds are moving through from July, with a peak in August. Very few stay here as the main wintering area is south of Sahara.

THE PLUMAGE IS very curlew-like, but darker, and the crown, if seen closely, has a pale central stripe, and the face a noticeable eye-stripe. Unlike the curlew, whimbrels rarely probe deeply, taking insects from the upper layers of soil, and worms from the mudflats.

Breeding whimbrel extend up to the arctic, often far inland. Britain is at the extreme south of their breeding range, with Shetland the stronghold, where some 500 pairs breed among short heather or blanket bog. Elsewhere they are rare, with just a handful on Orkney and scattered in north Scotland and the Western Isles. Whimbrel often breed in loose groups, and make shallow nests lined with fragments of vegetation.

SIZE

IDENTIFICATION

HABITAT

POPULATION

MAP

Like a small version of a curlew, the whimbrel's trilling flight-call often gives it away.

Greenshank

30 cm (12 in)

SIZE

IDENTIFICATION

HABITAT

POPULATION

MAP

SPECIES INFORMATION

SCIENTIFIC NAME	Tringa nebularia
RELATED SPECIES	Redshank, Spotted Redshank, Green Sandpiper, Wood Sandpiper
CALL	Flight-call a fluting 'tew-tew-tew'. On breeding ground a harder 'kji-kji-kji'. Song a fluting 'klivi-klivi-klivi', often in flight over territory
HABITAT	Breeds on open moorland or on heath with bushes or isolated trees close to water. Outside breeding season mainly coastal, in small groups or individually
STATUS	North-west Scotland about 1500 pairs. Migrates to coasts in autumn and winter

LARGE, RATHER PALE grey wader with long, slightly upturned bill and long, greenish legs. Outside breeding season (and juveniles) paler and greyer above, white beneath. In flight the legs extend well beyond the tail.

GREENSHANK OFTEN LOOK very pale, and the legs usually do look green. Like many waders, there is nothing remarkable about the plumage, but there is an attractive mix of grey brown and black on the back and wings, a streaked breast turning to spots and then to pure white underparts.

The long, slightly upturned bill, used for feeding in the shallows, is very distinctive. A wide range of food is taken, including small fish, shrimps, shore crabs and worms. Greenshanks often feed by sweeping the bill from side to side, with the tip just in contact with the surface and opening and closing gently. On its breeding grounds it takes mainly insects and other small invertebrates.

Ratcliffe describes the contributions made by the Nethersole Thompson family to understanding the breeding biology of what he calls 'the most special bird of the deer forests'. 'Greenshanks' writes Ratcliffe 'mostly return to their Scottish breeding haunts during early April and for two to three weeks afterwards are conspicuous and vocal in pairs as they court and stake out territories. It is then that the male gives his thrilling song dance in undulating flight high over his chosen area, advertising his possession to all his neighbours. This is a water's edge feeder, probing and picking for the wide range of invertebrates along the margins of lochs, lochans, bog pools and rivers or on the seashore.

By early May, greenshanks are to be found nesting singly. They rise to the intruder with an alarmed 'tew-tew-tew' and rapidly distance themselves before pitching to resume their quiet search for food. The absent mate is sitting on eggs in some secret place on the moor: it may be near or far but there is not the least clue to suggest where.'

Greenshank country is the high rainfall areas of western Scotland – notably Sutherland, West Caithness, Wester Ross, west Inverness and the Western Isles, dominated by pools and blanket bogs.

Among the haunts loved by Nethersole Thompson and greenshank are places where 'great cliffs and precipices, grim, moist, black and forbidding, soar above a wilderness of scree and rock table overlooking the scars, pocks, furrows and craters of a bog, in which the roots of an ancient forest project like the snouts of primeval monsters snuffing in ebony, porridge like scum'.

An elegant wader, the greenshank has quite a long, very slightly upturned bill.

SPECIES INFORMATION	
SCIENTIFIC NAME	Asio flammeus
RELATED SPECIES	Long-eared Owl
CALL	Territorial males have soft 'doo-doo-doo-doo' in spring, female replies with 'tjair-op'. Alarm call at nest is a barking 'kwe'
HABITAT	Open country with low vegetation. Moorland, heath, overgrown lake margins, damp meadows and reedbeds
STATUS	Resident and partial migrant. In BI about 2,000 pairs (almost absent as breeding bird in Ireland)

Short-Eared Owl

38 cm (15 in)

MEDIUM-SIZED, LONG-WINGED owl, often active by day. Has short 'ear' tufts, often invisible. Plumage light brownish-grey. Eyes yellow and surrounded by broad black circles. In flight appears pale and narrow-winged. Wing tips dark; often glides with wings held in V shape; tail wedge-shaped.

SHORT-EARED OWLS breed on heather moors, coastal marshes and young plantations where new growth gives cover to small mammals. When voles do not occur, as in Ireland, there are few owls. In winter these long-winged diurnal hunters can turn up on downland, heath or coastal dune, and when they settle, the boldly streaked underparts and yellow eye may be seen.

Wintering birds are highly nomadic, and half of the ringing recoveries mentioned in the *Winter Atlas* were more than a hundred kilometres from where they were ringed. These wanderers will take what food they can, but small mammals dominate, although some birds also feature.

If food supplies of small rodents are steady, owls will be consistent in their breeding but where voles come and go, as they often do among young forestry plantations, the owls do likewise. Their real favourite is heather. Here short eared owls can be conspicuous whether sitting on a roadside post, beating about slowly over the ground in search of prey, or showing their aerial antics in courtship and territorial display.

The short ears of the name are usually invisible, but the face, buff white with black patches is striking enough in its own right. Striking also is the advertising call of the male, a hollow 'doo doo doo', likened to the distant puffing of a steam engine, frequently repeated. A barking call, hoarse and hissing, is used in a variety of contexts.

The Scandinavian countries have good populations, up to 10,000 pairs in Norway and Finland, while the extensive Arctic tundra of Russia has many more. The range extends across Northern Asia and North America, and it is one of few Palearctic birds that breeds in South America.

SIZE

IDENTIFICATION

HABITAT

POPULATION

MAP

Top left and right
Despite its name, the short tufts (which are not ears) of the short-eared owl are usually invisible.

Bottom
They sometimes turn up on downland in the winter.

Ring Ouzel

24 cm (9.5 in)

SPECIES INFORMATION

SCIENTIFIC NAME	*Turdus torquatus*
RELATED SPECIES	Blackbird, Song Thrush, Mistle Thrush, Redwing, Fieldfare
CALL	Alarm call 'tok-tok-tok'; flight-call 'tsreet'. Song consists of short, repeated rather rough-toned fluting phrases
HABITAT	Hills, moorland and mountains. On migration also in lowland and coastal pasture
STATUS	Summer visitor. In BI about 10,000 pairs (only about 200 in Ireland)

SIZE

IDENTIFICATION

HABITAT

POPULATION

MAP

SIMILAR IN SIZE and shape to blackbird, but with white breastband (male), slightly longer wings and tail and 'scaly' underside, particularly in winter. Female has fainter breastband and browner plumage. Juveniles are speckled brown below and on throat.

EVERYONE WHO LOVES the hills and knows something of their birds loves the ring ouzel. One reason, as Ratcliffe describes, is that it 'shares with the wheatear the claim of being the earliest of our upland summer migrants to arrive, usually towards the end of March. From this time onwards, dawn chorus in the mountains often begins with the clear triple note of a cock ring ouzel carrying far across the hill.

While evidently preferring heathery hills, ring ouzels are typical birds of the sheep walks, especially where there is much

rocky ground. Nesting habitat varies widely, but one of the most favoured is the steep, rocky bank of a secluded little stream, preferably grown with long overhanging heather or other rank vegetation … The nests are beautifully made and durable structures of tough hill grasses such as *nardus*, and will last for several years in sheltered sites.' These secluded little streams are often free of sheep, and the mountain plants, roseroot and mountain sorrel, globeflower and starry saxifrage survive to add to the ambience of the ring ouzel's haunt.

Ring ouzels really are blackbird-like, although the scaly plumage has not the gloss of its lowland relative. The males white bib is 'cleaner' than the female's and she is not as dark. Both have pale yellow bills. Autumn migrants, which may turn up where there are good berry supplies, have almost lost their crescent bibs, but the silvery wings, due to pale fringes on the wing coverts, help identification. Ring ouzels turn up regularly in early spring along the coasts, especially on grazed pasture. Our birds may only move as far as Southern Spain, but some may go on to winter in the Atlas mountains.

The scaly plumage and white throat crescent distinguish this upland species from the blackbird.

SPECIES INFORMATION

SCIENTIFIC NAME	*Oenanthe oenanthe*
RELATED SPECIES	*No close relatives in British Isles*
CALL	*Alarm-call 'chak'. Song, not often heard, is a short, rapid, warbling phrase made up of hard notes and soft whistles*
HABITAT	*Open stoney or rocky country, pasture, moorland and heath*
STATUS	*Summer visitor. In BI about 70,000 pairs*

Northern Wheatear

15 cm (6 in)

RATHER ACTIVE, STURDY bird with striking white rump and tail markings, long, black legs and upright posture. Male has grey back, black cheeks and wings, and white stripe above eye. Female and autumn male brownish, without contrasting head markings. Juveniles finely speckled.

WHEATEARS ARE BIRDS of rocky grassland, particularly if there are loose boulders or screes. Hiding among these screes, or showing themselves on close-cropped turf the striking males, a pattern of pale orange, grey-blue and black, with striking whiteness on rump and sides of tail, are good company. Where the male's wings are black, the female's are browner, her back is brownish grey rather than blueish, and her chest lacks the orange tone. Adults in autumn retain the characteristic tail pattern, which is shared by a number of other wheatear species, but the birds are essentially buff, with the vaguest trace of the breeding male's pattern of black face and white eye-stripe.

Frank Fraser Darling (1940) describing bird life in the *Summer Isles* wrote about wheatears: 'It would be impossible to pass through the springtime country of sea pinks, where heaps of lichened stones add their saffron and green to the brilliance of the whole, without seeing wheatears. They are brilliant also, and no bird more graceful. Would that their voice equalled their plumage.'

Peter Conder (1989) explains that 'one of the actions which has prime significance in a wide range of displays is the exposure of the rump by fanning the tail out sideways and drooping the wings a fraction.' On all occasions of excitement the tail is fanned and the rump exposed. He also mentions bobbing at the approach of any intruder, including rabbits and sheep, when the 'tuc tuc' call is usually given.

> '*The wheatears come in early spring*
> *And sit on tufts of higher ground*
> *Bobbing smartly as they sing*
> *Synchronously with the sound*'
> Robert S. Morrison WORDS ON BIRDS

SIZE

IDENTIFICATION

HABITAT

POPULATION

MAP

The usual sight of a wheatear is of a lively bird flitting close to the ground or landing on a pile of rocks. Watch for the tell-tail white rump.

Meadow Pipit

14.5 cm (5.5 in)

SIZE

IDENTIFICATION

HABITAT

POPULATION

MAP

SMALL, RATHER FEATURELESS common bird of open country. From similar tree pipit mainly by voice and habitat. Breast has less yellow, and is more delicately streaked. Flight rather undulating.

MEADOW PIPITS HAVE streaked breasts, brown backs and white outer tail feathers. They may not impress one, but their friendly presence, 'tseep' call and tinkling song as they glide down to grassy slopes is part of the hill scene in summer. On many walks in the mountains they are just about the only bird to be seen. In autumn many leave for Iberia, while others winter in loose flocks in lowland fields or by the sea.

Irish legend has it that if a meadow pipit host climbs into a cuckoo's mouth, which it often appears to be trying to, the end of the world will come.

Meadow pipits are common on upland pasture and moorland.

Twite

14 cm (5.5 in)

SPECIES INFORMATION	
SCIENTIFIC NAME	*Carduelis flavirostris*
RELATED SPECIES	Linnet, Siskin, Redpoll, Goldfinch, Greenfinch
CALL	Call is a nasal 'chweet'. Song is a rattling twitter, slightly slower than Linnet's
HABITAT	Breeds on rocky coasts, in mountains and moorland. In winter on coastal meadows, saltmarsh and stubblefields; rarer inland
STATUS	Resident and partial migrant. Winters mainly on north and east coasts. In BI about 68,500 pairs

VERY SIMILAR TO female Linnet, but browner, and with less white on wings and tail; has yellow-brown, not pale chin. Male has pinkish rump.

AT A DISTANCE, twites and linnets are very similar, but the male twite's pink rump, more distinct wing bars and honey buff face, together with longer tail are good field characters.

A gathering of twites on telephone wires in north Skye is my only lasting memory of these inconspicuous finches that are as much birds of coastal rough pastures as of mountains, particularly in winter. The 'chweet' call may separate them from linnets but they have the same bouncy flight and twitters. Always as inconspicuous as female or juvenile linnets, their yellow winter beaks and honey-coloured throats may set them apart. Twites are in long term decline in Ireland and, like other finches, suffer as so much agriculture, even in the hills, becomes cleaner.

The main breeding areas are on the Scottish coasts and highlands, and the Pennines. Those breeding on the English moors move to the coast for the winter, whereas the Scottish birds tend to be sedentary. On their return, the S. Pennine flocks rely heavily on patches of burnt purple moor grass where they exploit its fallen seeds, before dispersing to heather-dominated parts of the moors. Here the heather and bracken offer the birds safe and concealed nesting places. Throughout the breeding season they travel to and from agricultural pastures where they feed on weed seeds.

SIZE

IDENTIFICATION

HABITAT

POPULATION

MAP

The linnet-like twite is a rather unobtrusive moorland bird, sometimes seen in winter on saltmarshes.

Raven

65 cm (25 in)

SPECIES INFORMATION

SCIENTIFIC NAME	*Corvus corax*
RELATED SPECIES	Rook, Carrion Crow, Hooded Crow, Jackdaw
CALL	Call a deep, hollow 'grok', or 'krrooap'
HABITAT	Mainly mountains and other rocky sites
STATUS	Resident. In BI about 10,500 pairs

SIZE

IDENTIFICATION

HABITAT

POPULATION

MAP

LARGEST BLACK CROW, with very deep call and wedge-shaped tail. Very powerful black bill.

WHEN, IN THE 1930s, only one pair of ravens bred in Dorset, Llwelyn Powys, quoted by Hawkins (1991), described how, 'Their dark shadows cross and recross the sloping shoulders of the downs, but they are always flying alone, the male and the female, with solitary, mutual love. In February, when they prepare for the first clutch of eggs, they are self sufficient, and in mid winter, when they come in Swyre Head after a morning's scavenging on the Chesil Beach, it is the same. What a massive self absorption is suggested by the croak of a raven: no wonder to primitive minds this harsh utterance seemed to conceal hidden meanings, dark occult messages, decrees of a dolorous fate.'

Aloof though the ravens are, there is one bird that breaks in upon their proud isolation. For some obscure reason the heavy, dark flight of these giants of the air is exasperating to peregrine falcons. A peregrine falcon will pester a raven in its flight for several miles together, soaring high up above it and then with a deadly swoop darting downwards. I have seen them knock feathers out of the ravens body, but never do serious harm and it is astonishing how the great bird knows when to turn upon its back in mid air at the very instant when in its downward rush the peregrine is ready to strike.

There are certainly plenty of raven stories and superstitions. To the old St Kildans it meant battles, mayhem and death in a big way, and wayward children in Yorkshire are still told 'the black raven' will get them. In Denmark, ravens contain the unbaptised dead, and in Languedoc it is wicked priests. There was the hoarse raven in *Macbeth* and a swarthy one in the *Anglo Saxon Chronicle of 938*.

John Fowles maintains in *The Nature of Nature* that 'if I see or hear ravens something in me always rises with and to them'. They are good, if often distant company on even the worst day in the mountains. Obviously large crows, their guttural call, wedge-shaped tail and acrobatic flight distinguish them.

'The boding raven on her cottage sat,
And with hoarse croakings warned us of our fate'
John Gay THE DIRGE

Top left and right
Large size and very heavy bill typify the jet-black raven.

Bottom
In flight, the wedge-shaped tail is a good field character.

SPECIES INFORMATION

SCIENTIFIC NAME	Corvus corone cornix
RELATED SPECIES	Carrion Crow, Rook, Raven, Jackdaw
CALL	Hoarse cawing call, often repeated three times
HABITAT	Open country
STATUS	Resident and partial migrant. Replaces carrion crow in north, east and south-east Europe, and in north-west Scotland and Ireland. In BI about 450,000 pairs

Hooded Crow

47cm (19 in)

AN IMPRESSIVE BIRD to spot out of context, for example flying over Bardsey, or at a refuse dump in north London or, where there are no carrion crows, rampaging among the seaweed on an Irish beach.

BELONGS TO THE same species as carrion crow, but clearly different in plumage, with grey back and underbody. They are sufficiently alike in physiology and behaviour to be able to interbreed along a line across Britain, northern Europe and the Mediterranean. Although the hybrid zone moves, it is surprising that it does not widen. In Britain most hybrids are found in central Scotland, the north-east tip of mainland Scotland, and in the Isle of Man.

Pure hooded crows live mainly in Ireland, the Isle of Man and western and northern Scotland.

SIZE

IDENTIFICATION

HABITAT

POPULATION

MAP

Hooded crows, like ravens, often nest in rocky sites.

Freshwater and Marsh Birds

THE RIVER I have known best is the Lledr, a tributary of the Conwy in north Wales. It collects first from wet deserted grassland in the hinterland between the Crimean Pass and Moel Siabod, cascades through a deserted village at the point the railway disappears into a tunnel in the hillside and flows peacefully through the farmland of, so-called, Roman Bridge.

AFTER ANOTHER CHANGE, a surrounding of sessile oaks, it is joined by two tributaries, both now thickly planted around with conifers. Just below Dolwyddelan is a meandering stretch, where for several years I carried out a Waterways Bird Survey, and then torrential falls below Pont-y-Pant bridge.

It is a typical young upland river, with shingle banks and rapids, but 'my' stretch was not typical for the gradient is slight, allowing marshy areas and emergent riverside vegetation. The resident moorhens and a pair of reed buntings must have been the only ones for miles around, as was the occasional

sedge warbler. By contrast, the dippers, grey wagtails and common sandpipers were typical of rivers in the hills. As dippers declined, perhaps because of increasing acidity, goosanders appeared, to produce another welcome touch of impressive colour.

THE RIVER THAMES

THE THAMES IS very different, an old lowland river with a tendency to accumulate mud. It has a long history of pollution, and not only in the very lowest reaches. In 1940 Robert Gibbins mentions a walk along Strand-on-the-Green 'The houses are charming, but the river is filthy. Talk about the sacred Ganges. It is nothing to the Thames at Chiswick. And there were children bathing, swimming in water the colour of beer, with a sediment on its surface thick enough to be the beginning of a new continent.'

Twenty years on the accumulated mud was black, smelly and oxygen-deficient outside the Houses of Parliament, and so was the water. The lower river was an avian void except for gulls.

Top
The grey wagtail is almost always associated with water, usually flowing water at weirs, or along a stream.

Bottom left
Bewick's swans are regular winter visitors to open water, such as at Slimbridge or the Ouse Washes.

Bottom right
The smart dipper lives up to its name by ducking underwater and feeding along the river bed.

THE CLEAN-UP OPERATION

THE START OF the cleaning-up operation was described in the *London Bird Report* of 1972. In the late 1950s, the Port of London Authority and the Greater London Council had started an anti-

pollution programme involving the closing down of small overloaded sewage works and establishing regulations that made sure that polluted wastes should be channelled through new plants.

By 1963, dissolved oxygen was present throughout the year, although locally in very small quantities, and the foul smells, often due to hydrogen sulphide, were decreasing. It was still dirty enough for tubifex worms, who thrive on organic waste, so there was plenty of food for ducks. Peak counts over the five years from 1968, along what had been a birdless stretch of river, were 1,490 mallard, 1,500 teal, 200 wigeon, 388 pintail, 800 tufted duck, 4,000 pochard and 3,000 shelduck. In the 1960s, some 2,500 dunlin

took to roosting on new dredging beds and soon birds actually started feeding; 7,000 dunlin, 800 redshank and 100 ruff by 1972–73.

The creation of this prime new bird habitat in what seemed a hopeless situation gave hope for other polluted waters, but it involved plenty of scientific research, a vast input of money and the drive of the Chairman of the Port of London Authority.

Paradoxically, when waters get cleaner bird populations may fall. There was a time when 20,000 scaup thrived on distillery discharges in the Firth of Forth, but they are gone and tubifex worms, often used as indicators of pollution, are often a duck's best food in the Mersey. London, perhaps because the evil-smelling water passed the terrace of the House of Commons, had shown what could be done, and other rivers have followed the Thames to a far healthier state.

Top
Wigeon sometimes gather in enormous flocks at suitable feeding sites.

Middle
A female tufted duck. This species feeds mainly by diving below the surface.

Bottom
Shy and unobtrusive, the teal (female shown) is our smallest duck.

Cotswold Water Park

ANOTHER WAY THAT man can create good wildlife habitat is as a product for his search for minerals. In this section Jim Harris, Head Ranger at The Cotswold Water Park describes this situation.

OLD GRAVEL PITS

THE COTSWOLD WATER PARK is an unusual and unique place formed as a result of man's activity. Gravel quarrying, which started in the early 1900s and peaked in the 1970s, has created what is now a fascinating area of lakes and wetlands. There are now well over 100 lakes within an area of approximately 100,000 ha (25,000 acres) on the boder of Wiltshire and Gloucestershire border which includes over 1,000 ha (2,500 acres) of open water. The gravel deposits were laid down in the Jurassic era (some

Top
Tufted ducks are common at the Cotswold Water Park.

Middle
Coots build their nests close to the water, using reeds and other vegetation.

Bottom
This coot is accompanied by a young bird.

165 million years ago) by glacial meltwaters in what now forms the Upper Thames Valley. The quarrying has created the largest area of man-made lakes in Britain, about half as large again as the Norfolk Broads. Every year over two million tonnes of gravel are excavated, opening up approximately 55 ha of new ground which will later flood and form new lakes, hence the area will continue to grow for many years. The deposits and therefore the resulting lakes are not particularly deep, being between two and seven metres, provide an ideal habitat for a wide variety of wildlife.

Not only wildlife benefits from all this open water, humans flock to the area, as it is a mecca for watersports enthusiasts, naturalists and families visiting the Country Park. Watersport clubs and facilities: jet ski-ing, sailing and angling use some 40 per cent of the lakes. This causes fewer problems to wildlife than might be expected as much of the disturbance happens after the breeding season and before the winter, when there is a huge influx of over-wintering wildfowl. However there is a policy for zoning the different recreational activities to keep those ones which cause most disturbance away from the best lakes for wildlife. English Nature has drawn up conservation guidelines for 64 lakes including nine which have Site of Special Scientific Interest (SSSI) designation. These SSSIs are an unusual feature of the area as they are 'Marl Forming' lakes. Normally only found in upland limestone areas, they deposit

calcium carbonate out of the water which accumulates on the lake bed resulting in an unusual flora including often rare species such as stoneworts. These provide a very important food source for over-wintering diving ducks.

BIRDWATCHING IN THE AREA

Birdwatchers find it daunting to know where to start, but it is worthwhile persevering, especially from late autumn, when large flocks of wildfowl can be seen through to when the spring migrants arrive to breed. However all year round there can be surprises – squacco heron, red-footed falcon and white-winged black tern to name a few. In summer a huge variety of insects, especially dragonflies and damselflies, can be seen. These attract birds such as hobbies and sand martins which nest in the quarry faces. The bird life becomes very tolerant of the large quarrying

machinery and often the bare quarry floors can be worth scanning carefully to spot waders such as a visiting Temminck's stint or perhaps a nesting little ringed plover. This should only be done from the safety of the extensive rights-of way-network. In the lake margins you may be lucky enough to spot a real rarity, a little egret or even an overwintering bittern.

In autumn hundreds of golden plover arrive to feed on the surrounding farmland and then, as winter starts to bite, flights of wigeon can be heard whistling as they fly in at dusk. This is the start of the winter

build-up. The Water Park is nationally important (having over one per cent of the total GB population) for six species: gadwall, pochard, tufted duck, great crested grebe, shoveler and coot. There are many other ducks that you are likely to see, such as goosander, smew, goldeneye and the unusual red-crested pochard, which has its UK stronghold in the Water Park.

There is a Ranger Service that operates from Keynes Country Park, which covers the whole of the Cotswold Water Park. A wide variety of conservation work is done to improve habitats, often with help from volunteers, including woodland management, lake management and general landscape improvements, such as hedgelaying. One particularly large scheme, started in 1997, is attracting a lot of interest; the creation of the largest inland reedbed in southern England – some 10 ha (24 acres) of reed on 17 ha (42 acres) of land that has been quarried and partially infilled. The hope is that the bitterns that overwinter at present will no longer need to leave the area to breed, and the otters that have been sighted occasionally will become resident. A Biodiversity Action Plan has been devised with various target species and habitats.

Top
Great crested grebe. The beautiful head feathers are spread out during spring displays.

Middle
Goldeneye is a pretty winter visitor to the coast and some inland lakes.

Bottom
Pond with a good range of aquatic habitats.

211

Ponds, Fens and Marshes

APART FROM RIVERS and gravel pits, the range of freshwater habitats is extensive, with vast man-made reservoirs and extensive natural lakes ranging in size from Lough Neagh in Northern Ireland to the smallest mountain lochan, and from the wet vegetation, nutrient-rich meres to the clear, almost plant-free, nutrient-poor lakes in the north and west.

Top right
Chesil Bank and the Fleet, Dorset. This coastal lagoon attracts large numbers of wildfowl.

Middle
A farm pond – a typical moorhen habitat.

Bottom
Redshank are still common marshland birds, although their numbers have declined in many areas.

PONDS

THERE ARE THE numerous ponds which people have made for a variety of reasons; these are constantly filling naturally, being used as dumps, or cleared in the interest of tidiness or agricultural convenience. Their reduction has not had the same effect on birdlife as the draining of extensive marshes and fens: moorhens may suffer, but not as much as newts and frogs.

THE FENS

OLIVER RACKHAM (1994) DESCRIBES three great phases to draining the Fens through which the Great Ouse flows. The Romans, he explains, had the most elaborate fen engineering technology that Europe has experienced and they created the Car Dyke, the biggest artificial watercourse the Fens have ever seen,

a channel that ran for 145 km (90 miles) between Lincoln and Cambridge. When they left, their drainage system largely lapsed.

Viking place names show their involvement in the next long phase, with Anglo-Saxons and then Normans helping to make the Fens the most prosperous part of rural England by the fourteenth century. The Normans created a 96 km (60 mile) earthwork that stood for 500 years and protected more than a million acres of land.

The third drainage phase is well known, with the creation of the Old and New Bedford rivers in 1637 and 1651, not for immediate local benefit, but in the hopes of good profits, through improved grassland and arable land.

Other wet areas, such as the Somerset Levels or Romney Marsh, have similar long histories of use and periods of lapsed management. Most of the great river estuaries were not embanked so they too were wet in a way we find hard to grasp. Lagoons are formed where a river is deflected by beach material like the Fleet behind Chesil Beach in Dorset or

Slapton Lea in Devon. Flashes are shallow ponds produced by subsidence when disused mines collapse or, as in Cheshire, when rock salt is pumped out, while the Norfolk Broads were holes left by a large industry of peat digging. The population density of Norfolk and Suffolk in the eleventh century was high and they had little wood, hence the use of vast amounts of peat for fuel. They could only dig because sea levels were lower then. Peat can accumulate on slopes, retaining water and forming blanket-bogs, while if it accumulates on level ground, raised bog, a great dome of sphagnum moss, results as it did over much of Ireland before peat-fired powerstations and bog reclamation began.

BIRDLIFE

WHAT BIRDS MIGHT have been in these wet habitats as human life ebbed and flowed and prosperity came and went? Fitter (1945) gives an interesting list of birds consumed in the household of a Tudor nobleman in 1512. They included 'crannys (cranes), redeshankes, fesauntes, sholards (spoonbills), knottes, bustards, great byrdes, hearonsewys (herons), bytters (bitterns), reys (reeves), kyrlewes, wegions, dottrells, ternes and smale byrds' all of which, except the bustards for which they might have had to go to the wild heaths of Hounslow, would have been obtainable in the marshes flanking the Thames.

Three hundred years on Fitter mentions G. Graves who recorded all three harriers from the south London marshes. The hen harrier was no uncommon sight skimming over fields by the Kent Road. The bearded tit seems to have been a common bird from Oxford to the Thames estuary, and the spotted crake was said to occur in great abundance. The large number of black terns that used to nest on the Norfolk Broads are another indication of the birdlife the old wetlands supported.

RECREATION OF OLD WETLANDS

ONE OF THE most encouraging things is how the recreation of old wetlands can so rapidly bring birds

back. In the winter of 1997–98, the RSPB had almost 50,000 waterfowl of 22 species at their West Sedgemoor Reserve on the Somerset Levels, including 10,000 teal and 20,000 lapwings, while more than 5,000 waterfowl, mainly teal and wigeon, were attracted to newly-created lagoons at Pulborough Brooks in West Sussex. It is the speed with which birds colonise that is so impressive. At Holkham, Norfolk, the co-operation between English Nature, the Earl of Leicester, Lord Coke, and the tenants of the estate, has transformed a large, relatively dull area into one of high value to wildlife as Marren (1994) describes: 'There have been immediate and in some cases dramatic increases in visiting and nesting birds, including exciting ones like marsh harrier and avocet. In 1993 the nesting density of redshanks, at around 15 pairs to the square kilometre was as high as anywhere in Britain... The greater depth of water in the dykes has benefited birds like little grebe and coot. The biggest increases have been achieved by geese and wigeon.'

Many of these successful reserves are where sea and land meet, so it will be fascinating to see how the RSPB develop their reserve in the heart of England at Otmoor, and it will be interesting, too, to see how climate change influences that vital zone at the edge of the sea.

Top
The male bearded tit is a beautiful, almost exotic-looking bird. Bearded tits are reedbed specialists.

Middle
Little grebes love weedy lakes, and are adept at diving for their food.

Bottom
An adult coot leads its newly-fledged young out onto the open water.

Lough Neagh

MANY NATURAL LAKES are rich in bird life, and the largest of them all has plenty. It is years since I have been to Lough Neagh, but it is ancestral country and E.A. Armstrong, writing in 1940, uses an approach that takes history, a long history of folklore and fairy, as part of his way of looking at birds.

'IF YOU VISIT Lough Neagh expecting to see scenery like that of the English Lakes or Scottish Lochs disappointment awaits you. No craggy headlands jut forth into it, no lofty mountains mirror their high tips in its waters.

In days to come when planes and speedboats have turned Lough Neagh into a Bedlam and nobody hearkens to the wind nor heeds the fairies songs, what I have written may seem foolishness. But I testify of what I have seen and felt; and still those who care for simple things and quiet places may prove my testimony is true.'

VARIETIES OF BIRDLIFE

AFTER A NIGHT by the Loughside 'a redshank, passing hurriedly with a gleam of silver, whistles "Look out!" I do look out from my blankets and behold a pair of wagtails tripping over the stones with frequent eager leaps into the air after some luckless insect. Where there are wagtails there is peace. With noisy pinions a pair of red-breasted mergansers fly quacking along the treetops fringing the lough "QUORK, QUORK, QUORK, quork, quork." The receding calls remind me absurdly of the coughing diminuendo of a

locomotive pulling out of a station. From the heronry in the wood behind comes an uproar like the quarrelling of the damned, it is only mother disgorging her morning's catch to the youngsters!

As I swim out into the Lough there is discomfiture amongst the birds. "Kittie Needie" cries a sandpiper, the daintiest of water sprites, fleeing low with attendant reflection in the limpid lake. Moorhens sneak away with huge strides through the alders, coots call off their ginger-headed young,

crested grebes, scandalised, crane their necks and dive, a distracted shoveler quacks in agitation to her brood by the waterside amongst the yellow flags.

Top
A stately heron strides through the shallows in search of fish or frogs.

Middle
Common sandpipers can often be spotted along the banks of lakes or reservoirs.

Bottom
Radipole Lake, near Weymouth, Dorset is an RSPB reserve, excellent for wildfowl, and also passage birds during the migration.

THE DUCK POPULATION

IN MAY AND JUNE ducks are busy with domestic affairs. The shoveler is much more plentiful than formerly. On the reedy islands the tufted duck's nest is

fairly common – yet half a century ago it was unknown in Ireland as a breeding bird. The pintail has been reported from several counties; happily this bird of refined colouring and elegant figure has been found nesting on Lough Neagh. "There seems to be a kind of natural modesty in it which you do not find in other ducks," said Audubon. May it thrive and multiply.'

TRANSFORMATION OF WETLANDS

SIXTY YEARS AFTER Armstrong's writing we know so much more, but in Britain and Ireland as a whole the ordinary countryside, the ordinary rivers, the margins of the ordinary lakes grow more boring, more uniform, more sterile; we must make more of the ordinary places more like the best.

Now that the Government accept the diversity of birds as an indicator of the quality of life let us press for wetter wetlands and help the Environment Agency to make river quality and associated marshland a top priority.

> 'What would the world be, once bereft
> Of wet and of wildness? Let them be left
> O let them be left, wildness and wet;
> Long live the weeds and the wilderness yet.'
> Gerard Manley Hopkins INVERSNAID

Top
The male shoveler is a very smart bird – note the large, spoon-shaped bill.

Middle
Female pintail – note the marbled plumage.

Bottom
Water meadows such as this provide nesting sites for birds such as redshank, snipe and yellow wagtail.

Great Crested Grebe

50 cm (19 in)

SPECIES INFORMATION	
SCIENTIFIC NAME	Podiceps cristatus
RELATED SPECIES	Red-necked Grebe, Black-necked Grebe, Slavonian Grebe, Little Grebe
CALL	Raw 'gruck-gruck', hoarse 'rah-rah', mostly in spring
HABITAT	Large lakes with reedy margins, sometimes on small lakes or reservoirs
STATUS	Mainly central, southern and eastern England. Absent from much of Scotland. In Ireland mainly in the north and central areas. In winter often in flocks on large lakes, rivers and coastal seas. In BI about 12,000 birds

SIZE

IDENTIFICATION

HABITAT

POPULATION

MAP

OUR LARGEST GREBE. Striking head and neck feathers form a ruff in breeding season. In winter has dark cap, white cheeks and front of neck and a clear white stripe above eye. Juveniles have striped head and neck. Swims deep in water.

GREAT CRESTED GREBES were among the first birds to have their populations monitored by a national survey as reported in *British Birds* (1932). At that time the grebes were increasing due to the digging of gravel pits and the end of persecution for their feathers.

'Grebe furs', particularly the breast feathers, had been a fashion item supplied from the continent for many years before, and in the middle of the nineteenth century it was realised that to some extent the market could be supplied from home.

From 1870, the year of the first bird protection Act, several measures were introduced in rapid succession:–

1870 'Act for the preservation of sea birds'
1873 'Act for the protection of certain inland birds during the breeding season'
1877 'Act for the preservation of wildfowl'
1880 'Wild Birds Protection Act'

THE 1880 ACT created the first reasonable length of 'close season', from March to July, and grebes began to increase. The value of grebe 'furs' also went up, and the fashion for them did not end until 1907 or 1908.

Great crested grebes have another role in ornithological history because of Julian Huxley's pioneering work on behaviour and courtship, during which their black crests and chestnut and black tippets come into their own. The mutual head-shaking display is the commonest, but the weed ceremony – when their long pink bills gather weed, to present to each other they rise out of the water is just as impressive. At this time grebes are unmistakable, but in winter they lose their ornaments, become decidedly pale and could be mistaken for red-necked grebes but for their much whiter faces and necks and pink bills. In flight the great crested has a longer neck and larger white wing-patches.

Today great crested grebes are spread over much of lowland Britain with an increasing Irish population. In England almost 50 per cent nest on gravel pits while more natural sites, with peripheral emergent vegetation, are favoured in Scotland. The nest is a bulky mass of aquatic vegetation with spare material available for covering the eggs. Despite a repertoire of guttural clucks and growls it is not so vocal as many grebes. It is mainly a fish eater.

Populations are found in a broad swathe across the Palearctic as far as China and it also breeds in Australasia and parts of Africa. In much of its British range it is migratory with many moving to the coast. Large numbers remain at extensive inland waters like Rutland Water, Chew Valley Lake and Queen Mary Reservoir, while Lough Neagh and Belfast Lough have outstanding populations of more than 1,000.

Top
Great crested grebes perform delightful courtship dances, involving head shaking.

Bottom
Seen up close, this species is very attractive with its head plumes.

Little Grebe
25 cm (10 in)

SPECIES INFORMATION

SCIENTIFIC NAME	Tachybaptus ruficollis
RELATED SPECIES	Great Crested Grebe, Red-necked Grebe, Black-necked Grebe, Slavonian Grebe
CALL	Long, vibrating trill, mainly in spring; also a high-pitched 'bi-ib'
HABITAT	Well-vegetated ponds and small lakes, slow rivers
STATUS	In winter often in small flocks on rivers, lakes and ponds. In BI about 15,000 pairs

OUR SMALLEST GREBE, dumpy and short-necked. In breeding plumage has chestnut brown head and sides of neck, and an obvious bright spot at base of bill. In winter uniform grey-brown, somewhat lighter on flanks.

DESPITE THE WHINNYING call, the little grebe (or Dabchick) can be elusive in the breeding season appearing with young on small lakes where you have no previous suspicion of their presence. The little grebe seems just about tail-less, and hardly any neck either so that its name is very apt. They are smart birds in breeding plumage, with a yellow spot on the bill and chestnut neck, but less distinctive in winter when essentially a dull brown.

Little grebes like shallow-water breeding lakes, and can tolerate far smaller bodies of water than other grebes, as long as there is plenty of emergent vegetation and sufficient clear water surface to allow them to swim and dive.

When above the water it swims buoyantly with feathers often fluffed up to give a plump appearance. When it dives there is a distinct splash and when it flies, which it seems quite ready to do on a winter estuary, it goes low on rapid wing-beats. The fact that it appears on unlikely waters suggests more mobility than expected.

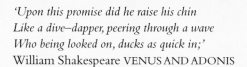

BWP describes its voice on its breeding grounds as 'wild sounding, shrill, rippling peal of notes like high pitched whinny of horse, with certain quality of laughter'. Perhaps its highly vocal summer is linked with strongly territorial nature. Little grebes are fond of molluscs and of any of all normal submerged, floating and aerial inhabitants of nutrient-rich lakes – insect larvae and crustaceans, amphibian larvae, whirligig beetles and adult flying insects snatched as the grebe swims rapidly to and fro.

'Upon this promise did he raise his chin
Like a dive–dapper, peering through a wave
Who being looked on, ducks as quick in;'
William Shakespeare VENUS AND ADONIS

'Now up, now down again that hard it is to prove
Whether underwater most it liveth or above'
Michael Drayton POLY-OLBION

 SIZE
 IDENTIFICATION
 HABITAT
 POPULATION
 MAP

Top and middle
Little grebe's nest, safely surrounded by water.

Bottom
A young little grebe seeking food from its parent.

Grey Heron

92 cm (36 in)

SIZE

IDENTIFICATION

HABITAT

POPULATION

MAP

COMMONEST AND LARGEST heron. Long neck and legs; long, pointed, yellowish bill. Plumage mainly grey; black stripe above eye, continued as two long drooping feathers. Young birds lack eye-stripe and plume feathers. Flies slowly, with heavy wing-beats and S-shaped neck, legs outstretched behind.

THE IMPRESSION CREATED by a solitary heron rising from a remoter pool is very different from that given by a group resting on the Thames foreshore, but the long legs, neck and bill and grey plumage are the same. As a large, gregarious tree-nester, with possible influence on fish populations, census work started even earlier than for great crested grebes, in 1928. Dips in population since then have often indicated cold winters.

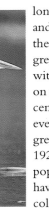

As counting began along the Thames it seems appropriate to quote from Robert Gibbings (1940). 'Watching the second bird I soon saw the cause of the trouble, for across the bird's beak was a large fish. The broad wings beat the air, the long legs of the bird trailed in the rushes, but the weight in its beak prevented it from raising its head. What misgivings there must have been in the poor creature's mind as it tried to rise, and what disappointment when it was compelled to drop its burden! In the momentary glance I had of the fish as it fell, I estimated it to be about two pounds in weight, but pink, trout or chub I failed to mark it.'

After early returns to breeding sites, the males issue far-carrying advertising call, perched conspicuously with head raised. Away from the heronry the harsh 'frarnk' call is common.

Top and middle
Typical views of herons standing or wading in shallow water

Bottom
In flight herons are heavy and ponderous, with slow wingbeats.

'*The old heron from the lonely lake*
Starts slow and flaps his melancholy wings.'
John Clare SELECTED POEMS

Bittern
76 cm (30 in)

A SQUAT, BROWN HERON, with relatively short neck. Plumage reed-coloured, legs and toes green (camouflage). Flight owl-like, with head stretched out in short flight, tucked in for longer flight. Clambers slowly among reeds. Stands motionless with head erect when disturbed, often for long periods.

THE BITTERN POPULATION is dangerously low with possible causes including pesticides, neglect of traditionally managed reedbeds, increased leisure boating and a decrease in the reedbeds themselves. It is included here as, even though rare, it is a keystone wetland species.

The booming call carries an extraordinary distance, but it is hard to find the caller. Bitterns may show themselves in open water in winter or be seen flying over the reeds when feeding young. Their ability to regurgitate frogs and fish of a size appropriate to their different-sized young is a special one, as is their ability to 'freeze' so that their mottled golden plumage merges with the reeds.

Because of their significance to birds, the proper management of reedbeds is important, particularly as fewer are now cut to produce a crop of thatching reed. Reedbeds, dominated by the common reed *Phragmites australis*, can be tidal or freshwater; neglected freshwater ones tend to dry out as dead vegetation builds up. The control of water level, by sluices and ditches, makes management possible for the reedbed must not dry out in summer. A regime that lowers the water level below the soil in autumn can allow cutting and prevent the build up of litter. Open water areas may add to habitat diversity, bitterns can feed in water up to 20 cm (8 in) deep and bearded tits flourish in beds of over 20 ha (49 acres); all these factors need consideration.

While traditional management for thatching might involve annual or biennial cutting, management for birds involves longer rotations, leaving plenty of cover, for species such as marsh harriers. As with grasslands, all cut material needs to be removed, but burning adds unwanted nutrients and piling around the fringes is labour intensive. The latter option may however create nesting sites for wildfowl as well as a habitat for beetles and hibernating grass snakes.

The varied diet of the bittern includes fish, amphibians, worms, leeches and molluscs as well as birds, lizards and crustaceans, but in winter sufficient food may be hard to find, and in most years reports of emaciated bitterns occur, often in unlikely places. In cold winters more continental birds arrive in Britain, and if there was enough suitable habitat perhaps more of them would stay. Foreign ringed birds tend to have come from north-west Europe where the Netherlands and Germany have good populations.

Bitterns are very secretive, skulking amongst the reeds, where their camouflaged plumage makes them hard to spot.

Mute Swan

150 cm (60 in)

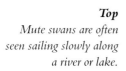

SIZE

IDENTIFICATION

HABITAT

POPULATION

MAP

SPECIES INFORMATION

SCIENTIFIC NAME	Cygnus olor
RELATED SPECIES	Whooper Swan, Bewick's Swan
CALL	Fairly silent, occasional hissing in defence. Wing noise in flight
HABITAT	Mainly freshwater. Lakes, gravel pits and ponds, even in urban areas. In winter often in large numbers on lakes. Breeds in lakes with rich vegetation and reedy banks; also banks of slow rivers and near the coast. Makes large nest of old reeds and other plant material. Semi-domesticated in many areas
STATUS	Partial migrant. In BI about 40,000 birds

LARGEST AND HEAVIEST waterbird. Pure white plumage, bill reddish with black base; obvious knob on bill, more developed in male, especially in spring. Juveniles grey-brown; bill grey, without knob. Swims with neck held in S-shaped curve. Flies with powerful wing-beats, with neck stretched out. Wings make distinct swishing sound.

SWANS ARE IMMEDIATELY recognisable, and the vast majority are of this species. The orange-red bill with its black knob, larger on the male when breeding starts, is diagnostic, as are the arched wings of aggression of swimming males and their graceful curved necks. Young birds, in their first year, also have a black base to their bill but grey-brown plumage. As the name implies, this species is normally silent but makes a distinctive throb, peculiar to the mute swan, with its wings as it flies and it hisses readily to protect nest or young.

In western Europe many swans are semi-tame, and very used to human activities, so that in parks they will readily take food, and on urban rivers, not only the Thames, they have built up large populations. On the Severn, and elsewhere, a rapid decline was linked to the ingestion of lead weights used by fishermen, but publicity about the deaths changed fishing practice. There are still problems with nylon fishing line.

The largest breeding colony, over 600 years old, at Abbotsbury in Dorset, is a popular tourist attraction. The brochure indicates the level of their wildness, encouraging visitors to help feed them at 12 and 4 pm daily, and visitors find the major attraction between mid-May and the end of June when over a hundred nests with six eggs each produce young.

Mute swans tend to like gentle waters, but whether these are river, gravel-pit, natural wetland or

Top
Mute swans are often seen sailing slowly along a river or lake.

Bottom
Mute swans traditionally congregate in large numbers at Abbotsbury, Dorset.

urban lake, does not seem to matter. There needs to be a supply of vegetation, of rushes and reeds, to create the large mounded nest which can be more than 2 m (6.5 ft) in diameter and which, as well as vegetation, has a lining of down.

Although not migratory in western Europe, there are local movements, Northern European birds are much more mobile, with movements from Scandinavia and northern Germany down to warmer wintering quarters, where water plants are not iced over. Much grazing, however, is at the water's edge, and on land, and some of the food is animal, including frogs, snails and worms.

Thames swans have been protected, at least since the time of Edward III in 1387, but even so, during that reign, swans were available in London markets at ten times the price of a goose. Swan upping, when young birds are caught and have their beaks marked, must have been very active in Elizabethan times for there were 900 recognised swan marks. A surviving aspect of this is any pub called the

'Generally speaking, I do not like swans. I think they are self opinionated and the flattery of human beings. Whenever they go they are pampered or treated with respect and indulgence. They have been glorified in the mythology of many countries.... But whatever may be said for or against the birds, there is no doubt that a swan on her nest has a truly regal appearance; and in the spring there are plenty of them to be seen on the islands in the Thames. There they sit, under canopies of budding willows, proud as queens upon their thrones, while their ever vigilant consorts sail majestically up and down the stream.'
Robert Gibbings SWEET THAMES RUN SOFTLY

'Swan with Two Necks' which is a corruption of 'Swan with two nicks', for the Vintners Company marked their birds with two nicks on the bill. Royalty have always been associated with swans, and in the time of Henry VII one could be imprisoned for a year and a day, as well as being fined, for stealing a swan's egg, but attempts to restrict the ownership of the swans seem to have failed, and swan stealing was rife. Since the end of the eighteenth century only the Crown and the Dyers and Vintners Companies have exercised their swan rights.

Introduced birds have made this already widely distributed swan even more widespread and with its capacity to live with man, but less happily with his dogs, this, our heaviest resident bird, must be our most conspicuous.

Top
A mute swan's nest is often a huge mound of vegetation, usually close to the river bank or lake side.

Middle
One of the heaviest of all flying birds, a mute swan needs a long run for successful take off.

Bottom
Mute swan courtship is a romantic sight.

221

Whooper Swan

150 cm (60 in)

SIZE

IDENTIFICATION

HABITAT

POPULATION

MAP

AS LARGE AS MUTE swan but slimmer. Bill has yellow wedge-shaped patch and lacks knob at base. Neck held straight. Juveniles greyer than young mute, bill flesh-coloured with darker tip. Flocks often fly in formation.

SPECIES INFORMATION	
SCIENTIFIC NAME	Cygnus cygnus
RELATED SPECIES	Mute Swan, Bewick's Swan
CALL	Calls frequently. Swimming flocks have goose-like nasal calls, loud trumpeting calls before and during migration
HABITAT	Breeds in bogs and around tundra lakes. Winters to washland and wet marshes
STATUS	Regular winter visitor in large flocks to North Sea and Baltic coasts, as well as to lakes and flooded rivers. Large numbers visit Ireland and Britain (mainly from Iceland). A handful breed each year in BI (about 5 pairs)

THESE MOST ELEGANT swans like shallow water and extensive grass and in favoured areas occur in large flocks. Our birds come from the western part of their tundra breeding range while Eastern birds move to Japan and China. Our whooper swans breed mainly in Iceland. Both whooper and Bewick's swans have yellow and black beaks with the Bewick's having more black than yellow, and the whooper the reverse.

Whooper swans gain their name from the bugle-like trumpetings, produced through a particularly long trachea, which are highly characteristic of flocks on the move or on the water.

A few whoopers stay in Britain for the summer and breeding has been recorded, as it has in Donegal.

The whooper swan has a large triangular patch of bright yellow on its bill.

Bewick's Swan

125 cm (48 in)

SPECIES INFORMATION

SCIENTIFIC NAME	*Cygnus columbianus*
RELATED SPECIES	*Whooper Swan, Mute Swan*
CALL	*Family groups make yodelling calls*
HABITAT	*Washland and flooded meadows*
STATUS	*Winter visitor*

BEWICK'S SWAN IS smaller than whooper, and has a variable yellow/orange bill patch. Regular winter visitor to north-west Europe from Siberian breeding grounds.

THE EXACT PATTERN on each individual Bewick's swan's beak is different, and students of Slimbridge birds, which have come to winter in the luxury of that Severnside reserve, having learned and named the individuals, can identify them on migration, on their distinct breeding grounds or on their annual return to Gloucestershire. Over a third of these Slimbridge birds carry some level of lead shot despite extensive protection.

Apart from bill colour and size, Bewick's are shorter-necked and shorter-bodied than other swans, and their bills are smaller than those of whoopers. The different bill size does not seem to reflect much difference in diet for both are largely vegetarians with leaves, shoots, roots and the like gathered by upending or grazing on land. Despite this their winter habitat seems very different,

although they overlap in protected areas like the Ouse Washes. Whoopers are far more northerly, happy with impoverished upland lakes of no great size and ready to graze on estuary eel-grass as well as agricultural land.

The Bewick's distribution is patchy, with very few in Scotland, but in Ireland there are plenty of whoopers.

Britain and Ireland are internationally important for both birds with eight English sites for Bewick's and 12 British and Irish sites for whoopers having more than one per cent of the international population. In 1995–96 there were almost 5,000 Bewick's on the Ouse Washes and almost 2,000 on the Nene Washes, while Lough Neagh and the Ouse Washes each had over 1,000 whooper swans.

> *'Here in my vaster pools, as white as snow or milk*
> *In water black as Styx, swims the wild swan, the ilke*
> *Of Hollanders so termed, no niggard of his breath*
> *(As poets says of swans who only sing in death);*
> *But, as other birds, is heard his tunes to roat*
> *Which like a trumpet comes, from his long*
> *arched throat.'*
> Michael Drayton

SIZE

IDENTIFICATION

HABITAT

POPULATION

MAP

Top
The patch on Bewick's swan's bill is variable in shape, but is normally smaller than whooper's; it is also more orange-yellow.

Bottom left
Wintering pairs are often accompanied by their offspring.

Canada Goose

100 cm (40 in)

SPECIES INFORMATION	
SCIENTIFIC NAME	*Branta canadensis*
RELATED SPECIES	*Brent Goose*
CALL	*Flight-call a nasal trumpeting, accented on the second syllable*
HABITAT	*Reservoirs, lakes, fishponds and ornamental lakes in parks. Introduced from North America; original habitat is marshy lakes and river banks, right up into tundra region*
STATUS	*Resident and partial migrant. About 60,000 pairs in Britain; about 700 in Ireland, where very local*

SIZE

IDENTIFICATION

HABITAT

POPULATION

MAP

VERY LARGE GOOSE (though the species is variable, with some small races) with long, black neck. Head black and white, tail, bill and feet black. Flocks often fly in V-formation.

THE LARGE CANADA goose has become familiar over most of England, and increasingly in southern Scotland, Ireland and lowland Wales. It has a dark head and white face patch, white belly and grey-brown body, and a dark tail. Canada geese are commonly found grazing in town or country. The winter flocks are highly mobile, making noisy honking calls as they fly.

This species was introduced into England in the seventeenth century and a glance at a selection of books will indicate its increase and change to a wider range of breeding sites. *Witherby's Handbook* (1939) says 'breeding local and to a great extent artificial'. Hollom (1952) in the *Popular Handbook* said much the same: 'widespread but local, breeding chiefly on private lakes'. The West Midlands has been a centre of increase, and the *Atlas of Breeding Birds in the West Midlands* says how flocks of 40 were noteworthy in 1950, whereas by 1970 flocks of 400 were to be found on some occasions. The first *Breeding Atlas* (1976) reported that 'following transportation by man there was a more marked tendency to breed on reservoirs with natural margins, flooded gravel pits, rural meres and town lakes', and by the *New Atlas* (1993) it had a catholic taste in breeding sites and was widespread in all English counties.

Although our introduced birds are mobile, they are not migratory except for moult migrations which have recently developed, with Yorkshire birds moving to Inverness. In North America there are northern moult migrations and extensive autumn movements to the south, with birds reaching Mexico. American birds cause taxonomic disagreements, with some authorities claiming four different species, and others claiming a varied range of subspecies. British birds are mainly of the subspecies *B. canadensis canadensis* but some seem too large for that. A white neck collar distinguishes some of these subspecies.

Canada geese breed close to water; very close if there are no islands on which to build their nests of a pile of vegetation, which may be on a raft of twigs or branches.

Top left
The white patch on the black neck is characteristic of the Canada goose.

Top right
Canada geese are fond of grazing.

Bottom
Pair with their brood of goslings.

Mallard

58 cm (23 in)

BEST KNOWN DUCK, the world's commonest, and ancestor of most domestic duck breeds. Breeding male has shiny green head with yellow bill, reddish-brown breast and curly black central tail feathers. Female brown and speckled.

THE MALLARD IS common on a wide variety of water, in town and country. The green head and white collar of the male is most familiar, as are the browns and buffs of the speckled females. Both have the violet speculum on the wing, while the purplish breast of the male is also distinctive. Males and females in eclipse are similar to other surface-feeding ducks so examine the beaks closely; the fine bill of the gadwall has orange patches pintail have a blue-grey bill, and wigeon much shorter ones. Mallards have longer bills than these, with the male's essentially yellow and the female's more orange.

Being highly adaptable, but liking shallow water, mallard can be found in town parks where artificially supplied food is welcome, or on small and even remote lochs, as long as there is vegetation. Some of this is used in nest building, as is down, but once again the bird is adaptable with some nesting in trees, some among ground vegetation and some under the shelter of logs or boulders. The downy young make spectacular descents from tree nests and often have to make substantial journeys to water; hence the newspaper's favourite pictures of policemen helping the birds across the road.

A very successful species across Europe and beyond it has also done well after being introduced in the southern hemisphere. As many breed in arctic tundra there are extensive winter movements. Those moving to Britain are more ready to use brackish and estuarine habitats in winter than for breeding. Here, and on island waters, there may be extensive flocking with much upending, surface dabbling and terrestrial grazing for plants which make up much of the food.

There is much variation through interbreeding with domestic ducks, and in some parks, or even small estuaries where feeding takes place, the range in size and colour is extensive, with few typical wild birds to be found. Whether wild or not, male sexual behaviour can be aggressive which could be the basis for the mallard having become a symbol of male promiscuity and fertility in the thirteenth century. Pope Gregory IX preached a crusade against a devil-worshipping cult whose symbol was a drake.

 SIZE
 IDENTIFICATION
 HABITAT
 POPULATION
 MAP

Like many ducks, male and female mallard have markedly different plumage.

225

Wigeon

46 cm (18 in)

○○○○○○○○○○○○○○○○○○○○○○○○○○○○○○

SPECIES INFORMATION

SCIENTIFIC NAME	*Anas penelope*
RELATED SPECIES	Mallard, Gadwall, Pintail, Shoveler, Teal, Garganey
CALL	Highly distinctive whistling 'whee-oo', with accent on first syllable (male). Rattling 'rarr' (female)
HABITAT	Lakes, muddy shores and estuaries
STATUS	Breeds on lakes, bogs and river deltas in northern Europe. In BI, about 450 pairs, mainly in the north. Regular winter visitor to North Sea and other coasts

SIZE

IDENTIFICATION

HABITAT

POPULATION

MAP

MEDIUM-SIZED DUCK with tucked-in head, high forehead and short bill. Breeding male has chestnut head with golden crown stripe; female similar to mallard female, but slimmer, with rusty-brown plumage and more pointed tail. In flight note the long wings and white belly, also large white wing-patches of male. Often forms large flocks in winter. Wigeon are vegetarian, grazing on land, or taking food from at or near the water surface.

WHETHER ONE HEARS them by a large reservoir, moving around on the edge of floodwater or on the mud of an estuary as the tide retreats, the whistling of wigeon is one of the great sounds of winter. They first arrive on our local estuary, visible from the road, in September, unimpressive in their eclipse plumage and unimpressive in numbers, but later there may be a couple of hundred and from the car, in the morning when the light is right, you can see the detail on the males. They now have yellow forecrowns on their chestnut heads.

The body is gently patterned grey, the silhouette distinctive, the chest pink and the rear end a contrast of black and white. As they dabble at the water's edge they whistle contentedly, paying no attention to the traffic and the female is seen to be just as distinctively shaped with her small bill, pointed

Above right
A large group of wigeon take to the air. The drake has a highly distinctive whistling flight-call.

Centre and bottom right
The drake wigeon is one of our prettiest waterfowl.

Bottom left
Grazing wigeon. At distance, the pure white at the base of the tail stands out clearly.

tail and high forehead. When the tide, or a passing dog, makes them fly, her white belly is characteristic. Both sexes have pointed wings and the white forewings of the males can still be seen as they gently descend some way off in the saltmarsh.

These birds will have come from Scandinavia, Finland, or Russia to winter on the Axe where, if we are lucky, we have 200 birds. More than 300,000 have made the journey to Britain. Estuaries, river valleys and areas of low-lying marsh will have more than 2,000, while the Ribble will sometimes have 100,000 feeding on eel-grass, sometimes called wigeon-grass, or grazing on grassland.

Of all the wintering wigeon, only some 300 pairs may be British breeding birds, mainly of Scottish origin. They breed scattered about upland bogs and lakes, in the Flow Country or on Loch Leven, with a few in northern England. Courtship is rather different from most dabbling ducks with hostility between courting males. The dominant males displays yellow crown in forehead-turning display. A tussock or a bit of shelter from scrub is needed to shelter the nest, a depression of grasses lined with down.

Gadwall
48–54 cm (19–21 in)

MALLARD-LIKE BUT slightly smaller and slimmer, with steeper forehead. Male relatively drab, with obvious black 'stern'. In flight both sexes show white belly and white speculum. Female has yellow-orange edges to bill.

THE DABBLING DUCKS have much in common so details of size and bill colour will be considered together. Male gadwall usually appear grey-brown with black back ends, and can easily be missed among duck as the white wing-patch is often obscure. In flight this becomes the identification feature while in good light the grey-brown, as Tunnicliffe mentions, becomes a complex of fine lines.

Gadwall are vegetarian and so like rich, shallow waters of the lowlands, and as even the young have much the same vegetable diet they avoid competition with, for example, the insectivorous ducklings of mallards.

SIZE

IDENTIFICATION

HABITAT

POPULATION

MAP

The male Gadwall's most striking feature is its jet black stern.

Teal

34–38 cm (13–15 in)

SPECIES INFORMATION	
SCIENTIFIC NAME	*Anas crecca*
RELATED SPECIES	Mallard, Wigeon, Pintail, Shoveler, Garganey, Gadwall
CALL	Melodious 'krick', often in flight (male). Female has a higher-pitched quack
HABITAT	Breeds on lakes with thick bank vegetation
STATUS	Widespread in N and E Europe, rarer further south. About 3,000 pairs in BI. Northern breeders move south for winter. Commoner outside breeding season, especially on flooded meadows and marshland

SIZE

IDENTIFICATION

HABITAT

POPULATION

MAP

OUR SMALLEST DUCK, with rapid, wader-like flight. Breeding male has chestnut and green head, and yellow triangle (bordered black) at side of tail. Female has yellow-brown spots and dark grey bill. Both sexes show white wing bar and green speculum in flight.

TEAL ARE THE smallest of the dabbling ducks. The male looks grey, with a brown head and buff black end. The green mark through the eye is often obscure but the white stripe along the scapulars is seen whether swimming, walking or flying past in a compact flock. The female, as with most ducks, is mottled brown with her green and black speculum and wing bars her most distinctive features. The very clear 'krit krit' call in flight is as good a winter sound as the wigeon's whistle and the two are often found together.

Any area of winter flooding may be the place for teal, and even smaller rivers get a few visitors. This implies a mobile population, moving according to weather and food supplies, and ringing recoveries confirm this. Hard weather movements to Ireland are characteristic. On their wanderings, seeds will be important, whether those of estuarine plants or farm weeds, but insects and molluscs, some flooded out of the soil, form a quarter of the diet.

Although they are wanderers, there are significant aggregations in suitable fresh water or estuarine conditions. While Mersey populations have fallen, the 1995–96 population on the Somerset Levels, where attempts are being made to keep water levels higher, rose to a peak of 24,000. Average populations on the Mersey, Ribble and Dee are also of international importance, while Lough Neagh and Strangford Lough have important populations in Northern Ireland. The breeding distribution is thinly scattered, concentrated on upland areas, where it is undisturbed, close to small moorland pools and bogs.

As already implied, most populations are migratory with northern populations moving south-west to winter to Britain and the Netherlands. The American subspecies, the green-winged teal, is an extensive migrant, moving as far south as the West Indies and Central America and sometimes appearing over here, as a vagrant. Adult males are recognisable by the absence of the white horizontal stripe on scapulars and the presence of a white crescent at the sides of the breast.

Top and middle
The drake teal has bright, pretty plumage.

Bottom
Teal in typical pose, resting close to the water.

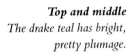

Garganey
37–40 cm (14.5–15.75 in)

SPECIES INFORMATION

SCIENTIFIC NAME	*Anas querquedula*
RELATED SPECIES	Teal, Mallard, Wigeon, Pintail, Shoveler, Gadwall
CALL	Breeding male has dry 'klerreb'; female a high-pitched, nasal quack
HABITAT	Breeds on shallow water or marsh with rich vegetation. Outside breeding season on lakes, flooded meadows and marshes
STATUS	Summer visitor to much of Europe (but absent from most of north-west and south Europe). Winters in Africa. In BI rare breeding bird, about 50 pairs

SLIGHTLY LARGER YET slimmer than teal. Breeding male has broad white eye-stripe reaching to back of head. Female like teal but with rather striped face pattern. Male in eclipse like female, but with blue-grey front of wing. Flight not as rapid as teal.

BWP SAYS THE garganey voice 'is characterised by the peculiar call of the male who lacks pure whistles in his repertoire and whose main utterance is a unique mechanical sounding rattle recalling the crackling noise of breaking ice'.

The drake garganey is a very beautiful bird, mainly mottled brown, with fine crescent markings on the breast, and a broad white band from the eye to the nape of the neck. The breast is brown, and sharply divided from the grey flanks and white underparts. The scapulars are blue-grey, black and white. The speculum is a bright metallic green, bordered with white in front and behind. On the wing the pale bluish-grey forewing is often conspicuous.

Garganey are unique among the *Anas* ducks in being wholly migratory, wintering in sub-Saharan Africa, even as far south as the Transvaal. In Britain it is on the edge of its range, and the small numbers fluctuate. Breeding is in sheltered, shallow waters with plenty of floating and emergent vegetation. The main movement to these breeding areas is in March and April, with eggs laid in late April.

> 'a kind of Teale which some fowlers call crackling teal from the noyse it maketh'
> Christopher Merrett (c 1660)

SIZE · IDENTIFICATION · HABITAT · POPULATION · MAP

Male garganey, showing the prominent white eyestripe – its most obvious feature.

Pintail

55–65 cm (22–25.5 in)

SPECIES INFORMATION	
SCIENTIFIC NAME	Anas acuta
RELATED SPECIES	Mallard, Wigeon, Shoveler, Gadwall, Teal, Garganey
CALL	Breeding call of male a low whistle; female a grating quack
HABITAT	Breeds mainly on shallow lakes in northern coniferous forest or tundra. Outside breeding season mainly on the coast, or flooded washland
STATUS	Summer visitor to breeding grounds. Winter visitor further south (mainly coastal areas). Rare breeder in BI, about 50 pairs

SIZE

IDENTIFICATION

HABITAT

POPULATION

MAP

SLIMMER THAN MALLARD. Male has chestnut head, grey body and long, pointed tail feathers. Female similar to mallard, but has more pointed tail and smaller, grey bill. Eclipse male very similar to female, but darker above. In flight (which is rapid) note long, pointed wings, slim body, long neck and white-edged speculum.

TUNNICLIFFE'S ANGLESEY PAINTINGS emphasise the black rear end of pintail males. They also have an elaborate vermiculated pattern on the back and flanks, which both appear grey at long range,

contrasting with dark head and clear white band down the side of the neck. When displaying, the drakes exhibit this striking nape and neck pattern, as a reminder that most or all the colours of birds have their appropriate significance. Slimbridge is a marvellous place to watch such elaborate duck displays, which focus on the brightly coloured parts

being exhibited by ritualised movements. The male pintail's tail is long and pointed but the female's is also pointed enough to help identification.

Although a few pintail do breed in Britain, they are essentially northern ducks ranging into tundra with a preference for moderately productive shallow pools and floods. Perhaps the often temporary nature of these explain why this mobile bird often nests as outlier populations well beyond its normal range. Pintail nest on the ground, usually but not always close to the water, lining a grassy nest with down.

The winter populations here are about half of the north-west European population, with Strangford Lough in Northern Ireland and Dublin Bay in the Republic holding significant numbers, but nothing like the 15 internationally important sites in England and Wales. The largest average populations recently have been 6,500 on the Dee and 3,300 on the Ribble. Pintail populations in the north-west emphasise the importance of that part of the Lancashire coast for estuarine birds.

Top and middle
The drake pintail has a very richly-textured breeding plumage, and the long, pointed tail which gives the species its name.

Bottom
In flight the long tail is very obvious.

Shoveler
47–53 cm (18.5–21 in)

 SIZE

 IDENTIFICATION

HABITAT

POPULATION

SQUATTER THAN MALLARD, with more pointed wings and long, broad bill. Male has dark head, white breast and chestnut belly and flanks. Female rather like mallard, but has pale blue forewing.

THE MALE HAS very distinctive plumage, but even the drab female can be identified with ease from the broad, flattened bill.

COMPARISON OF BILLS OF SEVERAL SPECIES

SPECIES	SIZE OF BILL	DESCRIPTION OF BEAK
Gadwall	50 mm (2 in)	Orange at sides (female)
Teal	36 mm (1.4 in)	Dark grey
Garganey	38 mm (1.5 in)	Grey; pale spot near base (female)
Pintail	56 mm (2.2 in)	Slim, grey
Shoveler	51 mm (2 in)	Broad, flattened
Mallard	58 mm (2.3 in)	Black and orange patches (female) Yellowish (male)
Wigeon	48 mm (1.9 in)	Small: grey-blue with dark tip

Male Shovelers, apart from their top heavy look, have green heads and a most distinguished contrast of chestnut flanks with white in front and behind and dark back. The blue forewing and green speculum are more visible in flight when wings appear small and pointed.

The bill can be used on the surface as a filter, being swept from side to catch crustaceans and other drifting invertebrates. The shoveler's filters are made up of intermeshing hair-like structures associated with both jaws, while the large bill allows much water to be sucked in.

Their breeding populations are scattered, being dependent on just the right sort of shallow water close to rough pasture or marshland. It is more territorial and less impressive in display than other ducks.

The main Palearctic populations are to the east, and it is some of these birds that make up our winter populations. These are nearly all freshwater, and there can be 500 or more on the Ouse Washes, at Abberton Reservoir, Rutland Water, Loch Leven or the Somerset Levels.

MAP

Top right
A pair of shovelers living up to their name.

Bottom
Apart from the bill-shape, drake and duck look rather different.

231

Pochard

46 cm (18 in)

S P E C I E S I N F O R M A T I O N	
SCIENTIFIC NAME	Aythya ferina
RELATED SPECIES	Tufted Duck, Scaup
CALL	Rather silent. Breeding male has low nasal whistle; female a raw 'cherr-cherr'
HABITAT	Breeds on rich freshwater lakes with large open areas and reeds. Outside breeding season on large lakes, reservoirs, ponds and slow-flowing rivers, often in large flocks. Sometimes tame in parks and lakes
STATUS	Resident and partial migrant. Summer visitor to north and east of range. Numbers in BI swelled in winter by migrants. Population in BI around 450 pairs

SIZE

IDENTIFICATION

HABITAT

POPULATION

MAP

PLUMP, COMPACT DUCK with domed head and steep forehead. Male has contrasting silver-grey back and flanks, black chest and tail, and chestnut-brown head. Female brown, with blackish bill and pale eye-ring.

MALE POCHARD, with brown head, black breast and patterned grey back and sides are handsome ducks. Females are rather nondescript brown, like many another duck, but the amount of grey among the brown, and the grey-banded bill make her recognisable. Like females, males have pale blue-banded bill and dark legs. They are fairly unusual among ducks in that there is no wing bar in flight, which is fast, with rapid beats of the broad wings.

The genus *Aythya* and relatives are medium-sized, diving ducks usually found on fresh water. Heads are distinctly large and bodies short; two features which are very clear when pochard and tufted duck flocks swim peacefully with beaks hidden as they doze on park lake, gravel pit or reservoir. As expert divers they have large toes and the legs are widely separated and set far back on the body, so are much more reluctant to move on land than mallards.

If sufficient food is offered, as it often is in town parks, they will move out near the water.

Although an expert diver, mainly to collect plant material, it is also a dabbler and upender, and its mixed feeding methods may have led to the name, with the old French 'pocher' meaning to poke about. The name pochard was not used until 1544.

Pochards breed in a broad band across Europe, avoiding the tundra and liking extensive shallow water as befits their feeding methods. They normally breed in thick vegetation, making a shallow nest of leaves and reed stems with the usual duck addition of down. In Britain there are only some 400 pairs, with a markedly eastern bias, but in winter a major arrival of migrants is heralded by the males, who arrive a fortnight before females in early autumn. Perhaps because of this, males and females often overwinter separately.

Top
Grey, black at both ends, and a rich chestnut head – defines the drake pochard.

Bottom left
Pochard in flight.

Bottom Right
Duck pochard has drabber plumage.

Tufted Duck

44 cm (17 in)

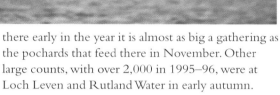

SPECIES INFORMATION	
SCIENTIFIC NAME	*Aythya fuligula*
RELATED SPECIES	Pochard, Scaup
CALL	Breeding male has guttural 'gee-gee-gee'; female a grating 'kreck-kreck'.
HABITAT	Lakes and reservoirs
STATUS	Resident and partial migrant. Numbers in BI swelled in winter by migrants. Relatively common breeding bird, occasionally in urban areas too. In BI population stands at about 10,000 pairs

SMALL, COMPACT DIVING duck. In flight shows white wing bar. Male black with white flanks, and long plume on back of head (which has purple sheen). Female dark brown, with head plume very short or absent, and sometimes with white spot at base of bill. Often forms large winter flocks. Not so quiet as pochard, the male whistles during the breeding season when females also call softly.

SIZE

IDENTIFICATION

HABITAT

POPULATION

MAP

TUFTED DUCK MUST be among the most popular of park birds; plenty of character, distinctive plumage and a spectacular dive help to make them attractive. The tuft is clear in breeding males but is little more than a bump on the back of the head of the female. The clear black and white pattern and black back of the male are unmistakable, but the dark brown female could be confused with similar, but white-faced, scaup or even a young male pochard, but it also has a paler face. The conspicuous yellow eye adds to their attraction, and the broad white wing bar in flight is very noticeable.

By becoming tolerant of humans, and ready to adapt diet to their offerings, the tufted duck has added park lakes to the other habitats, reservoirs, gravel pits, natural lakes and lowland lochs where it can be seen in winter. The number at Lough Neagh is of international importance, and with over 25,000

there early in the year it is almost as big a gathering as the pochards that feed there in November. Other large counts, with over 2,000 in 1995–96, were at Loch Leven and Rutland Water in early autumn.

Tufted ducks dive deeper than pochard and eat more animal food, some being sieved from bottom mud and some, like molluscs, being picked off underwater vegetation.

Although they need open water for feeding, without too much marginal encroachment, a degree of cover is needed for nesting to keep predation levels within bounds. Grassy tussocks close to water are favoured, but on islands, the ideal breeding site, they may make their nest of rushes and down further from the water. They will sometimes nest in the open among gulls and terns which give more protection to nests. After breeding, flocking starts early, with males collecting first after the break-up of the pair bond.

Top right
Tufted show a prominent white wing-bar in flight.

Bottom
The delicate crest trailing down the back of its head gives the tufted duck its name.

233

Marsh Harrier

48–56 cm (19–22 in)

SPECIES INFORMATION	
SCIENTIFIC NAME	*Circus aeruginosus*
RELATED SPECIES	Hen Harrier, Montagu's Harrier
CALL	Male has squawking 'quiair', alarm-call a snarling 'kike-kike-kike'
HABITAT	Marshes and lakes with extensive reedbeds. Hunts over reeds, water meadows, fields and open country
STATUS	Resident. In BI, mainly in south and east about 100 pairs

SIZE

IDENTIFICATION

HABITAT

POPULATION

MAP

BUZZARD-SIZED, BUT slimmer and narrower-winged and with longer tail. Male has pale grey tail and upper wings, contrasting with otherwise dark plumage and black wing tips. Female dark, with cream coloured head and shoulders. Flight slow, interspersed with buoyant gliding, wings held in a V-shape.

MARSH HARRIERS SHARE their reedbed habitat with the even rarer bittern, and both nest mainly in protected and managed reserves. The population is now recovering from a disastrous low, probably due to pesticides in the food chain.

They fly over the reeds with characteristic harrier glides, long tails and distinctive V silhouette of the wings. The male has grey patches on the wings and tail, and the larger female has a pale crown and throat. With one male often partnering more than one female we can talk of nests rather than pairs. In fact, some 15 per cent of males are polygamous and this may help explain the increase in recent years.

Brown (1976) describes their spectacular display: 'From this height they tumble earthwards in spectacular dives, during which they twist violently from side to side, or spin through 360°. The erratic movements display the contrasting grey and brown of their wings to advantage and the whole process is not only visible but the rushing sound made is audible for some distance. At the completion of the dive the male mounts again steeply, to repeat the

performance, sometimes after further acrobatics which may include looping the loop at the top of the swift steep upward swoop.'

He also describes the food pass, which is characteristic of all harriers: 'The male arriving with food calls the female off the nest with a characteristic mewing whistle. The female may answer with a higher pitched whistle. She rises from her perch, or from the nest and flies to meet the male. He often drops the food, which the female flying below him then  catches with a dextrous twist in mid air. Sometimes however, she flies up to him, turns over, and receives the prey by a foot to foot pass, a spectacularly agile and beautifully timed movement.'

In reedbeds the food passed may be a rodent, particularly voles, a bird or perhaps an amphibian. These are caught in low flight which is checked before descent with long legs extended. In arable fields, small birds, including young game birds, and rabbits are favoured.

Top left
A female marsh harrier looks out over the reedbeds from a vantage point nearby.

Top right
Typical harrier outline – very buoyant in flight, with a fairly long tail.

Bottom
Female marsh harrier – note the long, yellow legs.

SPECIES INFORMATION

SCIENTIFIC NAME	Pandion haliaetus
RELATED SPECIES	No close relatives
CALL	Whistling calls, usually heard near nest
HABITAT	Lakes, slow-flowing rivers and coasts. Regular at lakes, reservoirs and rivers on migration
STATUS	Summer visitor. Stable but small population in Scotland (about 80 pairs)

Osprey
55–69 cm (22–27 in)

VERY PALE BENEATH in flight, with long, narrow, angled wings. Dark brown above, mostly white underneath, with brown breast-band. Hovers and plunges to catch fish in talons. Dives almost vertically with wings half closed, often submerging for a short time.

OSPREYS HAVE RECEIVED much protection, particularly when they first returned to Scotland to breed, mostly in the form of direct protection of the nest site rather than of their habitat. This spectacular 'fish hawk' nests mainly in pines and, as it fishes, its white head, kinked wings and black wrist-patch make it easy to identify. More birds now appear at coastal and inland waters on migration.

In 1954, ospreys returned to build a nest near Loch Garten in Speyside and as Brown describes it: 'despite one failure through the maniac efforts of an egg collector which might have halted the entire process of re-establishment, the pair persisted, produced young in 1957, and the site is occupied to this day, observed day and night, and by many thousands of people annually. Never can any individual pair of birds anywhere in the world have given so much pleasure to so many people and never can any pair of birds done more for the cause of bird conservation.' By the early 1990s there were over 70 pairs.

Brown also describes its fishing habits: 'On sighting a fish it checks briefly in flight, sometimes hovers for a moment or two, then plunges nearly vertically towards the prey. It appears to dive head first ... but actually, at the last moment, the feet are thrown forward in front of the head and the osprey crashes feet first.' Short thick tarsi, spicules on the toes, long curved talons and a large cere which can close over the nostrils help this specialist fish eater.

Ospreys are very widely distributed over the northern hemisphere and also breed in Australia. Apart from some Mediterranean birds, those breeding in Europe are migrants, wintering along African river systems south of the Sahara. Migrant birds often delay at a suitable lake or estuary on the way, which is when most are seen.

> 'I will provide thee of a princely osprey,
> That, as he flieth over fish in pools
> The fish shall turn their glistening bellies up'
> George Peele THE BATTLE OF ALCAZOR

SIZE

IDENTIFICATION

HABITAT

POPULATION

MAP

Top
In flight, the osprey has rather angled wings.

Middle
In some areas osprey numbers have been boosted by the provision of platforms.

Bottom
Osprey bringing a fish back to the nest.

Moorhen

33 cm (13 in)

SPECIES INFORMATION

SCIENTIFIC NAME	Gallinula chloropus
RELATED SPECIES	Coot, Water Rail
CALL	Alarm call a guttural 'krrrk', or penetrating 'kirrec'
HABITAT	Still and slow-flowing water, ditches and small, overgrown ponds. Also common on streams and in ponds in urban parks and gardens. Feeds mainly on land
STATUS	Resident. In BI common except in north-west Scotland, about 315,000 pairs

SMALLER AND SLIMMER than Coot, with red, yellow-tipped bill and red frontal shield. Legs and toes long and green. White under tail coverts displayed as tail bobbed. Juveniles grey-brown with pale chin. Trails legs in flight. Nods head while swimming and walking, and repeatedly bobs tail.

IN TOWN PARKS moorhens are easy to spot with their flicking tails, red shield above the beak and white stripes below the wing. On land, collecting any additional food offered, their long flattened toes and smart green legs are easy to see, as they are if the birds are moving over water lilies or other surface vegetation. In reedy rivers they are often much more elusive, showing white under tail coverts as they head for cover.

Along the Lledr, in North Wales, it was surprisingly difficult to map their territories because of their elusive, sheltering behaviour, but on a winter evening they were often easy to count as they gathered to roost at the top of riverside willows. A breeding pair on the pond opposite our house in Devon was even more arboreal and

had their first nesting attempt about 9 m (30 ft) up an ash, concealed in ivy. They appeared most incongruous walking along the branches with long twigs for nesting material. This attempt was abandoned and later two broods were reared in more conventional sites. As so often happens with moorhens, the members of the first brood were most attentive helpers in the rearing of the second, but the apparently harmonious family life ended, with many chases over several days and a lot of noise, when the parents drove off the first lot of young birds.

British birds do not usually move far, whereas those from the north and east of the range, which extends across most of Europe south of 60∞, move extensively; a Scandinavian bird could reach north Africa or even south of the Sahara.

Moorhens are not demanding about breeding conditions, and are therefore widespread wherever water has sufficient emergent vegetation and is rich enough to provide adequate food. They therefore avoid upland areas and acid lakes.

The main features of the moorhen are the bright red bill and the white patches under the tail.

'Planing up shaving of silver spray
A moorhen darted out
From the bank there about,
And through the stream shine ripped his way.'
Thomas Hardy

Coot

38 cm (15 in)

<table>
<tr><th colspan="2">SPECIES INFORMATION</th></tr>
<tr><td>SCIENTIFIC NAME</td><td>Fulica atra</td></tr>
<tr><td>RELATED SPECIES</td><td>Moorhen, Water Rail</td></tr>
<tr><td>CALL</td><td>Male an unmusical 'tsk', and a sound rather like a cork popping. Female has a loud, barking 'kurrff'. Alarm call a sharp 'psi'</td></tr>
<tr><td>HABITAT</td><td>Lakes, reservoirs, ponds, and slow-flowing rivers with well-developed fringing vegetation. Also on gravel pits and on lakes in urban parks</td></tr>
<tr><td>STATUS</td><td>Resident and partial migrant. In BI common except in NW Scotland, about 55,000 pairs</td></tr>
</table>

BLACK, RATHER DUMPY waterbird with grey-green legs and white frontal shield above white bill. Toes lobed at edges. Dives for submerged food. Often gather in large flocks in winter.

SIZE

IDENTIFICATION

HABITAT

POPULATION

MAP

COOTS ARE LESS LIKELY to be celebrated in verse as they are noisy, quarrelsome birds with some insulting names. Michael Drayton in the sixteenth century wrote of the 'brain-bald coot' as well as casting aspersions on their sexual proclivities. Tennyson's brook came 'from haunt of coot and hern' but unless there were some lakes at the headwater it sounds an unlikely habitat. Perhaps there was an oxbow, but a brook seems to be too small for coots who like room to dive, with a distinctive jump, and a good expanse of open water.

Coots are larger and dumpier than moorhens, with all-black plumage, contrasting with their white bill and frontal shield. Juveniles can be very pale and are always less black, while the downy young, like moorhens, have distinctively coloured heads.

Arrivals of birds from northern Europe lead to some huge winter flocks. At the start of the breeding season there is much squabbling. The conspicuous shield is advertised when an aggressive bird lowers its head and raises neck and back feathers; if this is not sufficient and an intruder does not withdraw, actual foot-to-foot and beak-to-beak combat, with much splashing, follows.

Top left and right
The coot is sooty black, with a white bill and frontal shield.

Bottom
In winter, coot often congregate in large numbers at lakes and reservoirs.

Water Rail

25 cm (10 in)

SPECIES INFORMATION

SCIENTIFIC NAME	*Rallus aquaticus*
RELATED SPECIES	Moorhen, Coot, Corncrake
CALL	Like squealing pigs – 'kriek krruie krruie'; in spring a sharp 'zik-zik-zik' call, often ending with an extended, throaty 'tjuier'
HABITAT	Thick reed and sedge beds, especially at river or lake margins. Sometimes along ditches
STATUS	Resident. In BI commonest in Ireland and in parts of E Anglia. Total BI population probably around 3,000 pairs

SIZE

IDENTIFICATION

HABITAT

POPULATION

MAP

S LIM MARSH BIRD with long, slightly decurved red bill and black and white striped flanks. Upperparts brown with black markings; face, neck and breast slate grey; under tail coverts white. Juveniles pale brown below, with delicate stripes on neck and breast, and less stripy flanks. Secretive and difficult to observe.

WATER RAILS ARE noisy but elusive and live in well vegetated swamps. May be spotted for example as it searches the edge of a reedbed in shallow water, when the long red bill and impressively barred flanks, coupled with an actively jerking tail make it an attractive bird. When flushed it flutters off with trailing legs. When heard it is usually the grunts, groans and screams that are described, but the repeated 'pik pik' call is just as good an indication of a rail in the reeds. These noises are most frequently made at dawn or dusk. If one wants to see the bird in detail than a hide among the reeds can provide the answer.

Water rails, whose lateral compression allows them to stalk through reedbeds, have a very varied diet, including a wide range of wetland invertebrates, ranging in size from insects and their larvae to shrimps and molluscs, as well as vertebrates such as frogs and newts, and some vegetable matter.

Water rail are secretive, but sometimes come into the open, especially in the evening.

SPECIES INFORMATION

SCIENTIFIC NAME	Gallinago gallinago
RELATED SPECIES	Jack Snipe, Woodcock
CALL	Repeated nasal 'etch' when flushed. Song is a repeated, 'ticka-ticka-ticka', often from a song-post. Male makes high undulating flights over breeding ground, plunging downwards and producing a humming or bleating sound (so-called drumming), by vibrating the stiff outer tail feathers
HABITAT	Breeds in fens, bogs, damp meadows and other wetland areas with low vegetation. Also seen at lake margins, mudbanks, small ponds and ditches
STATUS	Resident and partial migrant. Numbers swelled by migrants from further north in winter. Common in BI, especially in north and west. In BI about 50,000 pairs

Common Snipe
26 cm (10 in)

M EDIUM-SIZED WADER with very long bill and camouflaged plumage. Back brown, with black and yellow markings. Dark stripes on cap. When flushed, tends to fly up suddenly, then pitch sideways, calling.

SNIPE ARE USUALLY hard to see on the ground, but the long straight beak and patterned upperparts are their most striking features when they are seen, often staying very still, beside a shallow pool. More often they are put up from a bog, calling as they zig-zag

away. With all snipe, on the ground or in the air, the long straight bills are the most noticeable features, but when well seen on the ground the cryptic patterning of browns, blacks and whites is marvellous.

Today breeding snipe look to be fairly widespread if one thinks in terms of 10 km (6 mile) squares, as in the *Atlas*, but even on that scale much of the west country, a swathe from there up to the Midlands, and many areas in the south-east are entirely without breeding snipe.

SPECIES INFORMATION

SCIENTIFIC NAME	Lymnocryptes minimus
RELATED SPECIES	Snipe, Woodcock
CALL	Song on breeding grounds said to resemble muffled galloping of a horse
HABITAT	Breeds in forest bogs and tundra of north-east Europe
STATUS	Regular as passage migrant and winter visitor to BI and European coasts. Breeds in far north-east of Europe

Jack Snipe
19 cm (7.5 in)

I T IS HARD to get a good view of jack snipe on the ground. They are usually seen when flushed from cover, when they make a brief low flight, showing a dark, wedge-shaped tail, and shorter bill.

SMALLER THAN THE SNIPE and much more secretive only taking flight at the very last minute. It has a slower, less zig-zagging flight than snipe and often flies back over the head of any intruder or diving in to cover. Despite apparently extraordinary noises it makes when breeding, any jack snipe here are likely to be quiet giving only a faint snipe like call. The head and back pattern show more clearly than on the snipe paticularly on a flying bird.

Common Redshank

26 cm (10 in)

BRIGHT RED LEGS, white rump and broad white trailing edge to wings (prominent in flight). In breeding plumage upperparts brownish, with darker speckles; at other times paler grey-brown above, and less speckled. Juveniles lack the red base to bill, have yellower legs, and are more reddish-brown above.

WADERS OF the genus *Tringa* are noisy, but some are heard more widely than others. Although breeding redshank in wet grassland are decreasing inland, their alarm calls there, or in winter estuaries, are a feature of the habitat, and their flight 'song' of sweet yodelling notes, often given in aerial display, seems joyous.

> '*A cry half of challenge, half lament, the very spirit of the estuary, of a life that chances and changes with wind and tide … No one who has ever heard the redshank cry in the wind over the saltings will ever after think of those waste spaces of water and ooze and sunlight without that haunting voice … and the lovely curves of that swift and slanting flight.*'
> Eric Parker ENGLISH WILDLIFE

SPECIES INFORMATION

SCIENTIFIC NAME	*Tringa totanus*
RELATED SPECIES	Greenshank, Spotted Redshank, Green Sandpiper, Wood Sandpiper
CALL	Loud, fluting 'tleu-hu' or 'tleu-hu-hu' flight-call is one of the most characteristic sounds of wetlands and coasts. Alarm call 'tjuk-tjuk-tjuk'. Song a yodelling 'tooli tooli tooli', often given in flight
HABITAT	Breeds in open marshes, mires and saltmarsh with short vegetation, especially near coasts. Outside breeding season on low-lying coasts, often in flocks on mudflats, or smaller groups in wet sites inland. Feeds mainly in shallow, muddy water
STATUS	Resident and partial migrant. Numbers in BI swelled in autumn and winter by migrants. About 35,000 pairs in BI. Declining over most of range

Bottom right
Redshank at its nest in marshland.

Top
The redshank takes its name from its long, red legs.

Bottom left
Redshank feeding in shallow water.

Little Ringed Plover

15 cm (6 in)

SPECIES INFORMATION	
SCIENTIFIC NAME	Charadrius dubius
RELATED SPECIES	Little Ringed Plover, Kentish Plover, Dotterel
CALL	Alarm call a loud melancholy 'piu' or sharp 'pitt-pitt'. Breeding song a trilling 'tree-tree-tree'
HABITAT	Gravelly and sandy river banks and islands; today mainly at gravel and sand pits, fishponds and flooded quarries. On migration mainly at coast, or on river mud
STATUS	Summer visitor. In Britain mainly in Midlands and S (about 1,000 pairs). Very rare in Scotland and Ireland

SMALL ROTUND WADER with black and white face pattern (breeding season), muddy yellow legs and yellow eye-ring. Smaller than ringed plover and lacking white wing bar.

LITTLE RINGED PLOVER and ringed plover are rather similar, and if you do not know them well or have not seen them for some time, they can be confused.

 SIZE

 IDENTIFICATION

 HABITAT

 POPULATION

 MAP

POINTS OF COMPARISON BETWEEN THE ADULT RINGED AND LITTLE RINGER PLOVERS

FEATURE	LITTLE RINGED PLOVER	RINGED PLOVER
Body	Slim	More robust
Eye-ring	Bright yellow	Faint orange
Legs	Pale flesh colour	Orange
Chest-band	Varied, but often narrow in centre	Wide
Head pattern	White border behind black crown	White eyebrow
Bill	Black	Orange at base

The crucial differences are that the little ringed plover has no wing bar in flight and 'pee-u' call rather than 'too-eep'. Young birds are brown where adults are black and have a uniform brown cap.

Here is a bird that has made great use of man-made habitats including gravel pits and reservoirs in their early days as they fill. The bird did not breed in Britain until 1938 but is now widespread, with recent colonisation of Wales along river shingle.

A similar picture emerges in Europe, with its versatility allowing it to spread in many countries, but with the largest populations in the north and east. To all these areas it is a summer visitor, mainly wintering in north Africa. Birds return to Britain in early April, display with territorial song-flight and lay from April onwards on bare ground.

Top
Little ringed plover – note the prominent eye-ring.

Bottom left
Pair of little ringed plover at their nest in shingle.

Bottom right
The female settles down on her eggs.

241

Black-tailed Godwit

38–44 cm (15–17 in)

```
○ ○ ○ ○ ○ ○ ○ ○ ○ ○ ○ ○ ○ ○ ○ ○ ○ ○ ○ ○ ○ ○
```
S P E C I E S   I N F O R M A T I O N

SCIENTIFIC NAME	*Limosa limosa*
RELATED SPECIES	Bar-tailed Godwit
CALL	Flight call 'eeka-reeka-reeka'. Song, in flight, a repeated 'keveeyoo-keveeyoo'
HABITAT	Breeds mainly in water meadows. In winter on estuaries, marshes and also on inland shallow water
STATUS	Summer visitor and migrant. Winters mainly around coasts. Breeds in Iceland, Netherlands, N Germany, southern Baltic, and scattered elsewhere. About 50 pairs breed in Britain, and a handful in Ireland

SIZE

IDENTIFICATION

HABITAT

POPULATION

MAP

LARGE, LONG-LEGGED, long-billed wader. Adult in breeding plumage has rust-brown neck and breast. In winter both sexes are a uniform grey. In flight shows white wing bar and white base to black tail. Legs longer than those of bar-tailed godwit, and bill longer and straighter.

AFTER MORE THAN a hundred years' absence black-tailed godwits nested sporadically in the 1930s when numbers were increasing in the Netherlands. They have nested on the Ouse Washes since 1952, with a peak of 64 pairs, from which birds may have spread to the Nene Washes, where the RSPB can maintain appropriate water levels for breeding waders. When water levels are right on the Somerset Levels black-tailed godwits occasionally nest there, as they do in Kent and Shetland.

'At the Ouse Washes, godwits begin returning to their breeding grounds in March, and the first nests are usually in the first two weeks of April. When breeding, they are loosely colonial (4-5 pairs per 100 ha) and such groups provide effective communal defence of eggs and young against crows, kestrels and other predators. Godwits nest in damp, tussocky pastures which have been grazed fairly heavily by cattle the previous summer.'

They feed mainly on earthworms, which they find by probing. Sites with a fairly high water table and

The black-tailed godwit is a majestic wader, with its long legs, long bill and russet summer plumage.

soft, peaty soils facilitate this method of feeding. They also take aquatic insects in shallow pools and ditches.

These large, graceful waders are very distinctive when flying, with their bold white wing bar, large white area of rump and tail-base and black terminal tail-band that gives them their name.

Black-tailed godwits are more commonly seen on our estuaries in the winter, when birds from western Europe are replaced by birds of the Icelandic race, the latter with shorter bills. British estuaries are vital feeding grounds for these birds. Prime sites include the Stour estuary in Essex, the Dee, Swale (Kent) and Poole Harbour.

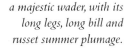

Ruff

26–32 cm (10–12.5 in) (male)
20–25 cm (8–9 in) (female)

SPECIES INFORMATION	
SCIENTIFIC NAME	Philomachus pugnax
RELATED SPECIES	No close relatives
CALL	Usually silent. A low 'wek' flight-call
HABITAT	Breeds on open bogs, damp meadows and on wet heaths; favours damp meadows with ditches and ponds, especially near to coast.
STATUS	Summer visitor to north of range. Mainly NE Europe (Finland holds about 50,000 pairs). Also Norway, Sweden, Denmark, N Germany and Holland. Rare breeder in Britain (about 5 females each year)

BREEDING MALE HAS remarkable ruff of feathers around neck, and head tufts, for lek displays. This varies in colour and pattern between individuals. Front of face with naked skin. Female and non-breeding male plumage dingy grey. Head small, and neck rather long. In flight shows narrow wing bar and white base to outer tail feathers.

MALES ARE LARGER than females and, in the breeding season they develop elaborate plumage, with a ruff of puffed out neck feathers. Different individuals have a different pattern of coloration – some being red, while others are white, black, mottled or barred.

The flamboyant males strut about, showing off their multicoloured ruffs and elaborate ear-tufts. Different coloured birds have different roles in the lek, with white-ruffed ones being 'satellites' who do not defend territories and serve mainly to attract females to the site. 'Independent' males, usually dark-coloured, may either be 'residents' who defend territories, or 'marginals' who do not. To complicate matters further, the satellite males are allowed on the residences, while the marginals are not. All this means, that a few males are responsible for all the matings, often with several females in a few minutes, and that the males play no part whatever in any subsequent incubation or chick rearing. It might be thought that the whole scheme would be an

evolutionary disaster and that, following a different line of thought, genes for white ruffs would die out. Satellites however are quite good at sneaking in to mate, without any display.

In Britain, ruffs are most often seen on their wintering grounds – muddy lakes, rivers and ponds, or at the coast. Features to watch for are the longish neck, medium-short bill, scaly back plumage, and, in flight, the white sides to the base of the tail.

Ruffs as breeding birds were once much commoner. An eighteenth-century Lincolnshire fowler netted 72 ruffs in a single morning, and 40–50 dozen between April and Michaelmas. These, when fattened, would sell for two shillings, or two shillings and six pence as table birds. No doubt this was one reason for their decline, but land drainage was probably more important, as this species likes hummocky marshes with shallow water for feeding, drier zones for displaying, and some cover for nest building. Another factor is that Britain is on the extreme western edge of the ruff's range, and any contractions of that range would mean a loss to us.

SIZE

IDENTIFICATION

HABITAT

POPULATION

MAP

Top and bottom
Ruff are relatively short-billed, with characteristically scaly plumage on the back.

Middle
In spring, male ruffs show a wide variety of plumages – this one has developed pure white feathering.

Common Sandpiper

20 cm (8 in)

SPECIES INFORMATION

SCIENTIFIC NAME	*Actitis hypoleucos*
RELATED SPECIES	Green Sandpiper, Wood sandpiper
CALL	Shrill 'kee-dee-dee' when flushed. Song, given mostly in flight, 'heedee-tititi-veedee-titi-veedee', often at night as well
HABITAT	Clear rivers, streams, lakes and on rocky islands with relatively sparse vegetation. Also on rocky shores with loose tree stands. Outside breeding season on gravelly or stoney ponds, lakes and rivers, and at sewage farms and estuaries
STATUS	Summer visitor and passage migrant. Scattered throughout most of Europe, becoming commoner towards N and NE (common in Finland and Scandinavia). In BI about 18,000 pairs

SIZE

IDENTIFICATION

HABITAT

POPULATION

MAP

A SMALL, SHORT-LEGGED wader with rather short, straight bill and dark rump. White wing bar is clearly visible in flight. Often bobs tail. Flies low over water with whirring wing-beats, interspersed with gliding on down-curved wings.

COMMON SANDPIPERS ARE white below, with the white looping up between brown wing and chest. There is a hint of an eye-stripe.

If redshank are the spirit of the lowland wetlands and estuaries, then common sandpipers fill a similar role by upland lakes and rivers.

Breeding sandpipers, with their excited calls and low flight on stiff wings, are welcome indeed when they return in April. Their presence, bobbing

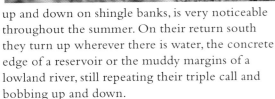

up and down on shingle banks, is very noticeable throughout the summer. On their return south they turn up wherever there is water, the concrete edge of a reservoir or the muddy margins of a lowland river, still repeating their triple call and bobbing up and down.

Along upland rivers, the amount of gravel exposed may vary rapidly after rain, and excited parents sometimes have to take their young into grassy cover after floods. The chicks are cryptically patterned, and difficult to spot amongst the stony banks, where food, in the form of beetles and fly larvae, can be found.

This rather short-legged wader typically sits, bobbing, close to the water's edge.

The common sandpiper tolerates an extremely wide climate range. Its range, always favouring the same fairly fast headwaters, extends across Asia to Japan. These eastern birds move into Australia, while European birds usually winter in the far south in Africa.

SPECIES INFORMATION

SCIENTIFIC NAME	Tringa ochropus
RELATED SPECIES	Wood Sandpiper, Redshank, Greenshank
CALL	Characteristic flight call is a sharp 'tluit-tit-tit', especially when flushed. Alarm call at breeding ground an incessant 'tick-tick-tick'. Song, given in circling flight, is fluting 'titti-looee, titti-looee'
HABITAT	Breeds on lightly wooded mires in damp, swampy woodland and wooded lake margins. On migration seen at lakes, often hidden from view alongside banks, or in ditches; creeks in saltmarshes; sewage-farms; and streams. Rarely on shore or mudflats. Breeds in Scandinavia and north-east Europe
STATUS	Summer visitor to breeding grounds. Migrates to south and west Europe in autumn and winter. In BI small numbers visit regularly as migrants

Green Sandpiper

23 cm (9 in)

MEDIUM-SIZED WADER with dark upperparts and white base of tail. Tail white, with 3 or 4 brownish bars. Juveniles have yellowish spots above. Shy, often sitting tight until flushed.

GREEN SANDPIPERS ARE largely passage migrants moving between their breeding areas in Norway (15,000 pairs), Sweden (30,000) and Finland (60,000) and wintering areas around the Mediterranean and into Africa. The huge Russian population moves to Turkey and Iran and on into China and the Philippines. Most migrants turn up around freshwater sites, which may be extensive wetlands, a steep-sided ditch or a river's edge: they can surprise you anywhere.

Surprise it can be for they rise steeply and noisily, calling 'klueet' or an extended 'tluit-tit-tit'. Apart from the white tail, rump and belly, the bird often appears almost black, flies fast and erratically before plunging back, snipe-like, to some hidden watery spot. The green of the name is never very evident, for the back, even of well-observed birds, is never more than an optimistic green-brown, peppered with small white dots. The neck and breast is streaked, with a clear boundary between breast and white belly.

Watercress beds or sewage farms are popular winter haunts and, as with passage birds, it is usually a singleton or couple who remain faithful to a chosen site for many weeks. The winter sites are likely to be southerly, whether in Ireland or in Britain, and may be abandoned if cold weather makes it difficult to get at the aquatic invertebrates and occasional small fish that make up the diet.

Green sandpipers' breeding habitat also requires freshwater, but often in very small amounts, with muddy margins and the presence of bogs and stands of alder, birch or pine. These trees are vital for nesting; some other bird's nest, or a squirrel's drey is often used.

SIZE

IDENTIFICATION

HABITAT

POPULATION

MAP

At a distance the green sandpiper can look very dark above, contrasting with its pure white plumage below.

Kingfisher

17 cm (6.5 in)

○○○○○○○○○○○○○○○○○○○○○○○○○

SPECIES INFORMATION

SCIENTIFIC NAME	*Alcedo atthis*
RELATED SPECIES	No close relatives in region
CALL	Flight-call a high-pitched 'tieht', or 'tii-tee', often repeated
HABITAT	Clean streams, lakes and rivers with steep banks in the vicinity (for nest tunnel). Outside breeding season on rivers, lakes, ponds, and also at the coast in hard weather
STATUS	Resident and partial migrant in west and central Europe. Summer visitor in north-east of range (avoids hard winters). Most of Europe, except far north. In BI about 6,000 pairs

SIZE

IDENTIFICATION

HABITAT

POPULATION

MAP

Top left
A kingfisher holds a fish lengthways in its bill, after a successful dive.

Top right
Watching the water below for suitable prey.

Bottom
When seen from behind, the shiny back contrasts with the somewhat darker wings.

BRIGHT BLUE ABOVE, with rapid flight, low and straight over the water. Easily overlooked when sitting quietly on a branch, and most often seen in flight.

APART FROM THE azure back, large bill and distinctive shape, the orange underparts and complex head pattern of blue, orange and white contribute to the appearance of a unique bird. Often, however, particularly on a misty winter's day it is the shrill call, frequently repeated, that makes you look up to see the bird disappearing down some estuarine creek. At that time of year more birds are down by the coast, but in summer, a fish supply, sandy bank and fishing post or branch are the requirements. The eggs, laid in the tunnel in the sandy bank, are usually round and, like many well hidden ones, are white and smooth.

Richard Jefferies (1879) has plenty to say about Kingfishers: 'Though these brilliant coloured birds may often be seen skimming across the surface of the mere, they seem to obtain more food from the brooks and ponds than from the broader expanse of water above. In the brooks they find overhanging branches upon which to perch and watch for their prey and without which they can do nothing.

His azure back and wings and ruddy breast are not equalled in beauty of colour by any bird native to this country. The long pointed beak looks half as long as the whole bird: his shape is somewhat wedge like, enlarging gradually from the point of the beak backwards.'

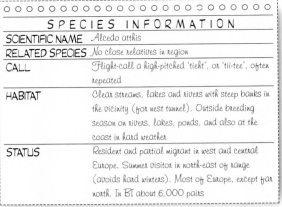

In Athens, when dried and hung up, kingfishers would ward off Zeus's lightening, they could calm storms, particularly during the halcyon days, the seven days they brood the eggs.
People in the Loire area knew that when hung up their beaks would turn to whichever way the wind blew. I like particularly the advice of Giraldus Cambrensis in 1186, 'these little birds ... if they are put among clothes and other articles ... preserve them from the moth and give them a pleasant odour'. I wonder how many of our present day activities will be seen as equally ridiculous.

Hopefully not the activities of the Environment Agency who, in our Local Biodiversity Action Plan needed to encourage and maintain the steep sandy banks favoured by kingfishers and sand martins for breeding. A 'well canalised', 'well disciplined' river would not create such things as it would not be allowed to erode and behave as rivers should. The Agency also works hard to keep rivers well-oxygenated, to prevent or clean up toxic spills and overflow from silage clamps. They are also much concerned with preventing fish-spawning gravels from being covered with sediment. In all these ways they help kingfishers, for without fish the fish-eating birds would starve.
Many eastern kingfishers, where population densities tend always to be lower, are migrants to the south-west. Not surprisingly if it is cold and the water icebound, kingfishers suffer and our relatively mild oceanic climate helps to make the British and Irish populations of great importance.

Sand Martin

12 cm (4.75 in)

SPECIES INFORMATION

SCIENTIFIC NAME	Riparia riparia
RELATED SPECIES	House Martin, Swallow
CALL	Very vocal. Scratchy 'tshrr' and repeated 'brr-brr-brr'. Song is a series of soft twitters
HABITAT	Sandy banks and quarries, usually close to water. Sometimes flocks gather in large numbers at reedbeds in late summer
STATUS	Summer visitor, wintering in tropical Africa. Throughout Europe, but distribution rather patchy. In BI about 200,000 pairs

SMALLEST EUROPEAN MARTIN. Tail is only weakly forked. Brown above and white below, with brown breast-band.

THEY ARE ONE OF the first of our summer visitors to arrive back, and seeing a brown martin with distinct chest-band over river or lake at the end of March is a hopeful sign of more spring arrivals soon. Colonies can be large, and are constantly alive with their twittering calls. Loss of habitat, and drought in the African Sahel where many of the birds winter, have combined to reduce numbers periodically. Notable crash years were 1968–69 and 1983–84.

A small nest area is defended, but essentially breeding birds are as gregarious as those on migration. Being early breeders, with eggs laid by the end of April, there is usually time for two broods. Sand martins dig out their tunnels in vertical sand or gravel banks, and a single colony may consist of hundreds or exceptionally thousands of pairs. In many urban areas, where rivers have been canalised and drains are needed to control water movements, artificial sites such as these drainpipes are sometimes used. Nests in Salisbury of this type usually seemed to be successful.

Sand martins rarely fly high, and although particularly associated with water are quite prepared to catch their insect prey wherever it is abundant.

'... the desolate face
Of rude waste landscapes far away from men
where frequent quarries give thee dwelling place
With strangest taste and labour undeterred
Drilling small holes along the quarries side'
John Clare SELECTED POEMS

SIZE

IDENTIFICATION

HABITAT

POPULATION

MAP

Sand martin nesting burrows in the sandy bank of a gravel workings.

Dipper
18 cm (7 in)

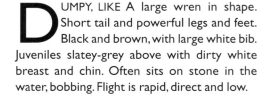

SIZE

IDENTIFICATION

HABITAT

POPULATION

MAP

DUMPY, LIKE A large wren in shape. Short tail and powerful legs and feet. Black and brown, with large white bib. Juveniles slatey-grey above with dirty white breast and chin. Often sits on stone in the water, bobbing. Flight is rapid, direct and low.

ON SOME WELSH streams I have found dippers with grey wagtails, but on others, where extensive forestry around the headwaters had led to acidification, the fall in invertebrates led to a consequent fall in the dipper population. Newton (1998) quoted studies from Wales and Scotland that showed that territories were longer and densities therefore lower, where the water was acid. This was in turn associated with decreases in suitable food items, such as mayfly nymphs and caddisfly larvae. Luckily, a recent survey in the Axe and its tributaries showed neutral water and plenty of invertebrates, but such dippers as there are prefer the shallower tributaries.

The territorial behaviour and unreadiness to move onto a neighbour's territory make dippers easy to map, and they are often easy to see if you stop, look and listen for instance on an old stone bridge. From there you may hear, as well as the murmur of the stream, the dipper's gentle babbling or its 'zit' call when disturbed from a mid-stream boulder. If you see one before disturbance, its bobbing action is as characteristic as its large wren-like shape, bright white chest, bordered below by chestnut, and the blackish back. It is the back, and whirring wings, that are most evident as it flies low to a new boulder or shingle bank.

In Ireland and western Scotland dippers have less chestnut below, and are darker above, while the Scandinavian bird that Linnaeus named has no chestnut at all. Four other races with a degree of overlap and variation are described within its European distribution, which appears scattered because of its preference for rapid flowing hill streams.

Dippers are very early breeders with laying eggs from the end of February, in a domed nest of moss and grass stems, often concealed behind a waterfall frequently on a ledge overhanging the water.

Turner in 1544, as many others since, called it a water ouzel, and the more appropriate dipper name did not appear until *Tunstall's Ornithologica Britannica* in 1777.

> 'Peradventure he may have the good fortune to see the common dipper walking, literally walking, at the bottom of the water in pursuit of its prey … precisely as if upon dry land.'
> George Pulman BOOK OF THE AXE (1875)

Top right
Dippers usually nest close to a river, such as underneath a waterfall or bridge.

Top and bottom left
The dipper is a rotund bird, with grey-brown plumage and obvious white bib.

SPECIES INFORMATION

SCIENTIFIC NAME	Motacilla cinerea
RELATED SPECIES	Yellow Wagtail, Pied wagtail
CALL	Sharp 'tseet-tseet'. Song is made up of high-pitched twittering phrases
HABITAT	Breeds along fast-flowing streams, shallow rivers, at reservoirs and gravel pits. Outside breeding season also on lakes and ponds
STATUS	Resident and partial migrant. Most of Europe, except for north and east. Absent from most of Scandinavia. In BI about 56,000 pairs

Grey Wagtail
40 cm (16 in)

YELLOW BENEATH, LIKE yellow wagtail, but has much longer tail, a grey back and dark wings. Male has black chin; in winter male, female and juveniles the chin is white. The bright yellow of the chest turns to even brighter yellow on the vent, and the smart grey head contrasts with white moustache and eye-stripe and black bib, which the female lacks.

THE GREY OF the name is wholly appropriate in winter when only rump and under-tail coverts are yellow. At that time grey wagtails are quite ready to move into towns where they may appear unexpectedly, especially where there is water.

In summer they often feed along rivers, but tend to breed up tiny tributaries, among rocks, by a bridge, or in a drystone wall. The song, an excited elaboration of its basic call is often delivered in flight, and may turn into a peaceful trill as the bird descends.

Away from the uplands, weirs and sluices can provide the breeding holes and cascading water that it likes and, using these, it has been spreading east in the lowlands.

Unlike dippers, they do not seem to suffer from acidification of watercourses, probably because they take a wide range of prey, including many of non-aquatic origin.

SIZE

IDENTIFICATION

HABITAT

POPULATION

MAP

Top right
A grey wagtail brings back a beakful of insects to its nest.

Top left
The grey-blue back contrasts with the bright yellow underside.

Bottom
This bird has caught a damselfly.

Goosander

58–66 cm (23–26 in)

○○○○○○○○○○○○○○○○○○○○○○○○○○○

SPECIES INFORMATION

SCIENTIFIC NAME	Mergus merganser
RELATED SPECIES	Red-breasted Merganser, Smew
CALL	Normally silent. Breeding male has various high-pitched calls, and breeding female a harsh 'skrrark'
HABITAT	Breeds on fish-rich lakes and rivers in forested areas, right up into the tundra. In winter on large lakes and rivers, and at coast
STATUS	Resident and partial migrant. In Britain about 2,500 pairs, mostly in Wales, N England, the border country and scattered in Scotland

SIZE

IDENTIFICATION

HABITAT

POPULATION

MAP

LARGEST EUROPEAN SAWBILL, with long, hook-tipped red bill. Male mostly white, with salmon pink flush underneath, greenish-black head and black back. Female mainly grey, with brown head and upper neck and white chin and neck.

THERE ARE FEW better colours than the pale pink underparts of male goosander. The combination of green head, long red bill and contrasting black back and white, merging with pink underparts are not always so clear, for it often seem a black and white bird. Females are rather merganser-like, but are more thick-set and have clearer demarcation to their white chin and a similarly clear separation between brown of head and blue-grey body.

It is not always popular with fishermen for the diet is almost entirely of fish. Photographs of goosanders fishing underwater show them as streamlined, with head and neck held out straight in front, strong-footed and versatile in the use of the saw-edged bill. When a fish is caught across the middle it needs realignment before swallowing.

Its distribution in winter is mainly on freshwater, spreading into southern England. As the evidence suggests that breeding birds do not spread far from their origins, the southern birds may be migrants from Scandinavia and Germany. The highest numbers are at Scottish sites, with several gatherings of 150 or more.

This large, fish-eating duck has a long bill equipped with sharp saw-like projections. The male is handsome indeed, with black, grey and pinkish-white, and a dark green head. The female is duller, with a brown head.

Smew

40 cm (16 in)

SPECIES INFORMATION

SCIENTIFIC NAME	*Mergus albellus*
RELATED SPECIES	Red-breasted Merganser, Goosander
CALL	Fairly silent. Male has rasping 'kairrr' as alarm call, or in courtship. Female a quacking 'gagaga'
HABITAT	Breeds on woodland edges and at lakes. Coastal in winter. Also at inland lakes and reservoirs
STATUS	Summer visitor in breeding range – northern and eastern Scandinavia. Winters south to coasts of North Sea, Baltic and Channel

SMALLEST OF THE sawbill ducks. Steep forehead and relatively short bill. Male pure white, with black lines on body, black eye-patch and back. Female grey, with red-brown cap, and white cheeks. Eclipse male like female, but with larger amounts of white on wings. Immature male has brownish-white wing patches. Sometimes seen with goldeneye in winter. Dives frequently, and flies fast.

THE DRAKE SMEW is truly impressive, with dazzling white plumage. In flight, both sexes show clear flickering white wing-patches. First winter males and females are 'red heads' and can be mistaken for grebes or goldeneye, as they are mainly grey, but the white on front of neck and side of face should identify them.

On their breeding grounds, smew, like goldeneye, like well-grown trees with holes but their southern limit is further north. Like goldeneye, also, they are divers with a winter fish diet appropriate to a 'sawbill'.

SIZE

IDENTIFICATION

HABITAT

POPULATION

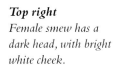
MAP

Top right
Female smew has a dark head, with bright white cheek.

Top left
Male smew has beautiful snow-white plumage.

Bottom
A flock of smew at sea. From a distance, the drakes look as pale as seagulls.

Red-breasted Merganser

52–58 cm (20–23 in)

SPECIES INFORMATION	
SCIENTIFIC NAME	Mergus serrator
RELATED SPECIES	Goosander, Smew
CALL	Normally silent. Breeding male has nasal 'qui-qui-air'. Female a grating 'aark-aark-aark'
HABITAT	Breeds on clear lakes and rivers of northern Europe and on shallow sandy or stoney coasts. Outside breeding season mainly at coasts
STATUS	Resident and partial migrant in Britain, summer visitor to breeding areas in northern Europe. Winters south to most coasts. Mainly in north and west Scotland, north-west England and Wales, and west Ireland. Total British and Irish population about 3,000 pairs.

SIZE

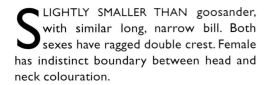

IDENTIFICATION

HABITAT

POPULATION

MAP

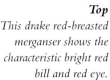

SLIGHTLY SMALLER THAN goosander, with similar long, narrow bill. Both sexes have ragged double crest. Female has indistinct boundary between head and neck colouration.

MALE MERGANSERS HAVE contrasting black and white and grey bodies with green heads, a fine double crest, and an impressive red bill. The red breast is much the colour of the female's ginger head. She can be told from a goosander by slighter frame, crest and absence of white chin.

E. A. Armstrong thinks that mergansers have never received the appreciation they deserve. 'Thousands of poets, artists and writers have lavished praise on the kingfisher, yet hardly a voice has been raised in honour of the merganser. The very name is clumsy, ugly and repellent.'

Some of the peculiar behaviour which delights him is described: 'As the birds career back and forth they constantly open wide their slender, serrated, red bills. They bob quickly and then shoot up head and neck into the air, gaping widely. It looks almost as if the birds were having spasms or

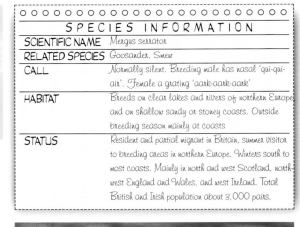

retching uncontrollably towards the heavens. The females, too, will occasionally stretch up their necks with a quick pump handle motion. Grace and pride of beauty are set aside and the agitated birds jerk and belch with what seems to the spectator painful vigour and intensity. "A mad world my masters", one might be inclined to say on first seeing this ludicrous pantomime amidst the still beauty of the Irish springtide.'

Top
This drake red-breasted merganser shows the characteristic bright red bill and red eye.

Bottom
The white double wing patch is clearly visible on this female merganser.

Sedge Warbler

13 cm (5 in)

SPECIES INFORMATION	
SCIENTIFIC NAME	*Acrocephalus schoenobaenus*
RELATED SPECIES	Reed Warbler, Marsh Warbler
CALL	Alarm-call a hard 'tseck' or rattling 'karrr'. Song is lively and scratchy, quite varied, usually beginning with a short 'trr' and with long trills
HABITAT	Reedbeds, marshy scrub, carr, banks and ditches
STATUS	Summer visitor. In BI about 360,000 pairs

SMALL BROWNISH WARBLER with clear white stripe over eye and dark crown. Streaked above, with unmarked rump.

THE MOST WIDESPREAD and numerous of the *Acrocephalus* warblers, whose cheerful chattering song livens up many a walk in marshy and reedy habitats. Sedge warblers also nest in scrub and bramble thickets, but usually require damp or swampy ground nearby.

Found over most of Britain and Ireland, but absent from upland country. The main strongholds are in south-east England, and the east coast of Britain generally, lowland Scotland and central Ireland.

SIZE

IDENTIFICATION

HABITAT

POPULATION

MAP

Sedge warblers nest hidden amongst damp scrub.

Reed Warbler

13 cm (5 in)

SPECIES INFORMATION	
SCIENTIFIC NAME	Acrocephalus scirpaceus
RELATED SPECIES	Sedge Warbler, Marsh Warbler
CALL	Alarm call hard 'kra' or 'vet'. Song similar to sedge warbler's but quieter, less penetrating, more continuous and faster
HABITAT	Mainly reedbeds, but also damp scrub
STATUS	Summer visitor. In BI about 60,000 pairs (fewer than 50 in Ireland and few in Scotland)

SMALL AND RATHER drab warbler, mainly brown, with white throat. Bill is relatively long.

THE REAL REEDBED specialist is the reed warbler, whose large foot-span helps it grip as it sidles among the reed stems. The nest is slung between adjacent reeds, or built in nearby scrub. Oddly, reed warbler's nests away from the reedbeds are often more successful, perhaps because fewer are parasitised by cuckoos. Grasses and reed leaves are wound around vertical stems to produce a deep cup, often lined with dead reed heads.

Reed warblers are found mainly in the south and east of Britain, especially in East Anglia, but are gradually expanding in range towards the north and west.

The song is easy to confuse with that of the sedge warbler but it is less grating, and full of repeated phrases. Reed warblers, like the very similar but rarer marsh warbler, often mimic other birds. They also have a longer song period, probably because many start to sing again when they breed for a second time.

Reed Bunting

15.5 cm (6 in)

SPECIES INFORMATION	
SCIENTIFIC NAME	Emberiza schoeniclus
RELATED SPECIES	Yellowhammer, Cirl Bunting.
CALL	Call is 'tsieh'. Song is a short phrase 'tsip-tsip-tete-tsink-tet'
HABITAT	Lake and river margins with reed and sedge beds, and damp willow scrub
STATUS	Resident. In BI about 350,000 pairs

BREEDING MALE HAS black head, chin and throat, white collar and white moustache. In winter head and neck are mottled brown. Female and juvenile have streaky brown plumage with black and white moustache.

BOTH SEXES ARE rather sparrow-like, but the male's bold head markings stand out, with the white moustache accentuating the black. The rest of the bird is unremarkable, but the white-edged tail, with a clear fork, often helps to pick out birds in mixed winter flocks. Females have a distinctive face pattern with pale eye-stripe and a pale patch where the male has his moustache.

At a time of population growth in the 1960s, when many farms were losing damp areas of marginal land, reed buntings adapted to far drier breeding conditions, moving into young forestry plantations, farmland and even scrub on dry chalkland, beginning to overlap with the yellowhammer's niche. They avoid really wet reedbeds as they nest on the ground.

○ ○

SPECIES INFORMATION

SCIENTIFIC NAME	*Panurus biarmicus*
RELATED SPECIES	*No close relatives*
CALL	*Flight-call is a very distinctive nasal 'ting', often repeated. Song is short and squeaky*
HABITAT	*Extensive reedbeds*
STATUS	*Resident. In B about 400 pairs (virtually absent from Ireland)*

Bearded Tit

16.5 cm (6.5 in)

LONG, CINNAMON TAIL. Male mainly cinnamon-brown with grey head and broad black moustache, yellow bill and eyes. Female less colourful and without moustache. Juvenile similar to female, but with dark back and sides of tail.

BEARDED TITS OR reedlings are very strongly associated with reedbeds, and their 'pinging' call and flight, like little arrows with their long tails, can create excitement when they turn up unexpectedly, and consistent pleasure when in familiar situations.

Males have lavender-grey heads with a black moustachial stripe and yellow bill. The body is mainly tawny-brown. The female is duller and lacks the male's head pattern. In the reeds they move jerkily or descend to feed among the detritus below. They suffer

severely in cold, snowy winters, and only a few pairs were left in Suffolk after the 1946–47 winter, but good recruitment from Dutch polder reedbeds helped recovery, despite further setbacks with east coast floods in 1963.

As with other reedbed species, population estimates are difficult, but when numbers do build up, autumn movements may help to colonise new sites. A new design of 'reedling box' might also encourage higher breeding densities.

The main sites for this species are Humberside, which has the largest colony, and the coastal reedbeds of Norfolk, Suffolk, Kent and Essex.

Bearded tits are mainly insectivorous, gathering midges from wetter areas, or moth larvae and pupae from reed stems and litter. Their nests are built near the ground, in drier areas where sedge or fallen reed stems provide cover, and their long breeding season enables them to rear a large number of young, if the conditions are good.

SIZE

IDENTIFICATION

HABITAT

POPULATION

MAP

Bearded tits perch on reed stems and feed from their seedheads.

Coastal Birds

AN ESTUARY AT the mouth of a river may sometimes appear desolate and lacking in life, but beneath the extensive tidal mud are usually a mass of worms, molluscs and crustaceans – there may be as many as 25,000 tiny *Hydrobia* snails per square metre. The larger lugworm may, despite much smaller numbers, provide an equal mass of food. The importance of wetlands such as estuaries is indicated by the 1.5 million waders which were counted in January 1996.

location of the birds. They are often tiny dots in a vast expanse of sea and, except in bad weather, are seldom visible to the naked eye.'

A NEW RESERVE

A 1998 ACTION UPDATE from the RSPB told of their excitement about one of their newest reserves. Belfast Lough is an oasis for wildlife in the middle of an industrialised harbour. It is also within easy reach of more than half a million people.

The mudflats and lagoons of this Northern Ireland site are surrounded by docks, development and

ESTUARY SITES OF INTERNATIONAL IMPORTANCE FOR WINTERING WADERS

SPECIES	SITES	MAIN SITE	AVERAGE MAXIMUM	MONTH
Redshank	24	Dee	7,000	Dec
Bar-tailed Godwit	18	Ribble	17,000	Feb
Knot	18	Wash	170,000	Nov
Dunlin	14	Morecambe Bay	53,000	Mar
Grey plover	14	Wash	10,000	Mar
Black-tailed Godwit	12	Stour	2,200	Jan

SEA-WATCHING

J.T.R. SHARROCK (1972) describes how sea-watching is an art: 'Put an ornithologist, even a real expert, on a cliff, point out a sooty shearwater half a mile away and watch him fail to see it. A Manx shearwater is only slightly larger than a cuckoo. Yet identification at a range of three miles is simple. The major problem encountered by the beginner however is the initial

wasteland, but the potential of the area for birds is enormous. A feature on the Lough in the Wetland Bird Survey report for 1995–96 also mentions problems of refuse disposal, pollution and general disturbance.

The feature reported that the Lough was of international importance for redshank and turnstone – 2,000 redshank were counted at low tide with the main concentration, at more than 15 birds per hectare, close to the city itself. Oystercatchers were more on

Top
The oystercatcher is ever-present at most estuaries and coastal sites.

Bottom left
An estuary at low tide. An excellent habitat for many birds, including waders and shelduck.

Bottom right
Drake goldeneye. This attractive duck often visits estuaries in winter.

the east shore but the 5,600 counted were well spread and represented a population in Ireland second only to those in Dundalk Bay in the Republic. Nationally important numbers of lapwing were near the Belfast Harbour Pools where there were also plenty of dunlin, enough again to be of national importance. Populations of both godwits, curlew, ringed plover and knot were also of national importance.

E. A. Armstrong (1945), growing up there, found the Lough of great interest and could remember the din of the shipyards, a diffused clamour carried for miles on warm summer morning breezes. He was taken on board the Titanic. It was a memorable experience to peep over the embankment as the sun was sinking below the purple Antrim hills. 'There not far from land, swim the silent swan flotillas, a vast, scattered fleet. The wine red dimples of the lazy wavelets form a perfect foil for the snowy birds as they placidly float or dip their necks to feed ... Beyond, appearing only as dark lines on the rippled sea lie squadrons of ducks – wigeon, mallard, scaup, goldeneye and scoter. A belated heron flaps away into the glowing sky leaving loneliness in his wake. There is hardly a sound: only the lapping of the water on the rocks and the occasional whistle of a redshank or curlew.'

Of the ducks he mentions, scaup and mallard are present today in numbers of national importance, as are she40duck, eider and red-breasted merganser. Belfast Lough is one of the most important sites for great ccrested grebes in the British Isles, and low-tide counts found 1,112 in February 1996. It also found 169 scaup, 481 eiders, 20 long-tailed duck, 260 goldeneye and 173 red-breasted merganser.

CLIFF BIRDS AND THEIR FOOD

ONLY THE NUMBER of birds and the coastal situation link the estuaries with the steep cliffs and rocky islets that are home to large segments of the world's storm petrels, gannets, razorbills and Manx shearwaters. Britain and Ireland form one of the outstanding seabird stations in the North Atlantic, and to experience the birds on an exposed Hebridean island or the corner of western Ireland is unforgettable.

Nesting cliffs need to be associated with rich feeding grounds. When important food sources

decline, as Shetland sand-eels did in the late 1980s, birds suffer and few kittiwake or Arctic tern young were reared in those years. Whether the sand-eel fisheries, now closed, were responsible is uncertain.

Sand-eels are food to Arctic tern, shag, puffin and kittiwake, but also to the dwindling stocks of cod, haddock and whiting. There are commercial fisheries for these on the East Coast. Other groups of organisms liking sand-eels are minke whales, harbour porpoises, dolphins, sea trout and salmon.

The sand-eel fishing had been uncontrolled, but following pressure from RSPB and other pressure groups it was set at one million tonnes in 1998. Efforts are being made to control the sand-eel fishery so that sufficient food remains to support our internationally important seabird colonies. It would indeed be excellent if another marine food web could return to something nearer a proper balance between the interests of man and wildlife.

BIRD FACT
The Birds of the London Area (1957) includes 245 species seen within 32 km (20 miles) of St Paul's Cathedral. A quick look at some regional Bird Reports shows that London is not alone.

Top left
Shelduck liven up many an estuary, especially on the North Sea coast.

Top right
A gannet colony at Hermaness, Shetland.

Bottom
The strange beak of the puffin is actually perfectly adapted for catching and carrying small fish and sand-eels.

BIRDS OF THE HEBRIDES

THE HEBRIDES SUPPORT a million pairs of breeding seabirds, while one Hebridean island, Islay, can feed up to 90 per cent of the barnacle geese from east Greenland and 50 per cent of the white-fronted geese from the west of that massive land mass.

The petrels that breed in the Hebrides are pelagic for most of the year, the auks, apart from the black guillemot, are offshore species, but the gulls, with the exception of the kittiwake, are essentially coastal. All find the Hebrides among the best of breeding areas, and the large numbers make up 50 per cent of the seabirds of Britain and Ireland. Even so, of all the possible sites, few are used, for food is the limiting factor. At the southern end of the Outer Hebrides, where inshore water from the sea of the Hebrides or the Minch, meets oceanic water, south-west of Barra Head there is a rich food supply. Here the vertical cliffs of Mingulay and Bernsey have getting on for 10,000 kittiwakes, 10,000 razorbills and 15,000 guillemots.

By contrast with Mingulay, the Shiants, in the Minch and Treshnish Isles, off Mull, have cliff terraces with plenty of talus, loose material that has fallen from the cliffs above, providing ideal conditions for crevice-lovers like puffins, shearwaters and storm petrels. The Treshnish Isles, with 14 species of seabird challenge the 15 of St Kilda, which has most of the annets, 50,000; most of the fulmars, 65,000; storm petrels, 10,000; and thousands of the virtually uncountable Leach's petrels. Rum, with its extraordinary mountain Manx shearwaters, challenges St Kilda for shearwater numbers.

When these birds have returned to sea, almost 30,000 barnacle geese arrive in November to fill the fertile fields of Islay, just 20 km (12 miles) wide. Numbers are reduced when some disperse to Ireland and to Scottish coasts, but most remain, with the RSPB farm at Gruinart as their centre. They feed on improved pasture. Grazing is restricted elsewhere so numbers build up again and birds gain weight before their return migration in April. These numbers, concentrated on improved pasture, caused resentment among farmers who shot some birds themselves and let some shooting rights to others until, in the mid 1980s, Sites of Special Scientific Interest were established, with compensation paid to farmers whose land was in these protected areas.

When Irish populations of wintering white-fronted geese suffered from drainage, disturbance and shooting, the population of these geese increased in Scotland with Islay holding 5,000, or 50 per cent of British birds. They feed and roost at different sites from the garnacle geese, and in the late 1980s were threatened when their peat roosting grounds were wanted by Islay's distinguished whisky distillers and moorlands were wanted by forestry interests. After national debate and much strong feeling, legal and political pressures eventually favoured the geese.

Top
Barnacle geese are regular winter visitors, mainly to Scotland and Ireland.

Bottom
Kittiwakes roosting on a rocky headland.

CLIMATE CHANGE

'SOFT' COASTS; ESTUARIES, saltmarshes, sand dunes and anywhere a sea defence wall is needed are highly vulnerable to the consequences of global warming. With a rise in sea level, together with more storms and increased wave height, 100 ha (250 acres) of saltmarsh are already being lost each year and the

be coastal squeeze' as the sea rises, with a narrower belt of sand or shingle on which terns or ringed plover can breed.

English Nature firmly believes that these coastal habitats need to be allowed to move. If vital habitats are lost, and many are protected as Special Areas of Conservation under the Habitats Directive, they must be recreated. Much of the coastline between the Humber and Poole Harbour is subject to various degrees of flooding, with over 3,000 ha (7,400 acres) of wet grassland, 500 ha (1,200 acres) of saline lagoons, 200 ha (500 acres) of reedbed and over 100 ha (250 acres) of shingle and sand-dune likely to go. Those involved with shoreline management planning and the recreation of habitats are going to be kept busy.

maintenance of many sea walls, make no economic sense. The Essex coast is at present the most vulnerable, and managed retreat or realignment means a new sea-wall further back and flooding of grazing marshes and other land behind the old wall. The nature of what is lost will have different consequences for birds, for grazing marshes can be an important feeding ground, and reedbeds, quite likely to be lost, are a most valued habitat for bitterns, bearded tits and marsh harriers among others. Sea level rise can also threaten sand dune systems, saline lagoons and shingle – all vital habitats. There will also be gains, for after the flooding new intertidal mudflats, suitable for waders, will soon develop, while plants are quick to colonise, creating new saltmarsh. It the old sea wall were to be maintained there would

> '*There heard I naught but seething sea,*
> *Ice cold waves, awhile a song of swan.*
> *There came to charm me gannets' pother*
> *And whimbrels' trills for the laughter of men,*
> *Kittiwake singing instead of mead.*
> *Storms there the stacks thrashed, there answered them the tern*
> *With icy feathers, full oft the erne wailed round*
> *Spray feathered …*'
> Anon 'THE SEAFARER' (c 680 AD)
>
> *Translated by James Fisher – this may refer to the Bass Rock in the Firth of Forth*

Top
Low tide on an estuary, which is good habitat for brent geese and many other species.

Middle
Seabirds have to contend with fierce seas along the Dorset coast.

Bottom
Ringed plover eggs are very difficult to spot amongst the shingle.

BIRD SPECIES

Manx Shearwater
34 cm (14 in)

SIZE

IDENTIFICATION

HABITAT

POPULATION

MAP

BLACK AND WHITE seabird with long, narrow, stiffly held wings. Glides low over the waves; wing-beats shallow, rapid and intermittent.

MANX SHEARWATERS ARE nocturnal island visitors making a selection of weird gruff sound effects suitable for a horror film. On Bardsey Island the birds nest where the soil is deep enough for a burrow, and also along low-lying field boundary walls; 'rafts' of thousands of birds build up at sea in summer evenings. Away from their breeding haunts the long-winged tilting flight, using every movement of the wind, reveals at one moment, the black back and at another the white underparts. All shearwaters share this distinctive flight, but separation into species often requires great skill.

The largest colonies are on Rum in Scotland, Skomer and Skokholm in Wales and the islands off the coast of Kerry in Ireland. The British and Irish sites account for over 90 per cent of the world total.

Apart from Manx shearwaters, British waters are visited by a number of other shearwater species. Cory's is sometimes described, being rather featureless, as the garden warbler of the oceans.

Top
Manx shearwaters come ashore to breed.

Bottom
A sandy slope showing Manx shearwater nesting burrows.

SPECIES INFORMATION

SCIENTIFIC NAME	Puffinus puffinus
RELATED SPECIES	Sooty Shearwater, Great Shearwater
CALL	Weird screaming and wailing at breeding colonies
HABITAT	Oceanic, except when breeding. Feeds in flocks offshore
STATUS	Coasts and islands of Iceland, western BI, France and Mediterranean. Ranges widely over open sea outside breeding season. In BI about 300,000 pairs breed

CORY'S
45 CM (17.7 IN)
Heavy appearance with grey hood, brown back; white below. Scattered breeding around the Mediterranean

GREAT
43–51 CM (17–20 IN)
Dark brown-grey above with white collar; white below, with some dark markings. Breeds in south Atlantic

SOOTY
40–51 CM (15.7–20 IN)
Almost uniform dark plumage; pale panel below (mostly dark). Breeds in southern hemisphere

YELKOUAN
36 CM (14 IN)
Duller than Manx shearwater, with little contrast Breeds on Mediterranean islands

LITTLE
25–30 CM (9.8–11.8 IN)
Compact shearwater black above, with white face; white below. Nearest breeding sites Canaries, Madeira and Azores

One way to see these birds is described by Steve Dudley in the *Bird Watcher's Year Book* 1998: 'You need to find a boat, with a skipper who knows where fishing boats are operating. If fish are gutted on board or if you have an evil mixture of fish scraps and offal to throw overboard, gulls, and then petrels and shearwaters, are attracted to the commotion and by the smell, picked up miles away with their specially evolved "tube noses". Within minutes your very own group of feeding seabirds is trailing your boat, with views more akin to watching blue tits in the garden.'

Storm Petrel
15 cm (6 in)

SPECIES INFORMATION	
SCIENTIFIC NAME	Hydrobates pelagicus
RELATED SPECIES	Leach's Petrel
CALL	Strange purring and squeaking at breeding colonies
HABITAT	Open sea, except when breeding at offshore islands
STATUS	Coasts and islands of Iceland, western BI, France and Mediterranean. In BI from Shetland through the west of Ireland, south to Scilly. Outside breeding season ranges widely over open sea. In BI probably about 160,000 pairs

VERY SMALL, DARK seabird with obvious white rump. Flight fluttery, dipping to surface sometimes with legs dangling. Pale wing bar, most obvious on underside.

THE SMALL PETRELS are virtually impossible to locate at their breeding grounds on remote boulder-covered islands, where they are active at night. Even on well-watched Bardsey the best evidence of breeding is a pathetic predated corpse. The storm petrel has a distinct white rump and a square-ended tail. May sometimes be seen on sea-watches from a prominent headland or from a boat. When flying in storms, petrels appear to pat the water with alternate feet as if walking on the water. The name 'petrel' comes from St Peter, who also allegedly walked on the water.

Leach's Petrel
20 cm (8 in)

SPECIES INFORMATION	
SCIENTIFIC NAME	Oceanodroma leucorhoa
RELATED SPECIES	Storm Petrel
CALL	Purring song, interrupted by sharp whistles; cackling
HABITAT	Open sea, except when breeding at offshore islands
STATUS	Much more local than storm petrel, with main colonies in Shetland, Foula, Flannan Islands and St Kilda. In BI population around 50,000 pairs (may be more – difficult to census)

LARGER AND PALER than the storm petrel and with more pointed wings and less obvious white rump (V-shaped patch), and forked tail (may look ragged).

USUALLY SEEN AFTER storms on the western coasts of the British Isles, particularly on the islands of the west coast of Scotland between April and November. Leach's petrel spends much of its time out on the open sea but comes in to breed and nest on the cliffs and rockfaces along the coastline. A characteristic of the Leach's petrel is its bounding flight in relatively short bursts; it is also given to changing speed and direction. The Leach's is silent at sea but is given to making high-pitched churrs when in colonies.

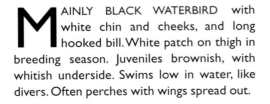

Cormorant

90 cm (35 in)

MAINLY BLACK WATERBIRD with white chin and cheeks, and long hooked bill. White patch on thigh in breeding season. Juveniles brownish, with whitish underside. Swims low in water, like divers. Often perches with wings spread out.

SPECIES INFORMATION

SCIENTIFIC NAME	Phalacrocorax carbo
RELATED SPECIES	Shag
CALL	Raw, grating, gurgling and crowing, usually only heard on breeding ground
HABITAT	Breeds in colonies on rocky coasts, also inland, usually on islands in large lakes, often in tall trees. Regular on larger lakes in winter, and in shallow coastal waters
STATUS	Resident and partial migrant. In BI about 12,000 pairs

CORMORANTS AND SHAGS are similar in many ways but avoid competition, with the smaller shag taking more free-swimming fish off rocky coasts, and the cormorant taking flat fish and shrimps in estuaries and 'soft' coasts. Perhaps there is less cormorant food there, for they are certainly gaining ground inland much to the chagrin of many fishermen. The white throat and, when breeding, white thigh patches of the cormorant, and the crest and green sheen of shags, when seen well, are clear distinctions. Young birds are harder to separate, but cormorants have more white. Both birds swim low in the water, and fly strongly with neck extended, but the shag avoids overland routes and stays close to the water.

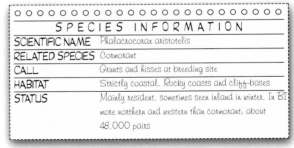

Shag

70 cm (28 in)

SPECIES INFORMATION

SCIENTIFIC NAME	Phalacrocorax aristotelis
RELATED SPECIES	Cormorant
CALL	Grunts and hisses at breeding site
HABITAT	Strictly coastal. Rocky coasts and cliff-bases
STATUS	Mainly resident, sometimes seen inland in winter. In BI more northern and western than cormorant; about 48,000 pairs

SMALLER THAN CORMORANT. Black plumage with a greenish tinge; upturned crest in breeding season. Breeds in colonies on rocky coasts. Less widespread than cormorant, but breeds in larger colonies.

THIS BIRD IS normally found on the open sea rather than sheltered water or estuaries; its nests on rocky shorelines but is seen inland after storms and galeas along the coast. It may disperse along the coast in winter.

Gannet

92 cm (36 in)

LARGE, GRACEFUL BLACK and white (adult) seabird, with pointed head and tail and long, rather narrow, black-tipped wings. Juveniles brown, gradually turning whiter over five years. Glides and soars, occasionally plunge-diving for fish.

GANNETS, WHICH REALLY are visible when sea-watching, are among our most spectacular birds with their size, distinctive shape and pattern, and magnificent diving making them unique.

The shape, with pointed tail, beak and wings is common to all gannets, but the pattern of black wing tips, contrasting with white plumage is for adults only, and takes up to five years to achieve. Before that the young will show various degrees of speckling and whiteness.

Our few large colonies are home to 70 per cent of the world's gannets, with half of the whole population in just five sites – St Kilda, Bass Rock, and Ailsa Craig in Scotland, Grassholm in Wales, and Little Skerrig in Ireland.

A fascinating feature of gannet breeding behaviour is that the egg is incubated below the webs of its feet. Nelson describes how 'the webs are placed in overlapping fashion over the egg ... They are adjusted by rocking movements, whilst the bird is slightly lifted, after which it settles back into the cup.'

SIZE

IDENTIFICATION

HABITAT

POPULATION

MAP

Top
Gannet colony on the Bass Rock, Firth of Forth, Scotland.

Bottom right and left
Adult gannet and the downy young.

Fulmar

45 cm (18 in)

○○○○○○○○○○○○○○○○○○○○○○○○○○

SPECIES INFORMATION

SCIENTIFIC NAME	*Fulmarus glacialis*
RELATED SPECIES	No close relatives in area
CALL	Rasping calls and also a softer flight call
HABITAT	Breeds in colonies on cliffs, rocky coasts and islands. Outside breeding season often at sea far from coasts
STATUS	Around coasts of northern Europe, Iceland and Norway, BI and south in to northern France. Seen mainly in Atlantic Ocean and North Sea; occasionally in Baltic. Population in BI about 575,000 pairs

SIZE

GULL-LIKE, BUT stockier, with thicker head and neck. Bill short and broad. Glides on stiffly held wings with occasional wing-beats.

IDENTIFICATION

FULMARS, WITH THEIR white heads and grey backs look a little like herring gulls on their breeding ledges, but the 'tube nose' bill and the straightness of the wings in flight make identification easy. Except for a time at the end of the year when they are at sea their distinctive flight, with flaps and long glides, can now be seen around most cliffs, for in just over a hundred years they have spread right round our coasts, from their St Kilda stronghold. Fulmars return from the ocean as early as the turn of the year.

'*Our most elegant companions were the fulmars, the premier acrobats of the waters, who glided in endless loops and circles around us for hour after hour riding close to the waves on stiff wings, their fat fluffy bodies like huge moths.*'

Tim Severin THE BRENDAN VOYAGE

HABITAT

POPULATION

MAP

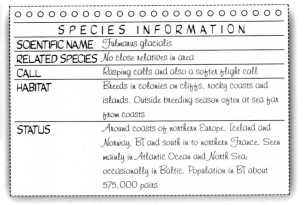

Top left
A fulmar glides in the wind on its stiff, narrow wings.

Top right
The tube-like nostrils are clearly visible on the beak of this bird.

Bottom
A fulmar pair going through the elaborate courting ritual.

Brent Goose

59 cm (23 in)

SPECIES INFORMATION	
SCIENTIFIC NAME	Branta bernicla
RELATED SPECIES	Barnacle Goose, Canada Goose
CALL	Deep nasal 'rott-rott-rott' or guttural 'rronk' when disturbed. Flight-call a short, hard 'ack', mixed with quieter, higher-pitched calls
HABITAT	Winters on mudflats and coastal fields
STATUS	Autumn and winter visitor to coasts of north-west Europe. Breeds in colonies near lakes in coastal arctic tundra

SMALL, DARK, RATHER duck-like goose with black bill and legs. White 'stern' contrasts with the rest of plumage.

TWO RACES VISIT Europe, a dark-bellied and a (rarer) pale-bellied form. Irish birds, and those in north east England are mainly of the pale-bellied race, while those visiting southern England and continental Europe are mostly dark-bellied. Usually forms large, loose flocks. Flight rapid. The dark-bellied form breeds in W Siberia, while the pale-bellied breeds in E Greenland and Svalbard (Spitzbergen).

The naturalist Armstrong describes the brent geese of Strangford Lough in Ireland:

'They come up in the mornings to feed if the mud banks are uncovered. What a sight it is as they advance! – flying in wide spreading arcs or chevrons, skein after skein, coming into view as long lines of tiny specks high above the water and swerving grandly as they come down to the slob land. As the smaller gaggles draw near, their resonant travel talk is heard, a virile "onk, onk, onk, orrck", but when the large flocks are resting on the water this busy chatter reaches the fascinated listener as a hoarse continuous clamour, rising and falling like the tumult from a vast encampment.'

SIZE

IDENTIFICATION

HABITAT

POPULATION

MAP

Top
Brent geese are rather restless and move about the estuary in small flocks.

Middle
At distance, brent geese appear very dark, with a white stern.

Bottom
Brent geese spend much time grazing in small flocks on saltmarsh and coastal grassland.

Barnacle Goose

64 cm (25 ins)

○ ○

SPECIES INFORMATION	
SCIENTIFIC NAME	Branta leucopsis
RELATED SPECIES	Brent Goose, Canada Goose
CALL	Flight-call a soft, puppy-like, yapping
HABITAT	Winters on saltmarshes, mudflats and coastal pasture.
STATUS	Regular winter visitor to Scotland, Ireland, and south-east North Sea. Breeds in far north, on cliffs above river valleys or fjords

SIZE

IDENTIFICATION

HABITAT

POPULATION

MAP

MEDIUM-SIZED GOOSE with small, black bill. From a distance looks black above, white below. The white face contrasts with the black neck. First year juveniles have a grey-white face and dark brown neck. Flocks of barnacle geese are usually unstructured in flight.

THIS SPECIES BREEDS mainly in East Greenland, Svalbard and Novaya Zemlya. Svalbard birds winter to Solway Firth, while those from Greenland migrate to West Scotland and Ireland.

Top
Barnacle geese are rather short-necked, with a large white patch on the face.

Bottom
A flock of barnacle geese grazing on coastal grassland Islay, Scotland.

Greylag Goose
75–90 cm (30–35 in)

<table>
<tr><th colspan="2">S P E C I E S I N F O R M A T I O N</th></tr>
<tr><td>SCIENTIFIC NAME</td><td>Anser anser</td></tr>
<tr><td>RELATED SPECIES</td><td>Pink-footed Goose, Bean Goose, White-fronted Goose, Lesser White-fronted Goose</td></tr>
<tr><td>CALL</td><td>Rather vocal, a nasal 'ga-ga-ga', 'angangang', or similar</td></tr>
<tr><td>HABITAT</td><td>Breeds on large inland lakes with thick fringing vegetation such as reeds, rushes or swampy thickets, or in bogs. Winter habitat coastal marshes and fields</td></tr>
<tr><td>STATUS</td><td>Resident and partial migrant. Iceland, Scandinavia, and patchily from Britain to E and SE Europe. In BI total population about 22,000 pairs, a large proportion (especially in the south) not of truly wild origin. Also resident as feral park bird, often with Canada Geese</td></tr>
</table>

LARGEST OF THE grey geese, and the ancestor of the familiar farmyard goose. Bill orange-yellow (western race) or flesh-coloured (eastern race), with intermediates; feet flesh-pink, grey in juveniles. In flight shows clear silver-grey leading edge to the broad wings.

SOME POPULATIONS ARE feral and semi-tame. However, those that fly into Scotland from Iceland or breed in the Outer Hebrides are truly wild. Graze on pasture or feed on estuaries and saltmarshes.

> '*And let us not forget*
> *The hopping gander*
> *Who gave a few quills to Bishop Morgan*
> *Giving the haven of its wings to the Welsh*
>   *language.*'
>
> Gwilym R. Jones PSALM TO THE CREATURES

SIZE

IDENTIFICATION

HABITAT

POPULATION

MAP

Top
The greylag is a large bird with a powerful bill.

Middle
A flock of greylag feeding on coastal meadow.

Bottom
In flight, the greylag goose appears heavy-headed.

White-fronted Goose

65–6cm (25.5–30 in)

SMALL GOOSE, WITH black horizontal barring on belly. Forehead white. Bill long and pink in Russian race; orange-yellow in Greenland race. Juveniles lack black belly markings and white patch, and bill has darker tip.

THE WHITE-FRONTED GOOSE is a medium-sized goose with sharp, angular wings and a square head. Juvenile birds do not have any white on their faces. The goose has a shrill, cackle-like call and is mainly a winter visitor to the grasslands of the British Isles, spending the summer months in arctic tundra. The nest is a shallow scrape on the ground, lined with vegetation and down from the female bird. Numbers have risen dramatically since the establishing of hunting restrictions in Europe.

SPECIES INFORMATION	
SCIENTIFIC NAME	Anser albifrons
RELATED SPECIES	Greylag Goose, Pink-footed Goose, Bean Goose, Lesser White-fronted Goose
CALL	High-pitched rapid 'kwi-kwi-kwi', or 'keowlyow'
HABITAT	Feed on coastal meadows and saltmarshes by day, spending the night on the water
STATUS	Winter visitor in flocks to British Isles – notably Ireland, W Scotland (Greenland race). Also North Sea and channel coasts of England, France, Holland and Germany (mainly Russian race). Breeds in tundra of northern Russia and Greenland

Bean Goose

66–88cm (26–35 in)

THE BEAN GOOSE is much rarer than pink-footed. It is also larger, and has an orange bill and feet. The wings are browner, and uniformly dark.

THERE ARE TWO populations of bean goose in Britain; one in the Norfolk Broads and one in central Scotland. The total British wintering population in less than one thousand birds. The call of this bird is louder than that of the greylag but quieter than the other geese, and it has a distinctive deep call. The nest consists of a shallow scrape on the ground which is lined with moss.

The goose is less laboured in flight than the greylag, and although slightly shy as a species, will feed among other types of goose.

SPECIES INFORMATION	
SCIENTIFIC NAME	Anser fabalis
RELATED SPECIES	Greylag Goose, Pink-footed Goose, White-fronted Goose, Lesser White-fronted Goose
CALL	Nasal cackle: 'kayakak'
HABITAT	Breeds in wooded tundra. Winters to coastal pastures and marshland
STATUS	Breeds in NE Scandinavia. Winters around coasts of Europe. In BI mainly SW Scotland (Solway) and E Anglia (but numbers small)

SPECIES INFORMATION

SCIENTIFIC NAME	Anser brachyrhynchus
RELATED SPECIES	Greylag Goose, Bean Goose, White-fronted Goose, Lesser White-fronted Goose
CALL	Very vocal. Musical calls include 'unk-unk' and a higher-pitched 'wink-wink-wink'
HABITAT	Breeds on rocky sites and tundra. Winters to pasture, stubble-fields and saltmarsh
STATUS	Breeds in Greenland, Iceland and Svalbard. Winters in large flocks to traditional sites in N Britain, notably Scotland, Lancashire and Norfolk

Pink-footed Goose
60–75 cm (24–30 in)

A RATHER SMALL, compact grey goose, showing pale leading edge to wing in flight (like greylag). Head is dark, and white upper tail shows clearly in flight. Legs pink; bill small and pink, dark at base.

IN 1939 PETER SCOTT wrote and broadcast about a pink-foot he called Annabel who had arrived one September at his lighthouse haven on the Wash.

'Greenland, Spitzbergen, and Iceland, the breeding grounds of all the pink-feet in the world, are dangerous places for a single goose. There are arctic foxes, and falcons, and men for all of whom a goose is just a very good meal. As October began I became apprehensive. There were also the dangers of the early autumn to be overcome, when the geese are stubbling in Scotland, and later in Yorkshire; a hundred possible fates might have overtaken Annabel. But none of them had, and, at noon on October 9th, I heard her shout high up in a dappled autumn sky. She was a tiny speck when I first saw her, almost straight above me, and with bowed wings she hurtled downwards. I called to her and she walked straight up to me. There she stood, a plump little round person, with her queer angular forehead, her unusually pink bill pattern and the few white feathers at its base.'

Fifteen years later Peter Scott was in Iceland to find out more of the breeding secrets of the pink-footed goose and to ring them during their flightless moult. Their breeding grounds in Spitzbergen had been found in 1855, in Greenland in 1891 and in Iceland in 1929 but the known sites could not account for the wintering numbers. Furthermore, the Severn Wildlife Trust had developed a technique of catching geese under rocket nets and in October 1950, 634 had been ringed in Scotland and perhaps a new Icelandic site would have some of these birds.

Eventually the expedition ringed and tagged 1,151 geese, estimated the population at 5,500 adults and 7,500 goslings, a major contribution to knowledge of pink-footed geese and their populations.

In 1950–51 there was a total of 30,000, including Greenland birds; by the 1990s there were over 200,000 in Britain and Iceland, an increase attributed to more favourable conditions in Britain in winter, where farming changes have led to an increased food supply, especially in east Scotland.

Their winter distribution correlates closely with areas of lowland farmland, where barley stubble, potato fields, winter-sown cereals and pasture provide them with their winter food. The low-lying farmland around the Wash was attracting flocks of 50,000, to feed mainly on harvested sugar beet fields.

The contrast between the dark neck and pale chest can be seen again in flight, when the dark underwing, grey forewing, shape and sound all help identification. The roosting sites used to be on the sandbanks and mudflats of estuaries but are now often on freshwater lochs and reservoirs. In the morning they will fly up to 20 km (12 miles) to find suitable feeding grounds.

SIZE

IDENTIFICATION

HABITAT

POPULATION

MAP

Top
A flock of pink-footed geese is a wonderful sight, accompanied by their musical calls.

Bottom
Pink-footed geese are regular winter visitors to several sites in Britain and Ireland.

269

Shelduck

61 cm (24 in)

SPECIES INFORMATION	
SCIENTIFIC NAME	Tadorna tadorna
RELATED SPECIES	Ruddy Shelduck
CALL	Piping 'tyutyutyutyu', and a trill (male). Female calls much deeper 'ga-ga-ga-ga' or 'ark'
HABITAT	Muddy and sandy coasts, and coastal lakes. Nests in holes and rabbit burrows
STATUS	Resident and partial migrant. Coasts of NW Europe, and patchily in Mediterranean. Common breeding bird of North Sea and Baltic. About 12,000 pairs in BI

SIZE

IDENTIFICATION

HABITAT

POPULATION

MAP

A LARGE, GOOSE-SIZED bird, looking black and white in the distance. Note the broad chestnut band around the body at chest region. Male has a knob at base of bill. Juveniles mostly grey-brown above, whitish below, with light grey bill and feet. Goose-like in flight, with relatively slow wing-beats, in lines or wedge formation.

SHELDUCK ARE EASY to identify, with both sexes having a dark green head and red bill above contrasting black, white and chestnut body. Young birds and adults in eclipse can cause identification difficulties however.

Tunnicliffe wondered where the Anglesey shelduck went from September to January, a time when many of them move to the Wadden Sea, where most of Europe's shelduck moult. Others go to Bridgwater Bay, but the succession of shelduck movements is very complex.

Shelduck need good feeding habitat for their mollusc and crustacean food, and also access to sand-dunes, for nesting. The nest burrows may be some way from water, so the ducklings may need to walk some distance. Once there, a number of young birds may form a crèche, with one or two parents who appear to have very large families.

Top left and right
The drake shelduck has an obvious knob at the base of its bill and distinct stripey patterning.

Bottom
In flight, the striking black and white pattern is very clear.

Eider

50–71cm (20–28 in)

SPECIES INFORMATION	
SCIENTIFIC NAME	*Somateria mollissima*
RELATED SPECIES	King Eider
CALL	Breeding male has a crooning 'ohuuo' or 'hu-huo'. Female a raw 'korr'
HABITAT	Breeds on coasts and nearby islands; outside breeding season in shallow bays and estuaries
STATUS	Summer visitor in breeding range. Winters mainly to adjacent coastal waters, south to English Channel. Coasts of Iceland, Scandinavia, northern BI about 32,000 pairs

LARGE SEA-DUCK, heavier than mallard, but more compact and shorter-necked. Breeding male mainly black and white. First-year males dark with partially white feathers, giving 'dappled' pattern. Female brownish, with darker stripes. Very sociable; often flying low over the water in long, straggling flocks.

THE EIDER HAS a peculiar head shape and the male has a black, white and lime-green head that distinguishes them from other ducks. They are highly social birds, spending all their time on sea water, and can often be seen around shorelines and on islands, chattering away between themselves. Take-off is laboured and their flight is relatively slow.

SIZE
IDENTIFICATION
HABITAT
POPULATION
MAP

Common Scoter

46–50cm (18–20 in)

SPECIES INFORMATION	
SCIENTIFIC NAME	*Melanitta nigra*
RELATED SPECIES	Velvet Scoter, Surf Scoter
CALL	Male has short fluting 'pyer' courtship call; female 'how-how-how' or 'knarr'
HABITAT	Breeds on lakes, mostly in tundra zone. Outside breeding season mainly at sea, often far from coast
STATUS	Summer visitor in breeding range. Winters to Atlantic and North Sea coasts, south to Gibraltar. Breeds in Iceland and Scandinavia; also a rare breeder in Scotland and Ireland (about 150 pairs)

Scotland. Velvet scoters may join flocks of common scoters at sea in the winter.

SQUAT, SHORT-NECKED sea-duck. Male is uniform black; bill black, with orange-yellow spot at base. Female dark brown with pale head and sides of neck. Flight rapid, in irregular strings.

COMMON SCOTERS AND the somewhat rarer velvet scoter are both strongly marine in winter when they will be seen as distant little blobs on a grey sea. Common scoter males are all black except for a yellow patch on the bill, but velvet scoters have a white wing-patch visible when they flap on the water. A few common scoter nest by limestone lakes in western Ireland and in the Flow Country of

SIZE
IDENTIFICATION
HABITAT
POPULATION
MAP

Scaup

48 cm (19 in)

SIZE

IDENTIFICATION

HABITAT

POPULATION

MAP

SPECIES INFORMATION

SCIENTIFIC NAME	*Aythya marila*
RELATED SPECIES	Tufted Duck, Pochard
CALL	Display call of male is a whistling 'pe-a-oo'. Female 'arr...arr'
HABITAT	Breeds on lakes in Scandinavia and Iceland. Winters to shallow seas and sheltered bays
STATUS	Regular winter visitor. A handful of pairs breed most years (mainly in Scotland)

SCAUP ARE ONE of the few ducks where females are easy to recognise, in this case by the white band around the base of her bill. The male, with dark head and breast and lighter body, can be confused with tufted or pochard, but black head and shoulder, pale grey back and white flanks should be sufficient for identification if well seen. In flight the wing pattern of white bars is similar to tufted.

> '*There is not a Shetland ornithologist who would not throw away his binoculars to confirm the calloo as a breeding bird*'
> J. L. Johnston
> NATURAL HISTORY OF SHETLAND
> ('calloo' is a local name for scaup)

Scaup may be confused with tufted ducks, but the grey back is distinctive.

Goldeneye
45 cm (18 in)

VERY COMPACT DUCK with large, domed head and yellow eye. Male black and white, with oval white patch between eye (yellow) and bill, and glossy green head. Female mainly grey, with brown head and yellow-tipped bill. Juvenile male similar to female, but with darker head, hint of white head-patch and uniformly black bill. Flight level, with rapid wing-beats.

THESE DUMPY DUCKS with their distinctive head shape have been increasing as breeders since nest-boxes have been provided to make up for a shortage of tree holes.

The idea of ducks in nest-boxes is peculiar to most of us, and the idea of boxes with porches and ladders that much more so, but Scandinavian boxes are of that type. Le Feu writing in the BTO's *Nest Box Guide*, 1993 describes the need for rough wood inside for the ducklings to get a firm hold, and a dark interior, and asks you not to worry about height as the ducklings can descend from great heights quite safely.

Goldeneye need molluscs, crustaceans and insect larvae, but they also like grain discharged from breweries and seed processing plants in Scotland, where sewer outlets are a favourite winter feeding place. At that time of year plenty do feed at sea, but they are also widespread inland, with a huge aggregation of up to or above 10,000 at Lough Neagh.

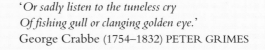
'*Or sadly listen to the tuneless cry*
Of fishing gull or clanging golden eye.'
George Crabbe (1754–1832) PETER GRIMES

SIZE

IDENTIFICATION

HABITAT

POPULATION

MAP

The drake goldeneye is one of our most attractive ducks, with its shiny green head, bright yellow eye and white face patch.

Long-tailed Duck

40–55cm (16–22 in)

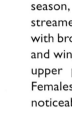

SPECIES INFORMATION	
SCIENTIFIC NAME	Clangula hyemalis
RELATED SPECIES	No close relative
CALL	Vocal. Male has melodious goose-like call, audible from a distance. Females 'ark-ark-ark'
HABITAT	Breeds on small lakes and slow rivers in Scandinavian tundra, and at coast. In winter usually well out to sea
STATUS	Common winter visitor to southern North Sea, Baltic and coasts around northern BI. Breeds in Iceland, Scandinavia and east Baltic

AN ELEGANT, SHORT-BILLED sea-duck with striking brown and white plumage. Plumage variable through season, but male nearly always has long tail streamers. In winter plumage mainly white, with brown patch on head, dark brown breast and wings. Breeding plumage male has brown upper parts and white area around eye. Females have mottled brown back and, most noticeable, a dark patch on the upper neck.

DRIFT NETS OF microfilament nylon are estimated to kill more than a million seabirds a year. Among British species some 10–20 per cent of long-tailed duck, velvet scoter and eider were killed in the southern Baltic between 1986 and 1990.

In winter, the drake long-tailed duck has very elaborate plumage. In summer, it is much darker on the head and back.

Avocet

42–46cm (16.5–18 in)

SPECIES INFORMATION

SCIENTIFIC NAME	*Recurvirostra avosetta*
RELATED SPECIES	No close relatives in the region
CALL	Musical 'pleet', repeated when alarmed
HABITAT	Saltmarshes, coastal lagoons and estuaries
STATUS	Mainly summer visitor. Winters in Africa, and south Europe, but also around coasts of north and west Europe (including south England). Breeds on North Sea coast (sometimes overwinters), parts of Baltic, Mediterranean, and in steppe region of Austria and Hungary. British population (mainly E Anglian coast) around 500 pairs

ELEGANT BLACK AND white wader with long, upturned bill and bluish legs. Juveniles have brownish cap and back markings. Legs extend well beyond tail in flight.

THE RETURN OF the avocet is for many people a symbol of the RSPB and of the growing interest in birds and conservation since the Second World War. It is as white and black as the oystercatcher, but totally different in every move and gesture. The liquid call is melodious.

They have favourite winter estuaries in the west, but Suffolk, Norfolk and the Thames are equally important. In winter, there is an average of 700 on the Alde complex, and nearly 400 on the Exe and in Poole Harbour.

Avocets breed near or in shallow water, and one of the main roles of the RSPB is in maintaining water levels to provide optimum conditions for breeding and feeding. The splendid bill is used to catch invertebrates by sideways sweeps, with the curved part, slightly open, passing through mud or water.

They are highly social birds with impressive displays as males circle females, getting closer and closer. This is followed by a lot of dipping and shaking of the bill in water. There are also complex distraction displays.

Avocets are normally found in shallow saline pools, muddy deltas and the like. There is a wide distribution outside Europe to Iran, Pakistan and Africa. Although the British wintering population is increasing, it is only about 6 per cent of the European birds.

SIZE

IDENTIFICATION

HABITAT

POPULATION

MAP

Top
The avocet, symbol of the RSPB, is quite unmistakable, with its unusual upturned bill.

Bottom
An avocet taking a bath.

Bar-tailed Godwit

33–42 cm (13–16.5 in)

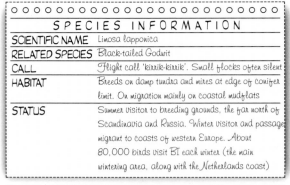

SPECIES INFORMATION	
SCIENTIFIC NAME	Limosa lapponica
RELATED SPECIES	Black-tailed Godwit
CALL	Flight call 'kirrik-kirrik'. Small flocks often silent
HABITAT	Breeds on damp tundra and mires at edge of conifer limit. On migration mainly on coastal mudflats
STATUS	Summer visitor to breeding grounds, the far north of Scandinavia and Russia. Winter visitor and passage migrant to coasts of western Europe. About 80,000 birds visit BI each winter (the main wintering area, along with the Netherlands coast)

SIZE

IDENTIFICATION

HABITAT

POPULATION

MAP

M EDIUM-SIZED WADER with rather long legs and long, very slightly upturned bill. Female has longer bill than male. Breeding male mainly rust-red, speckled brown and black on the back; female and winter male buff coloured. In flight legs extend slightly beyond tail. No wing bar. Tail with narrow bars.

BAR-TAILED GODWITS are one of those birds that turn up on those often beautiful but relatively bird-free sweeps of sand like those on the Northumberland coast, or along Cardigan Bay. Unlike the sanderling, which also occurs there, godwits really prefer a good muddy estuary, although they leave it to roost, sometimes some way off, on the

safest sand–bar available. Not only will they fly to roost, but they are mobile in response to food supplies. Some 18 British estuaries hold more than 1,000 birds, with the Ribble averaging 17,000.

Not as tall as their black–tailed relatives, these godwits are still taller than most of the waders they spend their time with. The typical winter wader plumage of streaked breast, brown upperparts, eye-stripe and pale belly is not distinctive against the mud, but when it flies, the long upturned beak, white rump and beautifully barred tail is easily recognised. The long bill, of course, is vital when probing, often in fairly deep water, for molluscs, crustaceans and annelid worms.

Breeding birds are much more spectacular, with much of the male's plumage over head, breast and belly being richly rufous. They have elaborate ceremonial display flights and a range of confusing calls. These can be seen and heard in Norway, Finland and Russia, and across Siberia into Alaska.

Top
A bar-tailed godwit in rarely-seen russet breeding plumage.

Middle
Here the bird is in the common winter plumage.

Bottom
Flock wading in an estuary.

Grey Plover

30 cm 12 (in)

SIZE

IDENTIFICATION

HABITAT

POPULATION

MAP

SLIGHTLY LARGER THAN golden plover, and with heavier bill. Greyer than golden plover in winter plumage. Breeding plumage (rarely seen) richly contrasting black, white and grey. Always has black axillaries ('armpits') and white rump. Often solitary.

GREY PLOVER NUMBERS peak in different months at different sites: as early as November on the Norfolk marshes, and as late as March on the Wash or in Chichester Harbour. In the 1995–96 winter it was present in internationally important numbers at 14 sites, at which at least one per cent of the international population wintered.

Large muddy estuaries are its favoured habitat, and there its short, stout bill separates it from most of its fellow waders. In winter, the plumage is pretty uniform grey, without the black chest and back 'spangling' of summer, but the black axillaries as it flies prevent confusion with the golden plover. The white rump of the young, which are more like golden plover because of their patterned backs, should also help to prevent confusion.

Top left and right
Grey plovers look timid and have rather a meek expression.

Bottom
A flock of four grey plover feed alongside a dunlin.

Knot
25 cm (10 in)

○ ○

SPECIES INFORMATION

SCIENTIFIC NAME	*Calidris canutus*
RELATED SPECIES	Dunlin, Sanderling, Curlew Sandpiper, Purple Sandpiper, Stints
CALL	Rather muted 'wutt-wutt'
HABITAT	Mainly sandy and muddy shores (winter)
STATUS	Winter visitor, mainly to NW European coasts. Mainly BI, Netherlands and France. About 90 per cent of European wintering birds (about 300,000) in Britain (notably in the Wash). Breeds in the high Arctic of Greenland and Canada

SIZE

IDENTIFICATION

HABITAT

POPULATION

MAP

MEDIUM-SIZED RATHER stocky, short-legged wader with short, straight bill. In breeding plumage rust-brown, with speckled upperparts. In winter pale grey upperparts, pale below. Wings rather long and narrow. In flight shows narrow white bars, and grey rump. Gathers in large, dense flocks, which in flight can seem almost cloud-like.

RESEARCH HAS SHOWN how knots, and no doubt other waders too, can detect crustaceans and molluscs under wet mud. When it pushes its bill into wet mud it creates a pressure wave in the water between the particles. This wave is reflected back and detected by cells in the horny layer at the end of the beak. Any objects larger than a grain of sand show up like aircraft on a radar screen.

The genus to which the Knot belongs, *Calidris*, is made up of small, short-billed Arctic breeders. They are extensive migrants, and while some winter here, others only occur on passage. All comparisons below are with dunlin.

KNOT
25 CM (10 IN)
Appearance: Stocky. Rusty underparts when breeding; short straight bill; pale grey rump; inconspicuous white wing bar in flight
Habitat: Feeds in masses on estuaries
Winter and passage

The knot is a medium-sized wading bird with few distinguishing features.

SANDERLING
20 CM (8 IN)
Appearance: Pale with black shoulder-patch; short straight heavier bill; very conspicuous broad white wing bar across dark wing
Habitat: Runs fast on sandy shores
Winter and passage

CURLEW SANDPIPER
22 CM (8.5 IN)
Appearance: Taller, scaly back, eye-stripe; larger, decurved bill; clear white rump and wing bar
Habitat: Often wades. Muddy shores and estuaries
Passage

LITTLE STINT
13 CM (5 IN)
Appearance: V on marked upperparts; tiny straight bill; grey outer tail feathers and narrower wing bar
Habitat: Often wades. Muddy shores and estuaries
Passage

PURPLE SANDPIPER
21 CM (8.25 IN)
Appearance: Dark, slatey and compact with yellow legs; yellow base to bill; Darker in flight
Winter

Dunlin

18 cm (7 in)

Ratcliffe describes their return in spring: 'Pairs or threes or fours will suddenly appear weaving their way at high speed through peat haggs with a thin, sizzling call. Alternatively flashing pale underparts and darker back as they zig-zag close to the ground, they are gone again... The nest will later be in a tussock, usually quite well hidden, and the neatest little cup, lined with cotton-grass leaves and containing four eggs.'

Adult dunlins in breeding plumage are smart little waders with quite a long, slightly decurved bill, streaked chestnut upperparts and a black belly. The first returning migrants, reaching estuaries in July, may still have this black belly, but when it is lost winter birds merge well with murky mud. The shrill flight call is a feature of autumn and winter estuaries.

Most winter on the coast, but passage birds will turn up by many inland waters, and sewage farms. At that time many moulting birds congregate in the Wash. The abundance of the bird, and the importance of British estuaries to it, is indicated by the facts that 14,000 or more are needed at one site to make the site of international merit, and that we have 14 sites of that importance. In 1995–96, the leading ones were Morecambe Bay (53,000 March), Mersey (44,000 Feb), Severn (41,000 Jan), Ribble (40,000 Jan) and Wash (36,000 Nov), while in Ireland the peak count of 5,316 was at Strangford Lough in February.

COMMONEST WADER IN northern Europe. Bill relatively long and slightly downcurved at tip. In breeding plumage belly is black. In winter grey-brown, without black belly patch. Juveniles brown above, with pale feather edges. Forms large flocks; flies in tight formation.

MOST PEOPLE WITH an interest in birds know the often abundant, but not very distinctive, dunlin and its tight flocks which so impress as they manoeuvre over winter estuaries. Many fewer know them on the wet grouse-moors and well developed blanket-bog of their breeding grounds.

SIZE

IDENTIFICATION

HABITAT

POPULATION

MAP

Top
A flock of dunlin in flight; the black bellies are very apparent.

Bottom right and left
The dunlin's bill is very slightly decurved.

Purple Sandpiper

21 cm (8.25 in)

SPECIES INFORMATION

SCIENTIFIC NAME	Calidris maritima
RELATED SPECIES	Dunlin, Knot, Curlew Sandpiper, Knot, Stints
CALL	Usually silent in winter. Flight-call 'veet' or 'vitveet'. Song fluting, from ground or in whirring song-flight
HABITAT	Breeds on bare, stoney plateaux, usually far from coast. Outside breeding season in small flocks on stoney and rocky coasts and jetties, often in surf zone
STATUS	Resident and partial migrant. Locally regular in autumn and winter at rocky coasts of north-west Europe, including BI. Breeds mainly in Iceland and Scandinavia. Very rare breeder in Scotland (two-three pairs)

SIZE

IDENTIFICATION

HABITAT

POPULATION

MAP

SMALL DARK, DUMPY wader with highly camouflaged plumage. Larger and shorter-legged than dunlin, with rather plump, rounded breast. Bill about as long as head, dark, with yellow base and slightly decurved. Legs grey-green.

IN BREEDING PLUMAGE back is blackish, flecked with rusty-brown and pale markings. In winter mainly dark brownish-grey with a pale belly, and pale orange legs. Dark in flight, with narrow white wing bar, black centre to rump, edged white. Relatively tame.

Fraser Darling gained constant pleasure from their tameness. 'The winter habitat is the barnacled rocks washed by the waves of every tide and there, apparently indifferent to the weather, the little bird quickly follows the receding wave, gathering small life unseen by us. And then a short fly back again as the new wave breaks on the rocks once more. How the ceaseless rhythm of the sea must have become part of the purple sandpiper, for in winter she is concerned wholly with the turbulent, changing strip of the intertidal zone.'

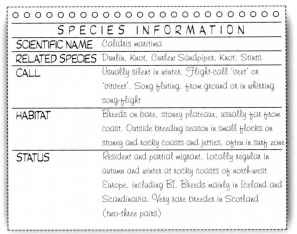

The purple sandpiper has dusky grey plumage and frequents rocky shores in winter.

Ringed Plover
18–20 cm (7–8 in)

```
○ ○ ○ ○ ○ ○ ○ ○ ○ ○ ○ ○ ○ ○ ○ ○ ○ ○ ○ ○ ○
```

SPECIES INFORMATION

SCIENTIFIC NAME	*Charadrius hiaticula*
RELATED SPECIES	Little Ringed Plover, Kentish Plover
CALL	Alarm call a soft 'tee-ip' or 'dooi', and a rapid 'kip-kiwip'. Song is a rapid 'drui-drui-drui' given in flight
HABITAT	Coastal sand and shingle, and on salt lakes. On migration regular on inland sand or mud banks
STATUS	Resident and partial migrant. Summer visitor in N of range. Also visits coasts of SW Europe in winter. Breeds at coasts of N and W Europe. In BI common, especially around N and E coasts, about 10,000 pairs

SMALL WADER WITH sandy-brown upperparts, black and white face pattern and orange-yellow legs. In flight shows clear white wing bar. Bill orange, tipped with black. Outside breeding plumage bill is black with orange mark at base. Juveniles resemble winter adults, but upperside feathers look scaly. Runs rapidly over sand, often stopping abruptly.

RINGED PLOVER ARE one of the few waders to be found on shingle beaches, but they also like sand. Disturbance is therefore a major problem, and breeding numbers have fallen on well-trodden beaches. As some compensation, the species has colonised some inland gravel pits and river shingles.

Males have a lovely 'song' and display flight, but you are most likely to hear liquid flight-call as it flits from one of the sandier parts of a winter estuary. Apart from the black ring across the white chest, which can immediately disappear when birds are among shingle, it has orange legs and bill and a brown back. The points separating it from the little ringed plover are listed in the freshwater section.

SIZE

IDENTIFICATION

HABITAT

POPULATION

MAP

Top
Stony ground near the coast is the preferred nesting habitat of ringed plover.

Middle
A ringed plover at its nest on the stoney beach at Dungeness.

Bottom
Close-up showing the bird's head patterning.

Spotted Redshank

30 cm (12 in)

SIZE

IDENTIFICATION

HABITAT

POPULATION

MAP

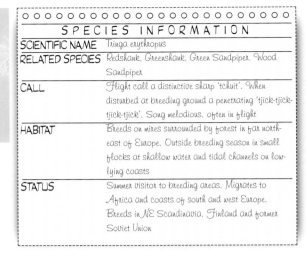

S OMEWHAT LARGER THAN redshank, and with a longer bill and legs. In breeding plumage (rarely seen) mainly blackish, with fine white spots on back (hence the name); legs dark red. At other times resembles redshank, but paler, and with black and white streaks from beak to eye. Lacks wing bar, but shows white in rump and back.

SPOTTED REDSHANK ARE among the pleasant, and very vocal, surprises when passage movements are on, and a few linger in the winter rather than heading on for Africa. Like other waders they often feed on rich tidal mudflats along the coastal wetlands.

SPECIES INFORMATION	
SCIENTIFIC NAME	Tringa erythropus
RELATED SPECIES	Redshank, Greenshank, Green Sandpiper, Wood Sandpiper
CALL	Flight call a distinctive sharp 'tchuit'. When disturbed at breeding ground a penetrating 'tjick-tjick-tjick-tjick'. Song melodious, often in flight
HABITAT	Breeds on mires surrounded by forest in far north-east of Europe. Outside breeding season in small flocks at shallow water and tidal channels on low-lying coasts
STATUS	Summer visitor to breeding areas. Migrates to Africa and coasts of south and west Europe. Breeds in NE Scandinavia, Finland and former Soviet Union

Wood Sandpiper

20 cm (8 in)

SIZE

IDENTIFICATION

HABITAT

POPULATION

MAP

M EDIUM-SIZED WADER, resembling green sandpiper, but more delicate and with slightly longer legs (visible beyond tail in flight).

SPECIES INFORMATION	
SCIENTIFIC NAME	Tringa glareola
RELATED SPECIES	Redshank, Spotted Redshank, Greenshank, Green Sandpiper
CALL	Flight call 'jiff-jiff-jiff'. Song incorporates 'tleea-tleea-tleea', delivered in high song-flight over territory
HABITAT	Breeds near water on mires with individual trees, in swampy woodland and in the tundra. On migration in small flocks on open mud, flooded meadows; often at coast
STATUS	Summer visitor to breeding grounds. Migrates to Africa and south Europe in autumn. In BI small numbers visit regularly as passage migrants (mainly autumn). Breeds mainly in north-east Europe (notably Finland and Sweden). Also a very rare breeder in Scotland (about six pairs)

ALSO HAS PALER, more heavily spotted plumage, and paler head and neck. Heavily spotted with white above, less clearly marked in winter. Juveniles with regular yellowish markings on back. Otherwise distinguished from green sandpiper by pale underwing and less contrasting upperparts. May nest in an old nest in a tree, but usually on the ground.

Oystercatcher

43 cm (17 in)

other countries, is thought to be genetic, and involves earlier breeding to coincide with a time of good food supplies.

LARGE BLACK AND white wader with long, red, slightly flattened bill, and red legs. Juveniles have pale throat markings and a dark tip to bill. In flight shows broad white wing bar and white rump.

NOISY OYSTERCATCHERS, with their black and white plumage and startling orange bills enliven many a rocky coast and estuary, but are also spreading as breeding birds inland, along northern rivers. This change, which has its parallels in

SIZE

IDENTIFICATION

HABITAT

POPULATION

MAP

Sanderling

20 cm (8 in)

SMALL WADER (roughly dunlin-sized), with straight, black bill and black legs. In breeding plumage, back, neck and upper breast rust-red with darker spots; white below.

VERY PALE IN winter plumage, with dark shoulder-patch. In flight silver-grey, with bold white wing bar. Often runs rapidly in and out of waves at the edge of the surf, and tends to stay close to the edge of the sea. The sanderling often nests in small hollows on the ground.

SIZE

IDENTIFICATION

HABITAT

POPULATION

MAP

Arctic Skua

41–45 cm (17 in)

SPECIES INFORMATION

SCIENTIFIC NAME	*Stercorarius parasiticus*
RELATED SPECIES	Long-tailed Skua, Pomarine Skua, Great Skua
CALL	Gull-like 'ee-air', often repeated
HABITAT	Breeds in open tundra and moorland with low vegetation, usually at the coast, or on grassy islands, and in some regions inland on boggy moorland, heath and in the tundra. Outside breeding season at sea
STATUS	Passage migrant, wintering in Atlantic. Regular off coasts of BI, mainly in autumn and spring. Breeds in Northern Europe and Arctic, south to Scandinavian coasts and N Britain (latter about 3,500 pairs)

SIZE

IDENTIFICATION

HABITAT

POPULATION

MAP

COMMONEST EUROPEAN SKUA. Two colour phases occur, with intermediates. Light phase (commoner in north) has whitish underside and dark neck band (sometimes missing). Dark phase (mainly in south) is uniformly dusky brown. Two pointed central tail feathers extend beyond tip of tail. Juvenile has shorter central tail feathers.

ARCTIC SKUAS, LIKE whimbrel, are Shetland birds but they also breed extensively on Orkney and have colonised Caithness and some of the Hebridean Islands. Plenty of the terns and gulls that it chases and robs breed much further south, but this may be too warm for the skuas. They breed successfully deep in the Arctic, and their plumage and metabolism is geared to the cold, so perhaps anywhere except the extreme north of Scotland is too warm for them.

Another peculiarity is that they exist in two forms, or phases. They are all dark sea birds with white wing flashes, like several other skuas, and most, 70 per cent or more, of the southern birds are dark phase individuals, which may be wholly dark below. Light phase individuals are pale below. Both phases are falcon-like in flight, well able to pursue terns and kittiwakes with agile twists and turns. Their chases often cause the victim to regurgitate its food, which the skua then consumes.

The ratio of light to dark phase birds increases as one moves north, with those in Greenland and Svalbard being virtually all pale. In 1977 Berry put forward an explanation based on a study of the Fair Isle birds. Dark male birds are less aggressive in relation to females, who initiate mating behaviour, and therefore dark males breed earlier as it takes less time before the male accepts the female.

When they first mate, those that pair with dark birds lay eggs some 11 days earlier. On the other hand, pale birds have an advantage over dark ones because they start to breed at a younger age and have a higher chance of surviving to breed, but their breeding season will be later. In the north, a late breeding season coincides with the peak population of lemmings and voles, while in the south early breeding helps the birds to time their breeding season to coincide with that of the gulls and terns.

Whether this version is true or not, most of us who see Arctic skuas see them on passage – for example harrying terns on the north Norfolk coast at Blakeney Point.

> ' …a pair of skuas arrived and this time there was no contest. The two terns fled for their lives, jinking and turning at wave crest level as the powerful skuas struck at them.'
> Tim Severin THE BRENDAN VOYAGE

Arctic skuas come in different colour phases: dark (below, left), pale (below, right) and intermediate (above).

```
○ ○ ○ ○ ○ ○ ○ ○ ○ ○ ○ ○ ○ ○ ○ ○ ○ ○ ○ ○ ○ ○ ○ ○
        S P E C I E S   I N F O R M A T I O N
```

SCIENTIFIC NAME	Stercorarius skua
RELATED SPECIES	Arctic Skua, Long-tailed Skua, Pomarine Skua
CALL	Deep 'tuk-tuk'; also 'uk-uk-uk' and 'skeerr'
HABITAT	Breeds on coastal moorland. Open sea and coastal waters
STATUS	Summer visitor. Migrates to North Sea and Atlantic in winter. Breeds in NW Europe: Iceland, Faeroes and N Scotland (about 8,000 pairs)

Great Skua

58 cm (23 in)

SIZE

IDENTIFICATION

HABITAT

POPULATION

MAP

LARGEST AND BULKIEST of the skuas, with short tail. Looks rather like juvenile herring gull, but wings more rounded. Wings show flashes of white at base of primaries. Chases other seabirds for food, and also eats fish, birds and eggs. Very aggressive at breeding grounds (will attack people).

GREAT SKUAS ARE BIRD pirates, chasing gulls, gannets, terns and auks to a point when the hapless victim disgorges the contents of its crop, upon which the skua swiftly swoops. They are also predators of other seabirds, killing adults and pillaging eggs and nestlings.

The great skua (or bonxie) can kill a bird as large as a gannet, and is the boldest of birds in defending its own nest site against an intruder – sheep and sheep-dogs can be harried and cowed by the diving bonxies and chased from the nesting area. Nearby, there are usually pools at which the bonxies bathe, preen and stand with raised wings, cackling. They rise to meet the intruder and then suddenly swoop in attack, sometimes striking the head with their feet before climbing away with a guttural 'tuk-tuk-tuk'. Though the birds are unlikely to cause serious injury to a person, they can draw blood and the onslaught takes nerve to resist, usually resulting in a hasty, head-down retreat.

Apart from its aggression, great skuas are remarkable for their distribution. In the western palearctic, populations are dotted around mainly remote islands, avoiding summer ice. In winter, birds may move at least as far as Brazil and the Gulf of Guinea.

Great skuas, as well as being pirates, predators and great travellers, are sturdy, brown, agile gull-like birds that look very dark in the distance, as when sea-watching, but with the darkness contrasting with white wing-flashes, both above and on the underwing. Outside the breeding season they are usually quiet.

Top left and below
The great skua is quite a bulky bird, with uniform brown plumage.

Top right
In comparison, the juvenile bird shows a rather streaky plumage.

Common Tern

34 cm (13 in)

SPECIES INFORMATION	
SCIENTIFIC NAME	Sterna hirundo
RELATED SPECIES	Arctic Tern, Sandwich Tern, Roseate Tern, Little Tern
CALL	Very vocal. Flight-call a short, repeated 'kick'. Alarm call 'kee-yah'
HABITAT	Breeds in colonies on sandy coasts, in dunes, and on islands. Also inland on gravel banks of undisturbed rivers, lakes and ponds
STATUS	Summer visitor and passage migrant. Scattered throughout, most numerous in north and east. In BI about 16,000 pairs

SIZE

IDENTIFICATION

HABITAT

POPULATION

MAP

COMMONEST EUROPEAN TERN. Very slim and elegant. Bill bright red, with black tip. Tail streamers do not extend beyond wing-tips when sitting. Winter adults and juveniles have dark bill and whitish forehead. In flight the dark outer primaries contrast with paler inner primaries.

TERNS RESEMBLE GULLS in their mainly white plumage, but are more graceful in flight, have pale grey backs and black crowns in the summer, when they breed on sand, shingle or low islands. This makes them very vulnerable to summer storms and to predators like foxes, rats and kestrels. Humans can disturb the birds too, sometimes causing them to abandon a site. Being long-lived, however, one successful breeding season can compensate for a series of bad ones.

Scolt Head Island in Norfolk is a typical tern nesting site. This is a natural ridge of sand and shingle about 6 km (4 miles) long, and separated from the mainland by a kilometre of intertidal mud and saltmarsh. As an uninhabited island which is also a National Nature Reserve it is ideal for nesting terns, and with protection the island became one of the largest tern colonies in western Europe, with several thousand pairs of sandwich, little and common terns in a good year. Since 1985 however, foxes have been crossing to the island at night and at low-tide, and an endless battle has gone on between the reserve manager and the foxes. All sorts of means, including electric fences, snares, cage-traps and a range of other inventive ideas have had to be employed to try to cope with this threat.

Top
The common tern's bright red bill has a black tip.

Middle
A pair of common terns copulating during the mating season.

Bottom
The common tern is extremely graceful in flight.

Arctic Tern

34 cm (13 in)

SPECIES INFORMATION

SCIENTIFIC NAME	Sterna paradisaea
RELATED SPECIES	Common Tern, Roseate Tern, Sandwich Tern, Little Tern
CALL	Not quite as harsh as common tern, and usually shorter and higher-pitched 'kree-errr'; also a soft 'gik'
HABITAT	Breeds entirely on coast, usually with other terns, in large colonies on sand and shingle banks
STATUS	Summer visitor. Famous for its long migration route – wintering around Antarctic pack-ice. Breeds mainly around Arctic region, south through Iceland to Scandinavia, BI and south North Sea. In BI about 46,500 pairs

SIZE

IDENTIFICATION

HABITAT

POPULATION

MAP

VERY SIMILAR TO common tern, and often hard to distinguish in the field. Uniformly red bill, shorter legs, and greyer underside. Tail streamers are longer, extending beyond wing-tips when sitting. In flight shows translucent primaries.

COMMON AND ARCTIC terns are often recorded in county bird reports as 'comic' terns because they are so hard to distinguish. Both are smaller, lighter birds than the sandwich, have red beaks and legs and forked tails. At close quarters in summer the arctic can be seen to have a uniformly red bill, while the common has a black tip to the bill, and, if seen perched, the short legs of the arctic are clear, if you are already familiar with the longer ones of the common. Arctic terns also have longer tail streamers, the length of which can be judged in relation to the wings when birds are perched: tail beyond wing-tip in arctic, but not in common. With their calls, too, familiarity with both species is the surest guide, but there is much to be said for enjoying the birds and not worrying about which is which.

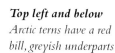

Top right
Arctic tern's nest in Shetland.

Top left and below
Arctic terns have a red bill, greyish underparts and long tail streamers.

Sandwich Tern

40 cm (16 in)

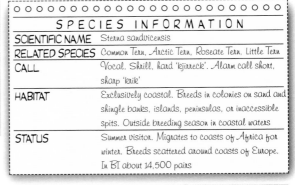

SPECIES INFORMATION	
SCIENTIFIC NAME	Sterna sandvicensis
RELATED SPECIES	Common Tern, Arctic Tern, Roseate Tern, Little Tern
CALL	Vocal. Shrill, hard 'kjirreck'. Alarm call short, sharp 'krik'
HABITAT	Exclusively coastal. Breeds in colonies on sand and shingle banks, islands, peninsulas, or inaccessible spits. Outside breeding season in coastal waters
STATUS	Summer visitor. Migrates to coasts of Africa for winter. Breeds scattered around coasts of Europe. In BI about 14,500 pairs

SIZE

IDENTIFICATION

HABITAT

POPULATION

MAP

RELATIVELY LARGE TERN, with long, black, yellow-tipped bill and shaggy crest on back of head. In winter has white forehead. Slim and narrow-winged in flight, with deep wing strokes.

THESE ARE THE largest British terns, less buoyant in flight than the others, and with relatively long, narrow wings. At its breeding sites the elongated feathers at the back of the crown may be seen, but most often birds will be seen flying out at sea and periodically diving for food. The black crown gains a white forehead after the breeding season; the beak remains black with a yellow tip. The noisy, rather creaking, calls have the second syllable higher pitched than the first, in contrast to common and arctic terns.

John Latham (General Synopsis of birds 1781–1790) said the sandwich tern was so called because some boys in that town told him about the birds.

Top
This is the largest of our local terns and has a white forehead in winter.

Bottom
A crowded breeding colony of sandwich terns.

SPECIES INFORMATION

SCIENTIFIC NAME	Sterna albifrons
RELATED SPECIES	Common Tern, Arctic Tern, Sandwich Tern, Roseate Tern
CALL	High-pitched raw 'kirrit', 'kirri-ik' or hard 'gik-gik'
HABITAT	Breeds on sand and shingle beaches, flat, rocky coasts, lagoons and on gentle banks of inland lakes. Usually in small colonies
STATUS	Summer visitor. Breeds scattered around European coasts, N to Baltic, and further E into Russia. In BI about 2,800 pairs

Little Tern
23 cm (9 in)

SMALLEST OF OUR TERNS, with white forehead even in breeding plumage, and yellow bill with black tip. Crown whitish in winter, grading into black of back of head. Juveniles have brownish crown and upperparts, with dark wavy markings. Wing-beats much quicker than those of other terns. Hovers frequently, often just before diving.

ALTHOUGH ALL TERN calls have plenty of similarities, the quick 'kirri-kirri, kirri-kirri' of this species on its breeding grounds is easier to distinguish than many. Little terns are often seen fishing, with characteristic hovering before diving. Little tern nests are extremely vulnerable, as they are placed so close to the high tide mark, and the terns also choose the same sorts of beaches that holiday-makers like: disturbance is therefore a major problem. In some places breeding sites are fenced off during the summer to reduce human (and canine) disturbance.

SIZE

IDENTIFICATION

HABITAT

POPULATION

MAP

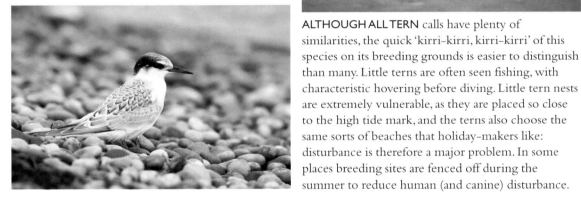

Top
Little Terns flying and wading in shallow water.

Middle
A juvenile little tern.

Bottom
Our smallest tern, the little tern has a white forehead, even in summer, and a yellow bill.

Turnstone

22 cm (9 in)

○○○○○○○○○○○○○○○○○○○○○○○○○○○○

SPECIES INFORMATION

SCIENTIFIC NAME	*Arenaria interpres*
RELATED SPECIES	*No close relatives in region*
CALL	*Flight call a rapid 'tritritri' or 'tuk-a-tuk'. Song a nasal 'tivi-tivi-titti', from song-post or in flight*
HABITAT	*Breeds on rocky coasts, islands, and in moss and lichen tundra of northern Europe and Arctic Canada. Winters on stoney or pebbly coasts.*
STATUS	*Summer visitor to breeding grounds. Winters mainly to coasts of North Sea and Atlantic. Breeds on coasts of Scandinavia and N Baltic*

SHORT-LEGGED AND dumpy wader. Breeding plumage is a very colourful chequered pattern. In winter duller brownish-black, with pale feather edges. In flight shows broad white wing bar and white tail with black band near tip.

SIZE

IDENTIFICATION

HABITAT

POPULATION

MAP

TURNSTONES ARE BIRDS of rock and seaweed. In spring, as they head for their northern breeding lands, they show a splendid contrast of black and white patterned head, black breast-band and chestnut back. They are more often seen in winter plumage, still with black breast-band, a suggestion of the summer face markings, but now with browny-black back. The orange legs provide the colour.

Turnstones are rather tame, but when they eventually move they fly off with a twittering call, and usually settle quickly, having shown their bold, pied flight pattern.

Armstrong describes the turnstone which frequent Strangford Lough all winter: 'They butt and bore into the wrack, using head and bill like a ram or ploughshare. Running briskly hither and thither the plump little birds poke under stones and generally behave as if they thoroughly understand the business of finding and devouring small marine organisms.'

Top left
A turnstone nest situated in the open tundra.

Top right
A turnstone at its nest in chequered summer plumage.

Bottom
The turnstone uses its strong bill to probe beneath stones and pebbles.

SPECIES INFORMATION

SCIENTIFIC NAME	*Larus ridibundus*
RELATED SPECIES	Common Gull, Mediterranean Gull, Little Gull; other *Larus* gulls
CALL	Very vocal 'kvairr' or 'kverarrr'; also 'ke-ke-ke' and high-pitched 'piee'
HABITAT	Breeds in colonies (often large) at reedy lakes, and on small islands and coastal marshes. Very common at coast and on inland waters (and fields) during the winter, also in built-up areas
STATUS	Summer visitor to north-east of range; resident and winter visitor further south. Breeds throughout Europe, especially in north and east. In BI about 200,000 pairs

Black-headed Gull

36 cm (14 in)

COMMONEST OF THE smaller gulls, and the commonest gull inland. Chocolate brown face-mask (not extending down back of neck), with crescent-shaped white mark around eye. Wing-tips black, bill and legs dark red. In winter has white head with dark ear-patch. Juveniles speckled brown above, with dark trailing edge to wings and dark tip to tail. In flight the narrow, pointed wings show a highly characteristic white leading edge.

NOTHING IS MORE recognisable than a gull, but the identification of individual species often causes problems. Even the attractive, common and widespread black-headed gull can create difficulties, as it has no dark head for much of the year, and, despite its name, never has a black head. Black-headed gulls are frequent visitors to park ponds, urban rivers, reservoirs, and rubbish tips, and will even take food in gardens. The *Garden Bird Watch Handbook* shows that ten to fifteen per cent of gardens have black-headed gulls early in the year.

The patterns of the wings of gulls in flight is crucial to their identification. Black-headed gulls are buoyant fliers, with pointed wings, which have a white leading edge when seen from above or below. There is a dark trailing edge to the upper wing and a generally dusky under wing. Young birds are very pale brown and white with dull orange legs and bill and they retain their mottled backs and distinctive tail-band into their first winter.

Breeding, which is always near shallow fresh water, occurs in a band across European middle latitudes.

Breeding behaviour is complex and much studied, with the head posture playing a crucial role. The nest around which all the display takes place is usually on the ground – a shallow scrape lined with vegetation. Where it is really wet, a mound may be built up.

Most of Europe's birds are migratory, avoiding the eastern continental climate and Scandinavian winters by moving as far south as the Persian gulf and the West African coast. Many also winter in inshore tidal waters around the North Sea, Baltic and Mediterranean.

Part of the success of the bird stems from the variety of its feeding methods, and of its food. All gulls, to varying degrees, share this versatility. They walk, as when following the plough, searching for worms, or investigating rubbish tips, fly with agility as when circling for flying ants in up-currents, for crusts thrown from London Bridge or for tideline detritus, or swim to feed at or just below the water surface.

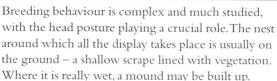

SIZE

IDENTIFICATION

HABITAT

POPULATION

MAP

Top
The chocolate-brown head of this gull appears black from a distance.

Bottom left
A black-headed gull proudly incubates its clutch of eggs.

Bottom right
When in winter plumage, only tiny smudges of dark remain on the head.

Herring Gull

60 cm (24 in)

SPECIES INFORMATION	
SCIENTIFIC NAME	Larus argentatus
RELATED SPECIES	Lesser Black-backed Gull, Great Black-backed Gull, other Larus gulls
CALL	Very vocal, repeated 'kyow'. Alarm call at breeding ground 'ga-ga-ga'
HABITAT	Breeds in coastal meadows, dunes, on shingle banks and small islands and rock ledges. In some areas even on buildings. Outside breeding season usually at coast, but also at inland water and rubbish tips
STATUS	Summer visitor to NE of range; resident and winter visitor further south. Breeds mainly in coastal areas of NW Europe. BI population is around 200,000 pairs

SIZE

IDENTIFICATION

HABITAT

POPULATION

MAP

COMMONEST LARGE GULL. White, with pale grey back and wings, and black wing-tips. Bill powerful, yellow, with red spot; eyes yellow; feet flesh pink. In winter, head has brownish streaks. Juveniles speckled brown, with black terminal tail-band, gradually attaining full adult plumage in the fourth year.

BOTH THE HERRING gull and the closely related lesser black-backed gull have begun to become more and more urban. Indeed, in some cities, such as Bristol, their populations have risen to the level at which they have become a bit of a problem. Herring gulls tend to remain fairly local, whereas lesser black-backed gulls wander further, more randomly and rather more inland.

Herring gulls, like many other gulls, have developed a great liking for refuse tips, sewage outlets and fish-quays; in fact for anywhere which provides rich pickings.

Top left
This young herring gull still shows signs of brown in its plumage.

Top right
A herring gull soaring overhead.

Bottom
A herring gull at its nest on a cliff-face in Wales.

Lesser Black-backed Gull

52–62 cm (20–24 in)

SPECIES INFORMATION

SCIENTIFIC NAME	Larus fuscus
RELATED SPECIES	Herring Gull, Great Black-backed Gull; other Larus gulls
CALL	Similar to Herring Gulls, but slightly deeper in pitch
HABITAT	Breeds on low-lying coasts and islands, usually with higher vegetation than Herring Gull; also on inland moors and bogs. Outside breeding season mainly at coasts, but regular at inland lakes as well. Hunts over open sea; occasionally visits rubbish tips
STATUS	Summer visitor; migrant and winter visitor from further north. Similar to herring gull, but breeds further N (to Arctic) and further south (to coasts of Spain and Portugal). BI population is around 90,000 pairs

SIZE AND SHAPE of herring gull, but with dark slate-grey back, and proportionately slightly longer wings. Legs yellow. In winter has streaky head and yellowish-pink legs. Juveniles difficult to separate from young herring gulls, but tend to be darker. Shade of colour on back and wings deepens from grey in south of range to black in Baltic area.

LESSER BLACK-BACKED GULLS used to be summer visitors to well vegetated cliffs and islands, but now some 80,000 winter on arable land, refuse tips and estuaries. The taxonomy of lesser black-back and herring gulls presents a complex picture on a world scale, with all sorts of grading of different coloured backs and legs, producing intermediate forms. Although this species can interbreed with the herring gull, it normally behaves as a good species, with differences in habitat, behaviour, leg, beak and back colour.

British lesser black-backs have lighter slate-grey backs than Scandinavian ones, so their wing-tips, which are black, provide a contrast. Apart from the back, the yellow legs in summer contrast with the pink of herring gulls and of the much larger great black-back. The legs in winter are a rather indeterminate grey. Young birds retain the mottled plumage typical of young gulls for a couple of years, but are always distinctly dark.

 SIZE

 IDENTIFICATION

 HABITAT

 POPULATION

  MAP

Top
In comparison with the great black-backed gull, the back of this species is somewhat paler than the jet-black wingtips.

Bottom
Lesser black-backed gull in full cry, with slate-grey back and yellow legs.

293

Great Black-backed Gull

68–78 cm (27–31 in)

SPECIES INFORMATION

SCIENTIFIC NAME	Larus marinus
RELATED SPECIES	Lesser Black-backed Gull, Herring Gull and other Larus gulls
CALL	A chuckling 'krau-krau-krau', deeper and slower than Herring Gull; also 'owk'
HABITAT	Breeds on rocky and stoney coasts, particularly on small rocky islands. Outside breeding season at coasts, often at rubbish tips
STATUS	Summer visitor to north-east of range; resident and winter visitor further S. Breeds in Iceland, Scandinavia, Finland, south to BI and north-west France. BI population about 23,000 pairs

SIZE

IDENTIFICATION

HABITAT

POPULATION

MAP

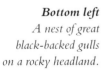

OUR LARGEST GULL, with back and wings black. Wings broader than those of lesser black-backed. Head large, bill deep, legs flesh-coloured. Juvenile similar to young herring gull, but larger, and head usually paler. Flight slow, with regular wing-beats and long periods of gliding.

THE VERY MUCH larger great black-back is more strictly maritime, has a genuine black back and can be beastly to almost anything that moves. Conservationists regret the killing that goes on at seabird breeding stations by this rather aggressive predator. Solitary nesters seem to be more bird directed in their food preference than colonial nesters. In fact great black-backs take a huge range of food, from live birds and small mammals to carrion, fish, eggs and worms. Along with crows and other gulls, they play an important role in cleaning up the bodies of sea animals from our beaches.

> 'It prefers a flesh diet, either recent or ancient, a dead rat, dog or whale is alike acceptable to the corpse eater.'
> T.A. Coward

Bottom left
A nest of great black-backed gulls on a rocky headland.

Top and bottom right
This powerful predator of the seaside has a back which is as dark as the wingtips, and flesh-coloured feet.

Common Gull

40–43 cm (16–17 in)

SPECIES INFORMATION

SCIENTIFIC NAME	Larus canus
RELATED SPECIES	Black-headed Gull, Herring Gull; other Larus gulls
CALL	Higher and more penetrating than herring gull. Flight-call nasal 'kyow-kyow', alarm call 'gleeu-gleeu'
HABITAT	Chiefly breeds near coast, in colonies in coastal meadows, bog and heath with low vegetation. Mainly coastal outside breeding season, but also on inland waters
STATUS	Summer visitor to NE of range; resident and winter visitor further S. Breeds mainly in N and NE Europe. Common in Scandinavia, and around Baltic Sea. Occasional breeder inland in central Europe. In BI mainly in N and W; about 70,000 pairs

LIKE A SMALL herring gull, but lacks red spot on bill. Rounded white head, relatively narrow yellow bill and dark eyes, giving rather a meek expression. Feet greenish-yellow. In winter head speckled brownish. Juvenile brownish above, with dark bill. In flight shows black wing-tips with white spots, and white trailing edge to wing. Back and wings of adult slightly darker grey than herring gull.

ALTHOUGH PLENTY OF herring, black-backed and black-headed gulls follow the plough, the common gull is the one most closely linked with farms, and earthworms, in the winter. It is fairly common at that time, but the name refers more to the absence of distinguishing features than any abundance anywhere or anytime.

The *Winter Atlas* shows a wide distribution in Britain, away from the mountains, but most Irish birds are around the coasts. J. D. R. Vernon, writing in the *Atlas* describes a 'preference for feeding at well grazed grassland, particularly on well-drained limestone soils, and often above 100 m in altitude. The short kept turf on airfields and playing fields is also exploited.' After heavy rain, flooded lowlands are visited for worms, often with black-headed gulls. Most of the wintering birds come from Scandinavia, Denmark and Germany.

The *Breeding Atlas* shows a very different picture. Most Irish populations are towards the north, and the main British concentration is in Scotland. Amazingly, 50 per cent of this population is in two colonies, on low heather-covered hills.

The common gull is usually identified on features of legs and bill, but those interested in gulls often rely more on features of wing and tail patterns. The small bill, like the legs, is yellow or greenish, while the wings, narrower than those of herring gull, have bold white wing mirrors on the outer primaries. Young gulls are always more difficult, but size, smaller bill, whiter underparts, white rump and contrasting black tail-band should distinguish from herring gull.

The common gull's diet is largely invertebrates, taken from land and water, fish, and eggs. The call is described as more 'mewing' than the herring gull's.

 SIZE

 IDENTIFICATION

 HABITAT

 POPULATION

 MAP

Top
A common gull at its nest guarding its eggs.

Bottom left
The common gull is a daintier version of a herring gull with a lesser bill and green legs.

Bottom right
This common gull has made its nest among the wooden slats of a pier.

Kittiwake

38–40 cm (15–16 in)

○○○○○○○○○○○○○○○○○○○○○○○○○○○

SPECIES INFORMATION

SCIENTIFIC NAME	*Rissa tridactyla*
RELATED SPECIES	No close relative in region
CALL	Flight-call a raw 'ke-ke-ke'. At breeding site a loud, repeated 'kiti-wa-ak'
HABITAT	Breeds in colonies on steep cliffs (sometimes on buildings). Otherwise a bird of the open sea
STATUS	Summer visitor to breeding areas. Winters in North Sea and Atlantic. Scattered around coasts of N and W Europe. In BI breeds on all coasts, except much of S and E (total about 545,000 pairs)

SIZE

IDENTIFICATION

HABITAT

POPULATION

MAP

GRACEFUL, MEDIUM-SIZED gull. Resembles common gull, but wings ('dipped in ink') lack white patches at tips. Legs black, bill yellow. Juveniles have dark zig-zag pattern on upper wings (see juvenile little gull), and black band across nape.

KITTIWAKES HAVE NO white tips to their primaries in flight, while black bands along the front of the wing and a dark patch behind the neck characterise young birds. Adults at the nest site might be mistaken for common gulls but for the site itself, their black legs, yellow bill and darker back. Non-breeding adults, like young birds, have a black 'splodge' behind the eye.

They are unusual among gulls in that they have adapted to life on vertical cliffs, while most gulls nest more or less on the level. The nest needs depth, and a firm base so parents trample mud to make the foundation. Unlike other gull chicks, kittiwake chicks remain fairly immobile – this keeps them safe on their precipitous nest site. Young kittiwakes also face the cliff wall. As they are always on the nest, there is no special parental food call and the parent recognises the nest not the young birds. This cliff-nesting which also calls for anatomical adaptations like strong claws and foot muscles, is an anti-predator device but some skuas have perfected the art of catching kittiwakes from the ledges. Kittiwakes get their name from the call, which can dominate the vicinity of their breeding cliffs.

Top
The kittiwake, arguably our prettiest gull, has a greenish-yellow bill and black legs.

Bottom
A pair of kittiwakes at their nesting site.

ADULT GULLS IN WINTER

BLACK-HEADED
Head: Dark mark behind eye; pale red bill
Back: Pale grey
Wings: White flash along front
Legs: Pale red

COMMON
Head: Streaked; grey-green bill
Back: Dark grey
Wings: Large white mirrors
Legs: Grey green

KITTIWAKE
Head: Spot behind eye; yellow bill
Back: Dark grey
Wings: White below with pure black tips
Legs: Short, black

LITTLE
Head: Dark eye patch; slight black bill
Back: Pale
Wings: Rounded, dark below
Legs: Reddish

MEDITERRANEAN
Head: Dusky side of face; strong red bill
Back: Very pale
Wings: Wholly white
Legs: reddish

GREAT BLACK-BACKED
Head: White; yellow, red-spotted bill
Back: Dark black
Wings: Very black
Legs: Pink

LESSER BLACK-BACKED BACK
Head: Some streaking; yellow, red-spotted bill
Back: Grey-black (but depends on race)
Legs: Yellow
Wings: Grey-black

HERRING
Head: White or streaked; yellow, red-spotted bill
Back: Grey
Wings: White mirrors to black tips
Legs: Pink

ICELAND
Head: Dirty streaking; yellow; red spot
Back: Very pale grey
Wings Pale: White-tipped
Legs: Pink

GLAUCOUS
Head: Dirty streaking; yellow, red-spotted bill
Back: Very pale grey
Wings: Pale, white-tipped
Legs: Pink

NB Iceland gull is size of herring gull; glaucous gull is size of great black-backed gull.

Top
A kittiwake soaring overhead, showing the 'dipped in ink' pure black wingtips.

Middle
Kittiwakes nest on precarious cliff faces; there is a dark neck band on the young bird.

Bottom left
At favoured breeding cliffs kittiwakes seem to occupy every ledge.

Bottom right
With dusty grey plumage and their yellow bills, these gulls are attractive.

Guillemot

40 cm (16 in)

SPECIES INFORMATION

SCIENTIFIC NAME	*Uria aalge*
RELATED SPECIES	Razorbill, Puffin, Black Guillemot
CALL	Grating 'aaarrr', 'uarr' at nesting site
HABITAT	Breeds in dense colonies on narrow ledges and small ridges on rocky sea-cliffs. Outside breeding season at sea
STATUS	Breeds on coasts of north and west Europe. Leaves breeding grounds in August to return in January. In BI over 1,200,000 birds

SIZE

IDENTIFICATION

HABITAT

POPULATION

MAP

BLACK AND WHITE seabird with narrow, pointed bill. Sits upright, penguin-style. Often has white eye-ring and narrow stripe behind eye (bridled form). In winter, cheeks, chin and neck white, and has a dark line behind eye.

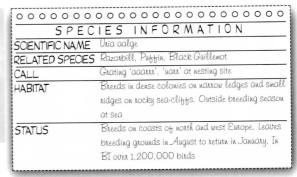

THEY ARE HIGHLY specialised and distinctive swimmers and divers who spend most of their time at sea. The guillemot is most easily told from the razorbill by its slender bill and its rather paler grey-black upperparts.

Guillemots are specialist fish-feeders and they nest close to seas rich in fish, which they bring in one at a time to their young. The largest colonies are in Scotland, where many have more than 10,000 birds each. On the east coast, the most southerly colony is at Flamborough Head, and there are no colonies between there and the Isle of Wight.

Top left

Guillemots standing, penguin-like, on a rock in the Shetland Isles.

Top right

A guillemot colony in the Farne Islands.

Bottom

The guillemot's streamlined body helps it swim and dive with ease.

'The guillemot and other auks all nest on rocky ledges.
Their eggs are conical to stop them rolling off the edges,
They sit in groups in coats of black like elders at a wake
But differ from the elders in the kind of noise they make'

Robert S. Morrison WORDS ON BIRDS

SPECIES INFORMATION

SCIENTIFIC NAME	*Alca torda*
RELATED SPECIES	*Guillemot, Puffin, Black Guillemot*
CALL	*Grating calls such as 'arrr' and 'orrr'*
HABITAT	*Breeds in small groups on steep cliffs, often with guillemots*
STATUS	*Breeds at coasts of NW Europe. Leaves breeding grounds in July, to return in February or March. In BI about 182,000 birds*

Razorbill

38 cm (15 in)

SIZE

IDENTIFICATION

HABITAT

POPULATION

MAP

SIMILAR TO GUILLEMOT but has larger head, shorter neck and heavier bill. Juveniles with smaller, uniformly black bill; easily confused with juvenile guillemots, but bill shorter and less pointed.

RAZORBILLS ARE BLACK on the back with white underparts and an odd bill, as its name implies. The bill is laterally compressed, looks a bit formidable, and is crossed by a white line; another white line runs towards the eye. Separating the two in winter is harder, but the guillemot is more pointed in front, the beak, and the razorbill at the rear, its tail. Flight appears fast, is usually low, and the wings are also used under water in pursuit of fish and crustaceans.

Top
Although they have narrow wings, razorbills and guillemots can fly quite well.

Middle
The razorbill has a thicker neck and wider bill than the guillemot.

Bottom
A group of razorbills perched on a seaside rock.

Puffin

28 cm (11 in)

○○○○○○○○○○○○○○○○○○○○○○○○○
SPECIES INFORMATION
SCIENTIFIC NAME	*Fratercula arctica*
RELATED SPECIES	Guillemot, Razorbill, Black Guillemot
CALL	Long growling at nest
HABITAT	Nests in colonies in rabbit burrows (or digs its own) on grassy islands or cliffs
STATUS	Summer visitor to breeding sites. Winters at sea (Atlantic, North Sea and west Mediterranean). Breeds at coasts of north and north-west Europe. In BI about 940,000 birds

SIZE

IDENTIFICATION

HABITAT

POPULATION

MAP

CLOWN-LIKE FACE, and unusual heavy, colourful bill. Dumpy, black and white seabird with bright red legs and feet. In winter, bill becomes smaller and darker. Flight straight, with rapid wing-beats.

THE PUFFIN IS the only one of our auks that does anything about preparing a home. It digs effectively, using its bill as a pickaxe, and its webbed feet as shovels to fling earth, or even soft sandstone, backwards. Having made the hole, or enlarged a rabbit burrow, it will take feathers, grass or seaweed into the burrow but may just as easily drop them at the entrance.

Everyone has seen pictures, tea towels or cards of puffins, with their remarkable triangular, brightly-coloured bills, but few are able to see these sociable birds at their breeding colonies. One of the pair spends much of the day in the isolation of the burrow, but when the egg is abandoned, for an hour or two on a summer evening, the pairs parade together, showing their bright orange legs among the orange lichens, or flap down to join rafts of birds on the sea below.

With their unusual bills, puffins are able to carry several small fish, such as sprats, at a time back to their young.

Top left and right
The puffin's bill is designed to catch and carry several sand-eels at once.

Bottom
Puffins at their burrows in the colony on the Shetland Islands.

SPECIES INFORMATION

SCIENTIFIC NAME	Cepphus grylle
RELATED SPECIES	Guillemot, Razorbill, Puffin
CALL	High-pitched whistle, 'ssiii' or 'piiiih', also repeated 'sist-sist'
HABITAT	Breeds in small colonies among rocks at the base of steep cliffs, on the lower slopes of bird cliffs and on small, rocky islands. Outside breeding season mostly in shallow coastal waters
STATUS	Resident or partial migrant. Coasts of N Europe. In BI about 40,000 birds

S MALL SEABIRD WITH black plumage and white wing-patches; feet bright red. In winter, white beneath, grey above, with pale feather edging. In flight the white wing-patches are conspicuous.

BLACK GUILLEMOTS SEEM to love their rocks and seaweed, and display beautifully early in the morning, near little islands in the north west. Their bright red feet, white wing-patch, slender bill and black summer plumage make them as distinctive as the almost pure white non-breeding adults, with dappled black and white backs in winter. Not surprisingly the white wing-patch is at all times a feature, but white underwings add to the bird's pied contrast when it flies or flaps in the water.

Black Guillemot
30 cm (12 in)

The main concentrations of black guillemots are in Shetland and Orkney, and along the western seaboard of Scotland.

In a chapter called the 'Playboys of the Western World' E.A.Armstrong describes the black guillemot: 'He is a quaint, jolly little fellow. The more you know him the queerer and the more likeable you find him to be. You appreciate him, indeed, because of his odd ways....If the black guillemot has his little whimsies and foibles it is only to say he is a real personality.'

'There is no more charming bird on Clerach than the black guillemot or tystie. The little bird is classed as an auk, but it is the least representative of the family in type. It is gregarious on the sea, or at least given to making up playful parties, but it nests in private, deep in some cranny and not necessarily directly above the sea.'
Fraser Darling

SIZE
IDENTIFICATION
HABITAT
POPULATION
MAP

The black guillemot stands out clearly in summer plumage with its contrasting black and white colouring and the vivid red of the legs.

BIRD SPECIES

Chough

40 cm (16 in)

SIZE

IDENTIFICATION

HABITAT

POPULATION

MAP

G LOSSY, BLUE-BLACK plumage, with long, curved red bill and red legs. Acrobatic in flight, showing deeply fingered wings and square tail.

SPECIES INFORMATION

SCIENTIFIC NAME	Pyrrhocorax pyrrhocorax
RELATED SPECIES	No close relatives in region (Alpine Chough in mountains of S Europe)
CALL	Jackdaw-like calls
HABITAT	Rocky sites in mountains; also on rocky coasts in west Europe
STATUS	Resident. Range includes S Europe, particularly Spain, Greece and Turkey; also Sardinia and Sicily and north-west France. In BI about 1,100 pairs, mainly in Ireland

*'How fearful
And dizzy 'tis, to cast one's eyes so low!
The crows and choughs that wing the midway air
Show scarce so gross as beetles: half way down
Hangs one that gathers samphire, dreadful trade..!'*

KING LEAR William Shakespeare

THE RED, CURVED bill and red legs make the chough instantly recognisable, but its call can be confused with a jackdaw's. In no sense is it a water bird, but over most of its British range it is closely associated with the sea, and there are few nest sites on mainland Britain, except in west Wales. RSPB research has shown a clear link between the length of grass sward and chough populations on Ramsey Island and Islay. On Bardsey chough populations have recently fallen, in line with a decline in rabbits, while a previous increase was linked to the introduction of a more intense grazing regime.

As well as low intensity agriculture, with short grass rich in beetles, choughs need caves, quarries or

derelict buildings in which to nest. Welsh, Scottish and Irish islands can produce this combination, and Islay, the Isle of Man and Ireland hold the majority of birds. Choughs are obvious 'corvids' and fine fliers, deftly using air currents up sea-cliffs and soaring, with well spread primary feathers.

I had always been led to believe, whether in English lessons or by birdwatchers who knew, that those caught were jackdaws, and that Shakespeare was wrong. However, there is a reference in *A History of Kent* (Dunkins, 1857): 'before the war of extermination was ruthlessly waged against the chough or red legged crow or Cornish chough – this bird was very plentiful among the Dover cliffs.'

The chough is a rather unusual member of the crow family, with its narrow, curved, bright-red bill. This rare bird is restricted to coastal sites in the extreme west of Britain and Ireland.

Rock Pipit

16 cm (6.5 in)

SPECIES INFORMATION

SCIENTIFIC NAME	Anthus petrosus
RELATED SPECIES	Meadow Pipit, Tree Pipit
CALL	Call 'weest'. Song given in flapping song-flight resembles that of meadow pipit, but with stronger trill at the end
HABITAT	Stoney and rocky shorelines
STATUS	Resident and partial migrant. Winters regularly around North Sea and Baltic. Breeds at coasts of north and west Europe. In BI about 45,000 pairs

LARGE AND DARK, with long bill and dark legs. Outer tail feathers are grey.

ROCK PIPITS ARE easy to miss, with their inconspicuous greys, olives and buffs blending with the seaweed as they search for food, among the boulders. Habitat alone is a good indicator when you do see them, but when joined by meadow pipits the more streaked back of the latter should be clear. The rock pipit has grey, not white, outer tail feathers and a call that is distinctive once you know it.

Rock pipits are very strongly linked to rocky shores and nest in rather inaccessible sites, on cliffs and among boulders. Their food includes a large proportion of marine animals, such as sandhoppers, small worms and marine molluscs.

'A sudden flip of olive green wings as we pass some stone or bunch of heather, and there for the trouble of kneeling and delicately parting the herbage with our hands we see a perfect, round nest of smoothed fibres and four mottled eggs. Happy and welcome little pipit! In our island winters you have become tame and graced our doorstep and only we can tell how grateful we are, for the island dweller in windswept places can have no fun from watching tits and robins and exciting newcomers at a bird table in the garden.'

Fraser Darling

SIZE

IDENTIFICATION

HABITAT

POPULATION

MAP

The rock pipit lives up to its name — making its nest in rocky sites along the coast. It is larger and darker than its close relative, the meadow pipit.

303

Rare or Local Breeding Birds

I N HIS INTRODUCTION to *Rare Birds in Britain and Ireland*, Sharrock maintains that: 'Most birdwatchers are fascinated by rarities. To some the occasional rarity is an unexpected but welcome excitement in the course of a normal year's birding, but to others the finding of rare birds becomes the *raison d'être* of their hobby.'

colloquially as "twitchers". Willing to travel hundreds of miles a years in the pursuit, twitchers undoubtedly include among their number some of our most skilled and energetic field ornithologists.'

'Are bird pager systems spelling the demise of traditional twitching? Too many younger rare bird enthusiasts are simply sitting at home waiting for the telephone to ring.'

RARITIES AND VAGRANTS

IN 1974, SHARROCK had written a book on scarce migrants, defined as those which occur annually or nearly so, in numbers ranging from a handful to a hundred or more. Two spectacular and one rather dull bird started this survey, with the striking hoopoe and equally striking but more elusive golden oriole being linked with the tawny pipit which, as he said, is distinctive as pipits go. Altogether he analysed some 7,000 records of 25 species, together with a collective look at the records of American waders and landbirds that appeared in Britain and Ireland. For most of us these are rare birds, but they do occur regularly, and many twitchers will have seen them.

Sometimes rarities and vagrants are just described and listed, but Cottridge and Vinicombe have attempted to make sense of the

ONCE KNOWN AS tally-hunters, tick-hunters or tickers, these rarity-seekers are now known

Top
The exotic ring-necked parakeet is now firmly established, notably in the southern suburbs of London.

Bottom
The ortolan bunting breeds over much of mainland Europe, but is only a rare vagrant to Britain.

competition following population falls of trans-Saharan migrants. They also ask the very pertinent question: 'If 615 yellow-browed warblers are recorded in Britain and Ireland in one autumn how many actually reach western Europe? As an extension of that, how many more left their breeding grounds heading in the wrong direction, and why? Similarly, if 25 red-eyed vireos from America reach this side of the Atlantic, how many set out?'

VAGRANTS FROM EUROPE

THEY THEN CONSIDERED short-range vagrancy from Europe, citing pre-migratory dispersal as a cause of autumn records of woodchat shrike, ortolan bunting and melodious warbler and, while not liking drift as a universal answer to the arrival of vagrants, used it to explain the spring arrival of bluethroats and icterine warblers. Some 15,000 redstarts, 8,000 wheatears, 4,000 pied flycatchers, 40 wrynecks, together with great reed warbler, icterine warbler, barred warbler, tawny pipit and ortolan bunting, were drifted onto a 3 km (1.8 mile) stretch of Suffolk coastline at Walberswick on 3 September 1965, so how many other vagrants could arrive?

Without adverse winds, birds can still make errors of judgement, with hoopoes not having to overshoot far to arrive from France, and bee-eaters, woodchat shrikes and southern herons sometimes arriving in the west country, having overshot from Iberia.

Bottom
The golden pheasant is a gaudy bird which breeds in small numbers at a few sites.

movements of vagrant birds. The increased records of Cetti's warbler as it spreads from the south, were a prelude to its colonisation, so will great white egrets and black kites be future colonists? They list ten eastern migrants that are occurring more frequently, and these may include species which will breed regularly in Britain in the future: citrine wagtail, thrush nightingale, river warbler, paddy-field warbler, Blythe's reed warbler, greenish warbler, penduline tit, rosefinch, and rustic and little buntings.

Perhaps their spread is linked with climate change, or perhaps, the authors suggest, with reduced

EFFECTS OF THE CLIMATE ON RARE BIRDS

CLIMATIC CHANGE WILL influence patterns of vagrancy, and perhaps has already done so through changes in wind patterns. It is possible that the surge in American landbirds recorded between 1950 and 1970 was not due to increased observers but to changes in the Atlantic weather systems.

Increased wind speeds at the spring and autumn equinoxes could affect spring over-shooting and autumn vagrancy from the east. It is also evident that some winter visitors like pink-footed geese, Greenland white-fronts, barnacle geese and Bewick's swan may winter nearer their breeding sites if conditions change.

LOCATION OF SCARCE SPECIES

SHARROCK PRODUCED A SERIES of maps showing where the scarce species turned up. Autumn icterine warbler, autumn greenish warbler and autumn pectoral sandpiper had a high incidence in Ireland, while spring icterine warbler, ortolan bunting and bluethroat were particularly Scottish. In autumn, barred, arctic and yellow-browed warblers and scarlet rosefinch were also more frequent in Scotland. Red-breasted flycatchers occurred on the east coast, hoopoes on the south coast, and autumn Richard's' pipits had two favourite areas, in Scotland and the south-west.

Bluethroat and red-breasted flycatcher are among the commonest and most attractive of the

AMERICAN VISITORS

RARE AMERICAN MIGRANTS are perhaps of particular interest because of the distance flown and the possibility of the birds having had assisted passages. Of the waders, most have been making landfalls in Ireland and south-west England. Tacumshin Lake, a brackish lagoon on the Wexford coast, has recorded almost all these American waders, with frequent buff-breasted sandpipers, and periodic lesser yellowlegs. American landbird records are concentrated on Scilly, Lundy, Skokholm, Bardsey and Cape Clear, in the first three weeks of October. There is good evidence that the majority of these, other than the seed-eating 'sparrows' and buntings, reach Britain and Ireland naturally.

Whether from the Atlantic or from the north, weather or food shortage can bring invasions, as with the 1995 irruption of arctic redpolls which led to 236 records, or the 315 nutcrackers in 1968.

Top
The little egret is a rare but increasingly regular visitor, now breeding in small numbers.

Middle
Little egrets are easily identified, even at some distance.

Bottom
Another rare breeding bird, the goshawk has taken advantage of coniferous plantations.

scarce migrants, with common rosefinch, barred and icterine warbler, wryneck and red-backed shrike also frequent. Both of these last two were still breeding in Britain when the original *Breeding Atlas* was produced, having been much more widespread before. Now, instead of breeding on south-eastern heaths, red-backed shrikes turn up in Shetland and Orkney, mainly in spring, while wrynecks, which have bred in every English and Welsh county, tend to appear on south and east coasts around September.

A long list of genuinely rare birds, in more or less increasing order of rarity might read: red-footed falcon, white-rumped sandpiper, subalpine warbler, alpine swift, night heron, rose-coloured starling and American wigeon. These are birds from a good spread of taxonomic groups, adapted to a range of habitats: will any of them come to stay?

Many species are seen only rarely, either because they breed here only in very small numbers, or because they appear infrequently on migration, or as rare vagrants. This section is divided into two parts – the first deals with rare breeders, and the second with rare birds which are mainly seen on migration or when blown off course by unusual weather systems.

Top far left and bottom
The snow bunting breeds in small numbers in the Scottish highlands, but winter flocks may be seen at the coasts further south.

Top left
The drake wood duck is a handsome bird. This species was introduced from North America, and now breeds wild in a few places.

Slavonian Grebe

35 cm (14 in)

SPECIES INFORMATION

SCIENTIFIC NAME	Podiceps auritus
RELATED SPECIES	Black-necked Grebe, Red-necked Grebe, Great Crested Grebe
CALL	Trills and squeals on breeding ground (recalls water rail)
HABITAT	Breeds on shallow lakes
STATUS	Regular but rare winter visitor to BI, mainly to coasts and estuaries. Northern Europe (Iceland, Norway, Sweden, Finland); small population in Scotland (about 75 pairs)

SIZE

IDENTIFICATION

HABITAT

POPULATION

MAP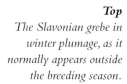

S MALL, SLIMMER AND somewhat longer-necked than little grebe. In summer it has black head, with golden 'horns', neck and rusty red underparts. In winter, grey with white neck and lower face, and black cap.

SLAVONIAN GREBES ARE as vulnerable to disturbance as the divers, and, as rare, beautiful birds, it can often be the birdwatchers who do the disturbing. As the *New Atlas* points out, there are hides on RSPB reserves where the birds can be safely watched without causing difficulties. From the hide you might see the chestnut red breast, neck and flanks, but most eye-catching is the contrast between the dark cheeks and golden crest tufts. Overall, this is a small, dumpy, rather stubby-billed grebe, with trilling calls and elaborate display. If you were lucky you could watch these and see the stripy-headed, downy young. Unfortunately, breeding success is not high, partly because of disturbance, but

also due to predation and changing water levels which can flood or leave nests stranded.

Slavonian grebes are far less distinctive in their winter plumage, and, as they may then occur with other similar grebes, identification features which differentiate them are summarised within the coastal birds section. Arthropods form a significant part of their diet when breeding, but fish are important at all times of year. When birds breed on more productive lakes they may reach breeding condition earlier, allowing the possibility of second broods. As a northern bird, breeding is determined by the period when lakes are frost-free, so second broods further north are rare. The nest is typical of grebes in being a heap of water weed and, in Scotland, is usually situated among sedges in a shallow bog.

In Western Europe, Finland has the highest population, but its extensive range in Russia, across Siberia, makes for many more birds. From their northern breeding quarters they move to mainly coastal wintering areas, with a few on the Atlantic coast south of Brittany, but other populations in the Adriatic and northern Black Sea. They usually stay within sheltered coastal waters, and in Britain few of these would have more than ten birds. However, internationally important sites in the Moray Firth and Forth estuary peak at more than 50, while Lough Foyle is an important site in Northern Ireland.

Top
The Slavonian grebe in winter plumage, as it normally appears outside the breeding season.

Bottom left and right
In breeding plumage it is very striking, with a golden tufted crest from its eye to the back of its head.

SPECIES INFORMATION	
SCIENTIFIC NAME	Podiceps nigricollis
RELATED SPECIES	Slavonian Grebe, Red-necked Grebe, Great Crested Grebe
CALL	Squeaky whistles
HABITAT	Shallow lakes with vegetation and little open water
STATUS	In BI breeds locally, in small numbers (about 30 pairs)

Black-necked Grebe

30 cm (12 in)

S LIGHTLY SMALLER THAN Slavonian, with upturned bill. In winter, neck and face are dusky grey. In summer, mainly black, with rusty flanks, and golden fan of feathers behind eyes. Look for the steep forehead, smudgy markings, and upturned bill. The red eye is sometimes visible. Summer birds look very different, with a genuine black neck and a less impressive spray of golden plumes than the Slavonian grebe.

SIZE

IDENTIFICATION

HABITAT

POPULATION

MAP

BLACK-NECKED GREBES are mainly passage migrants, but south-coast wintering, in a few sheltered waters, is regular, with Langstone Harbour and Studland Bay, for example, having good numbers. Also seen at reservoirs, such as Staines.

Like the little grebe, it is elusive even when present, and breeding haunts seem to change: a large Irish colony did not re-establish elsewhere after drainage, new birds have appeared in the English Midlands, and even in Scotland it is rarely certain where it will breed.

Disturbance and pike have been blamed for breeding failure, and drainage and natural succession for a moving population. It breeds in a wide swathe across Russia, and has some huge colonies in N America. In winter many birds move south to western coasts or the Mediterranean; with larger numbers further east.

The black-necked grebe has less yellow on its head than the Slavonian. The bill is slimmer and slightly upturned at the tip, and the forehead steeper.

Little Egret

48–53 cm (19–21 in)

SIZE

IDENTIFICATION

HABITAT

POPULATION

MAP

SPECIES INFORMATION	
SCIENTIFIC NAME	Egretta garzetta
RELATED SPECIES	Other herons and egrets
CALL	Raucous gurgling and snoring noises at nest
HABITAT	Breeds in colonies in large wetlands with bushes and trees
STATUS	Increasingly common visitor. A few now breed in BI

WHITE WITH BLACK bill, black legs and yellow feet. Long plumes on head and shoulders in breeding season, raised during displays. In flight has relatively rapid wing-beat, and rounded wings. Yellow feet most visible in flight. Sometimes runs rapidly in shallow water, stabbing to left and right for small fish, frogs and aquatic insects.

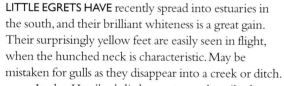

LITTLE EGRETS HAVE recently spread into estuaries in the south, and their brilliant whiteness is a great gain. Their surprisingly yellow feet are easily seen in flight, when the hunched neck is characteristic. May be mistaken for gulls as they disappear into a creek or ditch.

In the *Handbook*, little egrets are described as very rare vagrants, and when Sharrock described scarce birds in 1974 there had only been 12 records. They first bred in Dorset in 1996 and in Ireland in 1997. Twelve young were raised on Brownsea Island in 1997, and what 60 years before had been a vagrant was established as a breeding bird. In 1998 it bred in Somerset and Devon.

The little egret is a typical heron, but stands out well in its pure white plumage. The legs are dark, but the feet a bright yellow, though sometimes obscured by mud.

310

Egyptian Goose

68 cm (27 in)

PINKISH-BROWN BIRD with large, dark eye patches and huge white wing-flashes. The population is very much based in East Anglia, but it has bred at scattered English sites elsewhere, and on Anglesey. They need a gravel pit or similar refuge, short grass for the goslings, and a hole or old nest of buzzard or crow in which to breed.

SIZE

IDENTIFICATION

HABITAT

POPULATION

MAP

The large, dark eye patches and brown breast markings clearly distinguish the Egyptian goose.

Mandarin Duck

45 cm (18 in)

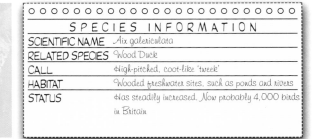

○ ○
SPECIES INFORMATION
SCIENTIFIC NAME	Aix galericulata
RELATED SPECIES	Wood Duck
CALL	High-pitched, coot-like 'tweek'
HABITAT	Wooded freshwater sites, such as ponds and rivers
STATUS	Has steadily increased. Now probably 4,000 birds in Britain

SIZE

IDENTIFICATION

HABITAT

POPULATION

MAP

MALE MANDARINS LOOK exotic, with their orange-yellow necks and wing sails, maroon breast with white stripes behind, multicoloured crown and red bill. By duck standards the female is also distinctive. Grey-brown above, distinct white spots below, and a white spectacle and eye-stripe.

ONLY THE WOOD duck is similar. Being small and compact, mandarins rise easily from land or water, fly with agility and perch readily. The spectacular sails are, of course, linked with breeding behaviour, and they and the crest are raised on many social occasions.

It is many years since I saw the only 'wild' mandarin ducks I have met, by Virginia Water in Surrey. This, and the neighbouring Windsor Great Park, has their preferred habitat, with old deciduous trees with holes, together with a mix of ponds and streams. As well as nesting holes, the trees produce the acorns, nuts and mast which are winter food for a species which lives very differently from any of our native ducks. Living among trees they need high manoeuvrability, which is partly provided by their relatively long tails.

Originally from Japan, China and Eastern Russia, the British feral population stems from birds that were released in various home counties in the 1920s and 1930s. By 1971 they were admitted to the British and Irish official list, and by the time of the first *Atlas* they were breeding, or suspected of breeding, far from their original centre. The Isle of Wight, Cheshire and Norfolk had birds, but these had not spread from the Surrey source, but from other wildfowl collections. The mandarin's stronghold is in Berkshire, Surrey and Buckinghamshire.

Top

The duck mandarin has much more sombre plumage than her mate.

Middle and bottom

Almost cartoon-like in its elaborate breeding plumage, the drake mandarin is a splendid sight.

```
 o o o o o o o o o o o o o o o o o o o o o o
    S P E C I E S   I N F O R M A T I O N
SCIENTIFIC NAME   Aix sponsa
RELATED SPECIES   Mandarin
CALL              Female has squealing flight-call
HABITAT           Water with trees nearby
STATUS            Introduced, and breeding wild, mainly in SE
                  England, but in much smaller numbers than Mandarin
```

Wood Duck

45 cm (18 in)

WOOD DUCK MALES have extra-ordinarily marked green heads, clear white throats, richer red, wine-coloured breasts, and dark patches under the tail. The female has some green on the crown, a broader but shorter spectacle and a white line around the base of the bill.

ALTHOUGH VERY SIMILAR to the mandarin in being a woodland, perching duck, the wood duck stems from America and has not been nearly as successful as the mandarin. A peculiar aspect of the relationship between the two, whose English ranges concentrate on Berkshire and Surrey, is that mandarins sometimes dump their eggs in wood duck clutches and leave the parent wood ducks with extra ducklings. The wood duck is not included on the British and Irish list, as most records are explicable in terms of movements of birds from free-flying collections, with breeding only occurring close to 'home'.

SIZE

IDENTIFICATION

HABITAT

POPULATION

MAP

Top
The female wood duck lacks the white spots along the flanks of the similar female mandarin.

Ruddy Duck

40 cm (16 in)

○○○○○○○○○○○○○○○○○○○○○○○○○○○

SPECIES INFORMATION

SCIENTIFIC NAME	*Oxyura jamaicensis*
RELATED SPECIES	*White-headed Duck (mainly south Spain)*
CALL	*Male makes low chuckling.*
HABITAT	*Reservoirs, lakes*
STATUS	*Introduced from North America. Probably at least 600 pairs, mainly in West Midlands*

SIZE

IDENTIFICATION

HABITAT

POPULATION

MAP

THE RUDDY DUCK has been in the news recently. From its very successful expansion in Britain, it has now spread to the continent, including Spain, putting the scarce, closely-related native white-headed duck at risk through competition and hybridisation. Control measures are being introduced in Britain in 1999.

THE OUTLINE OF the ruddy duck is highly distinctive, with its partly cocked tail used in display and broad, concave bill. Males have a chestnut body, and clear white cheeks, surrounded by black head and neck. Female is duller than the male with patterned face.

Top
The drake ruddy duck, showing its blue bill and obvious white lower face.

Middle
The short, stiff tail is so characteristic of this species.

Bottom
The female ruddy duck exercises its wraps.

Red-crested Pochard

55 cm (22 in)

SPECIES INFORMATION

SCIENTIFIC NAME	*Netta rufina*
RELATED SPECIES	Pochard.
CALL	Breeding male has loud 'bait' or slow, nasal 'geng'; female a harsh 'kurr'
HABITAT	Breeds at reedy lakes, mainly in drier regions
STATUS	Summer visitor, but resident south Spain and south France. Breeds in only a few places in Europe, mainly in southern Spain and Camargue (France), but also in Netherlands, Denmark, and south Central Europe (Lake Constance and southern Bavaria). Sometimes escapes from collections.

LARGE, THICK-HEADED diving duck, sitting rather high in the water. Breeding male has chestnut head (crown paler) and bright red bill. Female is uniform grey-brown with pale grey cheeks, (see also female common scoter).

THE HEADQUARTERS FOR this duck seems to be the Cotswold Water Park, and birds now breed in small numbers elsewhere in Britain. The females resemble common scoter. There is also a free-flying population in St James' Park, London.

The main world population is in Central Asia, west to the Caspian and Black Seas.

SIZE

IDENTIFICATION

HABITAT

POPULATION

MAP

Top
The female, though less colourful, is also distinctive, with pale cheeks and brown top to the head.

Bottom
The drake red-crested pochard has a prominent orange crown of erectile feathers.

315

White-tailed Eagle

80–95 cm (31–37 in)

SIZE

IDENTIFICATION

HABITAT

POPULATION

MAP

SPECIES INFORMATION	
SCIENTIFIC NAME	Haliaeetus albicilla
RELATED SPECIES	Golden Eagle
CALL	Very vocal, with a loud raucous 'kyowkyowkyow', especially near nest
HABITAT	Rocky coasts. Also near large forested lakes and rivers, even a few kilometres from water
STATUS	Resident and partial migrant. Regular on certain large lakes (e.g. in foothills of the Alps) outside breeding season. Norway, northern Germany and Poland. Re-introduction in west of Scotland is slowly proving a success, with about a dozen pairs now breeding

HUGE, WITH VERY broad, parallel-sided wings, head well extended, tail short and wedge-shaped. Powerful yellow bill and short white tail. Juveniles (up to 4 years) dark, even on head, tail and bill.

THE WING SHAPE of the white-tailed eagle, sea eagle or erne, is very different from the golden eagle, being broad, rectangular and deeply fingered. The bill is huge, the tail short, wedge-shaped and white in adult. Young birds are darker, with dark tails.

A reintroduction project started in 1975 and, for 11 years, eight-week old birds from Norway were taken to Rum for rearing and release. This involved fine levels of co-operation between many organisations, including the Royal Air Force who brought the young birds over. The species prospers in the Bodo district of Norway and taking birds from eyries with two eaglets, poses no threat to the Norwegian population.

The eagles needed to survive for five or six years to breed. By the early 1980s there were attempts, and in 1985 the first Scottish-bred sea eagle for 75 years flew in the Hebrides. There is now a young population there – in 1995 there were nine clutches and seven young, and in 1998, 15 clutches, with 13 chicks being fledged by 9 pairs.

'He clasps the crag with crooked hands;
Close to the sun in lonely lands.
Ring'd with azure world he stands
The wrinkled sea beneath him crawls:
He watches from his mountain wall,
And like a thunderbolt he falls'
Alfred Lord Tennyson THE EAGLE

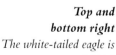

Top and bottom right
The white-tailed eagle is a very powerful bird which feeds mainly on fish and carrion.

Bottom left
Almost vulture-like in flight, its wingspan can be as much as 2.5m (8 feet).

SPECIES INFORMATION

SCIENTIFIC NAME	*Pernis apivorus*
RELATED SPECIES	
CALL	On breeding ground a high-pitched, melodious 'kee-er'
	Mixed woodland with clearings, pasture and fields.
HABITAT	Usually nests at woodland edge, hunting in open areas
STATUS	Summer visitor. Most of Europe, except far north and west. Rare bird (at edge of range) in Britain (about 20 pairs)

Honey Buzzard

55 cm (21 in)

BUZZARD-SIZED, BUT slimmer and longer-winged and with longer tail. Plumage variable – upperside usually dark brown, underside pale, almost white, or uniform brown. Head grey, eye yellow. In flight shows outstretched head, relatively narrow wings and long, narrow tail with one or two clear dark bands and black tip.

FOREST DESTRUCTION OCCURRED early in Britain and Ireland, and there is a long history of disturbance through hunting interests, and the demands for timber and more agricultural land. Honey buzzards may have been among the birds of prey to suffer from change and disturbance but they are on the fringes of their range here so climate too is important.

Fuller quotes its preference for forests larger than 250 ha (620 acres), for mixed forests in the Netherlands, although often nesting in fir or spruce, and a general preference for broadleaved woodland.

The scattered population of British summer visitors is spread over the south and east of England, with none in Ireland. It is unique in its diet, with its summer dependence on larvae and adults of bees and wasps; the larvae are crucial to the survival of the young.

SIZE

IDENTIFICATION

HABITAT

POPULATION

MAP

In flight, the honey buzzard shows its long, banded tail, splendid patterned wing span and rather narrow, almost pigeon-like head.

Goshawk

48–60 cm (19–24 in)

○○○○○○○○○○○○○○○○○○○○○○○○○

SPECIES INFORMATION

SCIENTIFIC NAME	*Accipiter gentilis*
RELATED SPECIES	Sparrowhawk
CALL	In breeding season 'gik-gik-gik'; buzzard-like 'hiair', accented on the first syllable
HABITAT	Wooded country, particularly coniferous forest
STATUS	Resident. Widespread (but secretive) in most of Europe. In Britain rare (about 200 pairs)

SIZE

IDENTIFICATION

HABITAT

POPULATION

MAP

LARGE SIZE (Especially the female which is buzzard-sized); long tail and relatively short and rounded wings. Male smaller and lighter than female. Upperparts of male grey-brown to slate-grey, female brown. Underside pale, with horizontal speckles, in juveniles yellowish, with dark brown spots. Look out for marked S-curve on trailing edge of wing, due to bulging secondaries, and remember that a male goshawk may be smaller than a female sparrowhawk.

GOSHAWKS ARE LARGER than sparrowhawks, and have more patterned faces and slate coloured backs. The rounder tail and longer wings, help separation from our other *Accipter*. Goshawks are on the increase, particularly in conifer woodland, but its exact status is difficult to verify because of its secrecy and doubts about the true status of some birds, which have escaped from hawking stock. It is unlikely that there are many more than 200 pairs, compared with over 40,000 pairs of sparrowhawks.

Sometimes British pairs breed as close together as 1.5 km (0.9 miles), so there is a potential for a very large population. It would be good to see more of these fine birds displaying over their nesting territories.

Top right and left
The goshawk is a powerful woodland predator, whose favourite prey is woodpigeon.

Bottom
A large eye and heavy bill are vital for an efficient bird-hunter.

```
○ ○ ○ ○ ○ ○ ○ ○ ○ ○ ○ ○ ○ ○ ○ ○ ○ ○ ○ ○ ○ ○ ○ ○ ○ ○
```
SPECIES INFORMATION

SCIENTIFIC NAME	*Circus pygargus*
RELATED SPECIES	Hen Harrier, Marsh Harrier
CALL	Shrill 'kek-kek-kek'
HABITAT	Breeds in low vegetation near water, but also in damp heath, especially on fens, and increasingly in open fields. Hunts mainly over wetlands with low cover, and in cultivated fields
STATUS	Summer visitor. Much of central and southern Europe. Rare breeder in BI (about ten pairs)

Montagu's Harrier
43–47 cm (17–18 in)

VERY SLIM AND GRACEFUL in flight (recalls seagull, or even tern). Male similar to hen harrier, but with narrower wings and longer tail, black band on wings, and brown stripes on belly. Female almost identical to female hen harrier, but wings narrower and white rump less marked. Juveniles like female, but with red-brown undersides.

ITS BEAUTY, AS with all harriers, is partly in its movement, on narrow, pointed wings. Kearton referred to it as the ash-coloured harrier, with the implication of a touch of dirty mottle to the male's grey upperparts. The dark wing-tips are shared with the hen harrier, but a black bar across the upperwing is diagnostic. The rump varies from pale grey to whitish. There are also black bars on the underwing, and brown streaks on the underside and underwing. Females can be distinguished from female hen harriers by their smaller size, narrower wings and narrower white rump; again there is a black bar on the wings, but as they are darker it is not so evident.

Montagu's harriers are summer visitors to Europe, wintering in sub-Saharan Africa, while an Indian wintering population summers well to the east. It is essentially a lowland species which will breed in dry as well as wet fields, including farmland, heaths, moors and peat bogs. Crops, given appropriate protection, provide the undisturbed taller cover it needs for breeding but when hunting it prefers lower vegetation.

Brown describes their hunting method: 'They fly low and slowly over the ground gliding against the wind if they can, but flying slowly and gliding if there is no wind, repeatedly checking in flight, hovering briefly above suspected prey, and dropping into the grass to catch it if it is finally located, or passing on if it is not.' He reckons that a day's winter hunting could involve 150 km (93 miles) of flying; certainly enough to take it a long way from its roost. Their manoeuvrability allows them to catch small birds, but voles and young rabbits are also important.

In an area of Dorset arable farmland, little groups of bird watchers can often be seen in summer in a lay-by on the main road. Although there is a magnificent National Nature Reserve nearby, that is not where the harriers breed. With co-operation between local farmers and RSPB this area of farmland has been one of the few strongholds for British Montagu's harriers in recent years. Rather than leaving uncut crops around the nest which might show where it was, the young are transferred to a box when harvesting, and this is tolerated by both parents and young. They are then returned to the nest after harvest.

SIZE

IDENTIFICATION

HABITAT

POPULATION

MAP

Formerly associated with heath and wet fenland, Montagu's harriers now nest mainly amongst crops, ideally with rough ground nearby for hunting. They are still very rare in Britain however.

Capercaillie

82–90 cm (32–35 in) male
58–64 cm (23–25 in) female

○○○○○○○○○○○○○○○○○○○○○○○○○○

S P E C I E S   I N F O R M A T I O N

SCIENTIFIC NAME	*Tetrao urogallus*
RELATED SPECIES	Black Grouse
CALL	Courting male has strange explosive, grinding and gurgling calls
HABITAT	Coniferous and mixed forests, with small clearings.
STATUS	Resident. Scandinavia, Scotland (about 1,500 birds), central and south-east Europe. Declined due to destruction of natural Scots pine forests, and through disturbance.

SIZE

IDENTIFICATION

HABITAT

POPULATION

MAP

LARGEST GROUSE. MALE is turkey-sized, black, with long spreadable tail. Female smaller, with orange-brown breast-band and rusty-red, black-banded tail. Take-off noisy, flight rapid with powerful wing-beats and long glides.

GIRALDUS CALLED THEM 'peacocks of the woods' and described them as 'abundant', but few of us get a chance to see the huge capercaillie in the mature pine forests of Scotland. Not only is it very big but its tail and wings are broad and the beak heavy. The male is dark with rich brown back and wings, velvet green shield on chest and white patches on the shoulder and on the flanks. The much smaller female could be confused with black grouse but is twice the weight and is paler. In flight, initial crashing among the branches gives way to agile but powerful flight between trees or away across a valley.

The song of the male is more complex than that of the black grouse. A tapping phase precedes a drum-roll of shortened clicks, often followed by a cork popping note. The end of the song is a rapid rhythmic gurgling or strangled squealing. The male also has a belch call, while females 'bray' at display area and 'cackle' when watching or anticipating display.

The capercaillie, except in its youth, is almost entirely vegetarian. From October until April it feeds on the buds and shoots of conifers, but during the summer months its diet is extensive and includes flowers, leaves, shoots of bracken, seed pods and berries.

Recent years have seen a marked contraction in range and numbers. The *New Atlas* suggests a reduction in blueberries, wetter June weather, more foxes and crows, collisions with deer fences, overshooting and habitat change as possible causes, pointing out also that over much of its wide range it is decreasing, as mature Scots pine and oak forests are felled.

Capercaillie males provide a wonderful spectacle in the mating season. Recent years have seen a decline in their numbers.

SPECIES INFORMATION

SCIENTIFIC NAME	Chrysolophus pictus
RELATED SPECIES	Lady Amherst's Pheasant
CALL	Noisy 'kercheck'
HABITAT	Young coniferous woodland
STATUS	Native of China. Introduced and now established, mainly in Breckland, South Downs, Anglesey and Galloway. About 1,500 birds

Golden Pheasant

60–115 cm (23–45 in), of which tail 30–75 cm

GOLDEN PHEASANTS RUN rather than fly and, being rather secretive birds, are hard to spot, despite their bright plumage. In February the males form small flocks on suitable territories and display to each other to claim ownership. By March these territories are established and the males dispersed throughout the suitable habitat, calling at dawn and dusk.

SPECIES INFORMATION

SCIENTIFIC NAME	Chrysolophus amherstiae
RELATED SPECIES	Golden Pheasant
CALL	Similar to Golden Pheasant
HABITAT	Young conifer plantations and rhododendron scrub
STATUS	Native of China. Introduced and now established, mainly near Woburn Abbey. About 200 birds

Lady Amherst's Pheasant

60–120 cm (23–47 in), of which tail 30–95 cm

LADY AMHERST'S PHEASANT is another Chinese bird and is arguably even more beautiful than the golden. It has an even longer, highly barred tail, scale-like pied feathers on neck, and a red and yellow rump (male).

Quail

18 cm (7 in)

SPECIES INFORMATION	
SCIENTIFIC NAME	Coturnix coturnix
RELATED SPECIES	Partridges and pheasants
CALL	Male territorial call is a repeated 'wick-wick-ic' (accented on first syllable), heard by day or night
HABITAT	Mixed fields with rough margins, hedges. Breeds in winter wheat, clover and lucerne crops, and in hay-meadows
STATUS	Summer visitor. Resident in Mediterranean. Mainly south and central Europe, north to BI. Widespread in lowlands, but generally decreasing. Normally rather rare in BI (about 300 pairs), but population fluctuates

SMALLEST EUROPEAN MEMBER of the partridge family. Dumpy, almost tail-less, with camouflaged plumage. Male has black markings on head and chin; female has heavily speckled chest. Secretive and more often heard than seen.

QUAILS ARE LONG-distance migrants, and their wings, relatively longer than those of gamebird relatives indicate this fact. They are, in effect, miniature partridges, and are easily confused, should you see them, with young partridges. More often the distinctive call is the only indication of their presence.

The 1988–91 *Atlas* included a 'quail year' in 1989, when instead of a few birds calling in Dorset and Wiltshire there was evidence of breeding in 233 10-km (6-mile) squares, and quail were present in another 571 squares. Male quail arrive first, set up territory, often among winter wheat, and call distinctively, with a sound that is often represented as 'wet-my-lips'.

Top
Arable landscape is the preferred habitat of quail, but they are almost impossible to spot.

Bottom left and right
The tiny quail likes to skulk close to the ground, under cover and seldom flies, except on migration.

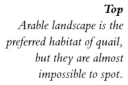

Corncrake

26 cm (11 in)

SPECIES INFORMATION	
SCIENTIFIC NAME	Crex crex
RELATED SPECIES	Other crakes, Water Rail
CALL	Male has rasping 'rerrp-rerrp', often continuing for hours, by night as well as in the daytime
HABITAT	Damp grassland, traditionally-cropped hay meadows; also in crops such as cereals, lucerne and clover
STATUS	Summer visitor. Mainly C and E Europe. In BI highly endangered and declining (about 450 pairs); mainly in Ireland and Hebrides. Populations in decline following habitat destruction, and mechanised hay-gathering

SIZE

IDENTIFICATION

HABITAT

POPULATION

MAP

SLIM, LONG-LEGGED. Upperparts light grey-brown, with dark brown streaks on back. Flight ungainly and fluttering with trailing legs and showing chestnut wings. Rarely seen, as usually remains hidden in vegetation.

'In the valley a corncrake calls
Monotonously
With a plaintive unalterable voice, that deadens
My confident activity.'
D. H. Lawrence
END OF ANOTHER HOME HOLIDAY

RICHARD JEFFERIES writing in 1879 told how 'the grass in the meadow or home field as it begins to grow tall is soon visited by the corncrakes, who take up their residence there. In this district they generally arrive about the time when it has grown sufficiently high and thick to hide their motions. This desire for concealment is apparently more marked in them than in any other bird; yet they utter their loud call of "crake, crake, crake!" not unlike the turning of a wooden rattle, continuously.'

It is not hiding now that makes corncrakes hard to see, for it is almost gone from Ireland, and only the activities of the RSPB and crofters allow it to maintain a precarious hold in Hebridean machair.

The persistent, rasping song of the corncrake has almost disappeared from our countryside now that this fascinating bird has become such a rarity.

Spotted Crake

23 cm (9 in)

SMALL MARSH BIRD, scarcely as big as blackbird, with dark, speckled plumage. Flanks barred white; undertail coverts yellowish. Bill much shorter than water rail's. Juveniles have whiter chin and paler undersides. Very rarely seen; lives in thick vegetation.

SPECIES INFORMATION	
SCIENTIFIC NAME	*Porzana porzana*
RELATED SPECIES	Other crakes, Water Rail
CALL	Male's spring song is characteristic – a short, repeated, 'huitt', like a whiplash, usually at dusk and at night. Other sounds include 'keck' or growling 'brurr'
HABITAT	Fenland, edges of rivers and lakes, particularly where reeds give way to sedges; also in wet meadows and ditch margins
STATUS	Resident in south of range, summer visitor further north (including BI). Most of Europe, except far north and south. Rare and decreasing, absent over large areas. In BI a rare breeder (about 20 pairs)

'Impossible little brutes to see'
John Buxton about the Norfolk Broads (1950)

IF THE BIRD IS seen, running away perhaps, the undertail coverts will not be as white as those of water rail, and the white freckles over the body plumage might be seen. With a better view, short yellowish bill with orange patch at base and yellow legs are very different.

Spotted crakes are summer visitors and probably were common when Britain and Ireland were wetter. By the time of the *New Atlas* there was breeding evidence from 11 squares, mainly in Cambridgeshire and eastern Scotland, and in 1989 there had been 21 singing males at ten sites.

Modern technology has come into crake-watching, and among the incredible crake numbers on the Ouse and Nene Washes in 1998, 15 were heard on one night, and two were caught and radio-tagged so that their use of the habitat could be investigated. They were followed for six weeks.

Spotted crakes rarely show themselves in the open, preferring to stay hidden in swamp vegetation. They dip around the river banks and are rarely seen.

Stone Curlew

43 cm (17 in)

LARGE WADER WITH short bill, large yellow eyes and long, relatively thick, yellow legs. In flight shows double white wing bars and black and white primaries.

THEY ARE LARGE-HEADED, long-tailed, thick-kneed birds with a striking wing pattern. In flight the black flight feathers contrast with the white patches on the primaries. Lovely though they are to see, their magic stems from the wailing calls which are striking by day, but positively haunting as dusk falls and the birds call in chorus.

More often heard than seen; secretive in behaviour and highly camouflaged in plumage. As T. A. Coward wrote in 1950, they are hard to see as 'from egg onward the life of the stone curlew is spent in hiding itself from view'.

There are two main population centres – the Breckland of Suffolk and Norfolk, and an area centred on Salisbury Plain. Stone curlew like free-draining, sandy soils with a high proportion of chalk rubble or flints, giving a background upon which the bird and

its eggs are well camouflaged. Another factor may be the tendency for free-draining soils to warm up early in the spring, and hence to have enhanced availability of the invertebrates upon which stone curlews feed. Many of the remaining patches of open ground with sparse vegetation only survive because of the activities of the military on Salisbury Plain and Breckland.

> '*He begins with the witching hour when the sun is down but the light not yet quite gone, the hour when the older shrubs and juniper bushes seem to take on uncanny shapes of things that do not appear in the hard light of day. Then from one side of the valley the quiet cour-lee steals forth, to be taken up afar by another bird out upon its evening business.*'
> G. K. Yeates
> BIRD HAUNTS IN SOUTHERN ENGLAND

SIZE

IDENTIFICATION

HABITAT

POPULATION

MAP

Top
The stone curlew at its nest in completely open country.

Middle
Although it often squats down low, the stone curlew has quite long legs.

Bottom
Stone curlew spend much of their time sitting very still, relying on camouflage for protection.

Dotterel

21 cm (8.5 in)

SIZE

IDENTIFICATION

HABITAT

POPULATION

MAP

PROMINENT WHITE STRIPE above eye, meeting behind head to form V-shape. Female slightly larger and more colourful than male. Black belly in breeding plumage. In winter much paler with yellow-grey upperparts, white belly and less clear breast band and eye-stripe. Dumpy and short-tailed in flight, with no wing bar. Often very approachable.

THE FEMALE IS the more highly coloured and larger of the pair, and she takes the initiative in the establishment of territory. White face and eye-stripe, dark cap, pinkish-grey chest with narrow black and white bands above makes for a mosaic of colour that is hard to describe. The yellow legs, white eye-stripes and chest band are present in all plumages, but non-breeding birds are far from conspicuous when they turn up on grassy hills, poor agricultural land or coastal heaths. These migrant birds winter in the Middle East and North Africa.

SPECIES INFORMATION	
SCIENTIFIC NAME	*Charadrius morinellus*
RELATED SPECIES	Ringed Plover, Little Ringed Plover, Kentish Plover
CALL	Flight-call 'kirr' or 'plitt'. Song a repeated 'pit-pit-pit', in display flight
HABITAT	Breeds on open tundra or mountain tops. Outside breeding season seen in small groups on dry, rocky areas, short pasture and on river banks
STATUS	Summer visitor. Regularly seen on passage at traditional sites. Breeds in northern Scandinavia, northern Britain (mainly Scottish Highlands). Also in a few places in the Alps, Apennines, and, more recently, on the Netherlands coast. British population about 900 pairs

Brewer's Dictionary of Phrase and Fable tells us that a dotterel is a doting old fool, an old man easily cajoled, and this plover is so called as it is easily approached. Despite this tameness, dotterel are not easy to count, partly, as Ratcliffe says, because their nesting habitat includes some of the bleakest terrain in our country – the windswept summit plateaux or broad ridges and upper spurs of the higher hills. Here the ground cover is sparse, with moss carpets, lichen heaths or open stony fell-fields. Sometimes the males, which do the incubating, sit tight until almost trodden upon. Knowledge of past population levels are sketchy and contradictory, but it seems now that almost 1,000 pairs may breed in Scotland. A further complication is that some birds attempt to breed in Norway and Scotland in the same year.

Right
Young dotterel can be hard to spot in rocky terrain.

Left
In all plumages, the broad white eyestripe is a tell-tale feature.

Red-necked Phalarope

18 cm (7 in)

SMALL, DELICATE WADER with fine, needle-like bill. Female has showy breeding plumage, with white chin and bright rust-brown band at sides of neck and breast. Male less colourful. Winter plumage is grey with dark on top of head and dark patch through eye. In flight shows prominent white wing bar. Often swims when feeding, turning abruptly on its own axis to stir up food items from sediment.

SIZE

IDENTIFICATION

HABITAT

POPULATION

MAP

Top
With phalaropes, it is the male which sits on the eggs and cares for the young.

Middle
Phalaropes swim and dabble in shallow pools.

Bottom
The female has the brightest colours in the breeding season.

Roseate Tern

36 cm (14 in)

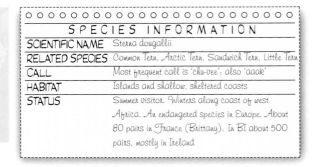

SPECIES INFORMATION	
SCIENTIFIC NAME	Sterna dougallii
RELATED SPECIES	Common Tern, Arctic Tern, Sandwich Tern, Little Tern
CALL	Most frequent call is 'chu-vee'; also 'aaak'
HABITAT	Islands and shallow, sheltered coasts
STATUS	Summer visitor. Winters along coast of west Africa. An endangered species in Europe. About 80 pairs in France (Brittany). In BI about 500 pairs, mostly in Ireland

SIZE

IDENTIFICATION

HABITAT

POPULATION

MAP

DIFFICULT TO DISTINGUISH from common and arctic terns, but paler grey above, and with faint rose tinge to belly in breeding season. Tail streamers extend well beyond wing-tips when sitting, like arctic, but legs are longer. Bill mainly black, and usually only red towards base.

However, it is rarely as rosy as some illustrations make out, and the amount of red on the mainly black bill varies: all red is lost after breeding. The call is said to be distinctive, but the impression of greater whiteness and the very long streamers are probably the best field characters.

The roseate differs from the similar common and Arctic terns in having a mainly black bill, and longer tail streamers.

Black Tern

23 cm (9 in)

SIZE

IDENTIFICATION

HABITAT

POPULATION

MAP

SMALL TERN, WITH very dark breeding plumage; head and upperparts grey-black, wings light grey, above and below. With its forked tail, looks rather like a large, dark swallow. In winter white below, with dark on top of head. Juveniles similar, but darker above, and with dark mark on body near base of wing. Hovers and skims water, taking prey from surface.

WHEN THE EAST ANGLIAN fens were more extensive, black terns bred in good numbers. They are, therefore, one of our lost breeding birds, except for an occasional success in sites such as the Ouse Washes.

Black terns are one of the marsh terns, liking fresh or brackish waters with plenty of vegetation and insects and perhaps amphibian and fish food. Most of the birds we see are on migration, with more in autumn, when they are certainly not black.

Spring passage birds are black, or rather dark grey, with whitish underwing coverts, and a rather square tail. Small and slim, they dip down to the surface of the water of lakes, reservoirs or estuaries to pick up insects or crustaceans. At any other time look for the long, slim bill, blackish shoulder smudge and grey rump and tail. Black terns may also be seen during seawatches as they head for coastal areas in tropical west Africa.

White-winged black tern, *Chlidonias leucopterus*, is similar, but with more contrast in plumage, a whiter rump (also a white leading edge to wing), and black underwing coverts. Rare vagrant to BI (mainly May–September) from breeding grounds North of the Black Sea.

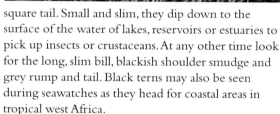

Top
The white-winged black tern breeds in eastern Europe and is a rare vagrant to Britain.

Middle and bottom
Black terns are dainty birds with a hovering flight pattern.

Ring-necked Parakeet

40 cm (16 in)

UNMISTAKABLE, WITH GREEN plumage and long tail. Flies fast and straight, usually singly or in small groups.

FIRST RECORDED IN 1969, it has spread and increased steadily. Although not featured in detail in the original *Atlas of Breeding Birds*, it had a page to itself by the time of the *Winter Atlas*. The populations are mainly in suburban areas, indicating its dependence on man for survival in this northern environment. It seems to manage well, even in hard winter weather.

It nests in holes, and therefore might compete with owls, jackdaws and woodpeckers, but there is no evidence that they are harming the prospects of any of these birds.

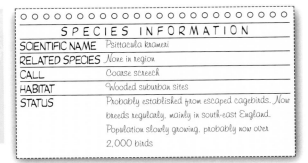

SPECIES INFORMATION	
SCIENTIFIC NAME	Psittacula krameri
RELATED SPECIES	None in region
CALL	Coarse screech
HABITAT	Wooded suburban sites
STATUS	Probably established from escaped cagebirds. Now breeds regularly, mainly in south-east England. Population slowly growing, probably now over 2,000 birds

Snowy Owl

55–65 cm (22–26 in)

VERY LARGE AND white (male) or white with black flecks (female). Flies powerfully on rather pointed wings.

There is always the chance that this magnificent predator will breed again in northern Scotland, but at present it is only a rare visitor.

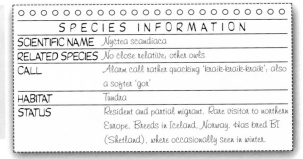

SPECIES INFORMATION	
SCIENTIFIC NAME	Nyctea scandiaca
RELATED SPECIES	No close relative; other owls
CALL	Alarm call rather quacking 'kraik-kraik-kraik'; also a softer 'gor'
HABITAT	Tundra
STATUS	Resident and partial migrant. Rare visitor to northern Europe. Breeds in Iceland, Norway. Has bred BI (Shetland), where occasionally seen in winter.

Black Redstart

14.5 cm (5.5 in)

○○○○○○○○○○○○○○○○○○○○○○○○○○○○○

S P E C I E S   I N F O R M A T I O N

SCIENTIFIC NAME	*Phoenicurus ochruros*
RELATED SPECIES	Redstart
CALL	Alarm call 'hit-tek-tek'. Song is a short, rapid phrase, starting with 'jirr-ti-ti-ti-ti', and ending with a scratchy sound, a bit like sliding gravel
HABITAT	On buildings in towns, villages and even in the centres of cities. Original habitat is mountain rocks and scree to over 3,000 m (10,000 ft) — now mainly in south of range
STATUS	Resident in south and west of range; summer visitor to north and east. Breeds in most of Europe, except for the far north and east. In BI about 100 pairs, mainly in the south (absent from Ireland)

MALE HAS DARK, sooty plumage with a pale wing-patch, and red rump and tail. Females are dusky grey-brown rather than dusky black, as are immatures, who also lack the white wing-panel of males.

OVER MUCH OF its range it favours cliffs and boulder-strewn terrain, but the presence of many potential nesting sites in walls and roofs of buildings has also led to a close association with people. Building sites often have weedy and bare areas as well as song-posts to recommend them.

Black redstarts attracted attention when they moved into London bombsites in the late 1940s, but their colonisation of Britain as breeding birds had started earlier. Taking examples from *Birds of the London Area* some salient stages in the London story appear. The book claims 'London is the metropolis

not only of man but of the black redstart in the British Isles. The story begins with three pairs taking up their abode within the Palace of Engineering in (1926) the year after the end of the Wembley Exhibition, and nesting on breeze-slab ledges about 18 feet from the ground every year... until 1941. In 1940 came the first breeding record for inner London, when a pair brought off two broods within the precincts of Westminster Abbey, and at least five other cocks were reported to be holding territories.'

The hoped for take-off in numbers, which might have led to colonisation of towns and villages as on the continent, has not occurred, but three pairs have recently (January 1998) turned up to interfere with work on the Millennium Dome.

David Glue, in his introduction to the species in the 1993 *Atlas* writes: 'The flash of bright orange-chestnut quivering tail announces the welcome spring arrival of a full-plumage male black redstart to brighten a scattering of built up environments. Others betray their presence through a scolding "tucc tucc" alarm call, still more by the short warbling song with characteristic metallic terminal flourish.'

Whereas breeding areas tend to be in the east of England, it often winters in the south-west, where it is closely associated with the sea. Cliffs have their own microclimate, as do city centres, and for a bird at the edge of its range this extra warmth may be important.

SIZE

IDENTIFICATION

HABITAT

POPULATION

MAP

Top
Black redstart are often now found in a typically urban setting.

Bottom
Sea-cliffs provide another suitable habitat for this species in some areas along the coast.

Cetti's Warbler

14 cm (5.5 in)

SPECIES INFORMATION

SCIENTIFIC NAME	Cettia cetti
RELATED SPECIES	No close relative
CALL	A very distinctive, rather explosive, loud and abrupt 'chut-chut-chutti-chutti-chutti', usually delivered from dense cover
HABITAT	Damp, overgrown habitats such as fen carr, swamps and ditches
STATUS	Resident. Breeds mainly in south and south-west Europe. Rare breeder in Britain, Netherlands, Belgium, and Switzerland. In B about 450 pairs, in south England and Wales. Absent from Ireland

CHESTNUT AND GREY warbler, with rather rounded tail. More often heard than seen. The male is some 30 per cent heavier than the female, and another strange feature is that the eggs are bright red. The rounded tail and dark chestnut upper parts can help separation from other reedbed warblers.

VERY DIFFICULT TO see among the reeds, and other dense vegetation. This interesting species has colonised the south of England and Wales, since the early 1970s, and now breeds locally in suitable sites. Suffers badly in hard winters, like Dartford warbler, which is another rare resident warbler at the edge of its range.

Savi's Warbler

14 cm (5.5 in)

SPECIES INFORMATION

SCIENTIFIC NAME	Locustella luscinioides
RELATED SPECIES	Grasshopper Warbler, River Warbler (rare vagrant)
CALL	Alarm call a short 'tsik'. Song reeling: shorter, faster and deeper than grasshopper warbler's, often beginning with accelerating ticking notes: 'tik-tik-tik-tik...'
HABITAT	Mainly reedbeds. Sometimes in rushes, and at overgrown lake margins
STATUS	Summer visitor. Mainly central, south and east Europe (notably Hungary and Romania). In Britain about 15 pairs, mainly in the south-east (absent from Ireland)

TAIL BROAD, ROUNDED and graduated. Plumage is unstreaked, rather like nightingale (but without chestnut on tail), or a dark reed warbler; inconspicuous stripe over eye.

THIS REEDBED BIRD, sounding rather more insect-like than the grasshopper warbler, disappeared from England for almost a hundred years, but finally returned in 1954. It broadly resembles the reed warbler but is in fact related to the grasshopper warbler.

The closely related river warbler, *Locustella fluviatilis* is a rare vagrant. It breeds in East Europe (mainly Poland and Hungary), West to Germany. Unstreaked above, but with spotted or streaked breast.

SPECIES INFORMATION

SCIENTIFIC NAME	Acrocephalus palustris
RELATED SPECIES	Reed Warbler, Sedge Warbler, Aquatic Warbler
CALL	Alarm-call 'tschak'. Song is loud, pleasant and very varied, mixed with squeaking and rattling notes: an unstructured medley, famously incorporating much mimicry. Often sings at night
HABITAT	Lush scrub near water, in tall-herb communities and nettle-beds
STATUS	Summer visitor. Mainly C and NE Europe. In B only about 12 pairs (but varies from year to year). Absent from Ireland

Marsh Warbler
13 cm (5 in)

 SIZE

 IDENTIFICATION

 HABITAT

 POPULATION

 MAP

VERY LIKE REED warbler, except for song. More olive-brown above and not quite so flat-headed.

MARSH WARBLERS ARE said to mimic 70 different species, from summer and winter haunts, in half an hour's singing. In addition, they blend these into their song, which is of striking beauty and vivacity.

Marsh warblers like sites with dense vegetation – such as nettles, meadow-sweet, umbellifers and willow-herbs. Plenty of such habitat is available, and the rarity of this species is something of a mystery. The main areas for breeding marsh warblers are now the Severn and Avon valleys in Worcestershire, and, more recently, Kent.

SPECIES INFORMATION

SCIENTIFIC NAME	Loxia scotica
RELATED SPECIES	Common Crossbill, Parrot Crossbill
CALL	Flight-call 'chip-chip-chip'
HABITAT	Scottish pine woods
STATUS	Resident. About 1,500 birds

Scottish Crossbill
17.5 cm (7 in)

 SIZE

 IDENTIFICATION

 HABITAT

 POPULATION

 MAP

THE SCOTTISH CROSSBILL is very similar to the common crossbill, but is slightly larger, and it has a somewhat heavier bill. It breeds only in the ancient Scots pine woods of the highlands of Scotland. It is Britain's only endemic species.

THE PARROT CROSSBILL, *Loxia pytyopsittacus*, is slightly larger, at 18 cm (7 in), with an even heavier bill. It breeds in north-east Europe, but has bred in East Anglia. It feeds mainly on pine seeds and, like a parrot, breaks a cone with its beak, then holds it with one leg to empty the contents.

Firecrest

9 cm (3.5 in)

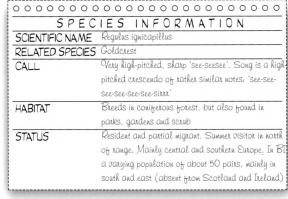

○ ○

SPECIES INFORMATION

SCIENTIFIC NAME	Regulus ignicapillus
RELATED SPECIES	Goldcrest
CALL	Very high-pitched, sharp 'see-seesee'. Song is a high pitched crescendo of rather similar notes: 'see-see-see-see-see-see-sirr'
HABITAT	Breeds in coniferous forest, but also found in parks, gardens and scrub
STATUS	Resident and partial migrant. Summer visitor in north of range. Mainly central and southern Europe. In BI a varying population of about 50 pairs, mainly in south and east (absent from Scotland and Ireland)

SIZE

IDENTIFICATION

HABITAT

POPULATION

MAP

SAME SIZE AND shape as goldcrest, but has black stripe through the eye and white stripe over the eye. Male has orange-red crown, female yellow. Juvenile lacks head markings, but has dark eye-stripe.

IN MOST RESPECTS firecrests are much like goldcrests, but a good view shows their beauty, with brighter plumage, striped head with white eye-stripe, and bronze shoulder patch. They are less committed to conifers than goldcrests, but some of the recently colonised British sites are in spruce, while others are in oak, beech and holly. To spot breeding birds the persistent, high-pitched song needs to be recognised.

Between the two *Breeding Atlases*, the firecrest had made large gains, with breeding records into Wales and as far as the Mersey, but the concentrations were in seven main areas: the New Forest, south-east Kent and the Suffolk coast. These birds would seem to be summer visitors wintering in the western Mediterranean.

The *Winter Atlas* shows a very different pattern, with a majority along the south coast and in the west country. Writing there, Marchant, who is obviously a firecrest enthusiast, says the places to look are in sheltered scrub or woodland edge near the coast. Many such sites hold small parties.

Top and bottom right
Firecrests are difficult to pick out as they flit amongst the branches, often in the company of goldcrests or tits in autumn or winter.

Bottom left
Look for the obvious eyestripe, which is characteristic.

Crested Tit

11.5 cm (4.5 in)

○ ○

SPECIES INFORMATION

SCIENTIFIC NAME	Parus cristatus
RELATED SPECIES	Blue Tit, Great Tit, Coal Tit, Marsh Tit, Willow Tit
CALL	Alarm call 'tzee-tzee-gurrr-r'. Song is similar to call, at alternating pitches
HABITAT	Pine, spruce or fir forests. In Britain, restricted to native Scots pine forests of the Scottish highlands and mature pine plantations of the Moray coast
STATUS	Resident. Breeds throughout Europe, except far N. and much of SE. In BI about 900 pairs (Scotland only)

BROWN ABOVE, whitish below, with cream coloured flanks, and black and white speckled crest. Juveniles have shorter crests.

THE BACKWARD POINTING crest is unique among our small passerines, giving it a distinctive silhouette. The crest is black and white, the patterned head with black 'C' on the ear coverts is also black and white, and the rest brown and white or brown and buff. It often draws attention to itself with its trilling, rolling call, which acts as a contact and alarm call.

Although widespread in Europe, in Spanish cork oak, Pyrenean beech, or other mixed southern woods, it prefers pine forest in Scotland. There it does also breed in pine plantations, but as a highly sedentary species any spread is slow, and the extensive mature and native pine along Deeside in Aberdeen has not been colonised. Martin Cook in the *New Atlas* asks, were they never there, is there some subtle ecological factor missing, or is it just the difficulty of dispersion across difficult ground?

The ecological conditions that do favour crested tits are extensive needle canopy, sufficient light to support ground cover or heather, and dead stumps for the excavation of nest holes. As with other tits, different times of year demand different feeding strategies, including the storage of seeds from pine cones, secreted under lichens on the branches.

SIZE

IDENTIFICATION

HABITAT

POPULATION

MAP

Top right
Crested tits dig their nest holes in dead tree stumps.

Top left and bottom
This species is well named, as it has a prominent crest at all times of the year.

Golden Oriole

24 cm (9.5 in)

○ ○

S P E C I E S   I N F O R M A T I O N

SCIENTIFIC NAME	*Oriolus oriolus*
RELATED SPECIES	*None in region*
CALL	*Call harsh 'kraa', or cat-like mewing. Song is a clear, plaintive, fluting whistle: 'peeloo-peeleoo'*
HABITAT	*Deciduous woods, parks, plantations (often poplar)*
STATUS	*Summer visitor. Throughout Europe except far N and NW. In B about 40 pairs, mainly in SE England (absent from Ireland)*

SIZE

IDENTIFICATION

HABITAT

POPULATION

MAP

BEAUTIFUL, WITH (MALE) bright yellow body and mainly black wings and tail. Female is green and yellow. Flight undulating (female can be confused with green woodpecker in flight).

FOR A LARGE, brightly-coloured bird, the golden oriole is notoriously hard to see. As the *New Atlas* says: 'in spite of the male's bright yellow and black plumage, the golden oriole is a bird more often heard than seen, even where it is known to have a nest. When eventually seen it is arguably one of the most spectacular of British breeding passerines. The female is a much duller green and black and is far more difficult to see against a leafy background. The cat like contact squawk or alarm call is the best indication that a bird is present.'

Golden orioles reach Britain mostly during early May, arriving all along the coasts from Cornwall to Suffolk, and then filter northwards to varying degrees. Many of these will be non-breeding first-year males.

The RSPB and the Golden Oriole Group monitor population levels in their stronghold of the East Anglian fens, and at the time of the *New Atlas* were hoping to promote the planting of new poplar cultivars, suitable both for commercial use and for golden orioles. In 1990 there were ten confirmed and 32 possible breeding pairs, but only 7–11 young were reared in 1995 because of bad weather.

A candidate for being one of our most beautiful birds, the male golden oriole looks quite stunning, and also has an attractive fluting call.

SPECIES INFORMATION

SCIENTIFIC NAME	*Serinus serinus*
RELATED SPECIES	None in immediate region; Citril Finch, Canary
CALL	Flight-call high-pitched trilling 'tir-ri-lillit'. Song is a high-pitched, rapid, jingling twitter
HABITAT	Parks, gardens, orchards and vineyards
STATUS	Resident in southern Europe; summer visitor further north. Breed in central and southern Europe; absent from most of north and north-west Europe. In BI about five pairs (south and south-east England)

Serin

11 cm (4.25 in)

THE SMALLEST EUROPEAN finch, with a very short bill, yellow head and breast (male), and streaked flanks. Female more grey-green. Shows yellow rump in flight.

THIS BOUNCY CHARACTER is everywhere on the continent, with its wheezy jingle-jangle song and erratic display flight making it a most conspicuous bird.

Since its range has now extended to northern France and southern Scandinavia, for a long time people have been predicting its arrival in Britain as a regular breeding bird, but it seems stubbornly unable to make the necessary leap across the channel.

The first *Breeding Atlas* (1976) had a map to show it spread across Europe from a Spanish and Italian base in 1800, until it had reached north and east to France, except Brittany, and southern Scandinavia by 1970. There had been some 185 occurrences in Britain by 1974, including two confirmed breeding reports. The *Winter Atlas* only had records from four 10-km(6-mile) squares, and the 1993 *Breeding Atlas* mentioned breeding pairs in Devon in the early 1980s, and the successful colonisation of Jersey.

SIZE

IDENTIFICATION

HABITAT

POPULATION

MAP

The serin is rather like a tiny canary. Its hurried, jingling song is a characteristic sound further south in Europe, though rarely heard in the British Isles.

Snow Bunting

17 cm (6.5 in)

○ ○

SPECIES INFORMATION	
SCIENTIFIC NAME	Plectrophenax nivalis
RELATED SPECIES	No close relative; other buntings
CALL	Flight-call a trilling 'tirr'. Song simple and tinkling
HABITAT	High mountains and tundra. Regular on north European coasts in winter, on open areas with low vegetation
STATUS	Resident in Iceland and Scotland. Elsewhere mainly summer visitor, wintering to shores of north and north-west Europe, and further inland in eastern Europe. In BI about 80 pairs (Scotland only)

SIZE

IDENTIFICATION

HABITAT

POPULATION

MAP

BREEDING MALE HAS white head and underside, black wings with large white patches and black bill. Female has less bright plumage and browner upperparts. Winter male has pale brown back and brownish cap and cheek.

THE MALE IS predominately white, strikingly pied on back and wings. The female is also white below, but has grey head and dark streaked back. More of us will see them not in the mountains in summer but perhaps on winter hilltops, or more likely on east coast saltmarshes or shores. On the ground they may not appear as bright as in summer, but as soon as a party takes wing; flickering and drifting, the white tail and wing markings inevitably remind the observer of a blizzard of snowflakes. When settled, they run fast and use their orange beaks to collect seeds, and when they fly again the musical rippled twitter is as attractive as the flying bird.

Derek Ratcliffe writes: 'last of the high mountain breeders in Britain, but by far the rarest and most elusive. This is a true Arctic species, with a virtually continuous circumpolar distribution'. Those breeding in Iceland, Scotland and southern Scandinavia, are more or less sedentary in winter, when the coastal migrants probably consist mainly of birds from northern Europe and perhaps Greenland.

Top
A female snow bunting approaches its nest amongst the rocks.

Middle
Snow buntings can sometimes be seen along the sea shore in winter.

Bottom
Female snow bunting feeding her young in a nest in a craggy rockface.

Their summer haunts in the Highlands are the upper slopes with boulders and rocky outcrops, where snow patches linger in sheltered spots until late in summer, or may even last the whole year through. The nest sites are deep inside crannies among the rocks.

Nethersole Thompson found that male snow buntings, which go through the motions of territorial behaviour, are concerned more with seeking and holding a mate than with defence of an area. In the Cairngorms it is usual for there to be surplus, unpaired cock buntings, which continue to sing and display, often ranging over large areas, while paired birds have eggs or young.

Cirl Bunting

16 cm (6.5 in)

MALE YELLOW BELOW, with greenish breast-band and yellow and black markings on head and neck. Female much drabber, rather like female yellowhammer, but with less yellow and with grey-brown (not chestnut) rump.

MALES START SINGING their rapid rattling song reminiscent of the lesser whitethroat in mid–March. They become more conspicuous, often perching openly but, even then, only a head may protrude from the tip of a tree. At other times, cirl buntings are often secretive in tree cover but will feed in the open for winter seeds.

'A map of the Roman Empire would give a tolerable idea of the distribution of the cirl bunting', wrote Nicholson. 'It is a bird of the Mediterranean but spreads some way across Asia Minor, up the Danube valley and through the mildest parts of western Europe. Like the Roman colonists it conveys an impression of tolerating best the most benign and genial spots in this dank northern island, in which it reaches both the most northerly and most westerly points of its breeding range.' He finds it difficult to define their exacting tastes. 'Their choice seems to fall not on a particular type of country but on the kind of spot to which a discriminating man might wish to retire after spending a good deal of his life in some much warmer climate than ours.'

A bit earlier than that the *Handbook* had given a map of cirl bunting distribution, with the bird widely distributed in north Wales, the Malvern–Cheltenham area, and from Cornwall to Kent, with an extension northwards into the Chilterns. Earlier in the century it had extended to Yorkshire and Cumberland. Now this attractive species is restricted to an area centred on south Devon, and it is counted amongst one of our rarest breeding birds.

The RSPB Cirl Bunting Project provides advice to land managers on beneficial management, and grants available, through site visits, demonstration sites and publications. The project officer draws up management plans and helps with grant applications that will benefit cirl buntings and other farmland wildlife. Of particular importance has been the MAFF Countryside Stewardship Scheme, which gives payment for provision of stubbles, vitally important for birds during the winter months. Cirl buntings seem to require weed-rich stubble fields in the winter months, a habitat which has declined considerably.

SIZE

IDENTIFICATION

HABITAT

POPULATION

MAP

Top and bottom right
Black chin and dark eyestripe distinguish the male cirl bunting, but it is hard to spot in among the branches.

Bottom left
South-facing farmland in the south west of England provides some suitable sites for this rare breeding bird.

Great Northern Diver

69–91 cm (27–36 in)

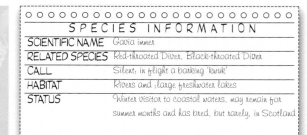

○ ○

SPECIES INFORMATION

SCIENTIFIC NAME	*Gavia immer*
RELATED SPECIES	Red-throated Diver, Black-throated Diver
CALL	Silent; in flight a barking 'kwuk'
HABITAT	Rivers and large freshwater lakes
STATUS	Winter visitor to coastal waters, may remain for summer months and has bred, but rarely, in Scotland

SIZE

IDENTIFICATION

HABITAT

POPULATION

MAP

LARGER, AND WITH heavier bill than red- and black-throated. Seen mainly in winter on coasts of north-western Europe. Usually seen at sea where they look really bulky, with heavy heads and powerful bills, and in winter with a dark crown and white throat. A comparison with other divers may be helpful.

THE GREAT NORTHERN DIVER has a steep forehead, with a dark collar that is almost complete. The back is slate-grey and covered with large spots. Preferred habitat is large lakes in remote areas during the summer months and they are often seen off sea coasts in the summer. The **black-throated diver** shows a clear contrast between white front and dark back of the neck. The **red-throated diver** has a whiter neck and face, and an upturned bill.

Red-necked Grebe

46 cm (18 in)

MORE COMPACT THAN great crested grebe, with shorter, thicker neck. In breeding plumage has rusty-red neck, white cheeks and throat and a black bill, yellow towards base. In winter plumage very like great crested, but with greyer neck and lacking the white stripe over the eye.

THE GREAT CRESTED GREBE is pale of plumage, with a long white neck. The flanks are pale brown and the back is dark grey. They are found in shallow waters such as large lakes with plants emerging from them, normally at low levels. Their courtship is intricate; they make extravagant use of their head plumes. The red-necked grebe has a yellow bill, with a medium-length neck, and is only slightly smaller than great crested. The **Slavonian grebe** is black and white, with a flat forehead. It is of medium size, between little grebe and great crested. The **black–necked grebe** is fairly uniform in colour, with a steep forehead, and is slightly longer than the little grebe.

SIZE

IDENTIFICATION

HABITAT

POPULATION

MAP

The red-necked grebe winters in the British Isles sometimes, but still not in large numbers. It does not have the crest of the crested grebe.

341

Purple Heron

75–85 cm (30–33 in)

SPECIES INFORMATION

SCIENTIFIC NAME	*Ardea purpurea*
RELATED SPECIES	Grey Heron.
CALL	Flight-call rather higher pitched than Grey Heron's
HABITAT	Extensive reedbeds; marshy areas with thick scrub
STATUS	Summer visitor. Breeds mainly in southern Europe, but north to Holland. Rare, but regular, visitor, mainly to SE England

SIZE
IDENTIFICATION
HABITAT
POPULATION
MAP

SLIMMER AND LONGER-NECKED than grey heron; plumage very dark, especially in flight. Often holds neck in snake-like curve (neck looks angular in flight). Juveniles paler, lacking black head and neck markings; easily confused with grey heron from a distance.

Night Heron

58–65 cm (23–26 in)

SPECIES INFORMATION

SCIENTIFIC NAME	*Nycticorax nycticorax*
RELATED SPECIES	Other herons
CALL	
HABITAT	Reedbeds, marshes
STATUS	Rare in northern and central Europe, with a few small colonies in Holland and southern Germany; somewhat commoner in Hungary and Czechoslovakia. Vagrant to Britain

SIZE
IDENTIFICATION
HABITAT
POPULATION
MAP

SMALLISH HERON, GREY and black (juvenile brown).

AS ITS NAME suggests, the night heron spends its days hidden in cover and is nocturnal. Although it can be seen feeding during the day the bird leaves its roost a dusk, setting out to hunt for food and thus avoids competition with diurnal heron species.

The night heron's bill is very thick, wide and rather short, this relates directly to its feeding habits as its varied diet includes not only fish, frogs and insects but even the chicks of marsh birds. The adult is balck on crown and back, wings are dove-grey and underparts white with yellowish legs and large reddish eyes. A vagrant from southern Europe.

○ ○

SPECIES INFORMATION	
SCIENTIFIC NAME	Ixobrychus minutus
RELATED SPECIES	Other herons
CALL	Flight-call a short, raw croak. Male also has low, repeated bark in breeding season
HABITAT	Thick reedbeds on lakes, damp, riverside willow scrub, marshes and flood-plain woods
STATUS	Summer visitor. Breeds in central and southern Europe. Local, and mostly commoner in the east of range. Vagrant to Britain (mainly in spring)

Little Bittern
33–38 cm (13–15 in)

EUROPE'S SMALLEST HERON. Male has dark cap and upperparts. Female less contrasting, streaked on neck, breast and flanks. Pale wings obvious in flight, especially in male. Flies low over reeds with rapid wing-beats, quickly diving down into fresh cover. Found in marshes, little bitterns climb up reed streams rather than walk along the floor of the reedbed. They migrate to Africa and spend the winter south of the Sahara and in Britain only odd birds turn up during migration

 SIZE

 IDENTIFICATION

 HABITAT

 POPULATION

 MAP

○ ○

SPECIES INFORMATION	
SCIENTIFIC NAME	Platalea leucorodia
RELATED SPECIES	None in region
CALL	Nasal grunts and wailing sounds at nest
HABITAT	Marshy areas, with reedbeds and shallow water
STATUS	Summer visitor (resident Spain). Often at coasts outside breeding season. Rare breeding bird in Holland, Austria, Hungary and Greece. Also SW Spain. Rare but regular visitor to Britain

Spoonbill
78–85 cm (31–33 in)

LONG SPOON-SHAPED bill with yellow tip. White plumage, with yellow-ochre chin. In breeding season has crest behind head and yellowish breast-band. Juveniles lack crest, yellow chin spot and breast-band, and wings have dark tips. In flight, head and neck outstretched; neck sagging slightly. Stands in water and sieves small animals by swishing bill from side to side. Flocks often fly in long lines or in V-formation.

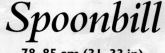

 SIZE

 IDENTIFICATION

 HABITAT

 POPULATION

     MAP

White Stork

95–105 cm (37–41 in)

○○○○○○○○○○○○○○○○○○○○○○○○○

SPECIES INFORMATION

SCIENTIFIC NAME	Ciconia ciconia
RELATED SPECIES	Black Stork (even rarer visitor).
CALL	Noisy bill clapping during breeding displays. Occasional hissing.
HABITAT	Damp meadows and fields in open lowland.
STATUS	Summer visitor. Resident in S Spain and Portugal. Breeds mainly in NE Central Europe, and in SW Spain and Portugal.

SIZE

IDENTIFICATION

HABITAT

POPULATION

MAP

VERY LARGE AND white, with black flight feathers; long red bill and legs. Juveniles have much paler bill and legs. Flies and soars with neck outstretched, unlike herons.

THE WHITE STORK breeds mainly on buildings and chimneys, often on a wheel provided specially for the birds. Sometimes nests in trees in river-valley woodland.

In western Europe has been decreasing markedly for decades, mainly because of habitat destruction, collisions with power lines and shooting in winter quarters. Occasional in Britain, and is found mainly April to August.

Crane

106–118 cm (42–46 in)

○○○○○○○○○○○○○○○○○○○○○○○○○○

SPECIES INFORMATION

SCIENTIFIC NAME	Grus grus
RELATED SPECIES	None in area
CALL	Loud bellowing or trumpeting call 'krooi-kruh', often in early morning.
HABITAT	Extensive wetlands, marshy lake margins, swampy woodland, bogs and isolated forest lakes. On migration also found in cultivated areas, or roosting on shallow water
STATUS	Summer visitor. Mainly in Scandinavia, N Germany, Poland and Baltic States. Irregular breeder in Britain (1–2 pairs)

SIZE

IDENTIFICATION

HABITAT

POPULATION

MAP

TALL, ELEGANT, AND long-legged with long bill (but relatively shorter than heron or egret). Mainly grey, with black and white on head and neck. In flight neck is extended and legs trail well beyond tail. Migrating flocks often fly in wedge formation.

THROUGHOUT THE YEAR, especially during spring, close to their breeding grounds they perform a distinctive mating ritual in which they leap up with raised wings, their tail plumes fluffed and erect and trumpet loudly.

They breed in open bogs on marshland, where they also take insects and other animal food.

Lesser White-fronted Goose

53–66 cm (21–26 in)

HAS A LARGER WHITE shield than its larger and much commoner relative. Smaller and shorter-necked, with rounder head and shorter bill. The white patch extends above eye, which has a characteristic yellow ring. Flight very agile. Numbers of these have risen dramatically in areas where hunting restrictions have been imposed, usch as in the Netherlands, Flanders and parts of Germany and the numbers wintering in Britain have remained stable.

RED-BREASTED GOOSE

Breeds in Siberian tundra; winters on estuaries and flooded fields, mainly around black sea. Very rare visitor to Britain, usually with barnacle geese. Small, mainly black and white, but with red breast and cheek-patch.

SNOW GOOSE

Very rare visitor from North America, but most are probably birds escaped from collections.

SIZE

IDENTIFICATION

HABITAT

POPULATION

MAP

These three species may be seen, though rarely, usually as single birds turning up in mixed flocks with other commoner geese.

Ring-necked Duck

37–46 cm (15–18 in)

SPECIES INFORMATION	
SCIENTIFIC NAME	Aythya collaris
RELATED SPECIES	Pochard, Tufted Duck, Scaup, Ferruginous duck
CALL	Wheezy whistle (male), growl (female)
HABITAT	Freshwater; estuaries
STATUS	Rare but regular visitor

SIZE
IDENTIFICATION
HABITAT
POPULATION
MAP

THE MALE IS BLACK with pale grey flank, outlined in white and extending up the neck. Takes its name from the dark neck-band (not obvious in the field). Female like female pochard, but has white eye-ring and black tip to bill. Both sexes have more peaked crown, and show pale trailing edge to wing in flight. Behaviour is much like pochard.

VAGRANT FROM North America, with a social disposition; often found consorting with other diving ducks. The species has been spreading throughout the USA and eastern Canada, which may help to explain, together with the growing expertise of birders, the increasing number of records.

Ferruginous Duck

38-42cm (15-17in)

SPECIES INFORMATION	
SCIENTIFIC NAME	Aythya nyroca
RELATED SPECIES	Pochard, Tufted Duck, Scaup, Ring-necked Duck
CALL	'Err-err-err' (female); 'chuck-chuck' (male)
HABITAT	Shallow lowland lakes
STATUS	Rare winter visitor, mainly to south-east England

SIZE
IDENTIFICATION
HABITAT
POPULATION
MAP

THIS SMALL RELATIVE of our other diving ducks has very dark plumage with a chestnut tinge, contrasting with a pure white or pale undertail. The male also has a white iris. In flight it shows a white patch on the belly and a broad, white wing-bar. Note also the rather long bill and sloping forehead. It breeds mainly on ponds and lakes in eastern and central Europe.

Velvet Scoter
53–58 cm (21–23 in)

```
SPECIES INFORMATION
SCIENTIFIC NAME   Melanitta fusca
RELATED SPECIES   Common Scoter, Surf Scoter
CALL              In breeding season female has a nasal 'braa-braa';
                  male a piping 'kyu'
HABITAT           Breeds at lakes in mountains, especially in northern
                  coniferous forest and tundra zones; coastal waters
                  outside breeding season
STATUS            Breeds in Scandinavia and around Baltic Sea.
                  Summer visitor in breeding range. Mainly to North
                  Sea and Baltic coasts as passage bird and winter
                  visitor. Rarer than common scoter
```

LARGER THAN COMMON SCOTER, and has white wing-patches (may be hidden when swimming). Male black, with white patch below eye. Female dark brown with pale patches at side of head (sometimes absent). Sometimes accompanies the common scoter or eider in winter flocks and in flight are immediately identifiable by the white speculum. In marine areas, their food consists of molluscs, but in freshwater they eat insects.

Surf Scoter
45–56 cm (18–22 in)

```
SPECIES INFORMATION
SCIENTIFIC NAME   Melanitta perspicillata
RELATED SPECIES   Common Scoter, Velvet Scoter
CALL
HABITAT           Open sea
STATUS            Rare, but regular, vagrant from North America
```

THIS SEA DUCK is about the same size as the common scoter, and smaller than the velvet scoter. In flight, the wings are dark, with no pale area or wing-bar. Male has heavy, orange and white bill with a black patch at the side, and a white patch on the back of its neck. Female is more like common scoter, but has heavier bill and more angular head. It is most often seen off the north coast of Britain, mainly between September and April.

Rough-legged Buzzard

53–63 cm (21–25 in)

○ ○

SPECIES INFORMATION

SCIENTIFIC NAME	Buteo lagopus
RELATED SPECIES	Common Buzzard
CALL	Cat-like mewing. Usually silent in winter
HABITAT	Mountains and tundra of northern Europe, mostly above or beyond tree-line. Numbers increase after rodent population explosions. In winter found mainly on moorland and heaths
STATUS	Breeds mainly in Scandinavia and Finland. In some winters it migrates south in large numbers, especially to eastern Europe, but also (in small numbers) to east coast of BI

SIZE

IDENTIFICATION

HABITAT

POPULATION

MAP

TAIL WHITE, WITH wide dark band at tip; hovers much more frequently than buzzard. Plumage variable, but usually has pale head, and more contrast than buzzard. Legs feathered to toes. Wings and tail relatively long, belly black, contrasting with pale undersides of the wings.

MOST BIRDS THAT reach Britain in an ordinary winter remain close to the east coast, in East Anglia or Kent. The rough legs and feathered tarsi, are not easy to spot, but the pale tail with broad terminal band, the very dark upperparts, and the dark belly patch are good field marks.

Rodent cycles have their influence on breeding success. A good spring lemming or vole population can lead to large clutches and, if the rodents continue to breed through the summer, the large clutches become successful broods. After years like that, more rough-legged buzzards are likely to reach Britain, but the main movement is south to south-east, taking birds to the Black Sea and Caucasus.

One of the best rough-legged buzzard winters was 1966–67 when there were 67 records. It seems that these were due more to a crash in vole numbers than to an unusually high rough-legged buzzard population. Even better was 1974, when the wintering population may have been 100 birds, and more were seen in passage in October.

East Anglian coastal heathland is a favoured haunt of wintering rough-legged buzzards. They pause and hover as they search the ground below for rodents.

Red-footed Falcon
21–31 cm (8–12 in)

SPECIES INFORMATION	
SCIENTIFIC NAME	Falco vespertinus
RELATED SPECIES	Kestrel, Hobby, Peregrine, Merlin, Gyr Falcon
CALL	Usually silent
HABITAT	Heaths and wetlands
STATUS	Rare, but regular, visitor to Britain, mainly in May–June

LIKE A SMALL, dainty kestrel. Female rusty orange beneath, grey with dark barring above. Adult male all grey. Adults have bright red feet. Often found perching on wires and posts.

A HANDFUL OF THESE elegant falcons reach Britain almost every year and causing a stir amongst keen birdwatchers. Agile in flight and reminiscent of the hobby, but also hovering frequently in the manner of a kestrel, they catch insects either in flight or on the ground. The female and male look very different, the former is almost all dove-grey, but with red under tail coverts, while the latter is grey above, with rufous crown and underparts. The falcon is the same size as the hobby but has a blunter profile.

SPECIES INFORMATION	
SCIENTIFIC NAME	Falco rusticolus
RELATED SPECIES	Peregrine, Kestrel, Hobby, Merlin, Red-footed Falcon
CALL	Coarse 'kerreh-kerreh-kerreh'
HABITAT	Breeds in tundra (Iceland and Scandinavia). Rare visitor to BI, mainly in winter, when seen most often at coast
STATUS	Vagrant to BI

Gyr Falcon
55–60 cm (22–24 in)

LARGEST EUROPEAN FALCON, the size of a goshawk. Wings are broader at the base than peregrine's, and wing-beats slower. Plumage mainly grey, pale grey or even white (mainly Greenland birds).

SIMILAR IN FLIGHT to peregrine, but heavier and with slower, more deliberate wingbeats. There is much variation in plumage, with the pure white form found mainly in Siberia and Greenland, a light grey form in Iceland and a darker grey type in northern Scandinavia. Although it is a rare winter or spring visitor, each year will usually bring a couple of exciting sightings of the magnificent Gyr falcon in the British Isles.

Curlew Sandpiper

18–23 cm

SPECIES INFORMATION

SCIENTIFIC NAME	Calidris ferruginea
RELATED SPECIES	Dunlin, stints, Purple Sandpiper, Pectoral Sandpiper
CALL	Flight-call a trilling 'krillee', softer and less nasal than dunlin's
HABITAT	Breeds in arctic coastal tundra. On migration, mostly on mudflats, more rarely on inland muddy sites and salt lakes
STATUS	Regular passage migrant in small numbers on coasts, especially North Sea. Larger flocks in eastern Mediterranean. Breeds in High Arctic of east Asia

SIZE

IDENTIFICATION

HABITAT

POPULATION

MAP

DUNLIN-SIZED, BUT less dumpy, with longer legs and neck. Bill also longer and more decurved. Breeding plumage brick-red (like knot). In winter plumage it resembles Dunlin, but has paler belly. In flight shows white wing bar and white rump.

CURLEW SANDPIPERS BREED in the far north of Asia – in the Siberian Arctic. In Britain they turn up regularly on passage to their wintering grounds in Africa, in spring or, more commonly, in autumn. They tend to be single birds, and are often seen in mixed flocks, especially with dunlin. Easily confused with dunlin, especially since some dunlins have longer, more curved bills than others. Look also for the longer neck of the curlew sandpiper, and the more obvious eye-stripe. Unmistakable in spring or summer plumage, with brick-red plumage on neck and belly.

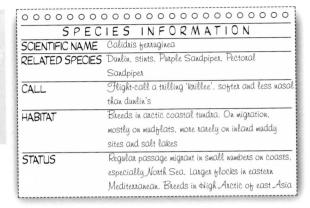

Curlew sandpipers are closely related to dunlins and look very similar; however, they are slightly larger in size.

Pectoral Sandpiper
19–23 cm (7.5–9 in)

SPECIES INFORMATION

SCIENTIFIC NAME	Calidris melanotus
RELATED SPECIES	Knot, Dunlin, Sanderling, stints, Purple Sandpiper, Curlew Sandpiper
CALL	'Chrook'
HABITAT	Breeds in N American and E Siberian tundra. Visits muddy and grassy shores
STATUS	N American species, but the most frequently seen American wader in Europe – mainly July–October

LARGER THAN DUNLIN, with a stance that often resembles a ruff. It has rich black and brown upper parts with pale stripes down the back. The pectoral band, with upper breast distinctly streaked, makes a sharp contrast with the white lower breast.

OFTEN TURNS UP in Ireland, at sites such as Akeragh Lough in County Kerry. However, as a quarter of records for pectoral sandpiper are from the east coast, some birds could be of Siberian rather than American origin. The legs are of a distinctive greenish colour. In small numbers, this sandpiper has become a regular transatlantic migrant, especially in the autumn months.

SPECIES INFORMATION

SCIENTIFIC NAME	Charadrius alexandrinus
RELATED SPECIES	Ringed Plover, Little Ringed Plover
CALL	Alarm call 'brrr brrr'; flight-call 'pit'. Song a trill, often in flight.
HABITAT	Most coastal of plovers, usually seen near to tidal zone on sandy coasts. Also on lagoons and saltpans
STATUS	Resident and partial migrant. Breeds in Spain, Portugal, France, and scattered around Mediterranean, Atlantic and (more rarely) southern North Sea. Also breeds inland in Hungary and E Austria, and further east around Black Sea. Rare visitor to BI on migration (mainly April–May or August–October)

Kentish Plover
16 cm (6 in)

LONGER-LEGGED THAN other ringed plovers, and with less black on face. Breeding male has chestnut on head. Bill and feet are dark, and neck band is incomplete. Female and winter male has paler plumage. In flight shows white wing bar.

OTHER FIELDMARKS USEFUL for distinguishing Kentish plover from ringed or little ringed plover are the sightly longer, narrower bill, the broad, rather flat-crowned head and the long, black or dark grey legs. In flight, look for the obvious white wing-bar and white sides to the tail. The plover's nest is a minimal scrape which has almost no lining, and both sexes help to incubate the eggs (normally two or three) for the 24 days that they take to hatch.

Grey Phalarope

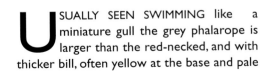

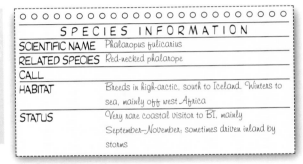

SPECIES INFORMATION	
SCIENTIFIC NAME	Phalaropus fulicarius
RELATED SPECIES	Red-necked phalarope
CALL	
HABITAT	Breeds in high-arctic, south to Iceland. Winters to sea, mainly off west Africa
STATUS	Very rare coastal visitor to BI, mainly September–November; sometimes driven inland by storms

SIZE

IDENTIFICATION

HABITAT

POPULATION

MAP

USUALLY SEEN SWIMMING like a miniature gull the grey phalarope is larger than the red-necked, and with thicker bill, often yellow at the base and pale greyish or black legs. Paler grey in winter than red-necked; bright brick-red summer plumage rarely seen in this country.

Little Stint

13 cm (5 in)

SIZE

IDENTIFICATION

HABITAT

POPULATION

MAP

SPECIES INFORMATION		
SCIENTIFIC NAME	Calidris minuta	
RELATED SPECIES	Temmink's Stint, Knot, Dunlin, Sanderling, Purple Sandpiper, Curlew Sandpiper	
CALL	Quiet vibrating 'tirr-tirr-tirrit' when flushed. Flight-call 'bit'. Song a soft, tinkling trill, in flight	
HABITAT	Breeds in damp tundra. On migration mainly at coast (especially muddy estuaries) in small or mixed flocks	
STATUS	Breeds on tundra of high Arctic. Summer visitor to breeding grounds. Migrates to Africa and S European coasts in autumn. In BI small numbers (mostly juveniles) visit regularly as passage migrants (mainly autumn)	

TINY WADER WITH short, black bill and black legs. In breeding plumage has reddish-brown upperparts with black and brown spots on the back; white below. V-shaped cream marking on upper back (very clear in juveniles). Dark streak along centre of crown. In winter, grey above, with greyish tinge to sides of breast.

Temminck's Stint

13 cm (5 in)

SIMILAR TO LITTLE stint, but slightly more elongated and shorter-legged. Legs paler, plumage greyer above. At the southern edge of its range in Scotland, where there is a tiny population, but plenty of suitable habitat. The Scandinavian population stands at over 100,000 birds, but few visit these shores.

 SIZE

 IDENTIFICATION

 HABITAT

 POPULATION

 MAP

Long-tailed Skua

35–58 cm (14–23 in) includes tail 12–20 cm (5–8 in)

MORE DELICATE THAN other skuas, with narrower wings. Very elegant in flight. Has sharply defined dark cap, with a white neck and upper breast. Tail streamers are longer than those of arctic skua. Juvenile has shorter central tail feathers.

THE LONG-TAILED skua is one of several Arctic and northern species whose populations fluctuate with the abundance of their prey – in this case mostly small rodents, especially lemmings. Records of passage birds in Britain increase following good breeding seasons.

 SIZE

 IDENTIFICATION

 HABITAT

 POPULATION

 MAP

Pomarine Skua

65–78 cm (25.5–31 in) includes tail 8 cm (3 in)

SIZE

IDENTIFICATION

HABITAT

POPULATION

MAP

SPECIES INFORMATION	
SCIENTIFIC NAME	Stercorarius pomarinus
RELATED SPECIES	Arctic Skua, Long-tailed Skua, Great Skua
CALL	'Gek-gek', or 'yee-ee'
HABITAT	Breeds on tundra. Winters mainly at sea (Atlantic)
STATUS	Breeds in arctic Russia. Summer visitor to breeding grounds. On passage off coasts, mainly in late autumn and late spring

LARGER AND HEAVIER than Arctic skua, with broader wings and heavier bill. Central tail feathers twisted into a blob. Pale phase and (rarer) dark phase occur. In juvenile the central tail feathers hardly visible (tail looks rounded).

Mediterranean Gull

38 cm (15 in)

SIZE

IDENTIFICATION

HABITAT

POPULATION

MAP

SPECIES INFORMATION	
SCIENTIFIC NAME	Larus melanocephalus
RELATED SPECIES	Black-headed Gull, other Larus gulls
CALL	Mostly silent outside breeding season. 'Eu-err' – more nasal, and shriller than black-headed gull
HABITAT	Nests in colonies at lagoons and lakes
STATUS	Scattered from S Baltic, through C Europe, to N Mediterranean. Rare breeder in England, with about 12 pairs, mainly in SE. Summer visitor to breeding grounds. Winters around Mediterranean, north to Channel.

SIMILAR TO BLACK-HEADED gull, but has paler and broader wings. In the summer the head is a true black (black more extensive than black-headed's brown); face has dark mask in winter.

THE MEDITERRANEAN GULL can easily be hidden in a huge breeding colony of black-headed gulls in summer or in winter. Either way, identification presents a challenge to the gull enthusiast.

SPECIES INFORMATION	
SCIENTIFIC NAME	Larus minutus
RELATED SPECIES	Black-headed gull, other Larus gulls
CALL	Soft 'kik-ki-ki' or tern-like 'kyek'
HABITAT	Breeds on shallow lakes with rich vegetation, often with black-headed gulls. Outside breeding season at sea and regularly on large inland lakes
STATUS	Mainly NE Europe, east of Baltic Sea. A few pairs in the Netherlands and north Germany. Mainly summer visitor to breeding areas (resident towards south). Winters around coasts. In BI regular on passage (has bred)

Little Gull

26 cm (10 in)

SIZE

IDENTIFICATION

HABITAT

POPULATION

MAP

OUR SMALLEST GULL is rather tern-like in flight. In breeding plumage resembles black-headed gull, but cap is black, and extends further down neck. The little gull also lacks white near eye, and has rounded wing-tips, without black tips. In flight, shows slate-black beneath wings, and white trailing edge to wings. Juveniles have dark, zig-zag pattern on upper wings (compare juvenile kittiwake), and dusky cap.

OUT OF THE breeding season, for instance when storm-driven winter birds are forced inshore, adult and young have a dark cap and ear-patch. Little gulls are buoyant fliers, and show their dark underwings and plain white wing-tips as they dip for food at the water surface.

Top and Middle
The juvenile little gull has a dark cap and a broad, black neck-band.

Below
The little gull in its winter plumage, with a dusky cap, dark ear-spot and general tern-like appearance.

Glaucous Gull

62–72 cm (24–28 in)

○○○○○○○○○○○○○○○○○○○○○○○○○○○○

SPECIES INFORMATION

SCIENTIFIC NAME	Larus hyperboreus
RELATED SPECIES	Iceland Gull, other Larus gulls
CALL	Similar call to herring
HABITAT	Breeds in high arctic – e.g. Greenland, Iceland, Svalbard
STATUS	Rare but regular visitor – mainly in winter

SIZE

IDENTIFICATION

HABITAT

POPULATION

MAP

GLAUCOUS GULLS AND Iceland gulls both have uniquely white wings, even at the tips. Immature birds have pale brown plumage, and in wintering adults there is a degree of brown streaking on the head. Immature birds mainly show a pink bill with a dark tip. Glaucous is slightly larger than herring gull, and the wings are relatively broader than Iceland's. Most glaucous gulls are ponderous, pot bellied birds although small birds may be seen. A winter visitor occurring in numbers around Shetland.

Iceland Gull

52–63 cm (20–25 in)

○○○○○○○○○○○○○○○○○○○○○○○○○○

SPECIES INFORMATION

SCIENTIFIC NAME	Larus glaucoides
RELATED SPECIES	Glaucous gull, other Larus gulls.
CALL	Similar call to herring
HABITAT	Breeds in high arctic – mainly Greenland.
STATUS	Rare but regular visitor – mainly in winter, mostly to NW of BI.

SIZE

IDENTIFICATION

HABITAT

POPULATION

MAP

Rather smaller than herring gull, with a slightly shorter, less heavy bill. Note that the wing tips are pure white. When resting, the long wings extend well beyond the tip of its tail. Immature birds are mottled brownish, but always have pale primaries. Iceland gulls prefer to stay over or close to the sea.

Wryneck
17 cm (7in)

SPECIES INFORMATION	
SCIENTIFIC NAME	*Jynx torquilla*
RELATED SPECIES	*No close relative in region*
CALL	*Call a hissing 'gshree'. Song a monotonous crescendo 'kyee-kyee-kyee' sung by both sexes, often as a duet*
HABITAT	*Open broadleaved woodland, copses, parks, and orchards*
STATUS	*Breeds scattered over most of continental Europe. In BI very few (perhaps five) pairs (Scotland). Summer visitor*

STRANGE-LOOKING WOODPECKER relative with nightjar-like, bark-coloured plumage and short bill. Could be mistaken for barred warbler, or possibly immature red-backed shrike.

THE WRYNECK AVOIDS dense woodland and feeds mainly on the ground. It is an uncommon but regular passage migrant to the British Isles.

The complex patterning of its plummage is unique. Its undulating flight is woodpecker-like and it nests in tree holes feeding on insects licked up with its long tongue. A sky-pointing display is used in courtship or when threatened.

SIZE

IDENTIFICATION

HABITAT

POPULATION

MAP

Lapland Bunting
16 cm (6 in)

SPECIES INFORMATION	
SCIENTIFIC NAME	*Calcarius lapponicus*
RELATED SPECIES	*No close relative in region; other buntings*
CALL	*Flight-call 'prrrt' or 'tew-prrrt'. Song resembles snow bunting's, but jerkier*
HABITAT	*Scandinavian mountains and arctic tundra. In winter to coastal meadows*
STATUS	*Breeds on arctic tundra. Winters around North Sea and Baltic coasts.*

THE BREEDING MALE is streaked above, with black head and face and chestnut nape. In winter similar to reed bunting, but has chestnut patch on wing, framed by two white wing bars with a yellowish.

THE LAPLAND BUNTING has bred in Scotland. Regular winter visitor, mainly along the east coast of England.

SIZE

IDENTIFICATION

HABITAT

POPULATION

MAP

Hoopoe
26–28 cm (10.5 in)

```
o o o o o o o o o o o o o o o o o o o o o o o o o o o
       SPECIES INFORMATION
```

SCIENTIFIC NAME	*Upupa epops*
RELATED SPECIES	*No close relatives*
CALL	*Raw, scratching territorial call. Song is a soft, but far-carrying 'poo-poo-poo'*
HABITAT	*Warm, dry, open country, especially cultivated areas, such as vineyards, light woodland, parks, orchards and pasture. Nests in holes in old trees, or in crevices in rocks and walls*
STATUS	*Breeds across much of continental Europe, north to Channel and Baltic. Rare but regular spring visitor to Britain (has bred)*

SIZE

IDENTIFICATION

HABITAT

POPULATION

MAP

THIS BIRD IS unmistakable. Often seen in flight, when seems floppy, almost like a huge butterfly, showing contrasting black and white barred wings and tail. Can be hard to spot on the ground. It has a fan-like erectile crest with a long, curved bill.

ONE OF THE JOYS of a continental holiday is to see and hear Hoopoes. The first sign is often the 'hoop-hoop-hoop' call, that excites with the prospect of a flying bird, boldly pied, and cinnamon-coloured, or of a bird feeding on the ground, using its long decurved bill and fanning its extraordinary crest. On Bardsey the rare possibility of a spring bird flying past the observatory and down the lane can clear the breakfast table, and a stray bird in a southern village soon gets known.

Although resident in southern Spain and North Africa, hoopoes are migratory over most of their range, and birds reaching Britain in the spring have probably overshot from France where it breeds in most areas.

Most European birds winter in sub-Saharan Africa.

Where it has declined, intensification of agriculture is probably responsible, for the larger insects and their protein-rich larvae and pupae are much scarcer in this insecticide age. Perhaps cool, wet summers have not helped, for it is decidedly a bird of warm, dry country, although it breeds successfully in a wide range of habitats.

Hoopoes have bred in Britain, for example four pairs in 1977, and nests are usually in a tree-hole. Territory is advertised with a 'pooping' display, involving calls and head movements from some conspicuous position.

Top right and left
The hoopoe cannot be mistaken for any other bird. The long crest is usually held furled, but is sometimes fanned forward.

Bottom
This lovely bird has begun to breed in the British Isles again and numbers may perhaps increase in the future.

Waxwing

18 cm (7 in)

SPECIES INFORMATION

SCIENTIFIC NAME	*Bombycilla garrulus*
RELATED SPECIES	*None in region*
CALL	*Flight-call a buzzing 'sree'. Song a mixture of humming and chattering calls*
HABITAT	*Breeds in open spruce or birch woods with rich undergrowth. May occur almost anywhere in winter*
STATUS	*Breeds mainly in NE Scandinavia and Russia. Summer visitor to breeding grounds. In autumn and winter, mainly to Scandinavia and E Europe. Further S and W (as far as Britain) in small numbers; in some years in much larger numbers, during 'irruptions'*

LOOKS BROWN FROM afar, but colourful when close. Starling-like in build and in flight, when white edges to primaries and the trilling calls, as a flock leaves its feeding place, help to distinguish them. The waxwing has sleek, pinky-brown plumage and crest of the same colour, black throat and black mask from bill and over the eye, and two bright yellow patches under the tail. The wings have bright red spots, like sealing wax, on the tips of the secondaries. Female has smaller red wing markings.

OCCASIONALLY, MANY WAXWINGS visit, as in 1996, when it was estimated that more than 10,000 birds arrived in Britain. Most records are from the east coast. In waxwing years, the birds can be easy to spot as they are tame and tend to congregate at berry-rich shrubs, often in parks and gardens.

SIZE

IDENTIFICATION

HABITAT

POPULATION

MAP

Top and bottom right
Suburban gardens with plenty of berry-bearing trees and shrubs are the places to watch for waxwings, which invade Britain from time to time in large numbers during the autumn and winter.

Bottom left
Waxwings have a distinctive pinky-brown crest with a black mask on the face.

Icterine Warbler

13 cm (5 in)

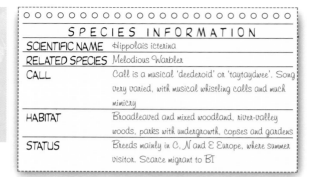

SPECIES INFORMATION	
SCIENTIFIC NAME	Hippolais icterina
RELATED SPECIES	Melodious Warbler
CALL	Call is a musical 'deederoid' or 'taytaydwee'. Song very varied, with musical whistling calls and much mimicry
HABITAT	Broadleaved and mixed woodland, river-valley woods, parks with undergrowth, copses and gardens
STATUS	Breeds mainly in C, N and E Europe, where summer visitor. Scarce migrant to BI

SIZE

IDENTIFICATION

HABITAT

POPULATION

MAP

THIS BIRD IS a little larger than wood warbler, its plumage mainly yellowish; and its posture reed warbler-like. It has a long orange bill with a pale patch on its wings

COULD WELL GO unnoticed unless trapped, or unless you hear the beautiful song – unlikely as most turn up in autumn.

Difficult to identify unless you are familiar with migrant birds, the icterine warbler is a rare visitor that turns up occasionally, mainly at coastal sites in autumn.

MELODIOUS WARBLER

Slightly shorter-tailed than icterine, and with shorter wings, lacking pale patch (13 cm (5 in). Only reliably distinguished from icterine in the field by song, a prolonged babbling warble although some individuals include mimicry

AQUATIC WARBLER

This rare visitor from central Europe is occasionally seen, mainly when caught at observatories. At 13 cm (5 in) tall, it resembles a sedge warbler, but is slightly yellower, with a darker crown with a central yellow stripe. Likes bushy country - olive groves, gardens, plantations and is often found in willows near water. Replaces icterine in S and W Europe. Summer visitor. Scare migrant to BI.

BARRED WARBLER

Large warbler, 15.5 cm (6 in), with powerful bill, double white wing bar and white tip to tail. Eye is yellow in adult. Female less barred beneath. Juvenile has dusky white underside, with indistinct barring, and dark eye. Young autumn birds are big, as warblers go, and have a heavy bill, but their sandy-grey plumage is not very distinctive. Breeds mainly in C, E and SE Europe, west to S Scandinavia and Germany. Summer visitor, wintering in E Africa. Scarce migrant to BI (mainly E coast, in autumn).

ARCTIC WARBLER AND GREENISH WARBLER

These two belong to an intriguing group, as several members of the genus *Phylloscopus* are so similar that identification sets a challenge. Greenish warblers, 11

cm (4.3 in), are the same size as chiffchaffs and willow warblers, with Arctic warblers slightly larger, 12 cm (4.75 in). The two species are greenish-brown above, whiter below than the common species, and with more prominent stripe over the eye, and small whitish wing bars. Arctic warbler has straw-coloured legs, while those of greenish are dusky.

Top right, middle right and bottom Arctic and greenish warblers are two species from north-east Europe, both rare autumn vagrants to Britain. They are very similar, and migrants are only reliably identified in the hand.

Bluethroat

14 cm (5.5 in)

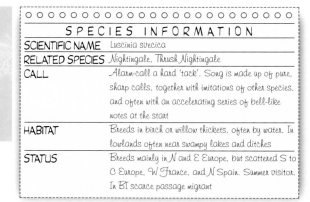

SPECIES INFORMATION	
SCIENTIFIC NAME	Luscinia svecica
RELATED SPECIES	Nightingale, Thrush Nightingale
CALL	Alarm-call a hard 'tack'. Song is made up of pure, sharp calls, together with imitations of other species, and often with an accelerating series of bell-like notes at the start
HABITAT	Breeds in birch or willow thickets, often by water. In lowlands often near swampy lakes and ditches
STATUS	Breeds mainly in N and E Europe, but scattered S to C Europe, W France, and N Spain. Summer visitor. In BI scarce passage migrant

SIZE

IDENTIFICATION

HABITAT

POPULATION

MAP

SIMILAR TO THE robin in shape and size, but with slightly longer legs. The base of its tail is rust-red with a pale stripe above the eye.

THE CENTRAL EUROPEAN race (*L. svecica cyanecula*) has a white spot on the blue throat, while the northern European race (*L. svecica svecica*) has a red spot. Female and winter male have white throat. Juveniles are similar to young robins, but with a red base to the tail. It is an extremely shy bird that likes to keep to the cover of its low vegetation habitat.

Red-Breasted Flycatcher

11.5 cm (4.5 in)

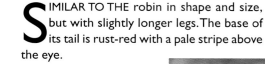

SPECIES INFORMATION	
SCIENTIFIC NAME	Ficedula parva
RELATED SPECIES	Pied Flycatcher, Collared Flycatcher
CALL	Alarm call 'doolii', and wren-like 'tsrrr'. Song is a descending, whistling phrase, a little like Willow Warbler's towards the end
HABITAT	Breeds in tall deciduous or mixed woodland. Also in parks in some areas
STATUS	Mainly C and E Europe, W to Germany. Summer visitor to breeding range. Scarce migrant to Britain (mainly E coast in autumn)

SIZE

IDENTIFICATION

HABITAT

POPULATION

MAP

SMALLEST OF THE European flycatchers, it is grey-brown above, creamy white below, with pale eye-ring and white at base of outer tail feathers.

ADULT MALE RED-BREASTED flycatcher has an orange-red throat bib with a greyish head. Female and first year male lack red bib.

SPECIES INFORMATION	
SCIENTIFIC NAME	Lanius excubitor
RELATED SPECIES	Red-backed Shrike, Woodchat Shrike
CALL	Sharp 'vaird' or 'shrrie' in two or three syllables. Sometimes a magpie-like chatter. Song consists of short metallic or vibrating phrases, and continuous warbling
HABITAT	Breeds on moorland and heath; also in hedgerows and orchards
STATUS	Breeds from N and NE Europe, through C Europe to SW Europe. Absent from NW, S and SE Europe. Resident; summer visitor to NE of range. In winter ranges over most of Europe, to suitable sites

Great Grey Shrike

24 cm (9.5 in)

LARGER THAN RED-BACKED shrike, with relatively short wings, and a long, somewhat graduated tail. Looks black and white from distance. Juvenile is rather duller, and darker below. Often sits on a high look-out perch. Flight slow and undulating; often hovers. Sometimes wedges food in tree branch, or impales it on thorns or barbed wire.

LIKE STONECHATS, great grey shrikes perch openly on heathland vegetation, but there the likeness ends. They are spectacular birds, particularly as they can appear suddenly, on a bleak winter's day, in a habitat where there appears to be little birdlife. As, particularly later in the winter, much of their diet is small birds, this means that a large hunting territory with appropriate hunting posts, is needed. On arrival in one of these territories, often heathland, there may still be insect life available, but as winter draws in, small mammals may be an alternative. As they too become less active and less visible, and as some birds weaken on a thinning diet, smaller birds may then become the chosen food.

The *Winter Atlas* shows a wide scattering of records. The heaths of the New Forest often attract this species, where meadow pipits, wrens, robins, finches, and even dartford warbler, feature in their diet.

The large insects which make up much of the summer diet are declining over most of Europe, with the intensification of agriculture and use of pesticides. Where these and small reptiles and mammals are available, they are caught following a wait and watch strategy from a good vantage point. After swooping flight and vertical pounce the shrike may eat the prey immediately or impale it for future use. Most British birds have Scandinavian origins, but the population centre is in the vast subarctic ranges of Russia which might hold a million pairs.

SIZE

IDENTIFICATION

HABITAT

POPULATION

MAP

A Great grey shrike in a typical pose at the top of a bush, from which it can scan its surroundings and watch the ground below for likely prey such as large beetles.

Red-backed Shrike

17 cm (7 in)

THE MALE HAS bright red-brown back, grey head with thick black eye-stripe, and black tail with white outer feathers at base. The female is red-brown above, pale beneath with crescent-shaped markings. Juvenile has rather scaly markings. Impales prey on thorns (or barbed wire) when food is plentiful.

SPECIES INFORMATION	
SCIENTIFIC NAME	Lanius collurio
RELATED SPECIES	Great Grey Shrike, Woodchat Shrike
CALL	Alarm call 'dshair', 'geck' or a hard 'trrt-trrt'. Song, seldom heard, is a varied warble, with short calls, interspersed with imitations of other birds.
HABITAT	Breeds on heaths, at woodland margins with thorn bushes, and in hedgerows
STATUS	Breeds throughout Europe, except for N and W. Virtually extinct as breeding species in BI (at north-west limit of range). Summer visitor, wintering in tropical Africa. In BI regularly seen on passage in spring and autumn

Woodchat Shrike

19 cm (7.5 in)

SMALL SHRIKE WITH rust-red head and conspicuous white shoulder-patches. Blackish above, pure white below. The female is slightly paler, with browner upperparts and less clearly marked black mask. Juvenile like young red-backed, but browner above, with paler shoulder and rump.

SPECIES INFORMATION	
SCIENTIFIC NAME	Lanius senator
RELATED SPECIES	Great Grey Shrike, Red-backed Shrike
CALL	Harsh calls, such as 'kshairr'. Song varied, with trills, whistles and mimicry
HABITAT	Open country — maquis, vineyards, gardens, orchards and the like
STATUS	Breeds mainly in S Europe, but north to Poland, and S Germany. Summer visitor. Annual vagrant to BI (mainly in May)

Scarlet Rosefinch

14 cm (5.5 in)

SPECIES INFORMATION

SCIENTIFIC NAME	Carpodacus erythrinus
RELATED SPECIES	None in immediate region; other finches
CALL	Soft 'djuwee', a bit like greenfinch. Song clear and whistling
HABITAT	Scrub and damp meadows
STATUS	Breeds mainly in NE Europe. In BI rare passage migrant, mainly in the north. Has bred in eastern England and in Scotland

A PRETTY FINCH. Sparrow-sized with stumpy bill. Distinctive red plumage on male, duller on female. Fairly common in Europe, rare in British Isles.

THIS BIRD HAS BEEN rapidly expanding westwards, and a pair were found with nest and eggs in the Highland Region of Scotland as recently in 1982. Singing males are becoming more common, other nests have been found on the east coast of Scotland, and it is hardly rare in the Shetland Islands in the spring months. Bright red plummage identifies adult males, but females, except for the powerful, stumpy bill, could be mistaken for the linnet as their plumage is dull. Occurs in thickets.

 SIZE
 IDENTIFICATION
 HABITAT
 POPULATION
 MAP

SPECIES INFORMATION

SCIENTIFIC NAME	Eremophila alpestris
RELATED SPECIES	None in immediate region; other larks
CALL	Flight-call a tinkling 'seet-dit-dit'. Song is a rapid, high-pitched twitter, in short phrases
HABITAT	Breeds in open mountain habitats on dry, stony plateaux. In winter on coastal meadows, waste land and fields
STATUS	Breeds on Scandinavian and Balkan mountains. Summer visitor in N; resident in Balkans. Winter visitor to North Sea and S Baltic coasts

Shore Lark

16 cm (6 in)

SANDY GREY ABOVE, whitish below. Yellow and black head markings, less distinct in winter, especially in the female. Breeding male has small black 'horns'. Slimmer, in flight, than other larks, and with rather pointed wings.

SINCE 1970, SHORE larks have bred erratically in the central Highlands, but certainly as breeding birds they are very rare. Seen regularly in winter along the east coast, although numbers have declined in recent years, reflecting declines in Scandinavia.

 SIZE
 IDENTIFICATION
 HABITAT
 POPULATION
 MAP

Useful Adresses

The Wildfowl and Wetlands Trust,
Slimbridge, Gloucester, GL2 7BT.
Tel: 01453 890333

The Royal Society for the Protection of Birds
and **Young Ornithologists' Club** (YOC),
(junior section of RSPB),
The Lodge, Sandy, Bedfordshire, SG19 2DL.
Tel: 01767 680551

British Trust for Ornithology,
National Centre for Ornithology,
The Nunnery, Thetford,
Norfolk, IP24 2PU.
Tel: 01842 750050

Birdwatch Ireland,
8 Longford Place, Monkstown, Co Dublin.
Tel: 012 804322

The National Trust,
36 Queen Anne's Gate, London, SW1H 9AS.
Tel: 0181 315 1111

Worldwide Fund for Nature,
Panda House, Weyside Park,
Godalming, Surrey, GU7 1XR.
Tel: 01483 426444

British Trust for Conservation Volunteers (BTCV),
36 St Mary's Street, Wallingford, Oxon, OX10 0EL.
Tel: 01491 839766

Royal Society for Nature Conservation (RSNC)
and **Watch** (junior section of RSNC),
The Kiln, Waterside, Mather Road,
Newark, NG24 1WT.
Tel: 01636 677711

The Woodland Trust,
Autumn Park, Dysart Road, Grantham,
Lincolnshire, NG31 6LL.
Tel: 01476 581111

The Walter Rothschild Zoological Museum,
Department of Ornithology,
Akeman Street, Tring, Herts, HP23 6AP.
Tel: 01442 824181

Scottish Ornithologists' Club,
21 Regent Terrace, Edinburgh, EH7 5BT.
Tel: 0131 5566042

**Royal Society for the Prevention
of Cruelty to Animals** (RSPCA),
Causeway, Horsham, Surrey, RH12 1HG.
Tel: 01403 264181

Selected Bibliography

Attenborough D., *The Life of Birds,* BBC 1998

Brooke M. & Birkhead T., *Cambridge Encyclopedia of Ornithology,* CUP, 1991

Bruun B. et al., *Hamlyn Guide to the Birds of Britain and Europe, 2nd ed.,* Hamlyn, 1992

Cannon A., *Garden Bird Watch Handbook,* BTO, 1998

Cottridge D. & Vinicombe K., *Rare Birds in Britain and Ireland,* HarperCollins, 1996

Du Feu C., *Nest Boxes,* BTO, 1993

Ferns P., *Bird Life of Coasts and Estuaries,* CUP, 1992

Fuller R., *Bird Habitats in Britain,* Poyser, 1982

Fuller R., *Bird Life of Woodland and Forest,* CUP, 1995

Gibbons D. et al., *The New Atlas of Breeding Birds in Britain and Ireland,* Poyser, 1993

Golley M. et al., *The Complete Garden Bird Book,* New Holland, 1996

Greenoak F., *British Birds: Their Folklore, Names and Literature,* Helm, 1997

Hayman P. & Hume R., *The Shell Easy Bird Guide,* Macmillan, 1997

Jonsson L., *Birds of Europe with North Africa and the Middle East,* Helm, 1996

Kightley C. et al., *Pocket Guide to the Birds of Britain and NW Europe,* Pica Press, 1998

Lack P., *Atlas of Wintering Birds in Britain and Ireland,* Poyser, 1986

Marchant J. H. et al., *Population Trends in British Breeding Birds,* BTO, 1990

Mead C., *Bird Migration,* Country Life, 1983

Newton I., *Population Limitation in Birds,* Academic Press, 1998

Pemberton J.E., *Birdwatchers Yearbook, 1999.* Buckingham Press, 1998

Peterson R. et al., *Birds of Britain and Europe, 5th ed.,* HarperCollins, 1993

Rackham O., *The Illustrated History of the Countryside,* Weidenfeld and Nicholson, 1994

Ratcliffe D., *Bird Life of Mountain and Upland,* CUP, 1990

RSPB, *Birds of Conservation Importance,* 1996

Sharrock J.T. R, *The Atlas of Breeding Birds,* BTO/Irish Wildbird Conservancy, 1976

Sharrock J.T.R, *Scarce Migrant Birds in Britain and Ireland.,* Poyser 1974

Snow D. & Perrins C.M., *The Birds of the Western Palearctic., Concise Edition.,* OUP 1998

Sterry, P. et al., *AA Field Guide: Birds of Britain and Europe,* AA, 1998

Tipling, D., *Top Birding Spots in Britain and Ireland,* HarperCollins, 1996

Glossary

Archaeopteryx
The name of an early fossil bird discovered in Jurassic rocks in Bavaria. The first specimen was found in 1861, and the state of its preservation is such that the structure of its feathers is clear. Archaeopteryx lived about 150 million years ago, and shows many features linking birds with reptiles.

Adaptive Radiation
The process by which a species evolves, through the isolation of different populations, into several new species. All birds have radiated out from an ancestral form, as they gradually adapted to different environments.

Allopatric Speciation
Occurs when populations are isolated for long enough, by some form of barrier, for their genetic makeup to become sufficiently different to make interbreeding between the members of the populations impossible. The isolated populations therefore become separate species.

Anting
This involves the use of ants by birds, or of the formic acid produced by the ants, together with peculiar movements, in what is probably an attempt to control parasites.

Aspect Ratio

Aspect ratio of a bird's wings is calculated by dividing the wingspan by the average width of the wing. A long, narrow wing with high aspect ratio is good for fast gliding.

Binomial Nomenclature

Introduced by Linnaeus (1758) to help with classifying animals and plants. Each species has a binomial (double-name), made up of the genus (or generic) name, together with the species (or specific) name. Both words are in Latin form. The generic name is placed first, with an initial capital letter, and the specific name afterwards, as in *Turdus philomelus*, the song thrush. By convention, binomials are always written in italic.

British Ornithologists Union (BOU)

This organisation aims to promote ornithology within the international scientific and birdwatching communities by, among other things, meetings, conferences and the publication of the journal *Ibis*.

British Trust for Ornithology (BTO)

A research and conservation organisation in which amateur enthusiasts co-operate with professional ornithologists in national projects, to count birds and monitor populations and distribution. For more details contact BTO.

Carpometacarpus

The name given to the fused bones of the hand of a bird, which provide a firm attachment for the primary feathers of the wing.

Cere

The fleshy covering to part of the upper mandible.

Climax Vegetation

The vegetation that would result if there were no interference by man, and if succession were allowed to take its natural course. In Britain, the climax vegetation of most normal lowland sites is woodland.

Cline

Occurs when a population shows a gradation in some feature such as weight, colour or tarsus length, from one part of its range to another.

Common Birds Census

A method used for estimating bird populations in woodland and on farms. Birdwatchers visit a site regularly during the breeding season, recording every contact with a bird on a large-scale visit map.

Convergent Evolution

The evolutionary process by which unrelated birds come to look similar or to have similar attributes. One example is the hummingbirds of Central and South America and the sunbirds of Africa.

Cloaca

The shared opening for three physiological systems: digestive, excretory and reproductive.

Density Dependent Factor

This reduces survival chances in a population when that population level is high. Too big a brood could actually reduce the number fledging.

Displacement Activity

Behaviour which appears out of context, as when a gull, at the edge of its territory, does not 'know' whether to advance or retreat: it may do neither but pull up grass instead.

Eclipse Plumage

Plumage taken on for a short time following a post-breeding moult in ducks. The males assume a cryptic, female-like plumage.

Ecosystem

A habitat defined in terms of the inter-relationships of the organisms living there, and their interactions with non-living factors like climate and soil.

Emargination

Emargination of primary wing feathers leads to an asymmetrical tapering towards the tip. This can help in identification, but its significance for the bird is that air can move smoothly through the wing-tips as it flies.

Endemic

Those birds found nowhere else. Thus many birds are endemic to Madagascar, but only the Scottish crossbill to Britain.

Eutrophic

Eutrophic of a lake or river, is when it is enriched, or over-enriched, with nutrients, particularly nitrates or phosphates. Contrast oligotrophic.

Family

A unit of classification with, in theory, all members sharing a common ancestor. Thus the family Corvidae includes the genus *Corvus*, crows, but also separate genera for jay, magpie and chough. They all belong in the Order Passeriformes.

Field Characteristics
The most important diagnostic features helping with wild bird identification.

Food Web
A way of representing who eats what in nature. Plants represent the lowest level at the bottom, and carnivores make up the top level. Toxic chemicals may pass up the complex food web to end up in the largest concentrations in the top carnivores.

Intraspecific Competition
This occurs between members of the same species, and interspecific competition occurs between different species.

Garden Bird Watch Scheme
A simple but scientific project by which anyone with a garden can contribute to knowledge of the populations of common birds.

Gene Flow
The exchange of genes between members of a population. It is reduced by distance and prevented by isolation.

Imprinting
A form of behaviour by which young birds, such as ducks, follow the first moving object that they encounter.

Integrated Population Monitoring
Uses information from all BTO surveys, to give the best possible indication of the causes of population changes.

Jizz
A term given to the impression a bird makes by its behaviour: for example the way it flicks its tail, moves in the reeds, or undulates in flight.

Leks
Elaborate, ritualised displays in which males compete to attract a female. Females are a passive audience, except when one enters the lek to mate with a dominant central male.

Lift
One of two components, drag being the other, of the force that acts when a wing moves. To keep a bird in the air, the lift must equal or exceed the weight of the bird.

Metatarsals
The bones of the foot, usually with three fused together and one free. The fused trio form an ankle joint with the long bone above. There are other joints with three toes below. The fourth toe, usually the backward pointing thumb, is attached to the free metatarsal.

Monophyletic
The monophyletic group has in theory a single ancestral form. Where convergence has taken place, those with different ancestors may be classified together, for instance in a family, because they seem similar. Such a group would be polyphyletic.

Niche

The combination of conditions that allows a bird to survive and reproduce. It involves environmental conditions like climate and food and habitat resources such as nest sites.

Nidicolous

Nidicolous young are hatched naked and are dependent upon their parents for a considerable time.

Nidifugous

Nidifugous chicks are immediately active and quickly leave the nest to become independent.

Nucleic Acids

Nucleic acids such as Deoxyribonucleic Acid (DNA), famed as the double helix, carry all the genetic information that determines an organism's inherited characteristics. The more closely related birds are, the more similar their DNA, and the more genes they will share.

Photoperiodism

A response to light, particularly to an increase or decrease in day length. The eyes, brain, hypothalamus, anterior pituitary gland and sex hormones are involved in bringing about associated behaviour changes.

Pishing

The making of vague 'pshu–pshu' sounds in an attempt to lure skulking birds out into a more open position.

Polygyny

This involves a pair bond of a male bird with more than one female, while polyandry is the reverse.

Polytypic

Polytypic species occur in a variety of forms, sometimes within the same range, sometimes separated in different areas. When closely studied, most species show this type of variation.

Pygostyle

The final part of the vertebral column with caudal or tail vertebrae fused or joined together.

Race

Race or subspecies, is made up of a population which is, or has been, geographically separated from other populations and has evolved its own characteristics of plumage, migratory behaviour or, for example, wing dimensions. The populations are still capable of interbreeding.

Resolving Power

This is the degree to which the lens system, in binoculars or a telescope, can make different parts of

an object distinguishable. Magnification by itself is not enough.

Royal Society for the Protection of Birds (RSPB)
This society champions the conservation of birds and biodiversity. It has a million members, manages more than 120 reserves and produces the quarterly magazine *Birds*.

Signals
Whether visual or auditory, signals release or stimulate aspects of behaviour. The coloured gape of a young cuckoo is a signal, releasing an instinctive feeding response.

Sonograms
A way of displaying bird calls and songs graphically in such a way that they can be accurately analysed and compared. The sonogram shows the changing frequency (kHz) over a period of time, and also gives an indication of volume.

Subsong
A quiet, modified song. It is often produced in autumn, or in spring when a low, but increasing, level of sex hormones starts to induce breeding behaviour.

Succession
The sequence of vegetational changes when bare soil or rock is colonised by plants or when grazing, burning or cutting stops. In Britain and Ireland such changes would almost always end in woodland, the climax vegetation.

Syrinx
A bird's organ of voice or song. It consists of a resonating chamber and vibrating membranes.

Transect
A line along which birds, or flowers or butterflies, are counted in a standardised way.

Zonation
Occurs when conditions change along a gradient; for example as one climbs a mountain or goes down the shore at low tide.

Author's Sources and Acknowledgements

AS WILL BE EVIDENT, books resulting from BTO surveys have provided much useful information for this book, helped by another thread that has run through a lifetime of interest in natural history; the 'New Naturalist' series published by HarperCollins, which started in 1945.

Two other bird books, of very different size, have been indispensable; the *'Birds of the Western Palearctic' (Concise Edition)*, edited by David Snow and Chris Perrins, and the genuinely pocket-sized *'Guide to the Birds of Britain and North West Europe'* by Chris Kightly and Steve Madge and illustrated by Dave Nurney.

Apart from these, and a few other recent references, I have delved into the past, as that is the nature of my library, so that I hope the book takes a historical perspective of the ever-changing habitats in which birds live.

History goes back a lot further than the written word, and birds are what they are because of millions of years of evolution. The world birds live in, whether it is one particular habitat or the whole of Britain and Ireland, is equally dependent upon the past, for most of which the two islands have had nothing like their present form. Only since the geologically recent changes of sea level and the action of ice have they been approximately as they are today. The presence of sea and ice has done much to shape the movements of our birds, and these cannot be separated from the rest of the world's geography. This book attempts at times to hint at the dependence of British and Irish birds on places far away and times past.

That the book exists at all depends on many people, starting from a comment from Helena Dean, my wife during the early *Atlas* years, about my lifelong interest in birds. This comment reached Polly Willis at The Foundry, who pursued the possibility of my writing something, and who has been a great support at all times.

The following is a list of all the sources I have drawn upon during the writing of this volume.

Allen, N. and Giddens, C. , 'Forty Years of Exmoor's Wildlife', *Exmoor Review*, Vol. 40, Exmoor Society, 1999

Armstrong, E.A. , *Birds of the Grey Wind*, OUP, 1940

Attenborough, D. , *The Life of Birds*, BBC, 1998

Aubrey, John, *Natural History of Wiltshire*, David and Charles, 1969

Bains, C. , 'Urban Areas', *Managing Habitats for Conservation*, Sutherland, W.J. and Hill, D.A. (Editors), Cambridge

Baker, R. (Editor), *The Mystery of Migration*, McDonald, 1980

Berry, R.J. , *Inheritance and Natural History*, Collins, 1977

Berry, R.J. and Johnston, J.L. , *The Natural History of Shetland*, Collins, 1980

Bibby, C. , Burgess, N. and Hill, D. , *Bird Census Techniques*, Academic Press/Collins, 1992

BOU, *The British List*, based on checklist of birds of Britain and Ireland, 1998 6th edition

Boyd, A.W. , *A Country Parish*, Collins, 1951

Boyd, J.M. and Boyd L.I. , *The Hebrides*, Collins, 1990

Brooke, Rupert, *Poetical Works*, Faber

Brooks, D. and Birkhead, T. , *Cambridge Encyclopedia of Ornithology*, CUP, 1991

Brown, L. , *Birds of Prey*, Harnlyn, 1979

Brown, L. , *British Birds of Prey*, Collins, 1976

Burgess, N. et al. , 'Reedbeds, Fens and Acid Bogs', *Managing Habitats for Conservation*, Sutherland, W.J. , 1995

Cain, A.J. , *Animal Species and their Evolution*, Hutchinson, 1954

Cain, A.J. , *Nature in Wales*, National Museum of Wales, 1984, vol. 3

Campbell, P.J. , *Blades of Grass*, Granary Press, 1986

Cannon, A. , *Garden Bird Watch Handbook*, BTO, 1998

Chaucer, Geoffrey, *The Riverside Chaucer*, OUP, 1987

Clare, John, *Selected Poems*, Dent, 1976

Colininvause, C. , *Why Big Force Animals are Rare*, Allen and Unwin, 1978

Conder, P. , *The Wheatear*, Christopher Helm, 1954

Condry, W.M. , *The Natural History of Wales*, Collins, 1981

Cooper, J.J. (Editor), *Brewers' Book of Myth and Legend*, Cassell, 1992

Cothridge, D. and Vinecombe, K. , *Rare Birds in Britain and Ireland – a photographic record*, Collins, 1996

Cranswick, P. et al. , *Wetland Bird Survey 1995-96*, BTO/WWT/RSPB/JNCC, Slimbridge, 1997

Dare, P. , *A Buzzard Population*, Devon Birds, 1998

Davies, S. , *The Wildlife of the Exe Estuary*,

Harbour Books, 1987

Diamond, J. , *Nature*, vol. 305, pp.17-18, 1983

Drabble, M. (Editor), *Oxford Companion to English Literature*, OUP, 1992

Du Feu, C. , *Nest Boxes*, BTO, 1993

Evans, I.H. (Editor), *Brewers' Dictionary of Phrase and Fable*, Cassell, 1987

Fisher, J. and Lockley, R. , *Sea Birds*, Collins, 1954

Fitler, R. , *London's Natural History*, Collins, 1945

Fitler, R. , *London's Birds*, Collins, 1949

Fowles, J. , *The French Lieutenant's Woman*, Jonathon Cape, 1969

Fowles, J. , *Wormholes*, Jonathon Cape, 1998

Fraser Darling, F. , *Island Years*, G. Bell and Sons, 1940

Fraser Darling, F. , *Natural History in the Highlands and Islands*, Collins, 1947

Freba, J. , *New Scientist*, 2.6.1976

Fuller, R. , *Bird Habitats in Britain*, Poyser, 1982

Fuller, R. , *Bird Life of Woodland and Forest*, Cambridge, 1995

Futuyama, D. , *Evolutionary Biology*, Sinaner Associated Ltd. , 1986 2nd Edition

Garner, M. , 'Identification of Yellow Legged Gulls', *British Birds*, vol. 90 Nos. 1 and 2, 1997

Gerald of Wales, *The Journey through Wales, The Description of Wales*, Penguin, 1978

Gibbings, R. , *Sweet Thames Run Softly*, Dent, 1940

Gibbons, D. et al. , *The New Atlas of Breeding Birds in Britain and Ireland 1988-1991*, Peyser, 1993

Glaves, D. (Editor), *Devon Bird Report*, 1996, 1998

Glegg, W. , *A History of the Birds of Middlesex*, Witherby, 1935

Gray J. , *How Animals Move*, Penguin, 1959

Greenoak F. , *British Birds, Their Folklore, Names and Literature*, A and C Black, 1979

Hale, W.G. , *Waders*, Collins, 1980

Harding, D.J.L. (Editor), *Britian since Silent Spring*, Institute of Biology, 1988

Hardy, Thomas, *New Wessex Selection of Poems*, Macmillan, 1978

Hardy, Thomas, *The Return of the Native*, Penguin, 1967

Harrison, T. and Hollom, P. , *The Great Crested Grebe Enquiry 1931*, Witherby, 1932

Harting, *Birds of Middlesex*, 1866

Hawkins, D. , *Hardy's Wessex*, Macmillan, 1983

Hayward, J. (Editor), *The Penguin Book of English Verse*, Penguin, 1983

Hearl, G. , *Bird Watching Guide to Menorca, Ibiza and Formentera*, Arlequin, 1996

Hickin, N.E. , *The Natural History of an English Forest*, Huychinson, 1971

Hickling, R. (Editor), *Enjoying Ornithology*, Poyser, 1983

Hollom, *Popular Handbook of British Birds*, Witherby, 1952

Hutchinson, C. , *Birds of Ireland*, Poyser, 1989

Huxley, J. , *Memories*, Penguin, 1972

Jeffries, R. , *Wildlife a Southern County*, Moonraker Press, 1978

Jones, G. (Editor), *The Oxford Book of Welsh Verse in English*, OUP, 1977

Jones, Hope and Bardsey, P. , *Observatory Report*, No. 40, 1996

Kaufman, K. , *Advanced Birding*, Boston, 1990

Kearton, R. and Kearton, C. , *British Birds Nests*, Cassell, 1908

Kennedy, P.G. , Ruttledge, R.F. and Scroope C.F. , *Birds of Ireland*, Oliver and Boyd, 1953

Kind, A.S. and McLelland J. , *Form and Function in Birds*, Academic Press, 1979

Kightly, C. et al. , *Pocket Guide to the Birds of Britain and Northern Europe*, Pica, 1998

Lacey, W.S. , *Welsh Wildlife in Trust*, North Wales Naturalist's Trust, 1970

Lack, D. , *The Natural Regulation of Animal Numbers*, OUP, 1954

Lack, P. , *Atlas of Wintering Birds in Britain and Ireland*, Poyser, 1986

Landsborough, Thomson A. (Editor), *New Dictionary of Birds*, Nelson, 1964

Leake, J. , *The Sunday Times*, July 10 1998

Lee, Laurie, *My Many Coated Man*, Andre Deutsch, 1955

Lee, Laurie, *The Sun My Monument*, Chatto and Windus, 1969

Le Feu, *Nest Boxes*, BTU, 1993

Lightowlers, P. , *New Scientist*, 5.5.1988

Lofts, B. , *Animal Photoperiodism*, Arnold

London Natural History Society, *The Birds of the London Area since 1900*,

Collins, 1957

Marchant, J.H. , Hudson, R. , Carter S. and Whittington P. , *Population Trends in British Breeding Birds*, BTO, 1990

Marren, P. , *England's National Nature Reserves*, Poyser, 1994

Mead, C. , 'Bird Migration', *Country Life*, 1983

Mitchell, F. , 'Shell Guide to Reading the Irish Landscape', *Country House*, 1986

Morrison, R.S. , *Words on Birds*

Mosley, J. and Hillier, C. , *Images of the Downs*, Macmillan, 1983

Moss, C. , 'Climate Change', *British Birds*, vol. 91 No. 8, 1998

Muldoon, P. (Editor), *Faber Book of Beasts*, Faber, 1997

NFU Countryside, *Conservation Frustrations*, NFU, 1996

Nelson, B. , *The Gannet*, Poyser, 1978

Nethersole-Thompson, *The Greenshank*, Collins, 1951

Newton, I. , *Finches*, Collins, 1972

Newton, I. , *Population Limitation in Birds*, Academic Press, 1998

Nicholson, E. M. , *Birds and Men*, Collins, 1951

Norman, D. and Tucker ,V. , *Where to Watch Birds in Devon and Cornwall*, Helm, 1997

Nuttall, N. , 'Ban on Eel Fishing', *The Times*, 30.9.1998

O'Conner, R. and Shrubb, M. , *Farming and Birds*, Cambridge, 1986

Oglivic, M. , 'Rare Breeding Species 1995', *British Birds* vol. 91 No. 8, 1998

O'Sullivan, M. , *Twenty Years A' Growing*, Chatto and Windus, 1933

Parker, M. , *Avian Physiology*, Zoological Society of London, 1975

Pemberton, J.E. , *Birdwatchers Yearbook 1999*, Buckingham Press, 1998

Perrins, C. , *British Tits*, Collins, 1979

Peterson, R. et al. , *A Field Guide to the Birds of Britain and Europe*, Collins, 1954

Potter, S. and Sargent, L. , *Pedigree; Words from Nature*, Collins, 1951

Prater, A. J. , *Birds of Estuaries Enquiry*, BTO/RSPB/WT

Pultman, G., *The Book of the Axe*, Longman, 1875

Rachan, O. , *The Illustrated History of the Countryside*, Weidenfeld and Nicholson, 1994

Ratcliffe, D. , *Bird Life of Mountain and Upland*, Cambridge, 1990

Ravenscroft, N.O.M., 'The Status and Habit of the Nightjar', *Bird Study*, vol. 36, 1989

Ricks, C. (Editor), *The New Oxford Book of Victorian Verse*, OUP, 1987

Rigg, D. (Editor), *So To The Land*, Headline, 1994

Roberts, M. (Editor), *The Faber Book of Modern Verse*, Faber, 1965

Roberts, P., *Birds of Bardsey Bird and Field Observatory*, 1985

Rogers, M., Rarities Committee, *Report on Rare birds in Great Britain in 1996*, British Birds vol. 90 No. 10, 1997

RSPB, *Birds of Conservation Importance*, 1996

RSPB, *Birds Magazine*, 1998

Ruttledge, R.F., *Ireland's Birds*, Witherby, 1966

Salim, A., *The Book of Indian Birds*, Bombay Natural History Society, 1964

Schmidt and Neilson, K., *How Animals Work*, Cambridge, 1988

Scott, P. and Fisher, J., *A Thousand Geese*, Collins, 1953

Scott, P., *Wild Chorus Country Life*, 1939

Severin, T., The Brendan Voyage, Abacus, 1978

Sharrock, J.T.R, *The Atlas of Breeding Birds*, BTO/Irish Wildbird Conservance, 1976

Sharrock, J.T.R., *Rare Birds in Britain and Ireland*, 1976

Sharrock, J.T.R., *The Natural History of Cape Clear Island*, Poysner, 1973

Sharrock, J.T.R., *Scarce Migrant Birds of Britain and Ireland*, Poysner, 1974

Shrubb, M., 'Birds and Farming Today', *Bird Study*, vol. 17, BTO, 1970

Simms, E., *British Thrushes*, Collins, 1978

Simms, E., *British Warblers*, Collins, 1985

Simms, E., *Woodland Birds*, Collins, 1971

Smith, M., 'Squawk on the Wildside', *The Independent*, 28.11.1998

Smith, S., *The Yellow Wagtail*, Collins, 1950

Snow, D. and Perrins, C.M., *The Birds of the Western Paleartic*, 1998 Concise Edition OUP

Spearman, D., *The Animal Anthology*, John Baker, 1978

Sutherland, W. and Hill, D., *Managing Habitats for Conservation*, CUP, 1995

Tinbergen, N., 'Behaviour, Systematics and Natural Selection', *Ibis*, vol. 101 Nos. 3-4, BOU, 1959

Tinbergen, N., *Curious Naturalists*, Penguin, 1974

Tinbergen, N., *Herring Gulls World*, Collins, 1978

Tubbs, C., *The New Forest*, Collins, 1986

Tunnicliffe, C., *Shorelands Winter Diary*, Robinson, 1992

Vaux, C., *Why Big Fierce Animals are Rare*, Allen and Unwin, 1978

Vosey-Fitzgerald, B., *British Game*, Collins, 1946

Vickery, J., Chamberlain, D. and Henderson, I., 'Farming and Birds', *BTO News*, vol. 216/217, 1998

Wardle Fowler, W., *Kingham Old and New; Studies in a Rural Parish*, Blackwell, 1913

Webb, N., *Heathlands*, Collins, 1986

Weiner, J., *The Beak of the Finch*, Cape, 1994

Wildland News, Nos. 43-44, Scottish Wildlife Group, 1998

Williams, I., 'Boosting Black Grouse', *RSPB Birds*, Winter, 1998

Williams, M. (Editor), *The Way to Lords*, Willow Books, 1983

Williamson, K., *Fair Isle and Its Birds*, Oliver and Boyd, 1965

Witherly, H.F. et al., *The Handbook of British Birds*, Witherly, 1941

Wordsworth, William, *Selected Poetry*, Penguin, 1992

Weiner, J., *The Beak of the Finch*, Cape, 1994

Wildland News, Nos. 43-45, Scottish Wildland Group, 1998

Wyatt, J., *Bird Watching*, July 1997

THE BOOK ITSELF would have taken a very different form but for the suggestions of Polly, the editor at The Foundry, which led Nicky, my present wife, into research on the non-ornithological aspects of wildlife; verse, folklore and the amazing world of bird names. Francesca Greenoak's book on *'Folklore, Names and Literature'* has been a rich source, and John Clare must have written more bird verse than anyone.

Nicky was also deeply involved in later stages, as deadlines approached, and she became tied to proof-reading, printer and computer. Her daughter Sarah was at the control of the computing world, converting my appalling scribble and constant changes of mind into a legible and coherent form.

The enormous contributions of Colin Varndell and Val Baker, from across the county border in Dorset, are enormously appreciated.

Finally many thanks to my father, my birdwatching companion for more than twenty five years until his eyes began to fail and he returned to plants. To have been able to show him four arctic-alpine species that were new to him, high in Cwm Idwal, was a special treat as he moved into his eighties. My brother Christopher abandoned birding after leaving our sandwiches on the train but was my companion in watching sport and drinking beer.

Nicky and I now run a bed and breakfast business in Devon which we advertise as 'friendly and different'; the aim of this book is to be the same.

NOTES ON THE EDITOR

MARTIN WALTERS is a keen ornithologist and naturalist, with a special interest in ecology and conservation. After studying zoology at Oxford, he has since worked mainly in biological publishing. He has travelled extensively and watched birds in many different regions, both in Europe and further afield. Martin has written and edited several books on birds, wildlife and natural history.

Picture Credits

Illustrations by Valerie Baker: 16 (tr), 14 (br), 17 (tl), 18 (l), 20 (l), 24 (t,b), 26 (tr,l,br), 31 (tl,mr), 45 (tr), 46 (bl,tr), 47 (tl,tr), 48 (tr) 80 (t,b), and **General Illustrations** by Jennifer Kenna and Helen Courtney.

Ardea London Ltd: 10 (t,bl), 11 (t,br), 12 (b), 13 (t), 14 (tr,br), 15 (l,br), 16 (l), 21 (tr), 36 (b), 37 (bl), 39 (tr), 41 (tr), 51 (b), 60 (b), 62 (tl), 64 (t,m,b), 70 (b), 73 (a), 74 (t), 76 (b), 77 (t,b), 79 (m), 115 (b), 146 (t,m,b), 155 (t,b), 161 (t,br), 172 (t,b), 174 (t,b), 175 (tl,b), 176 (t,b), 177 (b), 178 (b), 179 (tl,tr,b), 180 (t,b), 181 (tl,tr), 190 (b), 239 (b), 307 (tr), 313 (t,bl,br), 321 (tl,tr,bl,br), 324 (tl,tr,b), 332 (b), 333 (bl,br), 336 (bl), 344 (tl,tr,b), 345 (tr), 346 (bl,br), 347 (bl,br), 349 (t,b), 354 (tl,tr), 361 (tr,mr), 365 (t), 368 (b), 381 (t),

A–Z Wildlife Library: 17 (r), 20 (br), 23 (tl,tr,bl), 25 (l), 27 (ml), 29 (b), 33 (b), 34 (b), 38 (b), 40 (b), 43 (b), 44 (b), 46 (br), 47 (b), 48 (tl,b), 49 (t,m,b), 54 (t), 55 (tr,ml,b), 56 (tl,tr), 59 (b), 62 (br), 63 (tr), 64 (m,b), 66 (t), 67 (bl,br), 68 (t), 69 (t,mr,b), 72 (b), 84 (tl), 85 (t,b), 86 (r), 87 (tl), 96 (b), 97 (tl), 98 (tl), 99 (tr), 100 (m,b), 102 (t), 104 (br), 105 (bl), 107 (tl), 109 (br), 112 (tr,b), 114 (t), 115 (tl), 132 (t,b), 140 (t), 149 (t), 150 (bl), 157 (b), 161 (bl), 162 (br), 164 (c), 166 (tl), 167 (t,b), 171 (b), 181 (b), 182 (bl), 183 (r), 184 (tl), 188 (tl,tr,b), 190 (t), 184 (tr,br,bl), 185 (t,b), 192 (rl,tr), 197 (m,br), 204 (tl), 207 (l,r), 210 (m), 211 (t,m), 216 (b), 217 (t,m), 220 (t), 221 (t), 222 (t,b), 223 (t,bl,br), 224 (t,bl), 237 (b), 240 (br), 242 (t;.tr), 246 (tl), 251 (b), 253 (tl,tr,b), 254 (t), 256 (t), 257 (tr,b), 315 (t,m,b), 327 (t,m,b), 330 (bl,br), 333 (t), 335 (tr), 338 (t,m,b), 345 (tl), 353 (tl,b), 357 (bl), 373 (t), 379 (b),

Foundry Arts: 195 (mr),

Natural Image: 37 (tl,br), 50 (t), 51 (t), 53 (t,b), 71 (t), 72 (m), 73 (b), 74 (b), 75 (tr,ml), 76 (t), 78 (t), 79 (b), 96 (t), 97 (tr,b), 108 (tr), 110 (tr,b), 147 (t), 164 (b), 180 (m), 337 (t,bl,br), 346 (t), 365 (b), 382 (b),

RSPB: 118 (tl,tr,b), 124 (b), 131 (tr,b), 145 (t,m,b), 147 (b), 154 (tl,b), 159 (m), 160 (t,b), 165 (l,r), 169 (tr,b), 173 (t,b), 178 (tl,tr), 193 (m,b), 194 (t,b), 195 (tl,bl), 196 (t,m,b), 201 (tl,tr), 202 (t,b), 205 (t,m,b), 219 (b), 308 (t,l,r), 309 (tl,tr,b), 311 (t,b), 316 (t,bl,br), 317 (t,b), 318 (tl,tr), 319 (t,m,b), 320 (b), 322 (bl,br), 323 (t,m,b), 325 (t,m,b), 326 (br), 328 (tl,tr,b), 329 (t,m,b), 332 (t), 335 (tr,b), 336 (t,br), 339 (t,br), 340 (t,b), 341 (b), 343 (t), 348 (b), 354 (bl,br), 355 (t,m), 364 (bl,br), 366 (b), 370 (b), 378 (b),

Colin Varndell: 10 (br), 13 (b), 14 (l), 15 (tr), 18 (tr,br), 19 (tl,bl), 20 (tr), 21 (tl,br), 22 (b), 23 (br), 25 (t,br), 27 (tl,br), 28 (t,b), 29 (tl,ml,mr), 30 (tr,br), 31 (tr,bl), 32 (tr,ml,br), 33 (t), 34 (m), 35 (t,b), 39 (tl,ml), 41 (tl,b), 42 (ml,tr,b), 43 (t,ml), 44 (t,m), 45 (tl,b), 52 (t,bl,br), 54 (b), 55 (tl), 56 (b), 57 (tl,tr,b), 58 (tl,bl,br), 59 (al,ar), 60 (t,m), 61 (t), 62 (bl), 63 (tl,b), 64 (t), 66 (b), 67 (t), 69 (ml), 70 (t), 71 (m,b), 78 (m,b), 79 (t), 81 (b), 82 (b), 84 (b), 87 (b), 88 (b), 89 (t,bl,br), 94 (tl,tr,b), 95 (tl,tr,b), 98 (tr,b), 99 (tl,b), 100 (t), 101 (tl,tr,b), 102 (bl,br), 103 (t,b), 104 (t,bl), 105 (t,br), 106 (t,m,b), 107 (tr,b), 108 (bl,br), 109 (t,br), 110 (tl), 111 (b,t), 112 (tl), 113 (t,br,bl), 114 (bl,br), 115 (tr), 116 (t,m,b), 117 (t,m,b), 119 (t,m,b), 120 (t,b), 121 (t,b), 122 (t,bl,br), 123 (b), 124 (t), 125 (t,b), 126 (t, bl,br), 127 (t,b), 128 (t,b), 129 (t,br,bl), 130 (tr,tl,b), 131 (tl), 133 (t,m,b), 134 (t), 134 (bl), 134 (br), 135 (tl), 135 (tr), 135 (b), 136 (r), 137 (t), 137 (bl), 137 (br), 138 (br), 139 (t), 139 (b), 140 (b), 141 (t), 142 (tl), 142 (tr), 142 (b), 143 (tl), 143 (tr), 143 (b), 144 (t), 144 (bl), 144 (br), 148 (t), 148 (bl), 148 (br), 149 (m), 149 (b), 150 (t), 150 (br), 151 (t), 151 (m), 151 (b), 152 (bl), 152 (br), 153 (l), 153 (r), 155 (m), 156 (tl), 156 (tr), 156 (b), 157 (t), 156 (m), 158 (t,m), 158 (b), 159 (b), 162 (tr,bl), 163 (tr,tl,b), 166 (br), 168 (tl,tr,b), 169 (tl), 170 (tl,tr,b), 171 (tl,tr), 182 (t,br), 183 (l), 186 (ml,mr,b), 187 (tr,b), 191 (t,m,b), 184 (rl), 192 (b), 193 (t), 197 (tr), 198 (t,b), 199 (b), 201 (b), 203 (tl,b), 204 (b;.br), 206 (tl,tr,b), 208 (t,bl,br), 209 (t,m,b), 210 (t,b), 211 (b), 212 (t,b), 213 (t,m,b), 214 (t,m,b), 215 (t,m,b), 216 (t), 217 (b), 218 (tl,tr,bl,br), 220 (b), 221 (m,b), 224 (br), 225 (t,b), 226 (ar,cl,cr,b), 227 (t,b), 228 (t,m,b), 230 (t,m,b), 231 (tr,bl,br), 232 (tl,tr,bl,br), 233 (tr,b), 236 (t,m,b), 237 (t,m,b), 239 (t), 240 (tr,br), 241 (t,br,bl), 243 (t,m,b), 244 (t,m,b), 246 (tr,b), 247 (b), 248 (tr,tl,b), 249 (tr,tl,b), 250 (tl,tr,b), 251 (m), 252 (t,b), 254 (b), 255 (l,r), 256 (bl), 257 (tr), 310 (tr,l), 312 (t,m,b), 318 (b), 322 (t), 326 (r), 331 (l,r), 339 (bl), 345 (b), 347 (t), 351 (t), 352 (b), 353 (tr), 357 (t), 359 (t.bl.br), 306 (m,b), 307 (b), 367 (b), 369 (t), 371 (r), 372 (b), 380 (b),

Colin Varndell/Martin Cade: 234 (tr),

Colin Varndell/Peter Coe: 12 (t), 19 (br), 22 (t), 34 (t), 38 (t), 41 (ml), 50 (b), 61 (br,bl), 68 (b), 72 (t), 75 (b), 81 (t), 82 (t), 83 (al,ar), 84 (tr), 86 (l), 87 (tr), 88 (t), 132 (m), 136 (l), 138 (tl,tr), 141 (b), 175 (tr), 177 (tl,tr), 186 (b), 189 (t,b), 199 (ml,mr), 200 (t,b), 203 (tr), 229 (t,b), 234 (tl,b), 235 (t,mb), 238 (b), 242 (b), 245 (b), 251 (t), 256 (br), 306 (t), 307 (tl), 310 (br), 314 (t,m,b), 315 (m,b), 330 (tl,tr), 334 (t,bl,br), 342 (tl,tr,b), 343 (b), 350 (t,b), 351 (b), 352 (t), 355 (b), 356 (t,bl,br), 357 (br), 358 (tl,tr,b), 360b), 361 (tl), 362 (t,bl,br), 363 (b), 364 (tl,tr), 383 (t), 384 (b).

Colin Varndell/Peter Leigh: 36 (t), 39 (b), 83 (b), 361 (ml),

Windrush Photos: 361 (br).

Every effort has been made to contact the copyright holders and we apologise in advance for any ommisions. We will be pleased to insert appropriate acknowledgements in subsequent editions of this publication.

Index